PASSPORT TO LIFE

PASSPORT TO LIFE

Dennis Coughlin

authorHOUSE®

AuthorHouse™ UK Ltd.
1663 Liberty Drive
Bloomington, IN 47403 USA
www.authorhouse.co.uk
Phone: 0800.197.4150

Published by AuthorHouse   06/19/2013

ISBN: 978-1-4772-3093-0 (sc)
ISBN: 978-1-4772-3092-3 (hc)

Front Cover:

Children in a remote Muang village in Laos surrounded by murderous weaponry from the Vietnam War. The bomb casings are now used for house stilts, animal feeding troughs in the fields and for growing vegetables.

Back Cover:

My "class" after an impromptu English lesson in the centre of Lima, Peru.

By Jove I've Done It

Unless you experience the tangible immediacy of placing a Union Flag at the top of Everest or scoring a winning goal in a cup final the euphoria of realising a treasured dream or reaching a somewhat unlikely objective sometimes passes you by in the act of achieving it. This phenomenon dawned on me as I stood at the back of my English class. As I looked at the whiteboard in the distance, with my words and arrows looking like a map of the D-Day landings and despite the fact I had been teaching for a month, it was only at that moment of realisation I thought to myself. "I have actually done it"

It was several years earlier when I planned a dramatic life-altering move to avoid or at least delay my suicide. At that time I was drawing up a blueprint to create a new challenging and exciting lifestyle and I had an image engraved on my consciousness of me standing, chalk in hand, in front of young students in an exotic location in Asia. I now walked through the desks where about twenty young Vietnamese teenagers were scratching away with their pens amongst their whispered asides and then drew their attention to the answers of the exercise I had set. I deliberately took up the classical teacher's pose of facing the board then eliciting answers looking over my writing arm. I was recreating the stance I had imagined when the first seeds of what, at the time, seemed to be a rather whimsical and fanciful notion, first took root. The fact that in the intervening years the journey from plan to realisation was so tortuous and psychologically damaging that with my feeling of inevitable self destruction I searched suicide websites, added to my sense of achievement.

Less than two years earlier, at the age of fifty five, I was faced with the prospect of leaving the family home to live alone in rented accommodation which I knew would be fatal. The reason for my planned self-inflicted demise was unremarkably common . . . a woman, my wife, from whom I am devastatingly divorced plus the thought of what should have been, if not with her, with somebody else, dominated my consciousness through dark, silent, and often tormented nights.

The reasons for my eventual survival was the thought of the resulting trauma and stigma inherited by my son specifically, family in general, the choice of modus operandi, and the fact that eventually after many trials and tribulations I found meaning and incentive to carry on. During my darkest moments I had settled on checking into a hotel and taking an overdose washed down with a fine claret in fresh underwear. Hotel staff are trained to be unruffled by such discoveries. However having looked into the matter it seems that an overdose can cause severe vomiting and embarrassing survival. Even worse a coma rather than death could result, leaving me in a permanent vegetative state. A car exhaust pipe was my second choice but that would have involved being found up a country lane by an unsuspecting member of the public, maybe a child. I had no intention of dramatically throwing myself from a cliff or standing in front of a train, apart from the involvement with others, I intended to end up supine with my arms across my chest and all my features serenely intact. I was involved in a conversation about mushrooms when a work colleague informed a group of us that there is a specie of magic mushrooms that if more than the allotted amount that creates hallucinations is consumed, it becomes fatal. I intended to investigate further.

I'm not flippant about suicide and I am sensitive to desperate people who end their lives, especially the young and those often in a state of violent frenzy. Others are more measured, objective and reasoned. Some do not want to live on after the death of their partner, often going together. I considered myself in this group. In arguably the best film of all time, "It's a Wonderful Life," the morally upstanding character played by James Stuart is saved from suicide by the love of his wife, family and home. What happens if the home is a single rented flat after rejection from your wife? Jimmy, I believe, would have jumped in similar circumstances. The result of broken relationships is manifested in various ways and the most dramatic reactions seem to affect men mainly, where extreme violence is often involved against their partners, themselves and even their children. Often youngish and successful men who seem to have so much are ruined in moments of madness driven over the edge by these extreme violent emotions. They are young enough to start again. At fifty five my time had gone.

Because my suicidal ambitions couldn't be realised immediately after my marriage break up I decided, with some planning, to avoid the worst immediate after-effects of bed-sit blues and self pity by creating a dramatic and exotic lifestyle of travel and adventure. Despite my advanced years I decided to run away to the other side of the world to teach English. It would be my Foreign Legion. I was to plunge myself into new challenges and adventures away from the source of my misery and hopefully forget. I wanted to see the world before, at my own hand, I departed from it.

I had been a director of a small printing business for twelve years after working for a multi-national company for seventeen years so this would be a drastic move, although of course I had no plans for longevity as I was just filling in time living day by day. Leaving the family home at the end of 2002 with the shock of impending divorce and separation from my teenage son, plus the prospect of a single life in a one-bedroom apartment with old age beckoning, I needed this spectacularly positive response. My marriage had become loveless and sexless for some years so the timing of my exit was mine to choose. I waited until my son was mature enough before I put my plan of action into force, starting by securing a TEFL (teaching English as a foreign language) qualification which along with my Open University Degree more or less guaranteed a job abroad. This life-changing move was inspired by my life-long lust for travel and my interest in the English language. As I considered I had a good understanding of English I chose the most demanding and respected of TEFL courses which was CELTA under the auspices of Cambridge University.

Firstly I had to explain my leaving to my seventeen year old son, Ben. I had maintained a level of normality and civility at home but at seventeen he must have realised that his Mum and Dad would be expected to share the same bed. I decided I would ease him through in stages by just telling him I was to work in Asia for a while so that he could get used to me not being around. The permanency of my move would be put off until a later date. He thought working in somewhere like China was "cool" and was quite relaxed about the change of circumstances.

Although I was at a low ebb my remaining few years would be full of travel and adventure. What could possibly go wrong? There's a line from a favourite song of mine that goes "When you think you've lost everything you can always lose a little more." Well I lost a lot more in my initial attempts as one disaster followed another. You would expect that after my situation becoming even worse I would be pushed over the edge but I instinctively rallied to overcome these setbacks. My self esteem had always been high as I had nothing of which to be ashamed. I had after all been a victim of circumstance. I certainly had no intention of casting off my mortal coil in the midst of failure.

Flunking at Harrow

There are many schools and colleges around the country that offer a variety of TEFL courses and I chose Harrow House in Swanage because it was a large Edwardian building in a beautiful location. I arrived in a confident, bullish mood looking forward to meeting new people and to learn the intricacies of the English language. I assumed I would take the course in my stride and be amongst the leading lights of the class. I did well in the Literature module of my OU degree, had a knowledge of split infinitives and I never ended a sentence with a preposition. It was upon this I based my confidence.

There were about a dozen students including me with three men, including a retired naval officer. Several of the course members had already gained experience in teaching abroad but wanted the prized CELTA certificate.

After the first day it was clear the standard of the three rotating lecturers was exceptional. Over the next few days I was very impressed with the course structure and the vitality of our tutors. There was a huge workload and an intensity that I had never experienced on any other course. There was a lot more to the English language than I realised. In fact I printed a list of definitions of grammar terms and topics and it filled forty-four pages, and this wasn't fully comprehensive. Every other day each of us taught a class comprised of foreign students domiciled at the school. Standing in front of a class or any group of people doesn't faze me so long as I'm reasonably prepared. The lecturers and selected members of our class sat at the back with clip boards scribbling down comments for a post lesson critique. This debrief was often brutal and seemed on occasions pedantic and petty. Some of the girls were brought to tears after their lessons had been mauled by the tutors. The experienced ones did the best because they knew their topics intimately and could concentrate on class management, their very detailed lesson plan and the step-by-step method of successfully passing the course. They ticked the boxes that guaranteed the certificate. The rest of us had to first learn the topic, such as comparative adjectives, modals or conditionals, and then teach it with confidence, meticulously obeying strict classroom management instructions while following a detailed comprehensive lesson plan. An array of aids, props and exercises were expected which we had to prepare unaided.

We were warned before the course began that each individual must be of good health, free from worry and stress because no time could be allocated for sickness or a domestic crisis. No part of the course could be omitted. At the half way stage at the beginning of the third week I got toothache. I never get toothache. This toothache became, so I discovered later, a nasty bout of neuralgia. The whole of the right side of my head throbbed with agonising pain. I was up all night despite taking pain killers which turned out to be ineffective. I spoke to the lecturers the following day but their only concern was that I was prepared for my lesson that afternoon. The agony I was suffering was completely ignored. They implored me to teach my lesson despite the fact I hadn't prepared it and my face was contorted in pain. If I didn't teach that lesson I would fail the course. Even if I had taught that lesson, the content of which I was totally ignorant, I still had to catch up on two days work when we were struggling to manage the existing workload. This was also based on an immediate recovery. I flunked. I'm convinced I would have coped and passed if I had enjoyed good health. I base this on a fellow course member, Sue. She was in her early thirties and we became friendly on the first day and remained so. Apart from being over twenty years younger than me she was very attractive. I think she saw me as older and more sagacious and we worked together with her getting the better of the deal and me enjoying her glamorous company. She was also very hard working and tenacious often working to 3.00am before beginning another intense stressful day. For the remainder of the course I continued in class and helped Sue gain her hugely deserved CELTA certificate. There were two other failures.

Although I learned quite a lot during the second part of the course I felt a total failure. I felt I had deserted the others in the trench because of my lack of moral fibre. I was coasting, relaxing in the bar while they were studying till midnight, preparing lessons, experiencing the stress of their critically observed teaching, subsequently being verbally abused regarding their performances. I later convinced myself that my neuralgia was a psychosomatic cop out. It was the first time in my life that I had suffered this affliction but it wasn't long before I experienced another, again when under extreme stress. My second fortnight wasn't totally wasted, during that time I got a job . . . in China!

Day Trip to China

Towards the end of my time at Harrow I began applying for various TEFL positions, mainly in China. This was the obvious choice because there was great demand for English teachers as a result of the imminent Olympic Games in Beijing. If you have a good BA plus a CELTA with a few years experience you can secure the best paid jobs in the most desirable locations. Only having my BA (Hons) restricted my choice but it secured me a place in a school near Shanghai. The contract was agreed via the internet. It sounded like a good deal. The pay was fine and the contract included a fully furnished single apartment with cable TV, a computer plus other benefits. A week before I was due to leave, the destination was changed to Shunde. At first I was annoyed until I discovered that it was in the province of Guangdong and was only four hours by road from Hong Kong. I was to travel in February 2003 which meant I would be just in time for the Hong Kong rugby sevens in the March. I was happy.

I flew to Hong Kong where I was to spend a night at an expensive airport hotel. From there I called the contact number in Shunde. It was arranged that I meet a woman called Ning at noon the following day at a hotel near the bus terminal. At six the following morning I headed to the airport bus terminal to be confronted with a choice of six buses none of which depicted the city of Shunde. I showed my map to a uniformed employee and he casually pointed to a bus where the driver was sat in the driver's seat smoking a cigarette and reading a newspaper. I bellowed at him over the noise of the running engine. "Shunde?!" He looked over his newspaper, mumbled in Chinese and reverted back to his paper. There were a couple of people on board but departure didn't seem imminent. I wandered to the other side of the bus just as the baggage compartment door was being raised. I dragged my suitcase toward the man who instinctively heaved it inside. Again I said "Shunde?!" He smiled exhibiting his battered teeth amongst the gold fillings. This and the fact he had slung my bag in I took to be an affirmative.

I clambered on the bus and sat near the front not totally convinced I was heading in the right direction. It was bad enough heading into the unknown with my best prospect meeting Ning, a stranger, without the alternative of heading into mainland China on the wrong bus ending up who knows where, with the total inability to communicate. More people got on and as it began to fill up the driver's assistant jumped on and began selling the tickets. He must have noticed my furrowed brow and look of pleading concern. This happy smiling young man finally reassured me. "No problem, I will look after you" were his soothing reassuring words in broken English. I relaxed and began to look forward to the next four hours of adventurous initiation of this huge, mysterious and oh so alien country.

We travelled across bridges that gave full view of the famous Hong Kong skyline, circumnavigated the metropolis and headed off the island to cross into mainland China. Then we stopped and instructions were issued. Everybody began disembarking, not only that they began collecting their luggage. I followed, perplexed and annoyed. We entered a frenzy of activity that is unique to customs worldwide. I assumed that as Hong Kong was now again a part of China we would zip across into the mainland; not so. Being the only Caucasian on the bus I was separated from my group as I headed to the "Foreign Nationals" sign on the far side of a huge hall that was teeming with humanity. It took just under an hour of queuing, processing of documents and searching of bags before I appeared on the other side. I pulled my bag through the exit to be confronted by dozens of buses which were being gradually filled with travellers. Most of the buses had their baggage compartments opened as people jostled for position eager to offload their weighty burdens. I stood bemused before a uniformed transport official came to me, viewed my ticket and gently led me to my bus.

I sat looking through the window at all the activity, becalmed and thankful that the mini-crisis was now over. The bus eventually crossed into the mainland and stopped. The whole process was to be repeated. The procedure was the same as leaving one country and entering another. The traumatic experience was more or less the same as leaving Hong Kong. Again I stood frazzled next to my suitcase at the exit of customs looking at the dozens of buses and the multitudes that were boarding them. Again I asked for directions, and again I followed a less than precise pointed finger to a bus. I sought confirmation from a porter who nodded without conviction. I sat on the bus rather drained and unconvinced. I noticed a transport official with an air of studied professionalism and gravitas. I left the bus to seek confirmation that I was in fact on the road to Shunde. It transpired that I wasn't. The driver had to retrieve my suitcase and I was guided by my favourite Chinaman to the correct mode of conveyance. Then I really did relax.

I gazed through the window recording my first impressions of China. At first we travelled past built-up areas that resembled eastern bloc countries in the fifties. There were huge imposing tenement buildings which were grey and austere. Heavy industry was represented by Dickensian dark satanic factories with billowing black smoke snaking into the foreboding sky. This sinister, cheerless, concrete jungle was what I expected. This eventually gave way to rural China with paddy fields stretching out in the distance manned by thin, almost transparent workers wearing conical hats, up to their knees in the swamplands. I was now utterly relaxed as the changing landscape passed me by. After about three hours I became slightly more animated not wanting to go sailing past my destination. I spoke to the driver's assistant who in his own jolly way assured me that he would notify me when the time came.

We had travelled about four hours when we arrived at what I assumed was Shunde as there were no "Shunde Welcomes Careful Drivers" notices on the way in. Eventually we stopped in front of a smart hotel and everybody began to alight. As I fetched my case I was approached by an attractive woman of about twenty eight who greeted me in a formal business like manner. It was Ning. She led me into the hotel where we were to have lunch. She spoke very good English, was pleasant but always formal and business like. She explained that apart from the school in which I was to teach, the hotel was one of several private business contracts the school had and could be a source of extra earnings for me. I was disappointed that I was to teach conversational English to kindergarten aged kids, but it was my first TEFL job so it would be an easy introduction compared to something like teaching business English to adults. She then drove me to the school. What I expected was a building full of noise and activity staffed with a good sprinkling of native speakers from the likes of the UK, USA and the antipodes.

We pulled up outside a grey, dour, and unremarkable building. We entered a small courtyard and then a larger concrete quadrangle. This quadrangle had a few kids' activities such as a climbing frame and a see-saw dotted about. Around the quadrangle there were several small classrooms but there weren't many children about. I was led into a small office where I was introduced to another young woman who was very much like Ning with the same pleasing smiling visage but formal and cold. We sat alongside each other on a sofa as Ning disappeared back through the door. This new acquaintance, whose name escapes me, chatted as she gave me the once over. There seemed an air of disapproval in her manner. It could have been the fact that many men of my age work in China because of the easy access to young Asian women. She then made a rather surprising request. "I would like you to shave off your moustache." By this time the heat and the affects of jet lag were beginning to take its toll. My clothing was sticking to me and I was still lugging my suitcase. I had worn my moustache, on and off, (mainly on) since Sergeant Pepper and it had become the familiar furniture on my face. I refused and my indignation was barely concealed. Up until then I had passively accepted the role of the employee to her condescending employer role. My look of disdain created a slight panic in her demeanour and she became apologetic and suggested a tour of the school. There were four classrooms which were small with only a handful of tots in each. I noted there was a distinct lack of colour and the walls were bare and grey. I made a mental note to rectify this. We climbed the stairs and came to a door, with my guide proclaiming as she opened it "This is your room."

Now there are moments in our lives that define our fate and destiny. This was one of them. I stepped inside to experience one of those gut wrenching instantaneous moments that cause hyperventilation and acute nausea when no thought process or analysis is required. My reaction was instantaneous. There were no options, no alternatives. I was heading home on the next plane all plans and credibility shredded. I was confronted by a concrete cell with two bits of battered wooden furniture and a mattress. There was a gaping curtain-less, glassless window that looked down on the quadrangle below. My rigid silence was contagious as my guide looked at my stunned countenance open mouthed. Then I instinctively started frantically rifling through my rucksack before indignantly exhibiting my written contract highlighting the salient points with some vigour. And to think she wanted my moustache too!!

She panicked and ushered me out of the room. We descended the stairs as she jabbered on in mainly Chinese although I did detect a mood of contrition. Back in her office she claimed to have a better place for me and within ten minutes or so with my rucksack and suitcase still in tow we were driving through the busy streets of Shunde.

It was a short ride and we entered another building on a busy main street. Initially it looked like a small office block but as I sat in reception it transpired it was a school for the more mature such as teenagers and adults. I didn't see many students but about three young female Chinese English teachers regularly came to the foyer to ask me to explain points of English. They were very polite to the point of deferential. I think I was also a bit of a novelty which was actually quite depressing as I was getting the feeling that I was the only native English speaker for as far as Hong Kong. I sat on that sofa for nearly three hours becoming more nauseous, sticky, feeling more and more depressed and exhausted staring blankly at my unpacked suitcase. Dusk had arrived before my new "boss" returned. "They have finished now, it's ready." she announced. Apparently "they" were cleaning up my new flat. We arrived at a block of flats which was almost next door to the hotel we lunched at earlier. My pad was on the fourth floor, there was a lift and it worked. Despite the three hour renovation the flat was drab, depressing and a bit shabby. Assuming I was now happy it was arranged that I would be collected the following day. She left and I flopped onto the sofa and for quite some time sat there staring trance-like into the distance. What had I done?

I snapped out of it as I needed food, drink and toilet rolls so I descended in the lift and nodded at the uniformed man as I walked through the lobby. Nighttime had fallen as I entered the busy Shunde street and I negotiated my way across the busy road to a mini-market. I was aware that I was attracting a lot of attention because I looked so different. Apart from the eyes even at only five feet ten I was still much bigger and bulkier than the men and I totally dwarfed most of the women who were very slight. I was feeling self-conscious as I felt that my every move was being closely monitored. In one of the aisles a petite and smiling female assistant walked toward me with a pack of toilet rolls despite the fact that I had already secreted the very same in my basket. She continued to hold it out despite me pointing at my purchase. The puzzlement was rectified when she placed her toilet rolls in my basket while removing mine pointing to a miniscule tear in the packaging. She then coyly backed off down the aisle with a wonderful benign smile lighting up her face. I think she wanted partly to provide a top class service to a foreign VIP whilst creating an excuse to make contact with this alien being. I tried to be as gracious as possible as she slowly backed her way down and around the aisle maintaining her radiant smile.

Back in the flat because of my culinary limitations I ate a basic meal then flopped on to a sofa and attempted to plan my escape. Because an escape is what I felt it to be. I had heard that a minority of TEFL jobs in China can go wrong. I had also heard that passports had been collected by schools and not been returned until the basic contract, usually six months, had been completed. So paranoia began to consume me. My big problem was that I didn't know the route back to Hong Kong. I decided that at dawn I would head for the hotel where I left the bus a matter of hours earlier with so much hope and expectation. If the apartment hadn't been so close to the hotel I have no idea how I would have attempted my escape.

I arranged my clothes for the following day, packed my bags, set the alarm, and retired for the night. As I lay in bed I became totally consumed by a sense of dread. I was fifty five attempting to stave off self destruction for as long as possible by a new challenging exciting lifestyle which had now ended in miserable failure. I was stranded in an alien world fearing that I may have my passport taken and not knowing how to get back to Hong Kong. I have never suffered from claustrophobia or panic attacks but I was beginning to suffer from both. I jumped from the bed, dressed and left the apartment finding myself wandering the streets muttering inanities to myself, my face contorted by this demented response to total failure. I calmed myself down and decided to go back and get a good night's sleep.

I climbed back into bed and despite my attempts to relax and instil some sanity and normality into the situation I became consumed by this feeling of panic combined with nausea gathering in the pit of my stomach. I tried to contain it but despite convincing myself it wasn't the end of the world and I would be flying back home the following day I became totally engulfed, leapt from the bed, and found myself morosely patrolling the streets once again. I wanted to be instantly transported back to Cardiff and that impossibility was driving me insane. Looking back one of the reasons for this erratic behaviour was that I didn't have a home to go to. It seemed my feeling of desolation and isolation was exacerbated by the fact I was alone in a strange culture on the other side of the world without a home; I didn't belong anywhere. I felt I was floating alone in space. I returned to the flat but stayed outside on a chilly communal balcony for most of the night as time stood still. At the first hint of dawn I headed for the hotel hoping to glean some information about buses to Hong Kong. The security man in the foyer must have been perplexed by my nocturnal activities. I entered the large dimly lit lobby of the hotel and could make out a silhouette behind a large impressive desk. It was an overnight security man. He seemed a bit startled. I said "Bus for Hong Kong" He looked puzzled "Hong Kong" I repeated. He stood opened-mouthed and bemused. I mimicked a bus driver with sound affects and repeating more than once "Hong Kong" Surely the name Hong Kong was Chinese and not English. I couldn't make him understand so I left despondently.

I returned to the hotel at 6.30am with my suitcase planning to wait outside until I found how to get out of the place. The hotel was brighter and there were now two female receptionists. One of the girls helped me in my quest with good English as she informed me that the bus to Hong Kong would leave from outside the Hotel at

7.30am and not only that I could purchase my ticket from a table in the corner of the lobby at 7.00am

I sat in a comfortable chair in the corner feeling more relaxed. This calmness didn't last long as my paranoia set in again. Were either or both receptionists on duty the previous day to witness me lunching with Ning who had a contract with hotel? Would they inform her that I was about to make my dramatic escape? I picked up a Chinese newspaper and slid down behind it. Periodically, looking like a KGB agent, I peeked over the top of the paper to see a multitude gathering slowly, presumably to catch the Hong Kong bus, which added to my anxiety. Would I get a seat? At 7.00am sharp a man punctually took up his position at a table with a cash box and tickets and as inconspicuously as I could, I joined the queue. I felt convinced I was being observed as I shuffled forward. I handed my passport to the expressionless official who stared at it for what seemed like an eternity. He must have been puzzled at my short stay. He handed it back and I bought my ticket then returned to my seat to continue perusing my Chinese Daily. I couldn't relax until I was on the coach to start my long journey back home.

I sensed movement and joined the throng for the newly arrived bus. As I shuffled towards the entrance where the driver was checking the tickets I was still tense and half expected to re-enact the scene from The Great Escape when Richard Attenborough is led away as he is about to board a bus to freedom. The hand on the shoulder didn't materialise and ten minutes later feeling huge relief I was heading back to Hong Kong. I negotiated the border check with some experienced calm and took a taxi to the airport. After several attempts with various airlines I managed to secure the last and very expensive seat on a Virgin flight to continue my ignominious journey home.

At Heathrow I called my very surprised sister who agreed to put me up for a while. My first social occasion was the Sunday night pub quiz. My family and friends had joined me in a farewell "do before I left to pursue my new life and now only a few days later I walked into the Hollybush pub to stunned silence. During those few days the SARS pandemic was just coming to light so I was able to use this as my reason for my immediate return. So laughing off my experience I managed to mask the personal nightmare I had suffered. This nightmare, I realised later, was due more to my then unknown fragile mental state than the conditions I encountered. Normally I would have "hacked it" and enjoyed the experience of being probably the only non-Chinese person in Shunde. I could have become a local novelty, a latter day Lord Jim.

From Suburbia to Bohemia

I had reached advanced middle age when most men have attained a reasonable level of achievement. Most had a loving wife and adoring grown-up children in comfortable domestic harmony. They would've normally accumulated some wealth in the process. This certainly was the case with my peers. I, on the other hand, was unemployed and having joined the underclass and the dispossessed had moved into a large ramshackle building in the bed-sit land I had been determined to avoid. It wasn't even a bed-sit as it was one room in a shared house. I was in a state of shock after my Chinese debacle but I adapted reasonably well to my new environment and even enjoyed some of the bohemian nature of my new abode.

Until recently I had enjoyed a 27 year contented existence in suburban Cardiff. I had now decamped to densest bed-sit land. To provide the area with a modicum of anonymity my pad was about equidistant between The Locomotive and The Claude pubs. It was that part of Roath that will be forever Bangladesh, Iran, Estonia, Somalia; a latter day Ellis Island. The contrast between my new "manor" and the leafy glades of suburbia were stark and on many levels. In the suburbs people practiced a planned economy and lifestyle. The annual holiday and the triennial car change were budgeted well in advance. Most had some expectations for the future. The rituals that were the essence of organised family life were community wide, such as the weekend shop at Tescos, trips to B & Q on the bank holiday, and the Sunday flash floods through the estate as all the dads hosed down the Vectras and Mondeos while mum mowed the lawn as the veg simmered.

The people of bed-sit land had, in contrast, a philosophy of instant gratification. The first thing I noticed was the large number carrying a "must be seen with" accessory much like a Prada or Gucci handbag in more genteel society. This was a can of lager and the favoured designer label was Stella Artois. I witnessed this from dawn till dusk. Perhaps it had something to do with the street credibility of the local sub-culture. As a grey haired man walked toward me with his dog at 8.00 o'clock one morning I expected a nod of mutual recognition of old school values. As he passed he mumbled some incoherent verbiage as his dilated pupils stared vacantly over my shoulder into infinity. He was carrying a can of White Lightening. Booze played an important role in this neck of the woods and the area was full of party animals. On one occasion in the honeycombed house I shared with many others, a party was not so much thrown as catapulted. Originally a band was booked. A rock band in the kitchen!! It would have been just like a scene from the Young Ones. However this didn't materialise but a DJ turned up with his twin deck plus a couple of huge speakers and blasted away as the booze flowed.

Stumbling over the bodies the next morning with the intent of breakfasting I was asked if I wanted a drink. Expecting a coffee, a can of Kronenbourg was thrust into my hand by an illustrated man with enough metal inserted into various parts of his anatomy that he could have shifted magnetic north several degrees. As I discarded it I noticed a couple of almost empty bottles of absinthe. This is the fuel that ignited van Gogh's tortured imagination and probably tipped him over the edge.

One Sunday afternoon a group of young women were sat on the wall below my window each drinking from the requisite accessory having a drink fuelled conversation full of rancour. They used expletives between every syllable and made Billy Connolly sound like the Archbishop of Canterbury.

The cacophony of noise in the area was as loud as it was wide ranging. Redevelopment and refurbishment was a constant with the sound of drilling and hammering unrelenting. To ensure the dulcet tones of DJ Jo Whiley could be heard above the din, the builders cranked up the volume to number eleven so it wasn't just our ghetto that got blasted because the Arctic Monkeys could be heard as far as Gabalfa. On one occasion my attention was distracted by a mantra being shouted in a ritualistic repetitive manner. An Islamic neighbour was systematically marching up and down the street stopping every six paces or so where he stood to rigid attention, stared wild eyed at the sky and bellowed the same chant over and over again like pre-programmed Gatling gun. We also seemed to have the noisiest and most aggressive seagulls in town. Often I had to fend off their belligerent dive bombing air raids with my umbrella, looking like a cross between Zorro and the man from the Prudential.

Complaints had appeared in the local press regarding students leaving piles of rubbish behind. Our road was a residential landfill site. Back in suburbia neat piles appeared once a week all washed out and segregated into the requisite bags. Back in God's very little green acre every day was bin day and no such refuse apartheid existed. Many of the tiny front "gardens" were covered in debris, mattresses, settees and the contents of gutted houses. There was a fridge freezer a few doors down that had been there so long a preservation order had been slapped on it. Adding to all this you continually had to play hopscotch around discarded takeaways, some of which having experienced a short period of ingestion having had a fleeting acquaintance with the owner's stomach.

When I crossed town I had experienced my own bonfire of the vanities. Despite what seems like a diatribe against that neighbourhood I had adapted to this new bohemian existence. Many of my adopted community were itinerants, such as students of various nationalities, people in low paid jobs on the first rung of the employment ladder, along with those creating their first foothold in a new country and culture. The area proved the adage that the people who have the least tend to give the most. This community seemed totally unfazed by the noise, clutter, and the inebriated nature of the area and for the most part were helpful, cheerful and friendly. I preferred the extremes of the area compared to the predicable blandness of suburbia, although I did miss the sedating effects of chilled Chablis alongside a trickling water feature of quiet suburban garden. Comparing the two communities using the analogy of colour I would describe suburbia as light beige and my new rather bohemian experience as a canvas created by Magritte on a psychedelic trip.

I was suicidal before my change of "career" so you would expect that after further disastrous failures and my new reduced circumstances that shoelaces, belts and any kind of blade should've been removed from my possessions. Also I was conscious of the fact that some years earlier, at the peak of attainment and self-esteem, I had a responsible position, a happy home life, and felt, at the time, a bravura of self-satisfaction verging on smugness—and now this. Looking back I wondered how I coped with my fall from grace. I think a part of me was determined to improve my lot so that when I did choose to go it wouldn't be the case of escaping the slings and arrows of outrageous fortune. In fact despite my desperate position I was usually upbeat and good company, maintaining my sense of humour. Also my life had become fragmented and unpredictable which after nearly thirty years of what seemed predetermined domestic bliss and solid employment I had to cope with the unknown and try to make things happen. This was challenging, refreshing and an education. I was on the ropes and I had to recover. However before I made my come-back I got knocked to the canvas so often someone should have thrown in the towel.

My new abode and fellow house-mates could have been fertile ground for "The Wednesday Play" or Jimmy McGovern's "The Street." There must have been about a dozen occupants. Mark was an enthusiastic, optimistic twenty one year old who worked in a MacDonald's and was desperately trying to pass his driving test so he could be eligible to drive a car he couldn't afford. Kath was in her early twenties and from Ireland. It seemed a shame that such a young, pretty, and lively girl was a cleaner. Perhaps this was an early lesson regarding my job prospects with the options of my youth no longer available. She liked to drink and stay out late, often ringing my bell in the early hours after forgetting her key. She borrowed money from me and always paid it back on pay day. She had a very warm personality and often cajoled me from my room to join her and others, mainly young, in the conservatory for drinks. Although I joined in the patter these occasions made me feel awkward and self-conscious as although we were all in the penny-pinching under-achieving echelon of life, they had youth on their side whereas sharing the battered sofa at my age, I felt, was a bit pathetic.

There was an older woman not much younger than me. She was quiet and kept her own counsel. I masked my discomfiture with humour and bonhomie but she made no attempt to hide her melancholy. She had an intelligent face and must have been very attractive in her youth. One night I was woken in the early hours by shouting and wailing. It didn't subside so I got dressed to search out the commotion. Two flights up a young woman in her early twenties sat slumped at, what I learned later, was the door of the mystery woman. The girl was in an agitated and highly emotional state. She was begging to be let it only to be continually rebuffed by the voice inside. The girl was finally removed by the other occupants. I was informed later it was the woman's daughter who had drug problems and had created similar scenes before. How poignant is that? I'm sure the woman had good reasons but to turn away the girl you brought into the world and as a child no doubt read her bedtime stories, and took to school hand in hand, was just so sad.

Gizza a Job

I think I must have anaesthetised myself when signing on and seeking job seekers allowance. At £56.00 per week it's not surprising that a person can become homeless very quickly. This paltry sum didn't even cover the £250.00 per month for my one drab room which was dominated by a lumpy bed with protruding springs. This hovel was only a step away from sleeping on the streets and I had to subsidise myself with my savings to avert that particular humiliation. I did seek housing benefit but the red tape and misinformation given by the various employees at the Housing Offices added further delay to the built-in substantial lag in any application. I concentrated on job applications and, with what I considered an impressive CV, I expected soon to be gainfully employed.

A lot had changed since 1968 when, after perusing the many pages of situations vacant, a short letter or a telephone call would guarantee at least an interview, often within days. I now discovered that even the most menial of jobs required the completion of an application form the size of the Dead Sea Scrolls. Immediately I suffered the ageism in employment that I had read about. Initially I was so confident of my ability to do the job advertised I was planning my strategy and approach to the job and the lifestyle it would create only to see the postman pass by each morning. Also I experienced the "equal opportunities" employers, usually large companies and local government, that dragged you through the whole turgid process of application and interview only to select the internal candidate they planned to select from the outset. By paying lip service to their external advertising policy they exploited, used, and emotionally abused some of the most vulnerable people in society.

My worst experience was with the Probationary Service. Their half page advertisement in the local press stated that they wanted a variety of the populace to apply with no age barriers and qualifications were not just based on the academic. They wanted a cross section of society. The application form was long and complex taking a couple of days, with breaks, to complete. It was the first part of the selection process. I made it to the second stage which was in the form of a written exam and took place a few weeks later in a college in the next county. I arrived at the college along with, amazingly, hundreds of other hopefuls who populated many of the classrooms. The invigilators synchronised their watches and, in the true exam day tradition, invited us to turn over our papers and begin. The questions were in the form of social and legal scenarios with the odd moral dilemma.

A few weeks later I was informed that I had successfully reached the final stage which was a two day screening process again some distance away. A group of about forty gathered for the final processing. Most were in their twenties, probably graduates, and I was by far the oldest. This I saw as an advantage as when you are asked questions, such as give an example of incidences of my problem solving ability, my longevity presents a host from which to choose. I also considered myself well read and travelled plus I had run departments in a large organisation, run a small business, as well as experience as a union rep to over sixty employees and a branch member. We had to give a presentation which I had done several times before and presented no problem for me. I was very confident of this last stage which I believed played to my strengths. My coup de gras was in the collective test. Eight of us were sat around a large table with our adjudicators sat in the corners clasping their clip boards. The scenario was that we were all members of a council and we had to allocate a set amount of resources to eight applications for grants. For the first few moments we attempted to read each application before eventually we could form an opinion. Then I had a death or glory idea. I suggested that each should be given an application to champion rather than attempting to digest all eight from the pages. It was accepted and as I contemplated my bold move I realised it was a winner. The debate was well conducted and each contributed equally with one exception. A young woman in her twenties who, we had discovered, was currently employed by the service and continually rambled on attempting to dominate proceedings, embarrassing herself in the process. During a coffee break an applicant in the know informed us that there were eleven hundred applicants which was whittled down to five hundred from the in-depth application form. The written exam further reduced it to fifty. The service intended to employ just fifteen!!

After months of effort I got the letter which informed me that my application was unsuccessful and that I could contact the service for advice on my failed attempt. I spoke to the woman from Human Resources in charge of the application process who informed me that many of the applicants had first class degrees in criminology and others with law degrees. She could not pinpoint any weakness in my application other than my BA (hons) 2:1 was not sufficient compared to others. I reminded her of the original advertisement which encouraged a cross section of the community, including those without formal qualifications, to apply but she still maintained that her selection process was based on a meritocracy. She became very agitated when I accused her of using a thousand applicants as cannon fodder to ensure that an exhaustive selective process tested the mettle of the highest flying graduates who were finally selected. To add to my anger I was convinced that the irritating Probation Service employee was selected. I felt as much anger for all those young people attempting to get on the first rung of a career ladder who had put in so much time and effort not knowing that they never stood a chance from the outset.

Another totally different example of an anger generating job application concerned a company that hired people to read meters. After a few months I had begun to realise that job hunting was going to be frustrating and time consuming so I replied to an advertisement hiring meter readers at £6.00 per hour. I was invited to an interview in Bristol. I drove the forty miles across the Severn Bridge and located the small industrial estate where the interview was to take place. I was led to a large conference room to join about twenty others sat behind tables around the room. At the front was a nondescript middle age man who began to enthuse about the size of the company and the services it provided. It seemed pretty obvious to me that to most of those around the table a job that pays six pounds an hour, which included weekend and evening work, was a desperate short term option. When he finished his sycophantic corporate spiel he handed out test papers which seemed unnecessary as the job only entailed copying numbers from a meter. In the preamble I did recall without much stress that he mentioned that we didn't have to complete the mathematical problems in any set order.

We turned them over and began. We had fifteen minutes to attempt fifty questions. After about ten I realised they seemed to be getting easier so began selecting the rest at random before the time was up. I completed about thirty eight, guessing the last couple. He called out the answers and we marked our own. Then he stunned us by saying those below thirty five could leave. I had something like thirty three. People began staring at each other and slowly rising. I asked him "What do you mean leave?" I detected a certain amount of pleasure and satisfaction when he replied. "Less than thirty five is failure so you have to go." My initial instinct was to smash my fist into his flabby smug face. A few shuffled sheepishly towards the door. He condescendingly stated that if we had started at the back as he suggested we would have performed better. I said something

been deregulated and privatised in the 1980's which had become big business and in my experience a multi-million pound meat market. I would spend eighteen months in what seemed a parallel universe of caged alien beings before I could rid myself of the fear and apprehension that accompanied any thoughts of returning to Asia

I arrived for my first day's training and induction at a company called Cartrefi Cymru. There should have been four of us at their HQ in Cardiff. We sat in a small conference room with two trainers, one of each sex, in their thirties casually dressed who used "cool" quite a lot. Two of the trainees hadn't turned up so I was accompanied by just one other trainee, a most effete, effeminate man who constantly and dramatically gesticulated and flounced at every opportunity. After a brief introduction both our trainers were called away, excused themselves and left the room. My gay companion twittered on about the kind of minutia reminiscent of an Alan Bennett monologue. I paid scant attention as I found myself in one of my regular "how the fuck did I get myself into this situation" self-recrimination moods. I had after all voluntarily opted out of my comfortable, high income, high esteemed lifestyle to gamble on a dramatic life changing direction with disastrous results.

Whilst I was engrossed in this depressive navel gazing I was unaware that my fellow trainee had slithered his puny white arm across the table and touched my arm with his cold clammy fingers. I instinctively recoiled as if it was a deadly black mamba. This hyper-sensitive creature was obviously hurt by what seemed to be my revulsion. I mumbled an apology and attempted to respond to his twittering as a way of proof of my liberal, inclusive nature that was devoid of prejudice. I had always considered myself a champion of minorities and a voice against bigotry arguing against that kind of mentality in places such as rugby clubs and macho work places. I also considered myself able to converse at many levels and with diverse groups of people. I could hold my own from the arts to the history of boxing. Partly due to my downbeat mood I found it difficult to connect to this particular man. Maybe I was prejudiced after all and my theory could not be matched in practice. I was uncomfortable stuck in this room with this alien creature and was relieved when our two trainers returned.

Most of the clients were placed in houses in the community and our brief was to help them cope with day to day life and to involve them in the community. We then drove to one of these houses located in the central area of Cardiff where I had evolved over the years and where friends and family lived. Recognition was a source of dread for me. I was hoping to keep my new circumstances limited but I knew that clients were accompanied in public places such as shops, parks, and bowling alleys.

The house was comfortable with modern appliances. We were introduced to Mandy a jolly middle aged woman who was the manager of the house. She in turn introduced me to my first client, Michael, probably in his sixties who shuffled forward, his gurning features included a tongue lolling in the corner of his mouth which was dripping in saliva and constantly agape. He was quiet and uncommunicative. George entered from the kitchen and was a large cumbersome man in his fifties and when introduced to us by Mandy shoved out a large gnarled hand, and smiled benignly. There were two other residents who were currently out with their support workers. We were taken upstairs by the male trainer and shown the bedrooms which were tidy and comfortable. As part of our duties we were expected to sleep over several times a month as back up to the support worker on the night shift. The bed was located in the office where the daily finances, diaries, and the medication were located.

Both of us new employees were to be located in this house. The trainer described the clients, but it was his description of George that troubled me. Although he was relatively happy and passive he could become agitated and aggressive if not allowed to pick up discarded soft drink cans and bottles and drink the dregs. This often happened in the nearby Roath Park. This is the park where I played schoolboy rugby, football, and cricket and rugby as an adult. If I walked through Roath Park at any given time I could guarantee I would bump into at least four people of my acquaintance. It wasn't the physical challenge that bothered me, it was the utter shame of being publicly outed as a lowly menial at such a late stage of my life.

I didn't suffer from depression, just periods of being acutely pissed off, and I was suffering from a rather severe attack as I arrived home that evening. Fortunately the post revived my floundering spirits. I had been accepted in a similar post but this time over the mountain in Caerphilly. Although I was employed at Cartrefi for only one day, I discovered that in the great scheme of things this wasn't a bad company to work for. I later met others who worked for them and although the pay and hours like the rest of the industry were appalling, their holidays were generous.

I was actually very impressed with the organisation and professionalism of my new employer. There was to be a two week training and induction course at their HQ in Caerphilly. Along with about fifteen of a new intake, I accumulated several certificates that covered such subjects as first aid, autism, and methods of restraint. At the end of this training we were allocated our places of work. There were a half a dozen locations in the vicinity and as I discovered later I struck lucky with my posting. It was the middle of a group of three terraced cottages on a farm in a small village just outside Cardiff. It was a beautiful large cottage with beams and an inglenook fireplace. There were four clients. Bob was a big rotund, loud character in his late thirties. His general demeanour belied his hidden demons which very rarely came to the fore. He knew his rugby, liked a bet on the horses, and mixed with the staff in a natural convivial way. Shaun was thirty, built like a prop, dark and swarthy with a pot belly which resulted from overeating and lack of exercise. He was totally institutionalised having been in care, foster and otherwise all of his life. He had never known his parents, had the scars of self-harming, had been to prison for arson and was now sectioned. He could be violent. In the past he had attacked female staff, the most recent smashing a saucepan over the head of a female support worker from behind.

Christopher was a passive, quietly spoken man in his fifties. He was self-effacing, apologetic and ever grateful for the merest kindness or favour. He came from an upper middle-class family. His brother visited him from Kent in his BMW quite regularly. He was deemed to be a threat to children. There had been incidents that had resulted in his sectioning, although there were some staff who surmised that the authorities weren't sure whether they were real or imagined as he hadn't actually committed a crime. When out in the community Chris was to be closely monitored when children were around. He would self-regulate often telling us he felt uncomfortable in a park or a shop if children came within range. I recall him on more than one occasion breaking out in a sweat and becoming agitated when children appeared unexpectedly.

Brian was the least attractive of our clients. He had an ugly face with bulging eyes, one bulging more than the other, behind thick glasses. He was tall and thin with an Elvis Presley fixation and often wore the rhinestone suite and an Elvis wig bought cheaply from a fancy dress shop. He had to be constantly encouraged to improve his hygiene, continually moaned, was a hypochondriac and was very devious. Although some of the clients seemed less than impressive human beings they were usually products of a dreadful early environment and Brian was no exception. His father was an evil man who treated Brain abominably.

The main reason why this chapter in my life was made bearable was the quality of the staff. I was in valley boys and girls territory away from the metropolis of Cardiff. The staff in the main were loud, funny, and generous, often providing the clients with gifts and little surprises to bring some cheer to their predictable institutional existences. There were two male support workers in particular, both in their late twenties and big lads whose infectious personalities lifted the spirits. In previous generations they would have been in mining or engineering but as heavy industry is a thing of the past in South Wales they were now forced to cook and fend for these broken people whilst earning a pittance. Reece and Dave not only had accepted this with good humour they were also resourceful. In 2003 the pay was less than six pounds an hour despite the unsocial hours which meant that you had only one weekend off in four. With a sleepover this meant you were, on occasions, on duty from 8am until 8am the following morning. There were no overtime payments so if you worked an extra shift to bolster the meagre wage it was on the flat rate.

Both Dave and Reece were married with kids so to supplement their incomes Dave sold pirate DVDs and CDs and Reese sourced and sold cars at an average price of around five hundred pounds. Both these sidelines seemed lucrative enough to take their families on boozy holidays a couple of times a year. The people of the valleys are generally much warmer than the average and have a philosophy of instant gratification of live now pay later. They ate, drank, and laughed to excess and they all smoked. We were discussing holidays one day and it seemed that the Iberian peninsula and its islands were the only and obvious option for my workmates. When I mentioned I was off to India it was met with open mouthed incredulity. "India?!! What the fuck do you want to go to India for?!!" they exclaimed in unison.

I settled into a groove of taking the "clients" out into to the community and helping in the cooking and the cleaning of the house. Initially I was content that I had attached a tourniquet to my haemorrhaging funds and away from any prying eyes in Cardiff. My regular run with Bob was to the gym and then the bookies. In the gym Bob, whose largeness when stripped was mainly due to blubber, had all the gear of an Olympic weightlifter including the leather back and wrist supports. He would dab his hands with talc and with legs akimbo lift the weights a couple of times, sit down and rest for twenty minutes, before heading for the bookies.

I would take Shaun on long trips out to mini zoos and community farms but he always refused to get out of the vehicle. He played on a theory that he was unnerved by the public and the great beyond, the other theory was that he was too lazy to move under his own volition. Brian was up for anything. His big night out was known by everyone, including the clients, as Freaky Fridays but officially was Friendly Fridays where support workers accompanied clients from similar organisations in the area for music, dance and competitions. He usually wore his Elvis gear. If we stopped at a shop or similar we would have to check that children and adults of a nervous disposition weren't around.

We all dreaded a secondment to other units because they were by degrees more demanding and often distressing. It did make us feel fortunate in our regular assignment. I was often sent for a few days or a week to a unit nearby when there were staffing problems. This particular unit made Bedlam seem like the moribund archive department in a public library. It was a secure unit so the staff were constantly locking and unlocking doors from one room to the next. The scene confronting a first time visitor was one few other people could have experienced. Mark was a six feet two black African who was slim, athletic and in his early twenties. He would sit bolt upright chortling in his chair for a period of ten minutes or so then rise, quickly run across the room and run backwards hurling himself back into his chair as his head sprung back perilously close the wall. He did this throughout the day.

Gerry was a tall man, again in his twenties with wispy fair hair. He was usually sat in his corner where staff engaged him in nonsensical meaningless chat that Edward Lear may have found entertaining but to me was a bit grating. This chat turned out to be a calming procedure because periodically he became frustrated got up walked across the room where he would clench his fists and shape to attack but would be put on the floor in restraint by an over-zealous male member of staff. After several visits I came to the conclusion that a couple of members of staff were routinely putting him on the ground and Gerry was actually passively accepting it. I wondered what would have happened if they backed off as Gerry seemed to be going through the motions without any great intent.

Sue was a squat, podgy faced Shirley Temple look-a-like. She had soft features with her hair often in ringlets. She must have been only four and a half feet tall. Despite her girlie appearance she was probably in her mid thirties and had a left hook as lethal as "Enry's 'Ammer." which she used regularly on off guard, unsuspecting members of staff. She couldn't speak but used quiet squeaks and guttural noises in an attempt to communicate. I was aware of her pugilistic prowess as she sidled up to me and sat down on the sofa looking up at me with doleful eyes with her fist in her mouth. I would spend time in her room as she shaded in her colouring-in book. As she reached out for a pencil I would find myself easing away and found myself flinching if her movement was a bit more rapid than usual. I had witnessed the kind of damage she could inflict. Arriving one day I met a new young attractive female support worker who despite a stitched-up eyebrow was happily and acceptingly going about her duties.

Eddie was always heard and very rarely seen. At the end of a short corridor there were several secure rooms shooting off down a flight of steps. Eddie's voice was a constant throughout the day as he bellowed out comments and requests often using his name in the third person. "Eddie wants cocoa pops now!" he would repeat without response. His loud ranting often made little sense, while other comments were about members of staff. Some were amusing which would draw laughter and members of staff would acknowledged him with brief shouted responses. Some of his vocabulary was quite advanced although the utterances were often unfathomable giving the impression of an innate intelligence sadly gone awry. When I finally got to see him he was short and pugnacious looking like John Peel without the beard. He was taken into the community occasionally but his mood and demeanour dictated the frequency. He had caused chaos and in one incident in a supermarket the police were called.

Katherine was in another of these rooms and was often violent so she was locked away there on each occasion I visited. She was in her twenties and quite attractive. Although she had been sectioned she was of above average intelligence and gave the impression she had a massive chip on her shoulder. After my initial introduction to her I had a reasonable calm conversation but was always aware of a look of cunning, evil intent in her eyes. Maybe I was influenced by my briefing. She had been involved in many marathon restraints lasting many hours. Despite all the psychological and psychoanalytical terminology banded about, the term "Kicking off" was the most frequently used. Katherine used to "kick off" big time. I arrived on one shift to be immediately summoned to relieve one of a group of four who had been pinning her down on the floor for over four hours. She continued in this position for most of my eight hour shift. We relieved each other after each hour before she finally succumbed to a call of nature. Attempts were made to talk her down but on each occasion the grip was loosened she responded aggressively.

Maki was a stout, solid young man in his early twenties of black African origin. He was severely autistic but usually had a pleasant smiling face and had a basic level of communication. However someone had inadvertently informed him that in the following month he would be going to a holiday camp for a week. Having no understanding of time his excitement at this treat turned into anxiety and frustration as each day he expected to be leaving to go on holiday. The plan was to tell him the day before he was due to go. When not querying his proposed holiday he spent his day anxiously rocking back and forth chanting his own personal mantra. This added to the overall madness of each day. On a bad shift while Mark was periodically bouncing around the room, Eddie would be yelling from another part of the house, as Gerry was being physically restrained with monotonous regularity. Meanwhile Sue would wander around twittering to herself with her fist in her mouth, while support workers were pinning down Katherine in rotating stints.

On the last couple of occasions I visited the unit there was a new client in residence. At first I thought there was a pile of washing or ironing in the corner of the room with a dish and spoon alongside it. Then a member of staff leaned over this little bundle and encouraged it to eat. Then I noticed a blink of an eye. This little scrawny black sheeted bundle was carried from her bed in the morning and carried back to it at night. Judging by the ease in which she was carried she must have been less than five stone. She was curled up like a cat with her black sheet pulled over her face. In the two days I was there I never saw her face or her move from this position. I heard her squeak a couple of times. I often wondered what kind of perspective on the world these grotesquely incapacitated people had and if they were suffering severe mental anguish.

I was thankful for my posting in the community house and was always relieved to get back there. There were a couple of other secure units in the area where we were occasionally sent on secondment. The largest one contained comparatively well functioning clients. Some had Aspergers syndrome and Autism. There was one young male client who was over thirty stone, dark, swarthy, and was usually prostrate on a sofa like a reclining Polynesian Buddha. He had a booming deep almost theatrical voice. Like many autistic people he was cerebrally overdeveloped in certain areas. His specialty was the retention of minute details of what seemed every film that had ever been produced, including make up artists and lighting technicians. He also, bizarrely, had a detailed knowledge of Health and Safety legislation. He had been known to "kick off" and I shudder to think of the challenge of restraint, especially when some of the support staff, including some of the men, were quite slight and of advancing years.

Occasionally I worked with a well spoken young man in his twenties who was very articulate with an impressive range of vocabulary. I was told that he had a thing about foxes. After engaging him in general conversation for a while he slipped into a world of what he expected me, not only to engage with, but to be fully conversant. That was the fact that not only are foxes very intelligent but they actually control the universe. This wasn't a theory of his as to him it was a Cartesian Truth accepted by all. Another client, a young man of black African decent, some years earlier had been transferred from Rampton Secure Hospital and was continually tormented by the thought of being sent back to the place that housed the likes of Ian Huntley, Charles Bronson, and Frank "Mad Axeman" Mitchell. This mentally damaged man had not committed any crime and was a victim of circumstance and his condition. I was told that when he first arrived the Rampton guards had him in leg irons and chains. A female sister at the unit instructed his guards to remove his fetters immediately and despite dire warnings from the guards they were removed. She then, alone, took him for a long walk around the extensive grounds and wooded area. He was simple minded, vulnerable and keen to please. If he felt guilty of something real or imagined or was criticised in a minor way such as being late for breakfast or leaving his coat in a vehicle, he would beg not to be sent back to Rampton. Despite constant reassurances that he would never go back his fears could never be quelled. I cannot imaging what he suffered and witnessed there.

The most demanding secure unit was an old Victorian house on three floors, where the most damaged and violent clients were located. One particular client called Oliver was notorious and as his second floor location was unlocked while on another secondment I entered with some trepidation. As I headed for the common room some clients stood in the doorways of their rooms, one of whom I was informed was Oliver. He looked a boyish eighteen, thick set with a benign expression which allayed my initial nervousness. However

I steeled myself again after another support worker whispered in my ear "He's lining you up" as he ushered me away down a corridor and into an office. Oliver was severely autistic and when there was even a minor change in routine he became very violent.

Later I went to the common room and after being gently introduced to him I slowly tried to engage him conversation. I tried to interest him an activity or one of the games that were dotted around the room. We ended up playing catch with a brightly coloured plastic ball. Stood only a few feet apart we mechanically threw the ball back and forth to each other in silence which went on and on for nearly two hours. My legs and arms were aching, and I was also dying for a piss, but I couldn't stop as the smile on his face indicated he was enjoying the experience and any stoppage could have resulted in him "kicking off."

I Fought the Law and . . . Drew

Meanwhile back at the ranch I arrived on shift to be informed that there had been an incident and Bob had been removed to a secure unit. Something had triggered him to wreck his room. Because of his size he was contained in a small area where he wreaked havoc until his ire was satiated. He was now deemed to be a danger to the clients and staff within the unit. I believed that although he was capable of violence with inanimate objects he would never harm anyone. I was saddened by his departure. His replacement was Alan, a stocky, sly, slow moving slothful man of about forty who had attacked his aged mother before being sectioned. Like Brian his personal hygiene had a lot to be desired and although I had adapted to my new position with surprising ease my occasional "How the fuck did I end up doing this?" moments usually occurred either mopping floors at three in the morning or supervising Brian's or Alan's bath times.

I had the occasional delusions of promotion, as a unit manager earned about twenty five thousand pounds per annum with the added attraction of only working days, Monday to Friday. However a couple of incidents scuppered that particular notion and resulted in me looking for an exit strategy. The first incident was when Malcolm, our jovial assistant manager, was suspended for two weeks. Against all established behaviour patterns Chris, the passive, inoffensive, and most accommodating of clients absconded from the house. Although the official terminology was absconder, basically he just wandered off to the local village. He was retrieved relatively quickly. When asked why he did something so out of character he replied in his soft, distant, other world manner, "I'm not really sure." This was a man who was considered a possible danger to children. It was the opinion of the staff in the house that Malcolm was made a scapegoat and had been hung out to dry by management.

The house was only locked late at night and at all other times we were duty bound to keep the doors unlocked. The only way it was possible to prevent any clients leaving was to stand by the door which was physically impossible when, at times, there were only two support staff on duty, which was the case on this particular occasion. The clients could wander through the rooms up and down stairs at will and slipping out through the unlocked front door was always a possibility. The clients were so institutionalised and reliant on the staff for all their needs that they, until that moment, never absconded.

Malcolm returned after his suspension a chastened man as he was married with three children and jobs were hard to come by in that neck of the woods. During this period similar alarming stories about the style of management were emanating from some of the stalwarts. A few weeks later I too was to become a victim of this organisation's blame culture style of management

I was always a conscientious worker, never absent, always early and did my best for the clients. The issuing of medication was a priority for me as some staff could be less than stringent in obeying the rules governing drugs. On one particular morning right on the eight o'clock chime while preparing the pills for the various pots I inadvertently popped the lunchtime pills for one of the clients. Rectifying the situation I labelled it for the lunchtime issue placing it in the cabinet and writing it down in the diary. A senior support worker witnessed this. After taking a couple of the clients out I returned to the house just before lunch to be confronted by an air of gloomy expectation from the other members of staff and I was soon summoned upstairs to the office to be confronted by the manager Steve.

"You've been removed from issuing medication" he said with a stern forcefulness I had previously never witnessed from him.

"Why?" I replied with some puzzlement.

"You bloody potted up in advance and we had a visit from Andrea O'Connell and Debbie McKay this morning and they went fucking ballistic!!"

These women were two senior managers from Head Office who made occasional visits.

"So what's wrong with potting up?" I queried

"What's fucking wrong? What's fucking wrong? It's against the fucking rules!!"

"But it's done all the time" I replied

"Not here it's not" he continued shouting, obviously angered by the position he thinks I've placed him in. I sat down and started to put things in place. After a few minutes while he was ranting on about my retraining and my luck at not being suspended or worse I said calmly.

"When I've gone at night to other community houses the managers have potted up for me before they went off shift, because it makes sense as they know the system and the clients and there is less margin for error."

"Well they shouldn't" he said a little calmer as I think he was realising what was coming next.

"You potted up at Christmas so you could all go early for the staff party" I declared. Silence.

Not just calmly but softly this time he sighed,

"Well the damage is done now and you are off medication until you are retrained".

"Am I fuck" I said in a thoughtful restrained manner as I rose to my feet,

"They may be used to walking all over their staff but they won't find me so submissive."

Over the next few days I compiled my case which became irresistible. When the clients went out for long periods the mid day medication was potted up in advance. When there was staff untrained in medication on duty, usually the late evening or night shift, the medication was also potted up in advance. I scoured the diary and shift patterns over the previous months documenting the many times when untrained staff were on duty and pre-potted medication was issued. I then wrote a formal letter to one of the senior managers involved, copied in the other and sent another copy to Human Resources as a matter of record. In this letter were documented dates and times of the potting up and I suggested that this procedure was also carried out at other units. I was immediately summoned to Head Office and led to a room where Debbie McKay and Andrea O'Connell sat with a senior nurse around a small table with a vacant chair for me.

Their demeanour was smilingly benign. They tried to insist that I was blowing this issue out of all proportion and that others had been retrained without a whimper. I explained that what I had done was custom and practice carried out daily and the issuing of medication would be hugely problematic if the system of potting up was jettisoned. I added that to be removed from a duty for incompetence or disobeying strict rules of drug issue was an unjust stain on my character. They countered this by insisting my character was unblemished and that the company held me in high regard. When this good cop approach wasn't having the desired effect Andrea tried a more hard line approach.

"Have you read the medication guidelines?"

"Well no" I admitted, "I didn't know they existed. I was just shown the ropes by a senior support worker"

"Well I suggest you read them" she replied triumphantly.

When I returned to the unit I sought out the medication guidelines. None of the staff had ever seen them and I rifled through draws, filing cabinets and manuals in vain. I informed Andrea via the internal post.

Eventually I realised that I was in a Kafkaesque situation with a dash of Catch-22 where the system eventually chews up and spits out the little man. Malcolm had recently been a victim now it was my turn. The "industry" was fraught with possible incidents and subsequent investigations. It was closely monitored by government agencies and all the clients had advocates from the legal profession. The training policy, of which I was initially very impressed, was insurance for the company against costly litigation. We all had a host of certificates from the various training programmes so if anything went wrong the company could be absolved of all blame. It was the minnows who were ultimately responsible. In my case the company were aware of the potting up procedure because without it great expense and chaos would ensue. What usually happened was the lowly unrepresented employee would passively accept retraining, the relevant documentation regarding this would be raised and when the government agencies carry out a periodic inspection, evidence of a rigorous tight ship would be presented.

I did achieve a minor compromise inasmuch as the management decided to send a representative of Boots (the drugs provider) to train all the staff on the issue on medication. In the meantime, a period of a nearly three weeks, when a support worker without drugs training was on duty another qualified member of staff had to be summoned from other units which caused knock-on effects at those units and major transport problems and in general, chaos.

It was obvious my days were numbered and the actual moment came in the middle of Pontypridd on a busy Saturday afternoon with Alan. Even with the best intentions it was difficult to find any redeeming features with Alan. Everyone in the unit smoked and the staff rolled twelve cigarettes for the clients in the morning based on one an hour through the day. The clients understood the reasoning behind this as they needed there regular fix of nicotine. Alan, using his right to access his property, often finished his allocation by early afternoon and would either bum some from the staff or go to bed early. On this particular sunny Saturday afternoon Alan was clamming for a nicotine fix and resorted to picking discarded stubbed-ends from the pavement. I was stood with him as he waited for someone to move on as he had earlier spied a now squashed cigarette only half smoked, a prize indeed. I tried to coax him along but he was stubborn and I couldn't move him physically because that was definitely against the rules. It was that kind of moment when I usually engaged in my internal outburst of "How the fuck did I end up like this!" But this time it was the defining "I'm outta here!"

There was another reason because a few days earlier after eighteen months of anonymity I was outed. I was with Alan in the bookies in Church Village when John Barry, an old mate from the rugby club, looked up from his betting slip. "Alright Den, what are you doing in this neck of the woods?" I was about to waffle my way out of the situation when Alan shuffled over and asked me to write his bet. John looked at Alan, looked at me, then back at Alan. The game was up. The whole circle of friends and beyond would now know the levels to which I had sunk. That night I went online and searched out various TEFL courses and a company called TEFL International caught my eye as they had courses all over the world. Despite all the historic and exotic locations on offer one stood out above all others—Saigon. When I got up from my computer I had spent $1200US and knew that in five weeks I would be in the heart of former Indo-China. I was elated, choosing not to recall my nightmare Swanage and China experiences. I gave a month's notice the following day.

I did leave with a bang, well actually two; one planned and one unplanned. We had been joined by another client, Carlo. He was twenty three but with a mental age of a ten year old. He was likeable and excitable but had a fascination with knives plus an unhealthy approach to teenage girls and perhaps younger. Incidents with knives and young girls resulted in him being sectioned. He settled in well but had black moods. During one of these he absconded to the local village where he was picked up by a member of staff in the local pub. This was swept under the carpet and there were no repercussions.

While chatting with other members of staff about Chris and Carlo absconding and the disgraceful punishment of Malcolm I asked if the near neighbours had any inclination of the nature and possible threat of our clients. We had three clients who were deemed to be at least a possible danger to children. The farmer on the right of us had young grandchildren who visited regularly, and on the left was a young couple with an infant boy and girl. When playing in the garden they could be viewed from bedroom windows and staff had often caught Brian staring at them from his room. The staff were adamant that the neighbours were not aware, which made sense as I'm sure they wouldn't have their children in close proximity to such possible danger. I proffered the hypothetical question that if there was an incident where would we stand legally and morally? We would have had fore knowledge of this possible danger. It was a scenario the staff chose not to contemplate.

I suggested that we pose this question to the management. There was an audible gasp. So I decided that as I was leaving maybe I could do my workmates a favour by posing these questions in writing to the management, in doing so I would be creating insurance against any backlash on them and the onus and responsibility would be on the management of the company and, for a change, not its workers. I chose the contents of the letter carefully.

20t June 2004

Dear Debbie,

As an individual employee I am concerned over the recent incidents of clients absconding. In both cases the clients have a history of sex offences. I would like to know the following.

(1) Are the clients involved on a list of sex offenders, i.e. are the police aware of their location?

(2) Are the near neighbours aware of who is residing in close proximity to them and their children?

(3) If an incident takes place what is the legal position of individual employees who are aware of the possible dangers to the local residents?

The nature of our community house makes it impossible to prevent clients absconding.

Best regards

Did I set the alarm bells ringing? I must have been summoned immediately the internal post was opened at Head Office and I was heading there within hours of posting the letter. I entered the meeting room to be confronted by five silent, stone faced managers sat around a table with a spare seat for me. There were furrowed brows and atmosphere of impending gloom. I commented about the formal nature and the numbers of managers involved and deemed the proceedings serious enough for me to require representation. This irritated them and Andrea intimated that the meeting was informal.

The fact that they had gathered so many busy and often dispersed managers so quickly seemed to belie this claim, so I bade them good morning and left.

Another meeting was arranged a few days later. They didn't want a union rep because of the medical confidentiality of the clients so they recommended another member of staff. I didn't want to expose anyone to further recriminations after I had left so I attended alone. The management team had only one point to make and that I was employed to protect and assist the clients and client confidentiality was paramount. They continually ignored my claim of duty of care to the public retorting that as an employee our main concern and responsibility was to the clients and their welfare. I asked them to put this in writing in case there was a future incident or at least respond to my letter by replying in writing but they refused saying that it may get into the wrong hands.

I felt I had gone as far as I could. They knew I was on the point of leaving so they prevaricated the best they could for the final few weeks. I left copies of my letter with members of staff as insurance against a future claim of negligence, hopefully reflecting any culpability back to the management team and the company in general.

The second bang was unplanned. Shaun's violent outbursts were rare and he chose his moments when there were women on shift or when weaker members of staff were in situ. One evening I was stood in the conservatory with Shaun and a middle-aged member of staff, Anita, who was sat having a quiet chat. Jeff was older than me and was upstairs in the office sorting out the finances. There were often petty jealousies among some of the clients. Shaun was aware that Carlo had a £30,000 inheritance and spent more freely than the others. With his limited resources it played on his well developed sense of personal injustice and often was disparaging towards Carlo. He was being unfairly critical of Carlo this particular evening accusing him of things of which he was totally innocent.

In a subtle way I tried to redress the balance but Shaun suddenly rose up and came at me swinging his fists. As part of our training what should have happened is that Anita and I calmly walk toward Shaun and on either side put our arms underneath his armpits walk him backwards to a seat, sit him down locking his arms and putting our near leg over his. This training is usually carried out with an average size compliant member of staff. The reality is very different with the overriding diktat, that the client must not be harmed. In the past Shaun, and I suspect any large aggressive male kicking off, would be contained in small space while they wreak havoc to furniture, fixtures and fittings. Anita begged him to stop as she ran to get Jeff. I instinctively moved into Shaun wrapping my arms around his flaying arms preventing movement. Like interlocking tight head and loose head props I stopped his initial surge and forced him back. He replied with a hefty shove and I again responded likewise. We were eyeball to eyeball, beak to beak. We inched one way and then the other. The stalemate was broken when we started crabbing sideways. Anita was at the bottom of the stairs screaming for Jeff as we shuffled sideways exiting through the conservatory door into the garden daintily negotiating the step. Without conscious design we found ourselves waltzing back up the step and back into the conservatory. It must have looked like a Monty Python sketch. Back in the conservatory we fell over the arm of a sofa sideways before righting ourselves. Anita was still screaming for Jeff who at last arrived and we both pushed Shaun down on the sofa in a sitting position. Jeff negotiated a cessation of hostilities before we let go. Shaun was now calm mainly because his lack of fitness rendered him exhausted. I was knackered too and I had damaged my back.

I should have had a week or so sick leave such was the pain and restrictions my back injury caused but I couldn't give Shaun the satisfaction. Again his violence resulted in no sanctions, punishment or relocation by the management whereas Bob a nicer, more docile

I recalled the last time I was in Kuala Lumpur in 1970 when I was twenty two. I was returning from Bangkok to Singapore on the long two day steam train journey that exotically snaked its way through the jungle down the Malaysian peninsular. My fellow airman and I met the only other non Asian passenger, Susan Lewis, from Australia. She was with a fellow nurse originally from Singapore but both then living in Queensland. My friend and I had spent all our money and the girls bought us a meal. During the two days we had together there was more than a hint of mutual attraction between Susan and me.

They left the train at Kuala Lumpur to fly back to Australia. On one of the platforms of the magnificent Victorian station we parted self-consciously. Then as she looked back from the exit we instinctively came together with a warm embrace and a parting kiss. What a place, and what an age to be as the world and my life lay gloriously before me. I had so much expectation. Now I reflected on the intervening thirty five years in this same city with all meaningful life now over and the great love of my life having turned out to be a fallacy.

Again another total mood swing after arrival in Ho Chi Minh City. Driving from the airport in a taxi I was totally seduced by the initial experience of the city. I found myself laughing out loud and commenting excitedly to the bemused driver at the vision and sounds of this teeming city as we wended our way through impossible traffic. We were confronted by what seemed like tens of thousands of motor bikes often a dozen abreast both ways with the ability to turn into each other at junctions, avoiding contact like bats in a cave. There was great contrast as expensive limousines along with peasants with conical hats and yokes across their shoulders attempted to negotiate this traffic. The noise and smells were overpowering and the pavements offered no refuge as they were cluttered with bikes and a little food stalls.

I went to the guest house in Co Bac in the District 1 area recommended by TEFL International and checked in. It was run by a young couple along with, whom I later discovered to be, a Cinderella character who was much put upon. The husband, Dung, was the owner and he informed me as he led me to my room that another course member had been in residence for two days and was looking forward to the arrival of other course members. I unpacked and despite my jet lagged fatigue with great excitement went out into the Saigon streets. It was to be hot every day being in the mid thirties and very humid. Within minutes my clothing was saturated and glued to me but I didn't care as I had become immediately enchanted with my local streets. They were filled with humanity, haggling, laughing, chatting, but mainly eating as I gingerly weaved my way around that human obstacle course. Both sides of the streets were strewn with culinary activities with mainly women scurrying back and forth with bowls of Asian delights prepared for others in what seemed a communal round robin of varying exotic dishes.

I returned to the guesthouse and knocked on the door of my fellow course member and Cindy answered it. We introduced ourselves and arranged to meet for dinner. Cindy Porter was from Chicago and I was encouraged that she was a mature woman and not too young. We settled on a restaurant in the backpacker area of De Tham a few blocks away. It was located a few flights up overlooking the bustling streets below with the near Saigon skyline as a backdrop. Cindy was a successful chemist working for a large pharmaceutical corporation and was taking a sabbatical. She had just spent three months in Italy and planned a six month stint in Vietnam. We hit it off straight away as she was a highly intelligent, feisty, anti-Bush liberal with a committed interest in politics but with a great sense of humour and fun. We chatted, laughed, wined and dined exposed to the steamy perfumed night in one of the most exotic and historic places on the planet and I was intoxicated by the whole experience. Although the setting was romantic I was just content to enjoy her company on that crucial first night. She did have beautiful dark, expressive eyes, a wonderful smile and laughed freely but I think I was just happy to meet someone mature and compatible so far from home.

About 11.00pm we walked back to the guesthouse through the still bustling streets which were even more exotic among the brightly lit Vietnamese signs and adverts along with the numerous single bulb wooden stalls. We bade our goodnights and I retired for a long refreshing slumber.

I climbed into my bed tired but happy. It was always at night that the negative thoughts borne out of my domestic and marital failure became unwelcome guests in my subconscious but I expected a trouble free night after such an uplifting evening. However I suddenly became aware of a terrible nausea in the pit of my stomach that was spreading to the rest of my body which brought on an increasing sense of panic, paranoia, and claustrophobia so much so I jump from my bed, switched on the light and pulled open the door. I looked at myself in the mirror gasping for air and tried to calm myself down with deep breathing. After a few minutes I slowly closed the door, switched off the light and climbed back into bed. Almost immediately this feeling of dread began to resurface and spread from the pit of my stomach. I had to get out. Within minutes I was dressed and out on the Saigon streets walking quickly in no particular direction. I had left the feeling of panic back in my room only to be replaced with an overwhelming outburst of self-retribution. I found myself stomping through the streets berating myself loudly. "You fucking Idiot!. You've done again! You stupid fucking twat!! Who the fuck to do you think you're kidding!? Within what seemed minutes I was walking through the main cultural park of the area populated by late night walkers and the elderly taking their ritual nightly bedtime exercise. These and the cylco drivers who were curling up in their carriages, along with the pimps and prostitutes were looking startled at this Caucasian marching through their city looking wild eyed at the moon screaming foul mouthed inanities. I made it to the famous

Ben Thanh market over a mile away before I stopped. Like my China experience I wanted to be back in Cardiff and now! The next flight home wasn't good enough as this demented seizure could only be quelled by instant repatriation.

I slowly began walking back to the guesthouse. I had calmed down and was beginning to notice for the first time on my involuntary route march, the nighttime sights, sounds and smells of this chaotic city. Although beyond midnight there was humanity everywhere. The steamy humid nights kept people on or near the streets eating, sleeping and chatting. I returned to the guesthouse where Cinderella unlocked the door for me to gain entrance. I shuffled reluctantly into my room, sat on the bed with the light on before steeling myself to seek some rest. I pulled up the lightweight sheet in my darkened room and began to reason with myself to ensure I was thinking and acting in a rational way. Within minutes I was back on the streets of Saigon walking frantically and mumbling to a new audience as I found myself heading in the opposite direction. After I calmed down again I returned and asked Cinderella to fetch Dung although it was now near 2.00am. I had decided that a new room, preferably with a window, could solve my problem. Although puzzled he duly obliged but this new room with a view was two flights further up on the fourth floor. Now I began to panic as my claustrophobia had taken on a new strand because the main entrance was too far away four floors down. Cinderella and Dung looked at my contorted features with a mixture of concern and perplexity. I wanted to explain that I wasn't a hypersensitive, over demanding neurotic basket case; on the contrary I had always been viewed as a strong character with an iron constitution who was always unruffled and took everything in his stride with little fuss or bother. My demeanour now was akin to Edvard Munch's "The Scream." I returned to my room, left my door half open, the light on, and managed to remain, slightly unhinged, for the rest of the sleepless night.

The following day I was remarkably upbeat considering the hellish night I had survived. I took a cyclo ride around the Saigon sights with a cyclist called Vo who was very garrulous and extremely interesting. Vo used to be a South Vietnamese soldier during the war and as a result was "re-educated" by the Vietcong. Although the expected carnage after the South was overrun didn't take place Vo, who was 57 like me, was consigned to being a cyclo driver all his life as he was debarred from any kind of advancement despite his undoubted intelligent and engaging personality. One of the places I wanted to visit was the American Embassy, the scene of the historic rooftop scramble to safety via helicopters. Who could forget the iconic scenes of citizens of the most powerful nation in the world grappling frantically to gain access to the rope ladders attached to the hovering choppers preparing a hasty departure from the advancing Vietcong? After a long and arduous ride (for Vo that was) he stopped and pointed at a bland functional single story building which was nothing like the imperial splendour of the American Embassy. It transpired after a discussion with Vo that this was the place where the embassy used to be before it was pulled down many years previously. I felt disappointed at this and Vo's glaring oversight in not pointing this out before we travelled the length of Saigon. I soon forgave him realising that he just knackered himself to earn a few bucks for his family. On the way back Vo provided the reason why he had such a happy disposition despite his tough existence. He explained the role of Ying and Yang in his adopted religion of Taoism, attempting to create my Pauline conversion on the road to Co Bac.

I had dinner with Cindy that night which was the Saturday before the beginning of the course the following Monday. We travelled to the plusher end of town to seek out a Thai restaurant that Cindy had located in a travel book. While I was confusing myself with a map leading us both astray, the impatience of an achieving Chicago dame manifested itself when Cindy removed the map from me with brisk economy saying "Gimme d'book." A few minutes later we were ordering our starter. We enjoyed another entertaining evening avoiding any mention of a certain mental breakdown of the preceding night.

That evening preceded another fitful night almost devoid of sleep with the light on and the door open but at least I didn't bother the good souls of Saigon with any demented distractions. The following day Cindy and I sought out means of transport to the school which was about three miles away. We hired a couple of bikers. Mine turned out to be Elvis. I can't remember if he introduced himself as such or that we christened him. He did have long greasy hair with a quiff and he played the guitar. He also liked a drink which meant the thrill of the Saigon traffic became more acute. A few more course members, Sam, Matt, and Amy had arrived at the guesthouse. They were all slightly built graduates in their early twenties. Sam was a softly spoken ex-public schoolboy from the home counties with an engaging sense of humour and refreshing radical left wing views. The only thing that separated Matt and Amy was their gender. Both were from New York, were smart, and extremely self-obsessed after, what I assumed, were overindulged upbringings.

The adrenaline of the first morning of the course just about overcame the lethargy brought on by tiredness. Most of the course members were young, although there was a Canadian, Steve, who was actually older than me, a Pilipino, Mike, in his late forties and of course Cindy. There were also two American ex-college girls called Simmy and Minty, the former having Vietnamese parents. Minty was quite an attractive slim blonde but pretty spaced out. Her wide vacuous eyes gave it away. If you asked her a simple question like the correct time, her response would be; "Oh yeah . . . . Wow . . . . time . . . yeah . . . . let me think . . . . time um . . . phew". It was pointed out to me that she had been badly injured in a car crash which may explain her less than grounded demeanour. But she did have innate intelligence that saw her sail through the course. She could do the business when it mattered.

The course was demanding but not to the extent of the CELTA, however we were experiencing 35C and a 100% humidity with broken air conditioning. I had the advantage of a CELTA course behind me with a more in depth grammar content. I felt my grammar acumen was actually superior to the tutors. Much of the content was about pre-programmed role plays where you had to stick rigidly to a script and choreography. I found this difficult and would often find myself out of sequence.

Back at the guesthouse the first few nights were horrendous. I would spend most of the hours up to midnight rehearsing my routines, lesson planning, creating materials and exercises then spend a largely sleepless night. I began to fear the hours of darkness when my bed would be an object of dread and foreboding. It became my enemy. I used to listen to a beautiful Christie Moore song called John O'Dreams with lines like "The prince and the ploughman, the slave and the free man all find their comfort in old John O'Dreams." Well there was scant comfort for me. I would will myself to sleep only to end up tossing, turning, and pacing the room continually haunted by my demons.

Looking for a resolution to my problems, to the bemusement of Dung, I checked into the expensive Windsor Hotel for three nights. The room was massive with huge windows and I was able to close the door and switch off the lights, but still no sleep. By now Cindy and some others were aware of my problems. Predictably Minty was having the same experience and kindly gave me some of her powerful sleeping pills. They helped. They got me to sleep but after a few hours I was wide awake and taking more which was, in effect, an overdose. This had the side affect of my zombie like appearance during the day. I returned to the guesthouse and my nights marginally improved. The weekends helped as copious amounts of alcohol knocked me out for several hours.

Midway through the second week I had to use improvisation to help my cause. We were set a task to record conversations of four different characters to present a scenario to a class in a local state school. This meant at the end of the day we would have to stay behind to get fellow course members to role play on each other's tapes. This began to drag on in the heat and noise of the classroom so I took my leave. Back in my room I recorded all the voices myself using a Colonel Blimp type character, a southern belle, a take on Sean Connery, and yours truly to complete the quartet. The following day in the class the children reassuringly responded to my characters without adverse reaction while my observers were in fits of laughter, tears streaming down their cheeks—job done!!

A few days later my zombie like performance resulted in a "fail" by the judges. I missed a chunk of my "routine" which I had realised but soldiered on, which was a bigger mistake. I was castigated for not returning and putting right my oversight.

On the Thursday night of the third week I reached the lowest ebb of my life. The neuralgia I suffered at Swanage returned with a vengeance. I've since discovered that stress can be a causal factor which results in tooth and gum ache reaching through a membrane to the head so that the whole of the side of the face and head are affected. At its most extreme it's immune to common painkillers. In the morning I had swollen gums and mouth ulcers exacerbating my existing deteriorating condition. I felt like the Elephant Man as my head seemed to weigh three times the norm and looking in a mirror my eyes were like slits making me look more Asian than the locals. My face also had become very puffy and bloated.

The third week of the course had become more demanding and intense and on that Thursday night having had a really bad night with little sleep, as well as the neuralgia and my swollen gums, I had what felt like lacerations to the palate of my mouth. In front of me was a day that began at 6.30am and would not end until about midnight. During that day I, like the others, would have my lesson observed by teaching experts and peers, also filmed for an in depth critique. It was the most important observed lesson for me, because another failure and I was out. The state schools had no air conditioning, and in up to 38c you become saturated in sweat by the end of the lesson. I had decided that I was in no state to continue. I had nothing left. At 7.15am I planned to see some of the others and tell them I was dropping out. I had definitely made up my mind after having most of the night to think about it and I knew this would have resulted in my inevitable suicide. A few minutes later I was showered and dressed ready to head for school. I can't explain the force that made me do this but I did not consciously change my firmly made up mind. This was a crucial unexplained life or death moment, because if I had returned to the UK having failed to complete this course I would have taken my own life. I could not face the ignominy of failing yet again and a bleak bet-sit existence mopping floors in the early hours to finance the miserable last chapter of my life.

At Last They Certified Me

Somehow I got through the day, and my lacklustre performance was just enough not to fail. At the end of the last week I met Cindy before mounting our bikes for the morning ride to school and announced.

"I slept last night"

"Oh my God that's wunnerderful" she beamed as she hugged me. She knew it was a big deal as she more than the others was aware of my torment over those weeks. At the end of that final week I began to blossom from my torpor and on the Friday I received my TEFL certificate. I was told by Nash, the lead tutor, that allowances had been made for my poor physical and mental condition, something that a CELTA course would have ignored and failure would have been guaranteed.

After a boozy, entertaining, celebratory dinner cruising up and down the Saigon River most of the course members went travelling in various directions. Cindy and Minty were heading for Hanoi and I was heading across the Cambodian border to Phnom Penh for a few days. Simmy, having Vietnamese relations in the north, had already secured a job in Hanoi and was first to leave. Minty was giving Cindy a hard time as a result of her indecision. She must have changed her mind a dozen times about actually going and then their mode of conveyance. Finally they left on open bus tickets. I set off a day later.

A Spot of R & R

I was to travel to the Cambodian capital by boat up the Mekong via Chau Doc near the border. After the strain of the previous weeks I was now experiencing the serene calm of a slow boat chugging up the wide expanse of one of the most iconic waterways in the world. Since a boy of about eight I had always had a sense of history and geography. Although my childhood was devoid of books I always devoured any newspapers and magazines I could get hold of. Even as a kid I had a good knowledge of politics, current and international affairs. Another major formative influence were films. My grandmother, who had four unmarried middle-aged offspring at home and who were a great source of a variety of reading material, had a rare TV to which I was transfixed at every opportunity. Although the BBC in the fifties was class riddled and stuffy they did show American films. While the adults were otherwise engaged I loved, amongst others, the movies of James Cagney, Robert Mitchum and Humphrey Bogart. None of their characters were like any other people I had met. They weren't bricklayers, dockers, truck drivers, or even barristers. They lived in an exciting twilight world of clubs, dancers, speakeasies, and often in exotic parts of the world mixing with dangerous foreign villains. Robert Mitchum would amble into a lively nightspot in somewhere like Cairo or Shanghai and among the milieu below the spinning fans would be a seedy, sweaty, fat man in a soiled white suit peering menacingly over a newspaper. It was Bogey's "To Have and Have Not" a Hemingway adaptation that stuck with me and created the desire to travel. I liked the idea of enjoying an adventurous life gun running or similar in the Caribbean. So at eighteen I attempted to join the Merchant Navy. My violent, drunken father provided few positives but when I informed him that I had secured a position on a ship as a fireman thankfully he did point out that this was the official job description of a stoker. I had visions of crossing the Equator in my fireman's uniform waiting for a fire to break out.

In desperation for travel and adventure I joined the RAF and had a wonderful time having been posted to Singapore, and travelling up the Malayan peninsular to Bangkok. I was also posted to the Maldives and went on rugby tours to Sri Lanka and back to Singapore before buying myself out after only three and a half years. I secured a job with an American multinational printing company but after a year I got the "itch" again joining Decca Navigator a company that supplied manpower to operate navigation equipment for waterways around the world. I was to spend my first assignment in Abadan, in southern Iraq north of the Persian Gulf, to be followed by two year tours to Indonesia, South Africa and South America. From these destinations employees were provided with return airfares back home twice a year or the equivalent to any destination in the world. My future was set for travel and adventure. However this future was put on hold for decades by a chance meeting. During my three month training I met my future wife, and totally smitten, left Decca Navigator securing my old job and settled down to twenty five years of "domestic bliss." So my rediscovered desire for travel and adventure was just taking up where I left off in 1975 after a rather long suburban interlude.

While up top soaking up the panorama of the wide expanse of the Mekong and feeling the thrill of heading to the historic, and exotic city of Phnom Penh I got chatting to Peter. He was Austrian in his seventies but tall, strong and in robust health. He had a shock of thick white hair and a matching well manicured goatee beard. He looked and sounded very impressive and must have been uniquely handsome in his youth, rather like a Charlton Heston. He was a retired engineer having led an interesting and varied life and exuded calm wisdom. The fact that he was older than me and still doing "his thing" helped me experience a level of comfort that was missing when I was in the company of young people, which was most of the time. He was with a lone traveller, a young English woman, April, a quiet post graduate who seemed to find safety, solace and protection with him. As we chatted about weighty matters and laughed at the more frivolous we waved constantly to the kids swimming around their riverside pontoons and occasionally their mothers laying out the washing. We offered mutual greeting to the various river craft that came our way. This was the most relaxed and happy I had felt for quite a long time. The sun was going down behind the riverbank jungle as we drifted slowly towards the distant jetty of Chau Doc.

One of the many things I liked about Vietnam was the cheapness and informality of travel. There were lots of tiny travel shops offering an array of mouth-watering trips for next to nothing. My Cambodian visa was sorted in Chi's Bar, my favourite watering hole and eatery, by the eponymous Chi. I just handed my passport to her from my bar stool and she returned it in order three days later for a small fee.

There was usually some price to pay for the initial low cost and at Chau Doc we were confronted with the first inconvenience, which was our mode of conveyance to our overnight stay. There were not enough vehicles, which were larger versions of tuk-tuks. I, along with Peter and several others volunteered to sit on a large cart with a motorised contraption at the front. So we set off sat around the rim of the cart with our legs dangling like toddlers in a high chair or youngsters going hop picking in Kent as black smoke billowed into our faces. This riverside track had the terrain of Mercury so the ride was extremely uncomfortable as we began to be covered in choking dust and carbon monoxide. It seemed it was only Peter and I who could extract any humour from our predicament.

We arrived at our destination which was another unexpected surprise; our overnight stay was to be in a rather splendid new single story hotel that spread in various directions within several acres of manicured lawns. We checked in and I headed to my room along a veranda. I entered to find a modern clean room with all the facilities of a four star hotel including cable TV. I turned to close the door and experienced a momentary, slight, yet terrifying sense of foreboding in the pit of my stomach that regularly engulfed me weeks previously. This was a shock as I thought I had removed this unwelcome guest. I took deep breaths and left the door ajar, then the brewing storm began to abate. I unpacked some fresh clothes, turned on the TV, watched something recognisable, like the Simpsons, then turned on the shower. I now felt better and in control. Slowly I closed the door and took a shower. I was fine.

I headed for dinner at 7.30pm and saw diners at tables dotted around the garden. I sensed someone was waving to me and headed towards Peter and the ingenue, April. I slowly got to know her, admiring her courage for travelling alone as she was so shy and vulnerable. We chatted a lot when Peter was elsewhere as I believed I communicated with her better being from the same culture and I had a lighter touch than him.

During dinner the waiters doubled up as masseurs. Without warning they would pick up a diner's hand and massage the fingers working up the arms to the back and shoulders. While chatting, mid syllable, I was accosted as my free hand was gripped rather sensuously by a waiter. It was all rather pleasant and everyone seemed to appreciate it except for Brigadier Ponsenby-Smyth. At a table near us we heard,

"Go on darling it's fun"

"Absolutely not!!"

"Come on darling don't be a stick in the mud."

"Would you kindly unhand me young man?

I looked across at a middle-aged military type and his long suffering wife. He was dressed in "planters." When I was in the RAF in Singapore I regret to say I enjoyed the occasional throw back to Empire, an example of which was that at an evening function planters dress was the code after 7.00pm. This was a correctly worn tie and shirt buttoned at the wrist, which, along with conservative trousers and polished shoes, were essential to gain entry. While everyone else wore loose and flimsy attire suited to the hot steamy evening the Brigadier was fettered uncomfortably in a stiff collar, tie, shirt buttoned at the wrist, cavalry twills and heavy brown brogue shoes. An Englishman abroad! After dinner a group of us wandered over to a gazebo for a night cap. Our chat and laughter against the backdrop of the night sounds of the jungle and the gentle lapping of the Mekong was an end to a perfect day. I returned to my room and thanks largely to the alcohol and a general mood of wellbeing, without a thought about inner demons I sunk into a long deep sleep.

The following day we were taken to the local village and several shops which was interesting but you realise after the cultural tour you will be hit with the sales pitches. Later we were taken to a crocodile farm where hundreds of very large crocs were on display. Large crocodiles are always impressive and terrifying in equal measure but to see so many of these magnificent creatures was extremely unnerving but a sight to behold. I just wish our guide hadn't told us that the farm supplied the Chinese market where crocodiles are a delicacy.

After an excellent lunch we were, by mid afternoon, back on the Mekong. After a couple of hours the slow chugging boat reached the border which was a couple of wooden huts a hundred metres apart. Despite the rustic location, as ever, the process of customs and border controls were formal and laborious. Nevertheless I soaked up the physical reality of being in the jungle near the Mekong in the remote no man's land between the borders of Vietnam and Cambodia. I had spent years in factories, offices, and in front of the TV, and while I waited patiently, wiping away the sweat and dust, for those few reflective moments, I wasn't.

I got to the stage where I was desperate to be on land and heading into Phnom Penh. That moment finally came as we all piled into a coach. Within minutes, as night fell, we were heading over potted roads towards the capital. Apart from Peter and April, I had become friendly with other younger travellers and as we chatted excitedly one of them shout "a six" and everyone leaned towards the window grabbing their cameras and began snapping away. I followed suit. Mopeds are a way of life in Vietnam and Cambodia and the merchandise they carry is beyond imagination. Their main use is for family transport, usually mum, dad and two small children with no protection such as helmets. In Saigon the traffic is congested and slow which creates an element of safety. This one was on the open road where a family of six were travelling at high speed over perilous terrain, which was utter madness. I took a snap. When it was later developed it turned out to be one of my favourite photographs. It showed a young boy of about four at the front between his father's arms which were holding the handlebars, with three older girls at his back but in front of the mother at the rear. Their legs were sticking out uncomfortably from the wheels and their hair was blown back with the motion. But the look of joy and happiness on their faces was a source of both inspiration and envy for me. This family living in one of the poorest and most violated countries in the world seemed to have everything I desired and was denied.

The coach in which we were travelling apparently belonged to the King Hotel which turned out to be a large guesthouse. Our MC and part owner of the hotel was at the front with a microphone and he expended so much energy and time selling his beautiful King Hotel that it turned out to be overkill. We were now in Phnom Penh. The long wide French colonial boulevards the brochures promised were now evident and seemed to dissect the city. They were bright and lively which contrasted with the side roads which were darker and weren't actually roads at all. It looked like the side roads had been dug up then left through lack of funds. We turned into one of these roads and rocked our way along before pulling into the hotel. We drove straight into the building and stopped at the reception desk! On the left was a busy bar restaurant. It looked good to me. We all clambered off and as the backpacks were being unloaded the passengers swarmed around reception. A slight altercation broke out and people began pulling away mumbling, "I'm not paying fifteen dollars!" Apart from a few, the majority, grabbing their bags, began an exodus led by the group to whom I'd been chatting and more alarmingly Peter and April were joining them. My heart began to sink as I frantically looked for my bag. Do I run after them? I located my bag, went outside and saw groups heading out of the dark side street toward the bright lights of a main thoroughfare. I saw the silhouettes of Peter and April engrossed in conversation, totally oblivious to me. My initial reaction was to shout "Wait for me!!" but I didn't as the thought of searching for accommodation in a dark alien city was more daunting than booking into the hotel I was stood outside . . . alone. I checked in feeling abandoned. I realised how much I needed the company of others. Peter had become my security blanket and now he was gone. I thought I had travelling companions for my short stay. Fifteen dollars for a single room was not extortionate as I discovered, especially for the guesthouse's amenities and location. If they did find a better deal how much could they have saved?, a couple of dollars a night at best. Peter wasn't a penny pinching gap year backpacker; he had no right to leave me in the lurch was my unreasonable reasoning.

I trooped up two flights of stairs and into my bare single room. My despondency began to resurrect my pit of stomach demonic presence and panic began to pervade. I showered and changed quickly, returned downstairs and took a seat at a restaurant table. I scoured the room taking in the diverse nature of the diners looking for a Peter substitute which didn't materialise. I was very hungry so ate a large meal washed down with copious amounts of beer. I then found a comfortable sofa after picking up tourist leaflets to plan the following day. At reception I booked a tour for the following day and after a few more beers retired to bed. I felt better with the booze inside me and was looking forward to the day I had planned for myself, which was a bit shameful, as I was to visit the Khmer Rouge Killing Fields and the notorious Tuol Sleng prison.

The following morning after breakfast I headed for the people carrier that awaited me at the front of the hotel. I must have been its first port of call as I was the only occupant. It was sunny and very warm and I felt invigorated. We set off and I tried to soak up all the images and activities of Phnom Penh as we manoeuvred our way through the traffic. I looked into the faces and eyes of those of about my age and wondered what they had endured and witnessed during the mass genocide of Pol Pot and his heinous regime. I suddenly realised we were beyond the city centre and heading to the open road. I gleaned from my driver that I was his only client for the day. This excursion was going to be devoid of the banter and shared experience of others but I was getting used to these setbacks and in the bright sunlight just enjoyed the open road. True travellers like Paul Theroux avoided conversation and minor distractions while on the move so that he could concentrate on the flora, fauna and any other natural delights that may pass him by. I convinced myself to do the same.

The Killing Fields at Choeung Ek is just outside the city. I paid my entry fee and wandered in to join the few small groups dotted around a field sparsely populated with trees. I headed for what seemed the main building. I tagged on to a group with an English speaking guide. I had spotted in the distance the well documented mainly glass memorial that housed thousands of skulls of the stricken. The gruesome details of the victims were graphically described by the guide. Most of the victims had their heads smashed with hammers to save on bullets. This was not the enemy but their own people from children to the very old who were innocent of any crime. As we wandered in silence we were informed that we were walking over the mass graves of up to 20,000 victims and he pointed out that articles of clothing, buttons and sometimes bone could still be seen appearing through the surface. We got closer to the glass Mausoleum that housed thousands of skulls. Despite inwardly questioning the reason for the macabre public display and my role of a voyeuristic tourist, I guiltily snapped away.

There was no respite from this gore as we headed back to Phnom Penh and the notorious Tuol Sleng prison, also known as S-21. This was more chilling than the Killing Fields. Pol Pot had commandeered a secondary school to house prisoners who were horribly tortured and killed. There were hundreds of photographs, the most harrowing being the very young, the old and the frail, who underwent grotesque torture and death. People were milling around in stunned silence. Nobody spoke. Even if you accidentally bumped into each other there was no "sorry" or "excuse me" as we were too caught up in the horror of it all. Those people who didn't die in this unimaginable way were forced into hard labour in the countryside on starvation rations where many more perished in appalling conditions. Pol Pot killed up to two million of his own people, twenty five percent of the total population. What really angered me was when John Pilger exposed what was happening in Cambodia with his "Year Zero" documentary in 1979, the West still supported Pol Pot. Because Vietnam was the enemy of Cambodia and the West, it was a case of any enemy of Uncle Ho was a friend of ours. The Khmer Rouge filled the post Vietnam War vacuum after Nixon and Kissinger had decimated neutral Cambodia with illegal bombing, using five times the fire power that destroyed Hiroshima. This is the same Henry Kissinger that later received The Nobel Peace Prize!

I spent the afternoon at more aesthetic sites such as the impressive Kings' Palace where the poverty of this country was more evident. Filthy, barefooted street kids, some very young, were to be found begging outside in small groups. Although it's usually my policy to give to the old and avoid the young as it may destroy any aspiration they may have, I emptied my pockets as the dearth of tourists meant they were probably starving.

While amongst the throng in the grounds of the palace I heard my name on the breeze. It was Peter with April in tow. After an initial gabbled conversation we found a sheltered area and reacquainted ourselves over iced coffee. There is something egotistically worldly and uplifting when you are alone in a place like Phnom Penh and you unexpectedly bump into people you know. Apparently their first night exodus turned out to be ill thought out and they suffered for having to book into the first place available. After a while Peter wandered off to view the object d'art that I had covered and April decided to stay put. I got the impression that the safety and protection that Peter offered had the price of an obvious generation gap. She needed a break from him. Maybe because I had a son her age and worked with teenagers, plus perhaps Austrians have the same sense of humour as the Germans, I was more compatible. She became more relaxed, less stilted and laughed a lot. Later we bade our fond farewells.

After dinner in the hotel I secured an interview for a job at ILA (Vietnam) in Saigon via the local internet café. The next day I paid the four dollars for my bus ride back to Saigon.

The interview didn't bear fruit which I believe was down to ageism. I had confirmed the appointment by telephone with a man of substance, Jake Heinrich (Director), who was positively effusive. I was shown to his impressive office and he was everything his voice and name suggested. Mid thirties, tall, confident, expensive clothes with, no doubt, a Porsche parked outside. He was also superficial and misjudged my age completely. Formal greetings aside I uttered not a word as he explained that such was his fantastic school and low labour turnover that vacancies were rare, ignoring the constant internet advertisements and those in the English press. He offered to take my details and to contact me in future. Without uttering a word, offering a handshake or a parting gesture I walked out, closing the door firmly as he was still offering his regrets.

Miss Chi Gives Me My Big Break

Miss Chi was altogether a different proposition. I popped into a school called VUS ESL (Vietnam United States) to make enquiries. This was a large modern building with an impressive reception. I was asked to take a seat. After twenty minutes I was shown the elevator to the sixth floor where I was led to an office larger than Jake's to be met by an interviewer much smaller than Jake but greater in stature, the diminutive and inscrutable Miss Chi. She took me to a smaller interview room where we discussed the programmes they run, hours I was prepared to work and pay. VUS was much bigger than even this six floor complex. There were five other schools dotted around Saigon. I promised the earth, such as any hours no matter how unsocial, and I would travel anywhere. She offered me twelve US dollars an hour subject to an unpaid lesson observed by her. She was very efficient, intelligent and was a highly qualified TEFL teacher in her own right. She smiled a lot but not with her eyes; she was not a woman to be crossed.

TEFL lessons are based on set books chosen by the schools and vary depending on levels, from beginners, intermediate, to advanced and the specialised, such Business English. My demo lesson was intermediate level based on comparative adjectives, with a set of new vocabulary. I used my artistic talents to produce the highest quality flash cards and used as many props as I could carry. I downloaded extra exercises from the internet and spent a whole day and most of the evening photocopying and cutting up text for board rushes and other games. Observed lessons are always unnerving but now I was a different animal from the zombie of a few weeks previously. I was energised, confident and as long as I was prepared, enjoyed performing, because a TEFL teacher more than any other teacher must give a performance. Humour, slapstick, and mimicry are great tools to bring to life the grammar, pronunciation and academic aspect of language. Miss Chi was impressed, her only negative comment was to buy a belt because my shirt came out at the back and that would never do would it?

I collected my first weekly timetable and so many associated textbooks it took two trips by taxi. I located Elvis on Co Bac to negotiate rates for my daily journeys to five different locations and two on Saturdays and Sundays as I worked in the mornings and evenings on the weekend. Elvis seemed to have an elevated position amongst the bikers. I supposed you could call him the king of the bikers, which, along with his flamboyant quiff and the fact he played guitar, the name Elvis did seem appropriate.

As I was now gainfully employed with many hours bumping up my income I began to look for suitable accommodation. I had outgrown my room having to store most of the books under my bed. My guesthouse hunting was quick, my new abode being located no more than a hundred metres away just along the alleyway near Dung's place. At first the place seemed uninviting as I felt my way through a darkened ground floor car park choc a bloc with many vehicles, mainly bikes, but at the end was a shaft of light that led up and up through the most picturesque of buildings. On each floor there were open areas inundated with a huge variety of exotic cascading plants partly concealing several rooms with stonework that was whitewashed with dashes of pastel colours in harmony with its Arcadian environment. Each floor had communal gardens as chill out areas with ornate stone tables and chairs. As I climbed to the sixth floor the views of Saigon became more spectacular. At the top there was a stone gazebo with two hammocks and what must have been the house guitar. There were tenants lounging about and several locals pruning and sweeping. One of them led me to the office down stairs where a young man called Si offered me what turned out to be a large bright room with a great vantage point for only 50 dollars a month more than Dung's place but with breakfast thrown in.

Cindy had kept in touch via e-mail. She and Minty had hired bikers to take them to the mountain tribes of central Vietnam and were having a ball. They had been gone two weeks and were only half way to Hanoi. After my first week of teaching I went to the bank across town to set up an account. It was a large, air conditioned impressive building, populated behind the counters by scores of beautiful Vietnamese young women. Obviously I had come across many Vietnamese women in the Saigon throng but even the more attractive seemed to be a bit hardened and sullied by mixing with westerners in the areas I had been frequenting. These bank employees were a different specie seeming to glide around as on castors under their blue and white long silk uniforms based on the national dress. Talking to a westerner through the grill created genuine curiosity and the conversations went beyond finance. I studied their flawless complexions, lush black hair, and their perfect white teeth exposed by the beautiful smiles through their glorious cherub lips.

Because VUS sent their teachers across Saigon to different schools it was difficult to build up friendships and I was on no more than nodding acquaintance with my fellow teachers as our meetings were fleeting. However I was regularly contacted by Patrick, in the main, as the course members stayed in touch and got together regularly. Patrick would text me mid lesson to meet after class often at an obscure rendezvous. Thankfully the top dollar I was paying Elvis paid off as unlike many of his co-bikers he had "The Knowledge" and would pick me up at nine, usually whiskeyed up, to transfer me, post haste, to the allotted watering hole. I'd turn up in collar, tie, and well creased trousers along with my bulging attaché case.

After my inauspicious beginning I discovered I was first to be meaningfully employed and with the most hours. Patrick was struggling because he hadn't completed his degree course and Linda, who performed very well on the course, was having great difficulty because although she was born in America her family were originally from Korea. One of the great selling points of any private school was using native speakers and Linda had Asiatic eyes which could put the punters off. At these gatherings I would chat to Patrick a lot because he was very sporty, loving boxing and Premiership soccer. I tried to sell him Rugby Union but was struggling until one night he collared me after witnessing England and the All Blacks on TV. He was hooked after witnessing the Hakka and a mass brawl minutes into the game. "Wow what was all that about man?!!" he begged before I explained the finer arts. Nick was middle aged but conversation was stilted as he was a very conservative catholic who was sending money back to his impoverished family in the Philippines.

You're on Your Own Kid

Despite my progress and improved circumstances I was missing Cindy and looking forward to her return. Elvis dropped me off at another rendezvous a few weeks later where the gang were sprawled around a table looking suitably casual compared to my conservative and sober appearance. As I began chatting while sipping my well earned cold beer I noticed Minty at the end of the table and slowly scanned around the group to seek out Cindy. She wasn't there. I went over and crouched down by Minty and after discovering what a wonderful time she had, ask the important question.

"Oh Cindy has decided to stay in Hanoi and look for a job there"

My heart immediately reposition itself in the vicinity of my ankles. I was momentarily stunned, swimming in a silent little world of my own, detached from the external noise and conversation. I then composed myself, putting on a brave face while holding meaningless, absentminded small talk with others before I left to find a taxi back to Co Bac.

Barmaid My Wife Doesn't Understand Me

A few days later while sat on a stool in Chi's Bar chatting intermittently to her and some of the staff I was reminded of my childhood ambition of living like Bogey and Robert Mitchum while realising that I was currently living out these childhood fantasies. I had settled into this far flung, hot, steaming, exotic location but I didn't realise that there would be a heavy price to pay. In Casablanca Bogey always had a face like a battered dap. He was not a happy man. The reason he was in Morocco was not through choice. It wasn't a career move. It wasn't planned. Fate, a woman and failure was this end result and was the price he and now I had paid. This is why I enjoyed Graham Greene novels as now I could identify with the main characters who are often middle aged men caught up in circumstances and locations that they never originally envisaged which were a result of unplanned destiny and not design. In the Quiet American the character Thomas Fowler is a middle aged world weary cynic frequenting similar Saigon bars to the one in which I was currently nursing a beer.

Although my natural public persona was generally upbeat I was cursed with a deep unseen melancholy that ate into my very soul.

The love of my life seemed so unique and secure. I was devoted to her, making her happy, mistaking this happiness for her love for me. She avoided many social occasions because of her extreme shyness and hyper-sensitivity. She had a pathological aversion to the social scene, small talk and late nights. She wasn't interested in cosmetics, jewellery, or fashion. She was attuned to nature and animals. She would prefer a bag of garden manure to an expensive necklace. I helped cocoon her from the big bad world which isolated us from others and made us closer. Often I would hear her dulcet tones from the bedroom singing songs such as Scarborough Fair as she expertly finger-picked her acoustic guitar. I was the strong protector while she was talented, gifted, intelligent, and serenely fragile. Everyone commented on what a lovely person she was and many men found her beguilingly attractive compared to the more aggressive assertive modern woman. She was enigmatic and hailing from Cornwall added to her mystique. It was like living with a cross between the Virgin Mary and Maid Marion and for me was perfect and idyllic. We were meant to be. But looking back she never loved me. Her enigma was more an innate neurosis which made her incapable of loving anyone. After ten years she gave birth to Ben after reluctantly agreeing to start a family. The pregnancy strengthened her, turning a butterfly into a ruddy faced land girl, but the social implications of looking after a baby exposed her mental frailties. Pushing a pram in public attracted unwanted attention and wasn't an option. I had to be on hand for Ben to experience the great blue yonder otherwise he would have been permanently housebound. Mo was struggling mentally and despite my support may have had a nervous breakdown. During the following years despite my sensitive attempts to revive what I thought we had, her eyes were dull and distant. To unexpectedly spot your wife and child in a crowded street is so warming and reassuring, so natural and beautiful that it eclipses any other emotion as your son runs joyfully into your arms. My wife would be stone faced and disinterested. I meant nothing. For the last

carried them around all night, every night. After a few months I had bought most of what was on offer, yet they still pursued my custom, always with good humour. One night one of them asked what book I would like and she would get it for me. After a while I thought of a classic I hadn't read that she could possibly locate, The Lord of the Flies. Excitedly she left her books with me and ran out shouting back from the door, "I'll get all three" This left me perplexed as I hadn't realised that William Golding's classic was a trilogy. She returned euphoric ten minutes later with The Lord of the Rings Trilogy. How do I break it to her that I had read these years earlier? She wasn't totally crestfallen as I bought Lonely Planets on Vietnam and Laos. I pored over these books in bars, restaurants, and in the hammocks atop of the guesthouse. I began to get more ambitious and pencilled in Burma via Thailand which was more business for the book ladies.

While teaching one Wednesday night I received a text message from Patrick saying his "Last Supper" was to take place on the roof of the aptly named Temple Club. I got there about 9.20pm. It actually looked like the Last Supper as there were a dozen people around a long oblong table. I asked him when he was actually leaving. He said his flight was 6.00am the following morning. He went straight from the piss up, collected his suitcases and flew out. Youth is a wonderful time. I would never contemplate doing that now, but I remember doing it several times when I was in the RAF. Ironically the uncomplicated Patrick, though not fully qualified, was the most effective teacher during the course. In TEFL classes usually the louder the class the more effective the lesson. At the school where our lessons were observed the laughter, chanting and the singing resounded down the corridors from his lessons. He was physical, funny, and infectious with boundless enthusiasm. The boys loved him because he was young and macho and the girls just loved him. He also had an emotional affinity with Vietnam as his father was one of the Vietnamese boat people who survived that hazardous escape route in the seventies.

At an ungodly hour I remember hearing a text message coming through which I checked later when I got up. It said "I want to tell everybody that I love them. I want to thank you for everything that you have done for me. I will never forget you all—Patrick." I know he was worse for drink at the airport, but knowing Patrick I think every word was sincere. After all he was from New Jersey not L.A. He was going back to the USA to get fully qualified and planned to return.

A Welcome Visitation from the North

My disappointment at losing Patrick was more than compensated a week later by an e-mail from Cindy. After months of fruitless job hunting in Hanoi she was heading back to Saigon. I was elated. I organised a room in Si's guesthouse just opposite me on the panoramic fourth floor.

Since the beginning Cindy was the strong decisive one while I was a quivering wreck. On her return I was an established, and I believe, a highly regarded teacher and I had set her up in a "wunnerful" guesthouse. I had returned to physical and mental normality and I think she noticed the difference. It didn't take her long to find a job which also widened my circle of friends. She worked at the same school as Donna Morang, a woman of a certain age, and a Canadian couple, Drew and Michelle, who lived in our guesthouse a few flights down. Drew was a 31 year old Canadian who looked like a taller version of Andre Agassi. After I got to know him I realised I had witnessed the "Second Coming." I know that Cindy basked in his light, as he just exuded goodness. He was calm, even tempered, so nice, so helpful, and was like the Oracle. He was the font of all knowledge. He was also tall, good looking, and worked out. All the teachers who worked with him say that the kids adored him over any other. He had tattoos which I think was a ploy to give him some "edge" and to deflect some of his St. Francis of Assisi image. If it was, it failed miserably.

Donna is a self confessed ageing hippy, who didn't give a damn about the material things, but cared passionately about the important things in life, especially her students. She was very independent, taught in Mexico for five years, and was heading to Guatemala for her next teaching assignment. One of her daughters had inherited her free spirit and visited her regularly wherever she was in the world. We all went out regularly for dinner and drinks, mainly on De Tham but also ventured beyond, usually without Drew and Michelle as they were saving to get married. We would occasionally visit the more up market bars and restaurants in the Dong Khoi area, a particular favourite being the Sax n' Arts jazz club which was near the spot that Michael Caine witnessed the explosion in The Quiet American. That appealed to my sense of theatre.

Cambodia Revisited

Although I had been planning my exit strategy Tet was looming and I was heading back to Cambodia, this time with Cindy and this time up to Siem Reap and the temples of Angkor. Cindy left a couple of days before me as her school holidays were different to mine. I felt quite worldly giving her advice on hotel, visa and travel arrangements. The four dollar bus trip took less than four hours excluding border complications. I shared a bus with mainly other holidaying teachers, most of whom were going to the beaches and islands of Sihanoukville. The main border crossing and customs were more time consuming than my previous trip. It was still mainly out in the open with swarms of dusty, sweaty humanity loaded down with bags attempting to make sense of the ensuing confusion. Guides pushed in with bundles of passports for their groups, and dollars were changing hands for preferential treatment. Eventually I was walking from the Vietnamese side to the Cambodian border chaos. This entailed tramping across a dusty track of a few hundred metres of no man's land like beasts of burden under the beating sun. I instinctively began whistling Colonel Bogie and to my delight and surprise, as most of my fellow trudgers were under thirty, everybody joined in. It's little magical moments like this that raises the spirits and live in the memory.

The bus on the Cambodian side had the same MC as the previous trip and with the same vested interest in the King Hotel where hopefully Cindy had booked us in. What was better he remembered me and greeted me warmly. Someone on the Cambodian border greeting me like an old friend; how "man of the world" and cool was that? It got even better when we arrived inside the King Hotel. As we all clambered off the bus, sticky, dusty and ladened with bags, an inviting Chicago drawl purred, "Hey Dennis I bet you could use this" as Cindy thrust an ice cold beer in my hand. Barbara Stanwyck and Montgomery Clift surely must have acted out a similar scene. Cindy had done the dark side of Phnom Penh retracing the steps of my first trip. We had a few beers, caught up a bit, and then prepared to hit the town.

After showering and changing we got a cab to the renowned nightlife along the Mekong. For Cambodia this riverside area is very chic with lots of inviting bars and restaurants but we played safe eating at a little Italian bistro that sold Happy and Happy Happy Pizzas. I had a Calzone which was so delicious that I extolled its virtues way beyond its merits. I think Cindy thought the drink had inspired this extravagant, effusive outpouring until a fellow diner explained the Happy and the Happy Happy referred to the amount of marijuana involved in the preparation. Later in Siem Reap a placard outside a restaurant displayed a cartoon of man with an ear to ear grin and dilated eyes advertising Ecstatic Pizza. We gave it a miss.

After visiting a few plush and atmospheric riverside bars we then called a cab to a notorious club called the Heart of Darkness. A few years later a distraught British mother ended up there looking for her missing student son whose last known whereabouts was in this bar. It was very lively but seemed safe with no obvious felons around.

The next day we headed to Siem Reap. Cindy and I were the only westerners on board the packed bus. It was a full day's drive up the centre of Cambodia so at lunch time we stopped in a tiny village for refreshments. I was perusing the food stalls when Cindy called me over to a lady with a large metal platter piled with enormous cooked spiders with their legs dangling over the side. They actually smelled quite aromatic having seemingly been cooked in garlic. We resisted the temptation and opted for something more mundane. We were informed later that these spiders were in fact tarantulas which breed in great numbers in some areas, so not only does consuming them reduce the numbers, they provide very high protein. Cindy was sat next to a Cambodian on the bus who slurped and crunched her way through her arachnid lunch. I just averted my eyes.

We spent our first morning at Angkor, which was just outside Siem Reap, climbing some of the ancient Khmer temples including Angkor Thom. In the distance was the imperious and foreboding Angkor Wat which was huge and the most well preserved. We returned to Siem Reap at lunch time to avoid the midday heat (between 35C-40C) and to have lunch and sink a couple of welcome ice cold beers. Later we headed back to the most famous temple, the stunning Angkor Wat. To get to the top you have to climb very steep steps. Vertically the steps are very steep, horizontally they're very narrow which adds to the apprehension. You climb up by using hands and feet and never looking down. Of course when you get to the top you have to contemplate getting back down which is far more harrowing and dangerous. Fortunately there was some other steps that were equally precipitous but had a thin iron rail to hang on to. We queued for an hour to get back down this way which was still quite nerve wracking.

In the evening we went to a large restaurant call The Dead Fish. It was the most way out, original and decorous nightspot I have ever visited. It was a mixture of lacquered wood and corrugated iron filled with mainly wooden tables and chairs. These wooden tables were segments of large trees low to the floor, Japanese style, and the patrons lounged on cushions. It is difficult to describe in words and do it justice, but suffice to say that you would have to wander around slowly in all the nooks and crannies, like in an art gallery, to appreciate all the weird and wonderful artefacts. It had an artificial well with toads and a toad house. I saw one of the diners walk across to a corner, look down and take a photograph. So I followed to find about fourteen pet crocodiles. There were baby ones but some were six and seven feet long, uncaged!! The food was delicious and cheap. The live music came from a delightful Khmer band which thankfully ignored any hint of western music or influence thus maintaining the other world experience.

Some of the bars and restaurants in Siem Reap as in Phnom Penh had wonderful natural ambiance and atmosphere, much of it coming from French colonial influences. One night we ate in the Red Piano. It was at a small intersection and there were similar restaurant/bars on each of the four corners and more down each street. With people dining on the balconies, so close it seemed like we could read each other's menus, created a very Gallic touch, much like a miniature New Orleans.

Our guesthouse was an impressive old French colonial building with much marble and an outside cocktail bar. Each morning we'd have breakfast on the ornate marble veranda with wickerwork furniture. I could visualise being in a place like this, some time in the future, wearing a white suit to match my hat, rather more portly, ruddy of complexion, sipping claret, and smoking a long pipe.

This was located in the guesthouse/backpacker area. Beyond there were many plush hotels and restaurants and many more in various stages of construction. There were a lot of beggars and victims of landmines and hopefully they would be getting some of the benefits of this increase in tourism.

The last day at Siem Reap was spent at one of the distant temples, Ta Prohm, that had been reclaimed from the jungle. I say reclaimed, but defiantly mother nature had not given up the fight. All over the site there were some extraordinary scenes where the roots of huge, aged trees like tentacles were wrapped around the ancient construction refusing to let go. Peter Jackson should have filmed the Ent's scenes from there when making The Lord of The Rings. Never has the personification of nature seemed so acute. I read somewhere that in its pomp between the eleventh and thirteenth centuries Angkor was amazingly the size of Los Angeles and its empire dominated the whole of Indo-China reaching as far as India. Today the site is still imposing and has great majesty. It was this past glory that inspired the deranged Pol Pot to return his country to year zero to create the same conditions of a millennium ago to inspire the birth of another empire.

Cindy had to leave two days before me and flew back to Saigon. I decided to go back the long way and use a boat via a place called Battenbang. When I left Siem Reap for Battenbang I had a sort of tingling of anticipation mixed with foreboding. I bought a boat ticket from one of the small travel companies who were to pick me up at 6.00am. However life was never that simple there. At 6.15am a pick up truck packed with backpackers and all their gear arrived. Even with the tailgate down there was obviously no more room. With only half a buttock making minimal contact with the vehicle and hanging on like a petrified limpet we set off for the boat, where ever that was. Totally oblivious to his load the driver hurtled towards our destination, which took a good 20 minutes, the last part of the journey was over a dirt track. The boat or launch that was pictured on my ticket looked like one owned by the oligarch, Roman Abramovich. The embarkation point was like a biblical refugee camp. It was at a primitive fishing village with dozens of wooden junks bobbing up and down and clattering into each other. We clambered on, stepping from one boat to the next, all handing over tickets and hopefully being directed to the right boat. The sun was just coming up and the whole atmosphere with fisherman, the villagers, noise, and smells, was just wonderful.

Nobody was aware of how long this journey would take. We had many responses, from four to nine hours. We set out on these inland waterways and it turned out to be an ideal way to experience the otherwise inaccessible heartland of Cambodia. We chugged through many inland fishing communities. The villagers, especially the children, were happy to see us and waved enthusiastically from the riverbanks and the water. I think the fishermen were a little irritated as they had to stand up from their bent positions as we manoeuvred around their nets. At one stretch the waterway became a very large lake with a floating village community, including a small catholic church, cross and all, bobbing up and down. At one stage we had to transfer to smaller boats because of the low level of the water. I had read that part of the journey at this time of year would be completed by bus because of the low water levels. In fact we all eventually clambered into three four wheel drive pick-ups on the riverbank. In each vehicle there was four plus driver in the cabin and five on the back with the gear. I was on the back. This was when the fun really started.

We assumed that we were being transported from the riverbank to a bus on a nearby road; no road, no bus. We set off in convoy across some of the most inhospitable terrain you could imagine. It wasn't just rough, but covered in ditches, steep inclines, narrow "paths" with tree branches and briars hurtling at us, and the open areas turned into dust storms with our passing. To add to all this the drivers drove like maniacs. At one stage our driver performed a

Michael Schumacher ploy by leaving the "track" to cut across land that was making contact with man for the first time since the Big Bang to gain pole position, sounding his horn in triumph. The other two vehicles, at different times, ended up in ditches at angles of about thirty degrees, each time fortunately being pulled out by tow ropes. In the back of ours, which I shared with a couple from Hong Kong and two women from Switzerland, we took it in turns to grab and pull back in those who seemed to be leaving the vehicle in an involuntary manner. We were constantly shouting "duck!", as briars that could do facial damage that no Californian plastic surgeon could repair, appeared on our immediate horizon. One of the women had her bandanna ripped off by a passing branch only for it to be skilfully retrieved by the lightening dexterity of a passenger on a following vehicle. We reckoned this part of the journey took about an hour and a quarter. We arrived in Battenbang exhausted and absolutely filthy, being caked in dust and dirt from head to toe. Despite the constant warnings not to veer from the roads, as Cambodia was one of the most concentrated areas of mines and unexploded bombs in the world, I don't think anyone would have missed it for the world. The journey will remain long in the memory.

I stayed in Battenbang for a couple of nights. The small town was more industrious than picturesque. However wandering out over the nearby river, spanned by a rickety wooden bridge, through the darkness and the swaying trees I spotted a cluster of newly built restaurants and clubs which were mainly deserted. I dined in a large beautifully designed restaurant along with about two others. The staff outnumbered the patrons about six to one. I felt that someone had been tipped off about an imminent Klondike and they were preparing for the rush. I returned to Phnom Penh sedately by coach then back to Saigon.

Contentment at Last

For the next couple of months I fell into a rather satisfying and enjoyable routine. I was very busy, working seven days a week, six until nine every evening and nine until twelve Saturday and Sunday mornings. The weekends were hectic as I taught my Tiny Tots in the mornings before preparing my intermediate evening lessons, then heading out again to the various schools around Saigon. In the evenings after lessons I would usually meet Cindy for dinner at a variety of restaurants and often Donna, Drew and Michelle would be in tow. Saturday nights we'd often "tie one on," as my American friends described it, in the more salubrious district of Dong Khoi, so my Tiny Tot classes were usually conducted with a hangover. This was challenging as I acted out role plays using puppets, Benny and Sue, and a chunk of the lessons involved a lot of physical activity such as standing, sitting, walking, marching, jumping, catching and throwing balls, playing "Simon Says", and of course singing and nursery rhymes. If I did have blanks in my timetable I would invariably get a call from the VUS H.Q. with a happy greeting from one of the lovely office girls saying

"Missa Dennis will you do substitution.?"

Because of the large number of teachers on roll there were regular, and usually last minute, absentees and I'm sure I was the first they called as I was a soft touch for their persuasive charms. Having taken a call I would charge across town with Elvis often arriving half an hour after the lesson should have started without any knowledge of the class or subject matter. Some of these lessons were the most enjoyable as the adrenalin pumped I sought spur of the moment inspiration, improvisation and they were often more energetic and successful that my prepared lessons. I even covered maths on one occasion, but fortunately it was based on the seven times table with a class of eight year olds.

Later sitting in a restaurant, tie loosened, as my clothes clung to me in the humid Saigon night, waiting for dinner with an ice cold beer, especially after particularly good performance, was just the best of feelings. The free moments in the afternoons up top slumped in a hammock reading were just so relaxing and satisfying. I was reading a lot and catching up on a misspent youth by concentrating on the books that most English teachers should have read before they are thirty. I also enjoyed reading books about Indo-China, such as The Quiet American and The Killing Fields, as it added another dimension and great atmosphere being on location.

Sweet Sorrow

Of course this blissful contentment couldn't last and Cindy informed me that she was heading home. There was a family occasion, and Cindy being very close to her aging parents brought forward her leaving date. A few weeks later I put her bags in the back of a cab and after an emotional farewell she was gone. Later I sat outside on the communal patio attempting to read but found myself looking across at her room. My great friend and emotional crutch had gone but this time I was strong enough to carry on.

I concentrated on planning my journey home, poring over my library of Lonely Planet guide books, fine tuning my itinerary. I was to fly to Hanoi, then on to Laos travelling to Vientiane, Phosovan, and Luang Prubang before crossing into Thailand, moving through Chang Mai in the north and down to Bangkok. Here I would hopefully obtain a visa for Burma, a country that excited me greatly. I was attracted by the scent of the Raj and Road to Mandalay. I read about Mandalay Hill and Fort, of the temples of Bagan, and I dreamed of sipping Pimms in The Strand Hotel in Rangoon like Kipling, Somerset Maugham and the last Viceroy of India, Louis Mountbatten.

I planned to go to Phosovan and the Plain of Jars, a mysterious phenomenon in the Equatorial Rainforest of northern Laos, where hundreds of stone pots, some weighing six tons, lie haphazardly across several large fields. Scientists have calculated that they are about two thousand years old but the reason for their existence and how they got there is still a mystery. This area was carpet bombed by the USA and there is a huge amount of ordnance still to be made safe, so further investigation had been stymied.

I had been in Saigon about eight months and I had only days of my six month contract left. I had been offered an extension but I had already made a positive contact with a school in Ecuador for my next contract and I just could not wait for the great adventure of my journey home. During the last few days of my time in Saigon I had begun soaking up and being more sensitive and alive to what I would be missing, probably never to witness again. I arrived there an emotional wreck, an object of pity to friends and family back home, and now I felt blessed to be alive; the world had become my oyster.

Saigon was a place of extremes. If I made a clinical list of pros and cons I am sure the pros would be in the ascendant. It's always oppressively hot. It can be 37/38c and higher with the daytime minimum around 33C. It hadn't rained since the of end of the November but the heavens duly opened in May right on schedule. Nature's clock extends to each storm, usually between two and four in the afternoons, which is very thoughtful as with good planning you can avoid the biblical deluge.

I discovered that there were 4 million motorbikes in Saigon. This unbelievable number, along with cars and buses, contest the roads each day. The pollution is choking. The very few rules of the road are often ignored. For example there was only one stipulation for roundabouts and that was to travel anti-clockwise. How and when you join and leave was entirely up to the individual. On the wide boulevards the cars, buses and bikes were up to fourteen abreast and more at rush hours, all accessing and leaving the roundabouts at the same time. With such congestion it became quite intimate in the communal horn blowing melee. However there was very little road rage. The horns weren't tooted in a fit of pique but just bat like indications of navigation and avoidance. The locals accepted the anarchy and the fact they all drove as crazily as each other. The type and amount of merchandise they carried was staggering. For example piles of boxes or plastic bottles could be seen travelling along the street unaided until you noticed at the bottom a couple of protruding wheels. Trapped at the lights in dense traffic one day, I noticed a pair of women's legs akimbo reaching up above the heads. When this mysterious load passed it turned out to be a young and rather embarrassed male pillion passenger carrying the bottom half of a mannequin. When I first arrived I found the whole traffic experience fascinating and entertaining. My attitude later was more reserved as there had been so many uninsured English teachers involved in accidents, one almost fatal.

I loved the street life and the characters both local and imported who were a constant source of fun and entertainment. I usually ate and drank "on De Tham," the backpacker area. The food and drinks were good and cheap. It was usually al fresco so you ate each day and night on or near the street. We regularly frequented this area and I, with others, some of whom had been here for years, became familiar figures, as opposed to the backpackers who only spent a few days before moving on. The atmosphere, especially at night, was quite exotic. While we were dining, especially if we were on or near the street, we would be approached by a regular stream of vendors each with their peculiar style and product. The book women of course were regulars carrying their huge pile of books in straps. Most of these women were tiny and carried these heavy loads for hours each day and night. They began to leave us alone after we eventually bought all the titles which never changed. They mainly targeted the backpackers who were just passing through. These books were photocopied and sold a lot cheaper than the originals. Occasionally the copying would be unclear so they typed in the word or words they thought should be there, often with hilarious Malapropisms resulting. I was convinced this kind of editing would have resulted in James Joyce's Ulysses becoming intelligible for the first time.

There were quite a few kids on the street selling roses, gum, or cigarettes, until very late at night. Some were very young and took cynical advantage of their cuteness. They were allowed to wander into the very deep recesses of the restaurants by the owners and waiters as long as they didn't harass the punters too much. One night I was dining alone in La Cantina after class, when two girls of about seven and nine, for whom the word cute was invented, came in with expressions of resigned cynicism to try to sell me a rose, despite the fact I was alone. They rather impertinently sat down at my table and asked me to buy them a coke, which of course I did. Then they bummed a pen off the waitress and gave it to me along with an upturned restaurant business card. This left me bemused until the waitress said they wanted me to draw a fish. It was then I slowly recalled that a few evenings earlier I was there with Donna and a few others and we had consumed a few bottles of Delat red. I could vaguely remember drawing pictures for them and they wanted a repeat performance. So I gave them another art lesson as they copied my little sketches. I'm not sure if the restaurant owners were annoyed about a reprint of their business cards, but it was just nice to see the two girls could still be kids given the opportunity.

The Vietnamese were very inward looking. They rarely crossed their own borders and despite satellite TV and the internet they mainly consumed their own culture and largely ignored or were oblivious to western influences. This is very admirable but makes teaching difficult. The only well known westerner the kids seemed to recognise was Britney Spears. I taught a lesson one evening based around George Washington and Nelson Mandela. I could understand ignorance regarding George Washington but nobody had ever heard of Nelson Mandela either. We also used songs and chants in teaching. I had attempted to change chants to rap to make it more fun and contemporary, doing an Emimem impression at the same time. The reaction was bewilderment and the begging of the question, "What is rap and who the hell is Eminem?". The kids liked to watch Asian drama such as a very popular series, which I think was Chinese, about ancient warlords, where the good guys and the bad guys have degrees of magical powers. It seemed very dramatic and mystical with the many fight scenes shrouded in mist with the protagonists blessed with superhuman abilities. On one occasion I was in the 333 Bar/restaurant dining after finishing at 9.00pm when a familiar duet strolled in, a girl about nine and her brother who was about seven. They were selling gum and cigarettes. The aforementioned Chinese drama was on the TV which was positioned directly above my head. They were eyeing the programme while doing their business, before they slowly sidled across to my table and without looking away surreptitiously sat on the edge of the chairs before shifting gradually into more comfortable positions hoping that nobody would notice their presence. They both sat there, cigarette packets in hand, necks craned almost vertically, mouths agape, eyes like organ stops, for about forty five minutes blissfully unaware of anyone else. It reminded me of being a kid in my grandmother's house quietly watching American movies hoping I wouldn't be noticed until it was too late and I would have to stay the night.

The Vietnamese people who wear conical hats seem to belong to an identifiable lower working class, much like the old cloth caps in the first half of the 20th century in the UK. When I first arrived this class was made up of mainly, what seemed, prematurely aged women, and generated sympathy and pity from western visitors. Many of these women were tiny and each day carried what appeared like three times their own weight via yoked straw containers full of fruit, vegetables, and other produce. They almost trotted along similar to the gait of a walking race, heel/ toe, heel/toe, as if they could not wait to get to their destination and unload. But later I came across these women having their version of elevenses. They were to be found sat on street corners happy, laughing, and chatting amongst their own. I witnessed this with other members of this class. There were the women, usually young, some very attractive, who sold stuff that few people wanted from a tray similar to the old cinema usherettes. These trays were filled with back scratchers, miniature scissors, nail clippers etc. They went to each street bar and restaurant throughout the day and night to sell their cheap merchandise. If their ratio of sales was one in a hundred they were lucky. They were very rarely pushy and although most prospective punters were civil and well mannered, they did have to put up with occasional ignorance and abuse. Despite this they always retained a quiet dignity. They also seemed to take a pride in their appearance in albeit cheap apparel. I took a couple of photos of these women that captured this serenity. It cost me 10,000 dong for another back scratcher though.

There were those of this class who were small vendors on the street. On one occasion I bought some combs from a wrinkled old dear in a conical hat who could only be described as the comb lady, as that was all she sold from a wooden tray. During the negotiations, hampered by the language barrier, she asked me if I wanted new ones or the cheaper second hand ones. I settled for the former. She obviously went around collecting old combs, hopefully cleaning them up, and selling them, creating a niche market in the process. I paid her, and she gave change from her wedge of dong (16,500 to the dollar!) that was stuffed in her pocket. She exuded independence and seemed as content and satisfied doing a "bit of biz" as any car room salesman selling a new Mercedes. Many of these people scavenged the rubbish from skips in the streets at night. They looked dour and dirty, but if you made contact with them for any reason they always had a ready, if somewhat toothless, smile. Without trying to sound patronising these people epitomised the dignity of labour much admired by Ruskin and Carlyle, neither of whom did a day's physical labour in their lives!

The Vietnamese were very sociable. Travelling regularly across the city I covered many a square mile and witnessed the locals of all classes "wining and dining" seven nights a week. On the streets there were swarms of humanity amongst the multitude of plates and cooking pots with a lot of scurrying around and sharing. The next financial strata filled large noisy well lit licensed canteens and the moneyed classes gathered in bright, brash, neon lit restaurants.

In a perverse way, as he overcharged me and endangered my life with drink, I would miss Elvis. Other bikers built up a rapport with their regular clients, each in turn teaching a bit of English and Vietnamese. If they passed you walking home they'd tell you to hop on for a free trip home, but not Elvis, he was totally mercenary. Why did I use him? Mainly because he had the "Knowledge". He knew Saigon better than all the others. On many occasions I received text messages while teaching at night to meet people at some obscure rendezvous, and he always knew how to get there. Lots of bikers were limited in their knowledge of Saigon and the ability to interpret the most basic of instructions. Most had families. From what we had see, Elvis was a free spirit. Talking about spirits, of course Elvis liked a drop, whiskey in particular. One of his regular haunts was on the corner of our alley, where he huddled with his cronies on little stools, singing and playing guitar, while hurling tumblers of cheap hooch down their necks with monotonous regularity. I accepted the odd invitation to join them creating surreal Jack Kerouac moments.

And so to the teaching. Throughout my early adult life during various occupations, I always thought I was meant to do something else . . . teach perhaps. This was borne out of the feeling of incompetence and inadequacy in the practical jobs into which I was initially shoehorned. I did develop a burning vocation after seeing Ken Loache's film "Kes" and from my own school experience where I was secondary modern created factory fodder. Only grammar schools were allowed to produce teachers. Fate and people kept putting things in my hands, like spanners and screwdrivers. By the time, in later adulthood, when my fencing, with more flying buttresses than York Minster, still collapsed three times in a fortnight, and my fitted wardrobes could accurately be described as rustic, I was resigned to my lowly position in the practical world. I knew the score. I had accepted my limitations. Imagine the painful learning period when I was still unaware of this level of incompetence that fate bestowed on me. In the RAF I failed the formality of the SAC practical board twice. Nobody can remember anyone failing it once! I came close to blowing up a transmitter hall on more than one occasion.

After my China debacle I thought the teaching idea was dead and buried. However the combination of time and realising the depressing alternative, I changed my mind after experiencing a "Turn again Whittington moment." The streets of Saigon were not paved with gold, but it had been a great experience working there. It was one of my better decisions. I taught a wide range of ages from five to middle aged adults and from the gifted to the less gifted. It had been demanding, but very rewarding. Probably the most inspiring were my Tiny Tots classes on each Saturday and Sunday morning, some of it during the historic Welsh Grand Slam campaign. Each Sunday morning with a celebratory hangover still pounding in my head I begrudgingly headed to school knowing I had to be a combination of Valerie Singleton, Doctor Spock and the Chuckle Brothers. I did have the assistance of Benny, Sue, Mike and Julie (puppets) and other props. However as soon as I walked into the classroom I experienced an unconscious metamorphosis from an old grouch to Mr. Entertainment. If you have ever walked past a primary school and heard singing from innocent infant school children, which must be the most beautiful sound in the world, you will understand. Imagine orchestrating and being amongst a class of twenty four, five and six year old Asian children happily, yet earnestly, singing "An Elephant is bigger than a Flea". Is there a better job?

It is said that people judge you by the friends you have. I have always felt comfortable with that. "Our" kind of people seem to gravitate towards each other. I found that at home in Cardiff, away in the RAF all those years ago, and certainly it was the case in Saigon. The original "crew" from our course always kept in touch. There was mixture of old and young, but that didn't prevent the unity that survived right to the end. The younger element did have more expensive tastes and racier lifestyles, but that's to be expected. Out of the younger crowd I will always remember Patrick, the uncomplicated New Jersey kid who exuded optimism, humour and enthusiasm.

Cindy was back in Chicago and prospering as ever but we continued to e-mail each other regularly. She was my closest friend, and helped me through my "Van Gogh" period. No, I didn't paint, but I was in danger of cutting off my ear. She said of my first weeks here, "I thought you were nuts" She was right I was temporarily unhinged. She once described herself as "a tough Chicago broad". I think she is tough and resilient, you have to be to achieve the level of success she has attained in what is probably a man's world. But she gave up a successful and lucrative career to teach and live in a far less comfortable environment. She's so tough that she was a strict vegetarian, was the softest of touches for all the street kids, and was as committed and protective towards her students as Donna. What she had was "bottle". During the first week of training the admin staff from the course asked for volunteers to teach on the outskirts of Saigon on the following Saturday morning. After three days training everybody including the most extrovert and confident shied away . . . except Cindy.

"Sure I'll do it, I like working from the seat of my pants"

She was a great success too, I know because I was there cowering at the back of the class. And how many women would travel through Laos, one of the most cut off, and remote countries in the world, alone?

A Stroke of Bad Luck

With only a few days to go I was floating on a cloud of expectation. Most of my clothes were laundered ready for packing and I had purchased my flight ticket to Hanoi. I had cleaned out my bank account of over 3,000 dollars to finance my planned six week trip. I had risen from the depths of despair of physical and mental torment to the astral plain of serene contentment. My renaissance was complete and nothing would get to me now . . . except maybe a stroke.

It was towards the end of my penultimate lesson when, after a period of pre-teaching, having set the class a written exercise, I bent to pick up a top of a board marker when I experienced stasis. Balanced on one knee I was paralysed in suspended animation looking at the class, who were blissfully unaware of my predicament, as their heads were down conscientiously continuing the work I had set. At first I though I was dreaming. Then I was aware of a sparking, like wires shorting, at the back of my head while a message from another part was telling me,

"You are not dreaming, you are about to collapse embarrassingly in front of the class."

Then I snapped out of it. The whole episode probably lasted less than ten seconds. I slumped at my desk as the students continued to work in silence and thought to myself,

"What the fuck was that?"

I finished the lesson tentatively while nursing a headache. Elvis took me to dinner. I sat alone attempting to make sense of what had just happened as I sipped my beer still nursing a pounding headache.

The following morning along with my headache I set off for Chi's Bar for a late breakfast. While walking along the now familiar teeming streets I felt that my feet, especially the left foot, was slapping down with a lack of feeling in my toes, but when I looked down I was walking normally. My arms were throbbing incessantly. I chatted with the girls in Chi's Bar and felt I didn't have total control over my lips. I went to the gents and stared in the mirror and began talking to myself. Everything seemed normal except for the fact I was talking to myself in the gents. I went back to my pad to prepare for my last lesson. I sat on my bed. Something was wrong and I felt it was serious. On top of what I assumed were stroke symptoms I began to feel acute nausea. Again I studied my features in the mirror looking for signs of slackness of the mouth or jaw but externally I looked fine. I felt that my nervous system was operating at ninety percent efficiency. My last lesson was surprisingly lively mainly because it had lots of great and lively characters in the class so I, despite my calm intent, took my life in my hands and was swept away with their joyous enthusiasm. I decided that I would continue with my travel plans hoping that the symptoms of whatever I had would abate and then disappear.

My last day in Saigon was perfect. I had contacted Nash, our course instructor, to request a reference. He informed me that someone had, on my recommendation, signed up with TEFL International for their course, and I was due $100 as part of their introduction scheme. So we arranged to meet for lunch. As well as the reference and the $100 we had a convivial chat mainly about Saigon. He said I looked different, and I did, as my recovered mental state had improved my physical wellbeing considerably.

I had requested a reference from VUS, but all I received was their statutory record of employment letter, with just dates. This was understandable as they had scores of teachers on their books many, like me, staying a short time. I had e-mailed the inscrutable Miss Chi with a litany of my attributes, i.e. never a missed lesson, always early, always a soft touch for substitutions, especially late ones, and always responding positively to the pleas of the admin staff. I even taught maths for God's sake! Miss Chi wielded the power in

VUS and although petite she had a presence. She could have played a sinister Asian spy in a James Bond movie. I requested that if a prospective employer contacted her she could at least confirm the above? She did not reply. After I left Nash I took all the books back to VUS. I got the feeling that the staff, who I liked very much, were genuinely sorry to see me go. One of girls gave me a letter from Miss Chi. I took it outside to read and it was an excellent reference from her. I went to her office and with a cheesy grin and a big thumbs up, from the doorway, mouthed the words "Thank You". As ever busily engrossed in her work, she looked up and gave me an instinctive beaming smile, eyes and all. Did I detect a chink, no pun intended, in her armour? She probably berated herself later for her moment of weakness.

The last evening was spent with Donna, Drew and Michelle in our regular haunt, La Cantina. The usual suspects of street kids must have heard on the grapevine that the three softest touches in Saigon were in situ, and appeared like bees around a honey pot. They were back and forth all evening and didn't leave empty handed. I like to think that although they were streetwise and had to make a buck, they liked our company, felt safe and wanted to be with us. I think this was confirmed when one of the girls fell asleep curled up in Donna's lap and slept blissfully for hours.

There was a youth, who looked about 17 but was probably older, who worked at the guesthouse. His job seemed to be to maintain the plants and keep the top floors spic and span. I had never seen him not working. He was never found leaning on a brush, against a wall, or sat down. He was always active, lost in continuous chores. He was always happy, smiling, and disarmingly deferential. Most of the people who worked in the guesthouse also lived there and were paid very little above their board and lodge. So I gave him my $50.00 CD player. If I have ever made anyone happier in my life I cannot recall the occasion. When I left my room on the final morning one of the women started calling out. She was calling him on his instruction no doubt. He ran up the stairs and with great bravado lifted my very heavy case on to his shoulders and carried it down the five flights of stairs. A beaming smile never left his face.

I wanted to leave tips, but wasn't sure whether to give money to individuals, with the danger of accidentally leaving somebody out, or giving a lump sum to Si, the manager, for him to disperse amongst the staff. I sought advice from the beatified Drew. He advised me to give it Si, but to leave it to the last minute otherwise I would see a big present outside my door. The staff, who had little money, witnessed our lifestyles and excesses, would have bought me a present with the tips that I gave them. Lovely people. A lot of the staff were there to wave me off, which was a nice touch. So it was goodbye Saigon and thanks for saving my life

Off to See Uncle Ho

I jumped into a mini-van at Hanoi airport which was packed with locals. The excitement of the moment seemed to override any health issues. I felt elated driving into Hanoi, a city that seemed to the West like an indefatigable diabolical citadel of mysterious evil intent in the late sixties. It was the location of the infamous Hanoi Hilton, the water cages, and the indestructible, charismatic poet, philosopher, and the man who outwitted and defeated the most powerful nation on the planet, Ho Chi Minh. This was one of the places, in my youth, that dominated my consciousness with images from newsreels, films like the Deer Hunter, and Apocalypse Now, and I never for one moment in those far off days thought I would travel there.

Well my Hanoi visit got off to a good start. I booked into a little guesthouse in the old quarter so close to the Hoan Kiem Lake that I could have almost dipped my toe in from the doorway. After checking in I went looking for a cold beer. I happened to be staying yards away from the main interchange of the old quarter near the six story building which housed the City View bar/cafe at the top. I climbed the stairs and sat out outside to sip my beer, taking in the view of the lake and the busy main square below me. As I lent on the balcony I noticed, a few feet away, a bloke about my age doing the same thing. He was wearing a Steve Howe T-shirt. The uninitiated would say "Steve who? To enlighten them he is one of the greatest guitarists in the world and plays with the band, Yes. The real philistines may say "Who are Yes"? It's the band I have seen and played the most since the seventies. OK Steve is a bit obscure to the masses that's why to see his name in Hanoi of all places made me thrust off my natural reticence and make a comment. My fellow Yes fan turned out to be a very open and gregarious American.

"My name's Tom, may I join you?" he said shaking my hand.

Tom was a physician who spent a month a year in Vietnam on secondment. He was involved with cerebral palsy and was part of a small team, including anaesthetists, funded by the US government. He didn't say what he specialised in, and as it's possible, let me use a bit of poetic license for this little anecdote and assume he was brain surgeon. So there was me and this brain surgeon high above Hanoi babbling excitedly, like high school kids, about Yes, Led Zeppelin, King Crimson, Dylan . . . etc. We also did politics, as he was another George W Bush baiting anti-war liberal. He was interested in the '84 miner's strike and we discussed the role of the miner's leader, Arthur Scargill, and his effect on the outcome. He used to live in San Francisco and had moved to a place called Fresno not too far away, but into Republican country where his neighbours looked upon him as a "woolly headed tree-hugging liberal". After an hour or so his wife and her friend turned up after a spot of shopping. By the look on their faces they had seen this scenario before and legged it back to the hotel.

Tom was a practicing Catholic (I didn't mention I had been lapsed for 45years) and a member of a Fresno congregation that included Neil Young who had a disabled daughter, I believe, with cerebral palsy. He had been involved, as member of an organisation to which Tom belonged, in creating acoustic benefit concerts with line ups that have included Eric Clapton, The Who, Macca, and of course Neil Young, to mention a few. We were there for hours hardly taking a breather. As I mentioned before our kind seem to gravitate toward each other. Unfortunately it was his last night in Vietnam and he had to drag himself away at about six to prepare for a formal farewell dinner. He said I would be very welcome to meet up with him at a jazz club later that evening. I didn't go mainly because I may have been a distraction, the odd one out, and of course my less than robust health. I'm not sure if his wife would have appreciated it either. I took a photo of him overlooking the Hanoi skyline proudly wearing the Steve Howe T-shirt and e-mailed it to him later. I wasn't tempted to ask him for a diagnosis of my condition as it seemed unfair and would have upset the mood of the afternoon. A few minutes after he'd gone I called for my bill only to find he'd paid my rather extensive bar tab. Talk about friends well met. Thank you Steve Howe for an entertaining afternoon.

I loved Hanoi, or at least the old quarter where I stayed. It's situated at the north end of the lake and is a warren of little streets that were originally built in the thirteenth century. It was like the narrow back streets of Paris, each one lined with trees. Each day and especially the evenings it thronged with humanity. The ubiquitous motor bikes dominated of course and the place buzzed with cyclos, markets, the locals scurrying to and fro, and a contingent of western tourists. I stayed in Mais On, a little guesthouse recommend in Lonely Planet run by a lovely old lady. She was so old she spoke French more readily than Vietnamese and we conversed with some basic French. Her guesthouse was littered with beautiful French pieces of objects d'art. Each day I'd spend some time sat on my little balcony looking down three floors watching the world of this charming little street and all the characters in it, go by.

I did the organised day long city tour with about eight others in a people carrier. We went to see Uncle Ho in his mausoleum looking resplendent after his recent periodic make-over in Moscow and several other tourist attractions including the very impressive Museum of Ethnology. It celebrated the cultures of the surprisingly very diverse ethnic mix in Vietnam. On the tour, which included lunch, I got chatting to another American Bush baiting liberal. Although he seemed a very serious and earnest academic we still revelled in the recent George Galloway destruction of his Senate inquisitors. There were two couples from Australia who reminded me of Rab C Nesbit and Mary Hen along with Jamesie and his missus. At each stop they ordered four beers quickly followed by four more. They were covered in tattoos, very funny, very likable and as I discovered had travelled extensively and they were genuinely interested in the local culture.

I had an alarming experience in the gardens of the Temple of Literature which unnerved me. While our group were gathering after the tour I sat on a bench to rest my weary limbs. A Vietnamese boy about ten years old sat at the end of the bench and engaged me in a brief conversation asking me where I was from and if I liked Hanoi, in reasonable English. After a pause I thought I had better empty my bladder before the bus trip back to the hotel. While relieving myself in the nearby urinal the boy appeared alongside me and posed the question,

"Do you want sex?" I felt the blood drain from my body. I consider myself an unflappable man of the world but I became totally flustered bellowing at him to go away, which he ignored repeating his offer. In an effort to immediately vacate the place I attempted to stop my gushing piss, zip up, an get out which I managed clumsily, with urine dribbling uncomfortably down my legs. Out in the daylight I mingled back into my group as they clambered back on the bus. I sat in stunned silence during the trip back.

I went to see the famous Hanoi water puppets which was very impressive. The accompanying live music was equally charming and they included a free CD of it with the entrance fee. It was now the wet season and on two consecutive nights I got trapped in a restaurant because of tremendous downpours and flooding. The first night I was drinking Dalat red by the glass and when I got to seventh, I noticed I was drawing attention to myself. Well I couldn't just sit there! The second night I bought the bottle. On this occasion the water came into the restaurant and those at the front ate with their feet up on chairs. When a large vehicle like a truck and especially a bus came past the wake created waves that lashed the back of the restaurant leaving debris throughout the restaurant when it ebbed. Both nights I waded home through knee high floods carrying my shoes.

I felt that my condition was improving as I was feeling reasonably good most of the time. However I suffered periods of nausea, throbbing arms and my head seemed to be experiencing a steady drone like the sound of an electric sub-station. Despite this I decided to be positive and booked my flight to Vientiane. I had a Gallic send off the following morning. My taxi came at 6.00am and as I was bidding farewell to my landlady she beckoned me down to her four feet nine and gave be a big hug, and kisses on both two cheeks, French style.

Feeling Lousy in Laos

Like Vietnam, Laos was a place I thought I would never visit mainly because until the mid nineties both countries discouraged travel and in parts of both Laos and Cambodia the Paten Lao and

Khmer Rouge rebels still controlled parts of their countries. During the eighties and nineties there were quite a few young head strong adventurers who paid with their lives in those parts. After arriving at Wattay International Airport I headed to the Soradith Guesthouse selected from Lonely Planet which turned out to be a wise choice. It was off the beaten track and the rooms that nestled amongst the picturesque foliage were air-conditioned, clean, comfortable, with hot showers and multi-channelled cable TV. All this for ten dollars, incredible.

Being off the beaten track, later in the evening I wandered to the local night market and plonked myself down on a small stool and ate with the locals in the warm sultry night. I was loving this trip and was determined to continue.

The following morning I took a tuk-tuk around the city. The wide French boulevards were the same as those in Vietnam but hardly used. Vientiane for the most part was quiet and sedate, what little traffic about was driven within the law. They stopped at lights, even late at night when there was no traffic around and nobody to bear witnesses to minor traffic violations. This calm seemed part of the national psyche or maybe the people were cowed after years of war and military government. I was experiencing a totally different culture to the vibrant and often manic Hanoi and especially Saigon.

Later my uncharted wanderings led me to the river front and I ambled along the Mekong in the sunshine. As I wandered absentmindedly I noticed a woman waving trying to attract my attention. We walked toward each other. I could see she was wearing well worn evening clothes with high heels carrying a handbag and looking a bit bedraggled. I thought I was about to be solicited but when we reached each other this relatively young woman asked me for money for food. She did look desperate so I walked her to a nearby café and gave the proprietor five dollars, more than enough for a good feed. Two men at a table looked at me, incredulously shaking their heads. She thanked me and I wandered on. I may have been naive but also I may have been a momentary straw for her to clutch at. A short while later I found myself walking back to that café and crossed over to the opposite side of the street. I looked into the café and saw the woman eating ravenously while the two cynical men chatted idly over their coffees.

During the afternoon I took another leisurely stroll from the guesthouse down several deserted rural roads. It was hot and my newly purchased straw hat protected me from the blazing sun. I reached a small village with an internet café and seeking refuge from the sun, went in, sat down, and logged on. As I was typing away I suddenly felt the onset of an ever growing nausea consume me. This was more frightening and debilitating than any other attack. I felt weak and found myself slumped forward with my throbbing arms and tingling fingers dangling almost to the floor. My head was pounding and I felt dreadful. I also felt vulnerable with fear and foreboding beyond this illness. I had refused to face up to the fact I had no travel insurance. To obtain travel insurance from a British company I would've had to insure in the UK. I had topped up my insurance from Vietnam which had now run out and this topping up procedure could only be done once. I could have used a Vietnamese company but that would not have given me peace of mind. I now had visions of being take seriously ill with the cost entailed bankrupting me and maybe a few family members. I realised I had to get back to the UK as soon as possible. The attack subsided and I slowly trudged my way back to the guesthouse convinced that my feet were slapping uncontrollably down. As soon as I got back I called a cab to a travel agent in the centre of the city and booked my flight home for the following day.

Later I felt a lot better physically and mentally as my relief of knowing I would be seeing my GP within days suppressed any major disappointment of a ruined trip of a lifetime. I got spruced up and headed for the Knob Chai Deu Food Garden. It was busy with mainly young ex-pats, embassy personnel and travellers passing through. I found a table in the exterior garden and got stuck into a few cold beers while studying the menu. Some of the tables had holes in the centre the size of a large platter where for certain dishes the waiter would provide hot coals in metal braziers lowered in by chains. The diners would then cook their raw meat as and when required to their own taste and specification. I asked a couple near me if I could take a photograph of this process and they duly obliged.

He was British with a cockney accent and invited me over to their table. His name was Mick and I would guess in his early fifties and his wife was Lao and half his age. He was affable as you'd expect from a cockney especially if they are boozed as he was. He was typical of many middle-aged ex-pat males in that part of the world. Divorced at least once with a young local partner and a big drink problem, but I was glad of their company. I got the impression that he was glad to be with someone from the old country. He was ex-RAF Armaments and was clearing mines and other ordnance in the country, which meant he would be gainfully employed for quite some time. When he discovered I was former RAF we became like ex-comrades. We reminisced and despite my three and a half years duty compared to his twenty two I held my own. The fact I went to Singapore twice elicited a certain amount of mock jealousy.

"Y' jammy git" he exclaimed.

He then began to explain that the one posting he coveted most but failed to secure was RAF Gan, a staging post on an island in the Maldives. Since its closure in the mid seventies it has been etched into service folk law, not just because of its exotic location but also its unique culture and traditions. As he was regaling us about tales he'd heard about this military Shangri-la he noticed my growing wry smile.

"Y'didn't didchu?

I began to laugh.

"That's not bleeding fair, I spent my life serving man and boy for twenty two years and what did I get? Cyprus and bleeding Bahrain!"

Although he was showing mock horror at the cards he'd been dealt it made me realise that I'd had lots of good fortune in my time and maybe now my allotted misfortunes were coming home to roost. He was well entertained by my anecdotes and stories of Gan as the beer flowed. Mick's wife was from Phonsavan and we chatted about her village. Unlike the Vietnamese who never mention the war and are very forgiving of the Americans she could not forgive them. Phonsavan is a relatively new community and is the result of the American carpet bombing of the early seventies. The most bombed area was a group of very small hamlets and the local people took refuge in caves where they lived until the incessant attacks finally ceased. Most of their homes were destroyed and the small town of Phonsavan was built as a result after the war. I tried to drag myself away but succumbed to a couple more rounds before bidding my fond farewell and heading back.

When I arrived back at the guesthouse there were a few people sat on the veranda amongst the dense lush plants. I ordered a beer and joined them. They were young Lao men who worked there. One of them was attempting to complete his English homework from a night school course and sought my help on a few questions. When, rashly, I told him I was an English teacher he invited himself to my table and I embarked on my last lesson in Asia. I helped him as I consumed several more nightcaps under a dim flickering light amongst the banter and laughter of his friends with the backdrop of a chattering, balmy tropical night. God I was going to miss all this. As I swayed unsteadily down the path through the luxuriant foliage to my bed, through anguished gritted teeth, I vowed I would be back . . . . and two years almost to the day, I was.

OK Doc Give It To Me Straight

On my return to Cardiff I was fortunate enough to time my arrival as my niece and her husband headed to New Zealand for a month to see the rugby test series between the British Lions and the All Blacks. So I house sat for them in their terraced cottage in Pontypridd about a dozen miles from Cardiff. I also had use of their car. At the first opportunity I headed for my GP. The nausea had disappeared but the buzzing in my head continued, along with periodical throbbing in my arms and fingers. I still felt my nervous system was under performing. As a layman I could only think of one diagnosis, that I had suffered a stroke. After some basic tests and discussions of the symptoms the doctor did indeed suggest transient ischemic attack (TIA), a mini stroke, but also mentioned the possibility of epilepsy which was a bolt from the blue. It was because of the latter that he banned me from driving, adding that he would have to contact the police and the DVLA in writing. I was to undergo a brain scan amongst other tests. I drove from Cardiff back to Pontypridd then abandoned driving for at least the immediate future. All my life I had been in rude health, rarely ill or absent from work. I was a non smoker, fit and healthy for my age and played five-a-side football, was always active and now I'd probably suffered a stroke or had become epileptic or perhaps both and had been banned from driving for health reasons.

I now commuted to Cardiff by train to undergo brain scans, various other tests and visit family and friends. One of the tests was to have my torso wired with electrodes front and back over a forty eight hour period. In the meantime after a long drawn out application process and telephone interview from Ecuador I had secured another teaching job in a beautiful place called Cuenca. It didn't start for another seven weeks and I had hoped to get a quick diagnosis so, if allowed, I could enrol on a month's Spanish Course in Peru beforehand. I received a notice of an appointment with the head consultant for two weeks before the job began which threw all my plans of a crash course in Spanish out of the window. I went to the hospital to inform them of my situation and to my nervous delight a sympathetic administrator slotted me in for that morning.

When my time came the consultant seemed harassed and wasn't happy having to read my file for the first time as I sat there waiting to be diagnosed. She asked me some pertinent questions, scanned my tests' details and then confirmed that I had in fact suffered a minor stroke. She instructed me to take an aspirin a day and that was about it. I was now officially a stroke victim. All my life when filling out forms that have referred to health I had always ritually ticked the boxes down the right hand side indicating no to all the ailments on offer. From then on when the question "Have you ever suffered from a stroke?" appeared I would be duty bound to tick one of the left hand boxes. Would I get insurance or a work visa? If I couldn't what was the alternative? A job as care worker living a bed-sit? No, this wasn't an option which left the black capsule scenario I hadn't considered for quite a while.

However fate stepped in which resulted in a second opinion that revived my fortunes and spirits. I had to make a personal appearance at the Ecuadorian Embassy in London to secure my work visa. By telephone an official there told me that I would be expected on the 28th July, less than two weeks before the start of the term and this was non negotiable. At the time I was annoyed and frustrated but this news turned out to be very fortuitous. A few weeks later my niece and her husband returned from New Zealand and I moved to Cardiff University students' campus quarters. The university hire out rooms when the students were away and I spent several weeks in a mainly deserted seat of education. All this delay and uncertainty was beginning to get to me plus I was now a bona fide card carrying stroke victim. Then while sorting out some papers I came across my original appointment with the head consultant at the hospital which was two days before travelling to the Ecuadorian Embassy. I had planned to be in Peru weeks previously but I thought a second opinion by the head honcho would be worth pursuing. The hospital confirmed that this appointment still stood and had not been cancelled. I saw this as a very outside chance as I never doubted the original diagnosis but still thought it worth a try so I presented myself more in hope than expectation. Again the consultant asked the familiar questions, did a few physical tests, and shone a torch into my eyes. He had only cursory glances at the contents of my file as he must have familiarised himself earlier. My heart was sinking as he seemed to be going through the motions until he smiled and said. "You haven't suffered a stroke and come off the aspirin immediately" I was elated and despite my questioning he couldn't give a coherent explanation but said he would contact me in writing.

Despite the Ecuadorian Embassy experience unexpectedly turning out to be a full day's third degree by various officials who gave the impression that they were determined to find reasons to prevent my entry, I got the rubber stamp. I filled out my travel insurance form ticking all the boxes down the right hand side with some flourish and soon found myself practicing my little grasp of Spanish on an unsuspecting fellow passenger over the Atlantic on route to South America. At this time the consultant was completing his findings sending a copy of the results to my marital home where my estranged wife and my son resided. It was nearly a year later when I opened and read it while my wife pottered around in the kitchen. It concluded.

> "On the basis of his story I do not think that we can make a diagnosis as I suspect that his dream like state was a consequence of his changing social set up and the stresses he was under. His insomnia may have also been relevant I do not think that there is any evidence to make a diagnosis of epilepsy or a TIA. I have recommended that he carry

on as he is and try to stabilise his lifestyle. I would not ordinarily consider this description a reason not to drive and I will encourage him to contact the DVLA and I will support him in getting his license back."

I looked accusingly at the source of my purgatory as she busily dried the dishes.

Welcome To Cuenca

I landed at Guayaquil, the largest city in Ecuador, situated on the southern coast. I spent a couple of nights there resting and overcoming my jet lag. On my second day a fellow guest advised me to turn right and not left when I set out. I had turned left the night before into the badlands but I didn't experience any hassle although some of the areas looked somewhat uninviting. I came to realise that Guayaquil could be a very violent place. However turning right led me to the Pacific with an impressive modern seafront and wandering back into the metropolis there were many modern shopping areas and malls surrounding ancient picturesque plazas with medieval churches in abundance. Alas it was Cuenca I long to see as it was described as the most beautiful place in Ecuador. The pictures and images of my prospective new home had generated great anticipation

The bus journey from Guayaquil to Cuenca took four hours. From the coast we climbed the Andes to a very precipitous 8,500 feet. The scenery became spectacular after the foothills when it seemed we were entering Mordor. The mountains were dark, steep, craggy, and very foreboding. They must have been between fifteen and twenty thousand feet. As we ventured upwards and onwards they appeared out of the clouds and as you focused on the most imposing one, another gradually peered out of the mists towering above it. The road skirted the mountains and the ever increasing steep drop was alarming, especially when there were several freshly lain flowers and crucifixes at the side of the road commemorating those who didn't quite make it.

Cuenca is nestled in a valley just beyond the main range. I alighted the bus at the station just outside town and dragged my wheelie suitcase towards the centre, map in hand. The town was bustling with a populace varying from suited attaché case carrying businessmen to indigenous Indian women with trilbies and long plaits. This was the old quarter with whitewashed buildings dominating the narrow cobbled streets. There was an abundance of busy shops housed in the original Spanish/Indian architecture. I booked into a recommended small hotel until I secured more suitable long term accommodation. My room was on the fifth floor which overlooked a busy market square with a backdrop of the Andean chain. I struggled to sleep for the first few nights but this time due to the altitude and not any mental fragility. I was reasonably comfortable when I was vertical but prostrate in bed I found myself gasping for air.

For the first few days I wandered around this beautiful town getting my bearings. Cuenca was easy to navigate as it had a New York type grid system but instead of locations such as fifth and west twenty third, Cuenca named its streets after luminaries and heroes that provided more lyrical locations that rolled of the tongue. The main street was Gran Colombia and locations such General Torres y President Cordova and Padre Aguirre y Simon Bolivar would become familiar to me although only the surnames would be used. I headed for the wonderfully named river, the Rio Tomebamaba. I stood on an arched stone bridge as it flowed clear, narrow and shallow, wildly cascading over the rocky river bed. In the distance I could see women washing clothes then laying them out on the lush green grassy banks.

The climate in Cuenca is like a good British May spring with occasional hot days and occasional cold days but mostly in between.

There is a rainy season but like Saigon it's very accommodating with a daily deluge most afternoons from two till four. El Centro was Parque Calderon dominated by the magnificent Cathedral of the Immaculate Conception with three impressive blue domes. Old churches, large and small, inundated Cuenca and the cacophony of pealing bells added to the magic of the place. Families came to the Parque Calderon to play, relax and frequent the many restaurants skirting the park. There were many shoe shines seeking business and on most nights there was music. On Saturday and Sunday nights after mass the bandstand was filled with musicians orchestrating dancing among the trees.

After a few days I made my way to Tarqui y Pio Bravo to present myself to my new employers at CEDEI (Centers for Interamerican Studies). I was on an initial three month contract which was to begin a week hence. It was a large new red brick building with a wide courtyard. Inside space didn't seem to be a problem either as a receptionist guided me to the first floor. I announced my arrival at the admin office where I was warmly greeted by Maria. She eventually directed me to a large cavernous area with banks of computers along two walls and a balcony that overlooked what seemed a dance floor surrounded by tables, a couple of which were occupied my small groups chatting over coffee. There were several people using the computers and as I logged on the man next to me introduced himself. "Hi I'm Rob France from Winsconsin" he ventriloquised in a long slow drawl through gritted teeth and a long thin mouth that barely flickered. He had completed his first three months and was enrolled for another stint. He had previously spent time in Ecuador and was fluent in Spanish. Although I found myself impatiently finishing his sentences Rob was very friendly and provided me with useful information and my fast talking Splott/Cardiff accent caused him a few problems too. I turned and read my e-mails, checked out the BBC News and then a Coronation Street update to see if Shelly was still being manipulated and bullied by Charlie when I felt a

Centro the bustling noise gradually abated until I reached the eerie quiet and stillness of my prospective new address. From the outside it seemed an impressive old colonial building with balconies and shutters in the Spanish style. I gained entry through large heavy wooden doors remotely controlled. Like many of the these buildings there was a small quadrangle open to the sky well lit by natural light surrounded by the building itself which reached up three storeys. A po-faced old lady pointed up the stairs which I began to climb. At the top I met a very old lady who was the mistress of the house. To picture this very old woman you would have to imagine a 100 year old Joan Crawford with pasty, parchment skin, covered in heavy black makeup and white face powder. She wore a long dark heavy garment that rustled as if she was wearing a bustle.

She then began a tour around her house which was large, dark and more cluttered than adorned with period pieces. I was beginning to take notice of the artefacts which were considerable. There were enough to keep the Antiques Roadshow going for several series. Joan only spoke Spanish oblivious to, or ignoring the fact that I couldn't understand a word she was saying. As we went from room to room I was becoming unnerved by the bizarre and somewhat chilling nature of the place. It was like a stereotypical start to Hammer House of Horror movie. Many of her possessions seemed to have been inherited from previous generations and her ancestors were proudly displayed on the walls in sepia photos and portraits. In each room surveying all the clutter, some of which I'm certain must have had some value, were many pairs of eyes belonging to a bunch of starchy, ancestral, misanthropic looking spooks. She showed me a collection of what looked like 19th century dolls which were very lifelike, more eyes. She demonstrated with one of the dusty dolls showing three different expressions that rotated, depicting different moods, none of which were happy. To add to all this there was a lot of extreme and overstated religious representation. In each room there was a shrine or altar. In one particular room there was a statue of Our Lady, to scale! This was surrounded by other statues of children and lambs. In another room there was a huge statue of the bloodiest crucified Christ I have ever seen. Those familiar with Gruenwald's famous and unnerving "The Crucifixion", well it was like that and some.

Joan next led me into a large, dark bedroom lit by the odd shaft of light squeezing through the closed shuttered window which housed a huge ornate four poster bed. Again I felt I was being watched. Instinctively I swivelled around. Behind and above me was a huge painting of the Sacred Heart. It wasn't flush but hanging buy a large chain at about 20 degrees from the wall. I looked up with a crooked neck and somewhat startled I recoiled as it was glaring right down on top of me.

I looked at my watch and tried to leave, until she reminded me of the purpose of my visit which was to decide if I wanted to make this my home for the foreseeable future. This was a place where Ouija board and occult fans would challenge each other to spend a night. It was two in the afternoon, so imagine returning home at midnight during an Andean electric storm and finding your way through this macabre grotesque other world. She eventually handed me over to her two unsmiling underlings, both at least eighty, who I followed as they scuttled down the stairs to the apartment which turned out to be a subterranean shack at the back of the building. I beat a hasty retreat and headed across the quadrangle towards the heavy double doors praying "please be open, please be open" when someone addressed me in Spanish from high up on a balcony. I looked up and the scene was Hitchcockian. It was a distant black silhouette against the shafts of sunlight permeating into the quadrangle. It was Joan, as I could make out her extravagant black wig which was probably nailed to her head. I shouted up "Mas Tardes" indicating I would be back later and headed for the doors. As I reached for the handle I heard the door click. Click to open or click to close? It opened and I stepped outside back into Calle Largo. It was like leaving another world, another epoch.

The following day I crossed the Rio Tomebamba and decided upon a $200 apartment and the experience could not have been more different. There were three beautiful modern houses set back from the road behind large metal gates with a wide cobbled courtyard. The biggest one was owned by a very nice couple who spoke good English and the wife's elderly mother, who would be the landlady, lived in the middle house. The daughter had three young children and her brother's family occupied the third house. The families were very affluent owning four wheel drives and BMWs. My apartment was across the other side of the courtyard and I would guess that the matriarch's offspring had renovated an old building to provide income for her. I had a large bedroom, an even larger kitchen, a lounge and a sun room which was in fact a sort of conservatory tastefully decorated. The houses were protected by, what seemed at first, a vicious Alsatian who lived permanently outside in a kennel and compound. Mimi was never allowed out from her cage except for a cursory and shamefully short run out each evening. She was never afforded any affection and was just a security measure. Having had three dogs over many years, after a tentative start, I gave Mimi the attention she craved. I would've loved to have taken her bounding through the woods and countryside like I did with my own canine family. My landlord and clan were bemused by the attention I gave Mimi but didn't object. In fact I got on very well with them being invited to dinner on several occasions and providing English lessons to one of the sons at 10$US an hour.

The area of Cuenca on my side of the river was more modern and residential. Cuenca had a reputation as the most affluent place in Ecuador and the houses and cars on this side of the river gave credence to that claim. In the days leading up to term I began my daily routine of crossing the Tomebama then up and into the old town walking through Parque Calderon and heading for school to use the internet and to say hello to the new intake of teachers that were assembling each day. On the day before lessons started we had an introductory session where Kacie sat the group of about twenty new teachers in a circle so that we could introduce ourselves. Most were in their twenties but reassuringly there were a significant minority who were older that included an Australian married couple in their sixties who were retired teachers. They were Ruth and Clive. As the weeks went by I socialised a lot with them, or rather Ruth with Clive in tow. Ruth was a softly spoken kind hearted liberal and we seemed to have a lot in common. Clive was more abrasive and opinionated, with an air of unmerited self-righteous sagacity

Most were postgraduates doing their thing before joining the rat race. I stated that I was on a gap year or two between work and . . . well death really. This generated amusement not realising the literal element in my comment. Kacie informed us that the school had a tradition of two teachers a week travelling to a poor village a couple of hours away called Jima (pronounced Hima) to provided free lessons on a Friday evening. She had organised an introductory trip there for the coming Saturday for which we all volunteered.

Jima—Estupendo

We climbed into a battered bus and headed out on a combination of modern roads and bumpy tracks. Everybody chatted excitedly as we journeyed higher into the Andes. Jima was like a nineteenth century Mexican border town with whitewashed hacienda type buildings with wooden first floor verandas and shutters. Dirt tracks linked the handful streets. No sooner had we begun walking from the bus when Jane leapt into our group with the fresh faced boundless enthusiasm of a Joyce Grenfell on Prozac. She was in her early twenties I guess, had blonde hair in pigtails and had such a glowing expression that it looked as if she'd just witnessed a divine visitation. She was stationed there by the Peace Corp and as the mover and shaker of the community the villagers turned to her to make things happen, a bit like a female version Conrad's Lord Jim. Today was a big festival for the village, one of the many Our Lady of . . . whatever time of year it happened to be. The villagers were very hospitable towards their gringo visitors, seeking us out, shaking our hands and engaging us in conversation. The indigenous Quechan Indian women wore various colourful costumes, and sprouting from their trilbies, long black plaited hair down to their waists and all the children were in their Sunday best. In the small square next to the most impressive building in the village, the church, there was a small stage with a band and an MC. There was a lot of music, dancing, speeches, parades, competitions and prize-giving against a beautiful mountainous backdrop. The mayor was the last to speak with a long emotive speech in the style of a cross between Fidel Castro and El Ducce, inserting liberally "Jima Estupendo!, Jima Excelente!, Jima la mejer! This was an opportunity to chat and get to know the other teachers and was far more inclusive than in Saigon where it was almost impossible to make friends with other teachers in VUS as we were sent to different schools around the city with little routine.

Embracing Polite Quencan Society

I had an inauspicious start to my teaching. My first lesson was with a class of intermediate teenagers. On the first day I drew a detailed map of Britain on the board to identify Wales to a questioning class. When I attempted to realign the Isle of Wight I discovered, to my horror, but to the great amusement of the students, that I had used a permanent marker. I had to write in red across my drawing of old Blighty for the rest of the lesson. The following day with a different class I opened my glasses case to find it empty. This caused me some panic as I could not read the text book or my notes. Throughout the lesson I had to lean backwards out of the window holding the book at arm's length to catch as much sunlight as possible to read from the text book. One of the terminologies in TEFL is "Icebreakers" which is self explanatory. These two instances proved inadvertently to be effective examples of that particular genre.

I had another disturbing classroom experience a few weeks later. When I arrived in Ecuador my headaches, buzzing and dizziness were still a problem but I didn´t notice it so much when I was busy. I had a ringing in my ears but rarely noticed it although it was a bit weird when it started and when it went quiet. It was like someone switching an out of tune radio on and off. On this particular occasion I was in full flow but when I turned quickly to the board I had a little wobble, so I steadied myself and carried on. About ten minutes later I experienced a mini blackout which lasted a fraction of a second. Later in the lesson the same thing happened. That night I was very concerned. The following night with the same class and room the same thing happened but the blackout lasted a few seconds. Fortunately the rest of the class experienced it as well because they all moaned at a student at the back who when leaning back on his chair nudged a light switch off, sat up and nudged it back on again. I slept a lot better that night.

I was happily getting caught up in a regular social scene. Cordelia was Canadian and in her mid fifties, cultured, refined, of delicate health but she had an adventurous spirit. We gelled very well. Leanne was also Canadian and a highly intelligent thirty nine year old and we hit it off straight away. She ensured I was invited to any soirée that was on offer which included my first Thanksgiving and mothered me to a certain extent such as keeping my glass replenished at parties. Marcel was very vivacious in a natural unpretentious way with thick black hair, dark flashing eyes and full sensual mouth. She was left wing, idealistic and committed, resulting in us having several heated political discussions representing different factions of the left. When she arrived I thought she had brought her unsmiling moody younger brother in tow. Kevin looked like a cross between Harry Potter and the Milky Bar Kid, but as I got to know him I learned not to underestimate him mentally and, despite his slight frame, he could drink me under the table. They were both brilliant, innovative teachers who had previously taught in Prague. Later they would set up workshops that few of the teachers ever missed. They also liked to drink, often heavily, especially when the local hooch, Zhumir, was only a dollar a bottle and Kevin made his own Absinthe!

A group of us became members of the CEDEI chapter of the Deportivo Cuenca Football supporters club. We met up for drinks before the first game. The younger element included Chris from Oregon, another Chris from Florida, Becky from South Africa, and Rebecca from Swansea. Cordelia, wearing the Cuencan football shirt, scarf and hat, and I, added maturity to the occasion. It was a top of the Seria A table clash with Nationale of Quito. Cuenca was in second place and needed to win to go above Nationale. Ecuadorian football was on the crest of a wave having just qualified for their second successive World Cup. There was a capacity crowd of 25,000. It was very noisy and colourful with huge drums and brass sections. Before the kick off there was an impressive firework display, and as the teams came out the pitch was festooned with what at first seemed like toilet rolls. In fact they were similar to cash register rolls, and being heavier they travelled further. Oregon Chris turned to see where these projectiles were coming from and copped a barely opened one right between the eyes. He was showing off his scar for days after. The game was very entertaining with good football and chances at both ends. Nationale were the more accomplished side and took the lead in the first half with a beautiful sweeping move. Cuenca were in the game throughout and overall had more chances. They deservedly equalised in the second half from a free kick. The ball was floated to the far post where it was met by a power header, and then pandemonium.

There were four yellow cards and a sending off, par for the course by South American standards. Right on half time there was a melee involving all 22 players which was broken up by the riot police. Just before full time the ref sent off Cuenca's main striker who was very reluctant to leave, while his team-mates swarmed all over the ref. The crowd were incensed and were baying for the ref's blood. Cordelia and Becky who both spoke Spanish were too embarrassed to translate the tirades of abuse. At full time all three officials stood in the centre circle while the Riot Police marched on to protect them. The police surrounded them with their riot shields at the side and above, then began inching their way from the centre of the field to the tunnel where they were met with a bombardment of missiles, such as bottles and cans most of which bounced off the shields. It was just so typical of this part of the world. Three of the teachers had never seen a live "soccer" game before and now were absolutely hooked. Although the Americans are interested in their baseball and American Football this results mainly through tradition, as they fully admit that their anaesthetised, corporate, and constantly interrupted national sports don't hold a candle to the passion they witnessed that night.

About a month in it was my turn, along with Florida Chris, to perform charitable good works in Jima. As soon as we arrived Jane and her pigtails came skipping down the street to greet us. She gushed out directions and information, was delightful and very helpful. In a later conversation she explained that she had been in Jima for four years! I was beginning to think that she was perhaps more Ben Gunn than Lord Jim. This was a poor but very tightly knit community. They seemed very happy and there didn't appear to be an ounce of malice in the village. They were very friendly towards gringos as well as well as each other. There was a great sense of bonhomie. I was looking for throat sweets late at night and through the grapevine a shop-owner was informed, appeared and took me through the back of his closed shop into his living room where he produced some Hall's Mentholiptus. The village seemed to be cut off and unsullied by the outside word. It was like Brigadoon.

Chris and I set up our lesson in an old cavernous hall which was only lit at one end. About ten of the villagers turned up. We handed out pens and paper but exercise and text books were non existent, which for us was unexpected so we had to improvise. Presented with a disparate group made up of a couple of teenagers, latecomers straight from the fields, an old toothless artisan, and the lady of the manor who owned the small new hotel in preparation for the mass influx of tourist that hadn't quite materialised, we began. We arranged some of the tables and chairs in the hall in the form of a restaurant, placing our students in twos on the tables and after pre-teaching vocabulary Chris and I role-played waiter and customer. Then it was the turn of the students who had probably never been into a restaurant in their lives. The results were hilarious and the lesson was deemed a success.

After the lesson we went for dinner in the only café in town which consisted of two tables. We were warned beforehand that there were only two choices on the menu, mackerel and chicken. After consuming the half dozen bottles of beer in the fridge Chris and I headed back to the new hotel where we were the only guests. There was a bonus on the Saturday morning of a big festival, which turned out to be bigger than the previous one. All the surrounding communities turned up for a parade of mainly children through the village with bands and fireworks. They eventually assembled on the square, where different groups of school children performed dances and songs and then El Ducci gave another long bravado speech full of the superlatives that was Jima.

Jumping Freight in Rio

A couple of weeks later I was heading for a weekend away in Riobamba, the big attraction being the train ride to the Devil's Nose.

I travelled with Kevin, Marcel and Leanne. The journey was seven hours north by coach and despite the stunning scenery, it was a long time. We thought after nearly eight hours that the bus was running late until we discovered we had passed our stop. So we got off at some desolate spot waited an hour on an open road and caught a local bus back. In Riobamaba Kevin lead the way to the designated cheap hotel. After what seemed hours and fourteen blocks again we realised we had passed our destination and had to walk about eight blocks back. However undeterred, with our spirits still high, we had our first cold beer, originally planned for 2.30, at 7.30., and quite a few more after that.

Riobamba was a beautiful town of 120,000 and was dominated by the snow covered volcano Chimborazo. Most people would think that the longest distance from the centre of the earth to the highest point on earth would be to Mount Everest, but because the earth is a sphere with widest point at the Equator, Chimborazo claims that title. There was also a volatile volcano called Tungurahua that smoked menacingly in the background. On the Saturday there was a huge market which was very lively and full of characters and a wide variety of merchandise. While we were there we bumped into Zoe a woman that Leanne and some other teachers met in Vilcambamba, in southern Ecuador, the previous weekend. She was with an English speaking Swiss man she met when they were checking in to the same hotel. We arranged to meet in up in the evening.

Zoe was quite a remarkable woman. She was 30, from Bath and had spent the previous year travelling around South America on her own. On top of this she was camping and carried a full pack including a tent, primus stove, and the rest of the kind of gear you need for camping. She had hiked miles and camped in such places as Patagonia and Terra Del Fuego. Previously she had done the same thing in India and New Zealand. In between time she was a librarian. She was not hardened at all by her exploits and seemed lovely and vulnerable. Mild mannered Bath librarian turns into Colonel John

Blashford-Snell every other year. Rete, the Swiss man was 36. He had quit his job to cover North and South America, and was inspired by his dad. He told us that his dad always intended to do what Rete was currently doing, only after early retirement. Unfortunately his father died suddenly at the age of 57, and Rete wasn't going to make the same mistake. As I was fifty seven at the time it was a sobering thought. Anyway all six of us went out for a meal, a laugh and a good drink then later, on a dark Riobamba street corner, we split with Zoe and Rete who headed off in the opposite direction, our paths never to cross again.

On Sunday morning the train from Riobamaba left at 7am., heading south in the direction of Cuenca. Most sit on top of the box cars. Kevin and I were trying to dig out hobo songs. Where was Box Car Willie when you needed him? We were advised by Zoe and Rete to wear several layers of clothing and gradually peel them off as the day progressed. This was good advice. Firstly it was quite cold, being exposed on the top of the train at speed. By midday it was very hot and we were down to our bottom layer. The train had been known to come off the rails which is a bit unnerving considering the hair raising journey in front of us. Some way into the journey we came to a shuddering halt—a derailment above a steep bank. The method of getting back on track was quite primitive. They used boulders of different sizes. I'm not sure if they carried them or they found them at the side of the track. They backed up the carriages a few feet and then moved them forward up over the rocks and with the help of leaves for lubrication attempted to lever the wheels back on to the tracks. After about six attempts and 45 minutes, to loud cheers and applause they managed it.

The journey took about six hours and we stopped off at a few Andean towns where the locals crowded around, fed and watered us. Travelling through the day was both spectacular and disquieting especially across high viaducts, over steep ravines and valleys passing volcanoes in the distance as our feet dangled precariously over the long drops below us, with the possibility of another derailment at any time. When we arrived near the Devil's Nose it seemed impossible to negotiate such an inhospitable landscape of steep craggy mountains and seemingly impassable gullies. Travelling down, then up the Devil's Nose involved switchbacks, which are like three point turns, backing up steep inclines, to get around sharp bends. The journey terminated at Alausi which was a two hour bus ride from to Cuenca.

Self-Destructing in Peru

Back in Cuenca the teachers were planning for the long Christmas break. Many of the younger group were heading to the beaches to party for three weeks, others were more adventurous with two of the girls bravely travelling through Colombia to Cartanega in the north while a few chose EL Oriente (the Amazon). I was off to Peru and Machu Picchu and perhaps into Bolivia. We had an end of term party on the Friday before heading to our holiday destinations. I planned to go on the Sunday but Leanne was keen for me to escort her across the Peruvian border before she flew to Cusco (Machu Picchu) and she was leaving on the Saturday. So in a rush with a sore head Leanne and I boarded the bus to Machala near the Peru border. Leanne had quit after her three month stint and was to meet a friend in Lima and after walking the Inca Trail she was heading back to Canada. South American coaches were clean, comfortable, often luxurious and was a cheap way to explore the continent. Unfortunately there was a variety of coach companies with different destinations and they all had their own depots in obscure parts of towns and cities. Consequently it was Leanne's cool and calm persona that got me to Peru. I would have been lost without her, literally. She was also under pressure as she had a plane to catch from Tumbes on the other side of the border. She also diplomatically manoeuvred me through the Ecuadorian border control. This was a wooden hut filled with hot, flustered, sweaty humanity. There were two scrum like queues and we discovered that you had to use one before the other and of course we got it the wrong way round. After battling to the head of the second we were confronted with a specimen who wore his cap SS style and must have been bullied at school as he was now exacting revenge on the world. He took my passport, look at it, looked at me then put it to one side and dealt with others whilst ignoring my repeated response in perfect Spanish.

"Problemo senor?" Leanne was telling me to calm down as the veins in my neck were protruding like sticks of rhubarb. Eventually he picked it up again, looked at me, now a picture of benign serenity, then my passport then looked down as he handed me my passport in a casual absentminded way. As I stretched out my hand to collected it with some relief, without looking up, as if he had done this a thousand times before, he retracted his arm for another look. Leanne instantly grabbed me as she saw my expression and must have anticipated my lunge forward. I felt like grabbing him by the lapels and dragging him over his desk and through the metal grill. He finally returned it and we were heading the few miles to Machala to change buses to cross the border. Again Leanne with map and instructions in hand located the bus company's depot. I was supposed to be escorting a nervous Leanne but without her I wouldn't have made it to the border and probably had ended up in stir.

The Peruvian border control official was very helpful and polite and a short time later the coach was pulling into a small private bus terminal on the outskirts of Tumbes that squeezed in a maximum of three coaches. We jumped into a tuk tuk to take us to the centre of town. Once there Leanne flagged a taxi to the airport and we parted company with big hugs in the middle of the road whilst holding up the traffic resulting in much horn blowing, more in humour than in malice at two gringos acting like Latinos. Then after waving her taxi around the corner I threw my backpack in the boot of a battered old collectivo opened up by a big swarthy man in a soiled vest and three days stubble. Collectivos are large battered saloons that wait until full before setting off.

I was heading to Zorritos, a chill out area on the coast a few miles outside Tumbes. I was sat in the back alongside the only other passenger, a teenage girl. I smiled politely but unlike Asia ready smiles in places like this don't come easily. Generally South Americans don't mask the realities of their impoverished daily grind. After ten minutes with no additional passengers, I thought bollocks to this. I remembered Oregon Chris saying it's best to take a white taxi. So I got out and flagged one down and drove off around the corner. The driver and I had a bitter disagreement about the fare, so I got out in a huff and demanded he open the boot so I could get my backpack. With a look of confusion on his face I realised the backpack was still in the boot of the Collectivo!! In a state of abject shock and panic I ran back around the corner praying it was still there. It was, so I sidled in as though nothing had happened, smiling benignly as the driver and a group of his mates expressed moods of anger and bewilderment. We finally filled up and set off on a journey which took a half an hour down the coast road, and only cost a dollar. During the ride, apart from feeling foolish, I gave myself a good talking to about acting impulsively in a culture and a geography that was alien to me. If I hadn´t had that disagreement with the driver of the white cab my backpack and I would have been separated permanently. The Collectivo driver and his mates were just honest Joes going about their daily business and making a living the best way they could.

To add to this little misunderstanding my experience in Zorritos wasn´t great. The first impressions of my hotel were positive, with bars and hammocks on the deserted beach, lots of palm trees, a pool side bar and the prospect of swimming in the warm South Pacific. While I was waiting for my room to be prepared I unwound with a cold beer on the beach under a palm tree. Now everything would be heavenly; or so I thought. I soon realised first impressions can be deceiving. The rooms were basic as often becomes beach accommodation. But having no furniture, no towels, and no hot water was annoying. The curtains were smaller than the windows, so privacy was a problem. The biggest problem was the mosquitoes with whom I did battle for most of the night. They won. There were eight splattered on the walls by dawn, courtesy of a Graham Greene novel. By morning the cover photograph of the author looked like he had sprouted a toupee of dead insects. It made him look twenty years younger. Those paled into insignificance compared to the bites I incurred. I think the score was 27-8, with three bites in a line down my cheek. I resembled Al Capone. I left the following morning to the relative luxury of the Hotel Cosmos back in Tumbes, that had furniture, air conditioning, hot water, towels, cable TV, all at half the price of my previous accommodation. During the drive back I had this terrible feeling I had mislaid my little black book with all my crucial banking and internet details. In fact I had it on my person but in different place to its usual secretion. I was still having nagging self doubts and a feeling of a self inflicted disaster waiting to happen.

I drew some money from a cash point to pay for two nights at the hotel. I had a meal at a pretty little restaurant near the main plaza and went back to my room to get organised. I threw all the important things on my bed so that I could get myself sorted. I would separate my bank cards and copy all important information into another book and keep them separate so if I lost anything I had backup. I soon realised that a self inflicted disaster had already struck. I had left my main Nationwide debit card sticking out of the cash point! What a pillock!! What a time to exhibit this level of brainless incompetent ineptitude. I was so distraught I went into a Basil Fawltyesque rage of a self recriminating, self loathing rant. I can't remember if I actually went down on my haunches holding my head in my hands or banged my head against the wall, but I do know tears of frustration welled up in my eyes. My only mitigation is that in South America the money is issued before the card is returned. It's vice versa in the UK. I calmed down and set about making decisions. I had my Barclays debit card with about three hundred pounds that was being slowly drained by standing orders and direct debits. That wouldn't last three and a half weeks. Do I head back to Cuenca a humiliated fool? After pacing my room in silence for a few moments I decided on a plan of action. I would send a mayday message to my brother, Terry, in Stafford requesting he forward five hundred pounds to my Barclays account. I stayed in Tumbes for two nights as my brother and I exchanged emails and I cancelled my Nationwide card. This course of action was fraught with possible dangers. If there was a hitch or a delay with the transaction I could end up penniless in deepest Peru, an unforgiving place when you're skint.

At 9am on the third day I was pulling out of the bus depot on a large coach beginning the twenty four hour journey to Lima. I had become reasoned and becalmed, now assuming the persona of a mature traveller who could take most eventualities in his stride as opposed to my alter ego of "Mr. Bean Goes Forth." The Pan-American highway was straight and smooth stretching through the Peruvian desert that mainly clung to the Pacific that lapped the long, deserted, sun scorched beaches. I was the only gringo on the bus which stopped regularly for toilet breaks and meals. The eateries were usually large, rectangular cantinas, lone buildings in the vast expanse of scrubland and desert. Their function was to shovel fuel into the passing travellers and get them back on their way. At one they scooped out the carne and rice and onto the passing plates. It was sustenance, it did the job, and speaking for myself I was never ill. As night fell, satiated, I wandered outside. These are not memorable moments when travelling, standing outside a large cantina filled with humourless people travelling long distances, not for pleasure, but necessity. The occasional vehicle trundled past as I looked beyond over the flat, vapid coastal scrubland as dusk settled and the chill set in. I felt quite alone but not despondent as the very fact I was stood on this spot at this particular time heading somewhere with a hint of danger and unpredictability a long way from the comforts of home was quite invigorating.

There were a few annoying stoppages by the police who would evacuate the bus and search it before we continued our journey. On one occasion this took place at three in the morning when most people were at least dozing. There was another occasion in the early hours when we were hauled off the bus to go through a checkpoint which included searching our bags. All very annoying but like my fellow passengers, who were used to this, I was calmly resigned.

We arrived on the outskirts of Lima as dawn was breaking so I witnessed the urban nightmare that are the infamous shanty towns and slums that surround the capital. These barrios are the result of urbanisation where growing numbers of desperate people move from the countryside in search of work of any kind and usually end up scavenging for anything of value.

I got a cab from the notorious but now brightly lit busy bus station to the Hotel Espana, a large guesthouse right in the centre of Lima. I booked a single bijou room at $8.00 per night. The building was sensational. It was a huge Spanish colonial architectural delight that had genuine chandeliers, lighting the many classical paintings on each of the three main floors. There was a plethora of sculptures around the building, including Aphrodite, Venus de Milo and two busts of David that seemed to be on the scale of the original in Florence. The top two floors were a recent extension. There was a glorious roof garden with overhanging plants and other various flora and fauna, including parrots and other birds on my top floor plus a monkey. There were several tortoises shuffling slowly around. Later I would come across the most animated tortoise I had ever seen which was intent on descending a spiral staircase before I headed it off. I had a panoramic view of Lima from my window. There was a roof top cafe where we had breakfast and late night meals and drinks. From my window I could look across and down at the famous San Francisco church next door.

I showered then ventured out for breakfast refreshed in the warm sunshine after a poor night's sleep. Within yards I was in the expanse of Plaza de Mayor with awesome medieval historic buildings on three sides with the highly guarded and fortified President's Palace, the monumental Basilica San Pedro, and the magnificent Archbishop's Palace. I loitered for a while before my ravenous hunger led me to the more modern and even larger Plaza de Armas.

I found a modern restaurant so that I could enjoy a breakfast with ingredients I would recognise that guaranteed dippy eggs, plonked myself down and ordered. As egg yoke clogged my moustache I became aware that someone had entered and was jabbering excitedly with a waiter. He then flounced past me to the door, turned and came back to my table and asked me if I could speak English. He was a well dressed American in his mid thirties and so obviously gay as he gesticulated extravagantly about having his money belt cut from him by a machete wielding hombre at the bus station. He wanted to borrow a hundred Sol, about thirty dollars, to fetch his bags from the bus station where the dastardly deed took place. He suggested he meet me at the roof-top café at my hotel lunchtime to repay it. I was convinced of his honesty just by the question, what would a middle class gay American be doing cadging $30.00 in the middle of Lima, a city that was hardly a bastion of liberalism and tolerance? It was after he had left with my sol that I mulled over the fact he knew about the roof top café, having just arrived, and why would he leave his bags at the bus station only to bum the fare back to collect them?

As I wandered around the Plaza de Armas taking in its splendours in the glorious sunshine I was approached by two teenage school girls who wanted to practice their English. I experienced a pleasant ten minutes or so as we ambled along. When I changed direction, effectively ending our brief encounter, they suggested I take them for something to eat and when I declined they demanded money. I had been in Lima for a couple of hours and had been targeted twice. More in hope than expectation I spent lunchtime sat up on the rooftop café; the seat opposite remained vacant. Welcome to Lima!

Earlier I had passed a big demo outside the Church of San Francisco where a few hundred elderly people with chains around their necks were being separated from a meeting of bigwigs by heavily armed riot police. The temptation to take a photo was offset by the possibility of confiscation. Later I stumbled on another larger demo around the Plaza De Armas where an orderly middle-aged group of earnest, chanting, banner-waving demonstrators were guided around the plaza then away down a wide busy avenue. From my phrase book I gleaned their angst was pensions related. Although the police were heavily armed they seemed pretty tolerant and I was surprised that open defiance and opposition was, to some extent at least, tolerated.

My main concern for that afternoon, apart from warding off predators, was to extract money from an ATM. I found myself in the plush retail and commercial area of Lima outside a large bank. There was a queue at the cash point and I found myself leering over the shoulder of the man in front of me desperate to find out if the instructions were in English. I found, through trial and error in Cuenca, that the button to press was "savings account" to access cash. My fear was to lose my last remaining cash card as Peru wasn't the place to be stranded penniless. I entered the bank hoping, with my card and passport, to access cash over the counter, and to my relief I did just that. There was one complication that I discovered later which was that if a note wasn't in pristine condition it failed to be legal tender. Even the finest nick would render that note void. I was given four one hundred dollar notes that nearly emptied my Barclays current account, one of which had the faintest of nicks. For all the time I was in Peru that note was useless. I tried folding it, passing it off in dimly lit restaurants, and to the many money changers on darkened street corners, but on each occasion it was returned. I even tried to use it to buy my coach ticket to Cusco.

Cusco

Soft drinks and sandwiches, always ham and cheese, were provided by the bus companies on such journeys. Munching on my second cheese and ham sandwich meant I was about halfway through my bus journey to Cusco. It was twenty hours in duration through and over the Andes into the heart of South America. It was an overnight journey and morning provided the most South American of vistas I had witnessed so far on the continent. We stopped for breakfast at a large wooden shack set in isolation in the middle of a huge flat valley of stony scrubland. This was not what I expected as I imagined I would be confronted by layers of steep mountains which we would have to wind our way around and up and down. With others I sat outside in the chill morning air sipping my regular fix of coca tea, the elixir of life, while devouring scrambled eggs and gazing on a landscape that ignited every aesthetic nerve in my body. Near our wooden tables were three alpacas, one of which was stood staring at me willing me to feed it. Alpacas are not beautiful animals, not graceful and self aware like llamas. In fact they look quite ungainly but in the cutest, fluffiest way with those huge doleful eyes you just long to give them a good home, mine. At this moment in time their presence helped complete the perfect scene as in the far distance beyond many square miles of flat desolation were about a half dozen perfectly formed volcanoes.

We arrived in Cusco about mid-day. The bus was full of tourists so a large scrum gathered where the locals attempted to entice the passengers to a "hotel very cheap." I moved away to sort myself out and to look at my Lonely Planet when a woman approached me selling her particular "Hotel very cheap." The advantage to responding to these offers is that they throw in a taxi and as I discovered in later journeys the places are at least reasonable and often excellent. On this occasion it was the latter. The accommodation was a very impressive old Spanish colonial building, a mixture of stone and imposing dark wood with balconies and a cobbled courtyard. The rooms were substantial with lots of tasteful paintings and heavy ornate furniture. It was excellent value at $15.00 per night including breakfast in the courtyard. My room was large and the eye catching features were a wide, dark, sturdy, carved wooden bed, and a large decorative defunct fireplace. I felt I was a guest of a Spanish Count and Countessa.

At nearly 11,000 feet altitude sickness was a problem in Cusco. An antidote or at least a great help was coca tea. In fact it seemed to be a remedy for many ailments real and imagined. I have spoken to others who have experienced it and they wax lyrical about its wide ranging benefits. It's cocaine of course and banned outside Peru. Coca tea consists of a few coca leaves with hot water and is quite refreshing to drink. It's about 3% the strength of the white powder that many of the professional classes in the western world snort as their chosen recreational drug, but in this weakened state it is definitely medicinal. Throughout Peru the workers, especially those in agriculture, chewed the leaves incessantly to sustain them in the fields.

Cusco is a beautiful town with a mild climate. The Plaza de Armas is the main focal point and draws you like a magnet. It has impressive architecture, a combination of Spanish and Inca buildings with colonnades and balconies all around the square. The park in the centre was lit up for Christmas. Most of the balconies were a part of excellent restaurants where you could cheaply eat and drink well while watching the world go by. Most South American plazas are dominated by a magnificent cathedral or two and here was no exception. Cusco is surrounded by Andean mountains with various suburbs sweeping up the foothills and when lit at night it gives the impression that you are looking up into a glittering cosmos.

I walked south from The Plaza de Armas and climbed up into a district called San Blas. This is the chic bohemian area with lots of art galleries, craft and pottery shops ensconced in petite whitewashed buildings and often authentic Inca buildings. The Incas used large smooth boulders choosing compatible sizes and shapes placed on top and alongside each other without cement and such was the quality of this stonework it has outlasted more modern buildings. Climbing these narrow cobbled streets was quite exhausting because of the altitude, but when I reached the top it was well worth the effort for the panoramic view. Cusco was the Inca capital and far more important than Machu Picchu. Machu Picchu is famed for its spectacular location and the fact that the Spanish knew of its existence but couldn't find it!

Excluding my unusable defaced, yet brand new virginal $100 bill, I was down to my last thirty dollars with my account yet to be replenished and began to panic despite my overdraft facility. I flushed it from my mind and sought out the nightlife of the buzzing down town Cusco. I have an aversion to the ubiquitous Irish Bar but I succumbed and visited Flaherty's Bar. It was packed with mainly young tourists and backpackers and I have to admit that the draught lager and the food were excellent. I got talking to a New Zealander, a 21 year old who had played rugby in Argentina, and had been on a student exchange in Peru for eighteen months and found it difficult to leave, especially now that he was fluent in Spanish. We had an in depth chat about rugby and discovered he was a product of the excellent Kiwi coaching system from a young age and was part of a colt side that included Daniel Carter amongst others of the current New Zealand side. He spent about five years going through the ranks with these players and found it a bit weird that his big mate he grew up with had recently been voted the world player of the year.

After nervously checking my account the following day I discovered, to my relief, that I was again a man of means as £500.00 had at last appeared in my account. After the nervous ordeal of using the local hole in the wall I realised that it was well timed as I received a text from Leanne. She was due to finish the four night camping and trekking challenge that is the Inca Trail and suggested meeting at a restaurant called Perca's that brewed its own beer. The Inca trail is as demanding as it's rewarding. It involves a steep trek in high altitude with camping for four nights among the Inca ruins and cloud forests climaxing when, after a final assent to a precipice, Machu Picchu, in all its glory amongst the lost world panorama in which it is located, is revealed below.

As I ordered a beer in Perca's, Leanne came running in, arms akimbo, ready for big hugs. She had brought some fellow campers with her including her Canadian friend, Richard. We sat around a large table drinking and swapping stories. The group had shared a large tent for four nights, so after experiencing each other's body odours, flatulence, and smelly socks, these former strangers were now on intimate terms.

Two of the gathering were English middle class young professional men full of bravado who laughed a lot and caroused. Richard was more thoughtful, and Leanne was just happy. I was sat next to the last of the group, an Australian man who was unusually quietly spoken and circumspect for a native of the Antipodes. He was a factory worker and seemed the antithesis of the two English gentlemen at the other end of the table. He had saved a wedge, quit his job and had been travelling for the previous few months in the USA and now planned to finish up a month later in Rio just in time for the Rolling Stones free concert on the Copacabana. He was thoughtful and intelligent and I liked him. I hope he fulfilled his planned itinerary. We ate and drank until the early hours, then it was hugs and handshakes as we all went our separate ways never to meet again. This is a common occurrence when travelling. All pals together in a brief moment of time then they leave your life forever. It is always comforting and reassuring to meet regularly with friends of long standing but these "ships in the night" moments are special and long remembered.

At breakfast I eased my hangover with coca tea. It may have been the placebo effect but I certainly felt better. Having purchased my ticket I headed for the train to Machu Picchu. It was obvious when wending our way through the mammoth, tightly knit, precipitous outcrops covered in clogging, dark green vegetation that disappeared up into the cloud, why this lost city wasn't discovered until 1911 and frustrated the Spanish for so long. I spent an uncomfortable period with my head on my shoulder crooked upwards hard against the window attempting to take in this amazing ever changing landscape.

We arrived at our initial destination which was a colony for tourists that included restaurants, gift shops and a small market. We utilised these facilities until we were designated a coach to complete the journey. The bus climbed, coughing and stuttering slowly up the steep circling road until we reached the top. The rest of the way was on foot. Gasping excessively we climbed slowly up several layers of steep steps until that moment when all was revealed. The view was the classic that is portrayed in millions of posters, photographs, and advertisements around the world and is no less breathtaking for it. What they don't portray is the overall setting. At the dawn of time when these mountains were formed there must have been a natural concertina effect that created a concentrated group of imperious and imposing mountains seemingly jockeying for position. Machu Picchu perched on top of a steep almost vertical mountain is surrounded by similar protrusions, only higher giving it protection and anonymity. The clogging thick vegetation adds to the inaccessibility. It is these protective mountains that are the magnificent and atmospheric backdrop to this lost city. One of the main ingredients to this unique atmosphere is the ever changing cloud formations which adds a surreal element to these dark satanic mountains. With the advantage of modern transport it still took us four hours via train, road and foot to reach this most hallowed of destinations.

I had been using Ben's 35mm camera for several years as the quality of the pictures was excellent. It was now looking so battered I was getting a bit self conscious about it. Apart from the funny noise it was making there were bits falling off which I had stuck back on with tape. When you're at an iconic wonder of the world standing next to people with the most modern camera equipment it's a bit disconcerting. However, if I may say so, I took another classic picture. There were many llamas wandering around and so used were they to the tourists I was convinced they were posing for photographs. I homed in on one particular llama who responded immediately. It was stood on a flat stone outcrop and although there was a grass verge below him the shot I choreographed gave the impression that it was on a narrow ledge over a sheer drop of thousands of feet. Anticipating the click of my shutter he calmly turned in to profile and regally raised his head; so with the swirling mists wafting around the demonic mountains in the background, I clicked.

On the crowded train from Machu Picchu I began chatting to a Chilean career army officer and his gorgeous Swedish girlfriend who was sat on his lap. She was bubbly, blond, and beautiful. He wore a cravat, had a noble bearing like a character from the Count of Monte Christo, and seemed the type, in another era, who would have rapped a few cheeks with his gloves and fought duels at dawn in his or somebody else's honour. He was good looking and had charm by the bucket-load. When I told him I was from Wales I expected the usual puzzled response I experienced constantly over there, but his face lit up with instant recognition. He asked me if I knew Sennybridge and Neath. Apparently he and his unit had been seconded to the British Army in that area and was involved in exercises in the Brecon Beacons. He told me about the difficulties that not only he had in locating and pronouncing the Welsh names but also his British counterparts who were not from the area. He met his girlfriend when he was on duty in Bosnia where she was an interpreter. This had a certain Je ne sais quoi that's missing from "copping on" down at the local pallais.

Titicaca

My next destination was Lake Titicaca. South America has always fascinated me since I studied it in Geography lessons when I was twelve years old. It was always described in superlatives. The biggest, the longest, the deepest, the driest, the wettest. etc. The names were also magical, such as Cotopaxi, and Titicaca. We never thought we would actually go to these places. In 1962 the furthest people went was Barry Island a few miles away, and our family rarely went there. At the age of twelve in an all-male school, where girls were an alien specie, the name Titicaca caused . . . well titillation. The journey from Cusco to Puno on the edge of the lake was just eight hours, a mere bagatelle. Puno was described as tacky but I thought it was pleasant enough. My guesthouse was a bit tacky though; formica, bright colours, and my small room was so full of mirrors I thought I may have booked into a bordello. The pluses were a big comfortable bed and friendly staff.

Straight after breakfast on a sunny but chilly morning I climbed gingerly aboard a decrepit looking wooden boat with an outboard motor joining about a dozen others of various nationalities. Lake Titicaca had just lost its position as the highest navigable lake in the world, but South America still held that accolade as it's now been discovered that Peru and Chile have higher ones. But I doubt if either are as beautiful or as interesting. The wide expanse of water, clear and pure, was circumnavigated by brilliant white fluffy clouds that clung to the mountainous surround looking like a giant halo around the lake. Above, there was a vast expanse of blue sky. This heavenly image was reflected immaculately in the still lake which created every shade of blue and green found in a printer's colour swatch.

First we visited the man-made reed floating Uros islands. For thousands of years the indigenous Indians have made islands, houses and boats with Totora (reeds) and live without electricity. The islands last about ten years, so the inhabitants start constructing a new island as the shelf life of the current one reaches its expiry date, then move everything across. It was while we were sat watching the Indian men and women dexterously weaving these reeds that Ben's camera met its untimely demise. We then travelled out further to the island of Taquile. We climbed the 2km to the top of the island. It seemed like 10km. This steep incline peaked at 13,000 feet. The view was magnificent with the distant snow-capped mountains of Bolivia reflecting on the eastern part of the lake.

This island was inhabited by a tribe of Indians who are fiercely independent and have very quaint customs. The men dress in similar bright red costumes and hats with subtle changes that separate the single and the married. The women have similar identity symbols such as slightly different coloured shawls. When we got to the main square the men were sat one side of it and the women on the other. It was a bit like my local rugby club on a Saturday night. Why do these Indians live such Spartan independent lives? Well they believe that the beginning of civilisation started on Lake Titicaca, and they are tied to the lake by an umbilical cord of faith. The lake, to them, is a natural deity. Most of them are Catholic but they can reconcile both belief systems.

When we returned to land I paid a derisory £10.00 for a camera which would at least provide basic proof my adventurous journey even if the picture quality was questionable.

I Know How You Feel Mate

My schoolboy fascination for all things South American simmered under the surface as I excitedly boarded the bus to La Paz. The novelty of travel remained undiminished and the thought of crossing the border into Bolivia created a childish glee. I was sat next to a rugged looking middle-aged bloke of fair complexion with thinning sandy hair. He was wearing a padded check shirt and seemed the outdoors, red neck, hunting and shooting type. He was irritating me because he was taking more than his share of the seat. I didn't bother to spark up a conversation, which is unusual for me, as I assumed we had little in common. We were travelling through a huge, flat, wide expanse with the main Andean chain on our right and in the far distance on the left, a string of volcanoes. I sighted the odd dot walking in this wilderness many miles from anywhere and not a logical destination in sight. What were they doing there? Where were they going? How would they survive?

Then my check-shirted neighbour broke the ice and mumbled something about the great wide yonder which stuttered into a long and revealing conversation exposing the fact that we actually did have a lot in common. George was Canadian, recently divorced with two grown up daughters. He told me he had quit his job painting schools for the local education authority. It was a bit like painting the Severn Bridge as once he'd finished all the schools it was time to start again. He had done this for over twenty years and hated every minute of it. This honest confession made me warm to him. Not many men would admit to this sense of loss, resentment and failure. He was entering another more satisfying chapter in his life. He was heading south and going fishing. He had the same problem and the same dilemma as me and our responses seemed to be identical.

I have mixed feelings about border controls. The exhilaration of passing into a country like Bolivia is tempered by the frustration of officialdom. This border crossing was relatively quick and friendly. Shortly after we crossed over we stopped for refreshments at Copacabana, a pretty little resort on the south side of the lake. Some of the passengers, including George, were leaving the bus there. I followed most of the passengers down a steep road towards an inviting sandy beach at the edge of Titicaca. I grabbed a snack then wandered across the busy beach until I heard someone call me. It was George relaxing in a deckchair sipping a cold beer. As I sat next to him he thrust a beer in my hand and we continued the conversation typical of middle-aged menopausal men. He planned to take a boat out on the lake the following morning for a spot of fishing. A half an hour later the bus was due to leave so we shook hands and warmly bade our farewells. I shuffled back up the steep incline towards the waiting bus mulling over what the future held for George, and more to the point what it held for me.

Breathtaking La Paz

I had read several articles claiming that La Paz stood alongside Rio, San Francisco, and Hong Kong as having the most dramatic sites in the world. But for sudden impact La Paz is unique. I was aware of the approach so I was prepared. The bus travelled through the outskirts which was a long congested road mainly full of small engineering works and scrap yards. Then after what seemed like an eternity of gridlocks there was a left turn which was met by gasps by half the passengers. On the right side La Paz was thousands of feet below in a deep natural basin, like a capital city in miniature. From the bottom of this huge natural bowl, buildings and communities swept up the sides into the lower reaches of the snow capped mountains and volcanoes that included Mount Illimani which towered at 20,000 feet.

I had been chatting to a seventy eight year old Irishman sat across the aisle to me. He looked frail and doddery but apparently he'd been travelling for months including in Africa. He said he found Ethiopia particularly demanding. The very fact he chose to travel there at his time of life I found astounding. How could he have possibly survived in such hostile environments? The answer was sat alongside him. He introduced me to a young teenager called Pedro or Pepe. He explained that his young "companion" had helped him enormously. He got off shortly afterwards before I could satisfy my curiosity. I had booked a room from Puno and I was later dropped off close to my hotel.

I was soon out exploring La Paz which was a maze of steep gradients and at 13,000 feet I was soon incapacitated. I was forced to stop at regular intervals to gasp for air. The dense traffic with the ancient buses and trucks belching black carbon monoxide didn't help my flagging respiratory system. I popped into a travel agent to enquire about trips to Potosi and Sucre near the huge salt desert of Salar de Uyuni with its famous surreal landscapes. I felt quite weak so I headed back to the guesthouse which I found difficult to locate. I knew I was close but because of the steep and erratic nature of the roads and buildings I retraced my steps several times and when you are confronted by what seemed one in two inclines it's both frustrating and very debilitating. I finally collapsed on my bed exhausted. Even then in the horizontal position it was difficult to breathe.

In the early evening I took a taxi up to the elevated outskirts of the city to take in the magnificent night view. It was like looking down into a huge inverted chandelier. Later I decided to build up my strength by taking on a full pizza and raise my spirits further by consuming a bottle of Chilean Merlot. Although at the time it could be described as just what the doctor ordered the short term physical and mental benefits soon evaporated when I attempted to climb back to my hotel.

Making my way up the steep cobbled streets I felt dizzy and light headed stopping every few steps and leaning on walls for support. I felt faint and vulnerable. A journey that should have taken me fifteen minutes took three times longer. Back in my bathroom I had a wobble and felt I was about to faint, so I lay on the floor rather that fall to it. After a few minutes I crawled into the bedroom and up onto the bed. This was when my troubles really started. Dehydration is major problem caused by altitude and litres of water have to be consumed. It was almost impossible to sleep because of the panic stricken gasps for air. When I did manage to doze I woke to find my parched lips fused together to be separated only by copious amounts water. It was a long, tortuous night. I discovered later that at high altitude alcohol abstinence is crucial and cheese is the worst food to consume.

Reluctantly I booked the first available bus out of town. This was the 5.00am from the bus station on the outskirts of La Paz. My destination was Arica on the coast of Chile. After another water guzzling distraught night my ancient taxi chugged its way up and out of the La Paz bowl to the uninviting, dimly lit bus station. The external desolation gave way to an impressive interior, slowly coming to life. After handing my backpack to a willing official I slumped into my allocated seat and closed my weary reddened eyes.

The eight hour descent from thirteen thousand feet to the ocean was directly proportional to my recovery. By the time we had crossed the border into Chile I was so refreshed and reinvigorated I was able to fully appreciate the wonderful scenery dominated by rows of snow covered volcanoes, looking like a chorus line of cloned Mount Fujis, which later gave way to the lunar landscape of the Atacama Desert.

Arica was a beautiful and restrained beach resort with a sunny year round, moderately warm, climate. I was disappointed with my shorter than planned stay in Bolivia. I have since compared notes with those who have travelled around South America and many cite the area in and around Uyuni as the highlight of their travels. There was not a huge amount to do in Arica except enjoy the beach and the laid back atmosphere. My accommodation was a small cell in a warren of small cells. The cost of living in Chile was a lot higher than Peru and Bolivia so you got a lot less for your fifteen dollars per night. I had a stroke of luck when stepping out of the shower in a cramped bathroom. In a split second I was staring at my feet horizontally in mid air after slipping and then landed flat on my back. I was surrounded by blunt instruments like a sink, toilet bowl and several sharp corners. I shuddered at the thought of a fractured skull or a broken limb so far away from Cuenca, never mind home.

The White City

I headed north across the border to Arequipa in Southern Peru. I discovered that buses weren't allowed to cross the border and the only mode of conveyance was a collectivo. At first I assumed it would involve a lot of extra hassle but it turned out to be an enjoyable experience. From the bus station I was led to what, at first, seemed a Havana Cadillac breaker's yard. There, dozens of American 60's Sedans and Cadillacs, many brightly coloured with swooping fins and whitewashed tyres, were being loaded up. My driver led me to mine, or ours, as a family of mum, dad, and two young children were already on inside. My backpack was stuffed into the bulging boot, then the driver secured the partly opened rear with rope. It was a tight squeeze with two of us alongside the driver. I assumed these type of cars were a tradition and a pre-requisite as I didn't see other more practical vehicles like vans, transits, or people carriers in operation.

Soon we were travelling north on the Pan American Highway with the South Pacific rolling in on the left and the northern Atacama

Desert on the right. The windows were down so clothing and hair were being rearranged by the resulting breeze. The driver held a cigarette in his driving hand and his other arm hung out of the window as he sang along to the Latin music being loudly emitted from the radio; no safety belts of course. All this was very liberating and uplifting. These exhilarating moments were accentuated by my schoolboy memories of studying the driest place on the planet, the Atacama Desert which was flashing passed us. The driver eased us through the border controls by collecting all our passports and removing the stress and hassle of queuing in the sun. My travelling companions were Dutch and surprisingly had family in Southern Peru but they didn't engage much seeming more concerned with internal wrangles of their nuclear family.

At the end of our short journey to the border town of Tacna was another home for aging Cadillacs. Next door was the bus station and after a couple of hours wait I was heading for Arequipa, the second largest city in Peru. When I arrived, four hours later, I was persuaded to be driven to a hotel "very cheap" by an effusive taxi driver. It was near their Plaza de Armas where I found myself soon after dumping my bags. Arequipa is known as the "White City" because many of the buildings have been created from sillar, a volcanic pearly white rock, in the Spanish colonial style, making Arequipa aesthetically pleasing with scores of handsome buildings. The backdrop, at eight thousand feet, is the snow-capped volcano, El Misti. Unlike Lima the roads leading from the Plaza de Armas are comparably narrow, creating a more congested, but snug, intimate and inviting atmosphere. Not far from the main square there were several large noisy street markets where the people were loud, humorous and friendly.

It was Christmas Eve and I was hoping to book a trip to the Colca Canyon but was afraid in this devoutly Catholic country the place would shut down for the holiday. Fortunately the power of commerce prevailed and I was booked on a two day trip to the Colca Valley.

143

There were many small and inviting restaurants in and around the plaza but I thought as it was Christmas Eve I would treat myself, seeking out a good vantage point directly overlooking the main plaza which had been beautifully decorated for Christmas. I wined and dined on the balcony watching families with their excited kids playing and dancing to the sound of the Christmas music played by a band on a specially erected stage. I did have some company from the under worked waitresses who took every opportunity to improve their English in the most light-hearted and amusing way.

Flight of the Condor

Early on Christmas Morning I, along with three Swiss and a German couple, set off for the Colca Valley and Canyon. The French speaking Swiss didn't speak much English but the young German couple did and we got along very well. One of the main priorities of this journey was to spot a giant condor. They only exist in South America and are very elusive. We stopped after a couple of hours in flat desolate country. Our guide pointed to creatures in the distant scrubland that he identified as vicunas. They are related to llamas and alpacas but are extremely shy. Even at several hundred metres we had to move with stealth otherwise they would nervously disappear. We were informed that their very fine wool was one of the most expensive materials in the world with a woman's sweater costing several thousands of pounds. Our guide then spotted a giant condor. We were a bit dubious at first having located this elusive bird so quickly and so far away from the Colca Canyon, their normal habitat. The added doubt was that the guide was the only person who could actually see it. With squinted eyes we followed his finger into the bright yonder until our eyes adjusted to a couple of dots high in the sky. I aimed my ten pound camera at them and clicked away. This sighting took the pressure off. We had achieved our quest where many others had failed.

We then began to climb steeply out of this flat valley over treacherous terrain of wet mud and gravel as the road slowly disappeared. For several tortuous miles we negotiated cascading streams and waterfalls, and seemingly impenetrable terrain until we reached the clouds then stopped for lunch in a remote shack. Half way through I realised I was having tomato soup and an omelette for Christmas lunch, with not a cracker or silly hat in sight. Later that afternoon we went to a volcanic spa to soak and loll in hot volcanic natural springs surrounded by the volcanoes that kindly provided this luxury. As I flopped about, smiling smugly, I though of those back home enjoying the usual and predictable traditional Christmas lunch.

We continued to battle the elements and the terrain until we reached an Andean outpost called Chivney where we were to spend the night. It reminded me of Jima, a throwback to the wild west with wooden homesteads and many horses. They had a couple of basic saloons where a few beers were consumed. We were billeted in tiny wooded rooms with no hot water. I wasn't complaining as a bit of deprivation adds to such experiences. In the evening we were led to what seemed like a church hall where we joined other travellers for what can only be described as an old fashioned dinner and dance.

The choice of food wasn't that inviting so, rather guiltily, I took the opportunity to try alpaca for the first and last time. I chatted with our guide, who, like many of his profession around the world, was highly intelligent, multilingual but with little scope or opportunity to realise his ambition and potential. I found myself, on Christmas night, discussing the Peruvian tax system, or rather the lack of one. He was frustrated that he wasn't paying income tax as if Peru had an efficient tax gathering system it would make huge inroads into solving their enormous social and economic problems. I was then yanked onto the dance floor in mid syllable to embark on a complicated Peruvian folk dance, which was a cross between the conga and the paso doble accompanied by the local band and dance ensemble.

At 6.00am the following morning we set off for the Colca Canyon, which our guide informed us was the deepest canyon in the world, and twice the depth of the Grand Canyon. It had absolutely pissed down for most of the night. The roads, bad enough before, were now flooded and there were signs of avalanches, so the progress was slow and often hair raising, with steep precipices inches away from the wheels, but I was cool. Unfortunately as the canyon got deeper the cloud got thicker. The deeper it got the less visible it became until everything below us was obliterated by the cumulus nimbus.

We spent much of the time looking for giant condors. As many of the travellers here fail to locate any because of their elusiveness we were very lucky to have a very good guide who spotted all of ours. He'd point them out, and even then we struggled against the panoramic background to pick them up. We watched them gliding on thermals high in the canyon. We must have had our necks craned for hours, on and off over the two days, transfixed to those elegant gliding scavengers, and in that time I didn't see a wing flap. I thought I spotted one but the guide looked through his binoculars and said that it was only an eagle, so we traipsed on. Then I thought hang on, an eagle, you don't see one of those every day, but when I looked again it was gone.

Later that morning we picked up two American sisters from a remote lodge. They were in their late twenties. One lived in California and the other lived in New York, although both had Bronx accents and were teachers. One was laid back and couldn't give a damn and the other was intense and animated. They were close enough to argue unconsciously in public which they did often and to the amusement of others. We got chatting in the back of the vehicle which often turned into uproarious laughter. They were a very comical double act. One thing we all agreed upon was to revolutionise backpacking—by not

146

using backpacks. Let's be honest you are veritable beast of burden, it does untold damage to the back, and it seriously undermines deportment. If you turn left in a shop, you unknowingly destroy six months inventory on the right. In a busy street a glance over the shoulder can result in knocking people into on-coming traffic. There is an undeserved cool attached to wearing a backpack. The animated sister, Laverne, after years of carrying one was now using a wheelie suitcase.

I actually bought a cheap backpack for this journey because the uncool image of using my wheelie suitcase was unpalatable. I also learned a painful lesson, don't buy a cheap one. My backpack, which I had hoped would last a month, had become virtually useless with only one strap left which was hanging by a few threads of cotton. My backpack had now become my frontpack as I walked down the street hugging it like a long lost relative. How cool is that? The street credibility and the proletarian image attached to the whole backpacking get-up is so misplaced. Top of the range specialist clothing, boots and backpack cost twice as much as the clobber the Queen wears at the state opening of parliament. We dropped the girls off at another lodge in the middle of nowhere and calm was restored.

Back in Arequipa I came across a gentleman who can only be described as the Lace Man. In one of the noisy, bustling main streets I spotted what seemed to be a large multi-coloured vulture with a scraggy human head. It was in fact a small gnarled ugly man, and aged before his time no doubt. He looked like Albert Steptoe after being battered around the head with shovels for an hour. He was buried under thousands of laces of every colour imaginable but dominated by black, brown and white. His shoulders rose high above his head with laces, hence the likeness to a vulture, and they hung thickly down and around his feet. His arms appeared and disappeared into his acquired plumage at different places depending on customer choice. He demanded you buy from him by screeching at the top of his voice exposing both his blackened teeth. I bought two pairs from him because I genuinely needed some. He conned me by charging three times the correct amount. Discretion being the better part of valour, I meekly accepted the oversight from this intimidating vulture.

In a nearby museum I visited the famous Juanita the Ice Maiden. She was a 500 year old mummy who was discovered in 1995 on Mount Ampato. She was chosen at the age of twelve to be a human sacrifice to the Inca gods. This was a great honour for her family. The doomed Juanita was taken like other young virginal sacrifices to the top of a high mountain to be slaughtered in a long drawn out ceremony. She was well preserved in the ice capped summit until discovery. There were few tourists so I had her to myself. She was sat hunched over her knees and even after all this time and because she was so well preserved I still felt an immediate sense of anger and waste at this sad and poignant scene.

I wandered many miles around the this beautiful city, calling into several museums and monasteries including the famous Santa Catalina Monastery which was like a city in a city. On leaving Arequipa I had to make a decision about The Nazca Lines. These mysterious giant geoglyphs are drawings in the earth found in the southern Peruvian desert near Nazca. They are huge drawings of creatures such as monkeys, llamas, sharks, and lizards, estimated to have been drawn about two thousand years ago and can only be seen from the air. I had heard tales that the pilots of these small aircraft like to show off by looping the loop and other aeronautical gymnastics. The result was much vomiting. Looking back I wish I had taken a flight but at the time my nerve failed me and I bypassed Nazca and headed back to Lima

I Left My Heart in Lima .... Along With Two Cameras, a Rucksack, My Specs, Bus Tickets, Photos, My Sanity, The Will to Live ...

I was back with the monkeys, parrots, and tortoises on the roof of the Hotel Espana in Lima next to the room I stayed in on my outward journey. I ventured out to buy my ticket to Tumbes. I intended to be on my guard and walked self-consciously across the Plaza de Armas feeling eyes were targeting me. I purchased my ticket for the following day, had an enjoyable meal in a restaurant used by the locals and headed back. After a short nap I decided to go to the cinema I had passed earlier showing King Kong. The cinema was nothing like the modern multiplexes, more like the old Monaco in Cardiff which was one of the last of the family run picture houses and had now closed. I enjoyed this retro experience. The cinema was almost full of mainly young people and the bonus was the film was in English with Spanish sub-titles. As I got engrossed in the film I completely lost all sense of geography and felt I was back home in Cardiff subconsciously planning a take-away curry on the way home. It was only when the lights went up at the end of the film that I became aware of the Spanish chatter around me and realised. "I'm in Peru!!"

The following day I was due to leave Lima at six in the evening and headed for lunch at the same restaurant as the previous day. Now the following sequence of events had me philosophising over pre-determination versus chaos theory for quite some time. Back in the restaurant where, the previous day, I had enjoyed the meal so much I left a generous tip, I felt I was being ignored. I hadn't noticed the waiters only serving their regulars the previous day. Had I done something to upset them? Surely not. Anyway I took my leave and headed to the Plaza de Armas where there was a KFC tastefully ensconced in an architectural delight. Surely I couldn't go wrong in a KFC. As there were very few people in this large outlet, service was not a problem. I carried my tray around a corner and was spoiled for choice with seating availability. I plonked myself down, placed a napkin on my lap but spilled my coffee as the table wobbled. I moved across to another table near the window and wall placing my rucksack between the wall and my leg. No salt. I got up and decided, favouring caution, to take my rucksack with me to the counter. I returned and ate. Looking around there was a group of Japanese students studying a map while devouring burgers. The only other person was a man sat at the top corner reading a newspaper. About ten minutes later I reached for my bag . . . . in vain. I looked down and there it was . . . . gone. I stood up nonplussed. Theft didn't immediately occur to me. The Japanese lads were jabbering away and the man reading the newspaper . . . . well . . . he was gone!! No, impossible, the bag was touching my leg away from the aisle and against the wall. I ran to the counter seeking help but the counter assistants were as puzzled as me. I ran back to the students seeking witnesses. One said he saw the man pick up the bag but he thought he was a taxi driver. What?!! So that's what taxi drivers do is it?! They have special dispensation to walk into buildings and take the property of unsuspecting owners. Now the Japanese were never my favourite race since the rape of Nanking, the fall of Singapore and the antics of their tourists around the world. This experience did nothing to modify my opinion.

Actually I was surprisingly calm. The thief got nothing of value. His eyes may have lit up at the sight of two cameras but neither were digital, one was broken, and the other was virtually worthless. I had lost what I thought were competition winning photographs, in reality this saved my friends and family hours of boredom. There were three Lonely Planet guidebooks that belonged to Florida Chris and he had already travelled south. My passport and wallet were safely in my pocket. My immediate problem was my stolen bus ticket so I returned to the travel agent. Karla was an angel escorting me down the road to the police station and then helped with the paperwork, red tape and translation. These formalities were necessary for a ticket replacement. While I was in the cop shop two Irish women came in. They had been travelling for seven months in India, Asia, and South America without a hitch and were within two hours of flying home at the end of their long trip before one of the girls had her expensive mobile phone stolen. There was jostling on a crowded pavement and the thief unzipped her bag and it was gone. We sort of admired the level of skill involved in each incident.

I arrived at the designated bus terminal in good time. This particular Lima bus terminal was large, very busy and chaotic. My replacement ticket caused some confusion but after speaking to several harassed officials it was agreed I was a bona fide passenger. There were lots of bags lying about with an assortment of backpackers keeping steely eyes on their possessions. Like me they felt there were predators about and we were the prey. I had heard many times that one of a group would be left to guard, say seven bags. However it's very difficult to stare intently at seven bags, as your gaze is bound to drift, then drift back. You count one to seven repeatedly until you return your gaze one more to time to count one, two, three, four, five, six, se . . . . and they've struck in a blink of an eye. Backpacking what joy.!!

My Night of Smack-head Debauchery

After a stop-over in Tumbes I arrived back in Cuenca and was relieved that the interminable bus journeys were over. After a long sleep and an epic laundry session I headed across the Tomibamba to see who was back in town. I spotted Kevin with Marcel and planned to meet up later then received an e-mail from fellow Saigon rat, Gordon. In the evening we met at a favourite little haunt of ours called Percal. It was on two floors and very cramped. We had to squeeze around small tables on bench like seats which added to the intimacy of the place. The food was great and they mixed the most potent cocktails in Cuenca. It also had an air of mystery inasmuch as there were unflagged periods of closure. We would turn up and it would be closed and remained so for weeks. Then someone in the staffroom would exclaim "Percal's back open" and we'd all troop back.

Florida Chris also joined us and we swapped our Christmas holiday adventures. Kevin and Marcel spent the entire period on the beaches of northern Ecuador with many other young teachers partying and doing coke. They came back early because they had run out of money. Chris went to the Amazon with his parents which was great for them but terrifying for him as he suffered from acute arachnophobia. He explained to me that when he was in Lima he also stayed at the Hotel Espana in a room on the roof, which could have been the same room I had slept in. When he heard scratching noises he was so unnerved he went down two floors and slept in a stairwell. So by sleeping in a wooden hut in the densest jungle in the world he was, with great personal sacrifice, obeying the fifth commandment in extremis. Under his mosquito net he would lay awake during the night listening to, not only the sounds of the jungle, but the pattering of strange tiny feet and mysterious squeaks. A call of nature would take him to basic ablutions that required him to squat or stand, eyes tightly shut, knowing that huge crunchy beetles, spiders the size of dinner plates and god knows what else were lurking in the shadows.

I had experienced my own arachnid moment. As I'd grown older I had become more mentally fragile, you know, vertigo, claustrophobia, a bit of paranoia and psychosis, a couple of nervous breakdowns, insomnia etc. Conversely this growing fragility had been inversely proportional to my hitherto morbid fear of spiders. Although I prefer not to share the same space as them, my shock horror reaction has all but abated. This was just as well as a while back I had encountered the biggest spider I have ever seen outside a zoo or a James Bond movie. Another teacher had mentioned evicting large spiders, which I equated to those found in Britain. With Cuenca having a temperate climate I hadn't expected much more. I was eating a meal in my kitchen when I sensed movement through an opened door to the next room which was dimly lit. When I investigated my reaction was JESUS CHRI . . . . This wasn't a spider this was a beast. It was the size of a tarantula but a different shape and colour. Its eight legs were bent high above its body and it was thick, black, and hairy. My response was not to recoil but to be drawn towards it in fascination. Its high action coordinated movement looked so graceful as it glided slowly across the floor. Bent double I followed, with my nose hovering only inches above it. It stopped in, what my landlady loosely described as, the sun room. I continued to study it intently before realising eviction was the priority. I fetched a cup from the kitchen but it was too small so returned it, replacing it with a saucepan and grabbed a brush. I went back to the sun room and there it was . . . . GONE!! Did it turn right into the bedroom? My fascination with this creature didn't stretch to sharing my bedroom with it. In a blind panic I ransacked the bedroom before returning to the sun room to find it sauntering towards the exit door. It seemed to know it was an unwelcome guest. I planned to open the door and with the broom, launch it, Freddie Flintoff style, over the long on boundary. But this magnificent creature deserved more respect, and anyway he was about to leave of its own volition and pace. He wasn't the scurrying type. I opened the door and aware of my presence, with some aplomb it ambled out past me and away. Holding open the door as it casually wandered through I felt like its butler.

Later that evening Chris declared that he had some good local "shit," much better than his Florida supply so they all decided to go back to Kevin and Marcel's pad to snort a few lines. It didn't surprise me that Gordon was an occasional user, but Chris? He was a short, blond, blue eyed, polite, angelic choirboy with rich conservative parents who had put him through college. I was aghast. If he's into it, who the hell isn't? I was then rather strangely apologetic about being a coke virgin but Marcel was quite understanding.

"That's OK, we'll start you with a couple of bobs." The notion that, especially at my age, probably older that Chris's parents, I may not approve didn't seem to register. I sort of took it as a compliment that even at my age I was still rock and roll. I had a couple of periods of marijuana use in my youth where I self consciously sat cross-legged faking the spaced out look before realising, being a beer and darts man, that I much preferred Guinness.

I had no qualms about trying cocaine as I believe all drugs should be legalised. I was looking forward to a new experience. It wasn't that radical as it seems that for most young and not so young professionals it is their chosen recreational stimulant. It was a bit weird though, participating in a scenario I had only ever seen on TV or in the movies. Chris expertly chopped up the powder on a mirror with a credit card then laid out two lines each, setting aside a couple of bobs for me. Then we took it turns, snorting through a fifty dollar bill. Then we all sniffed up another two lines, including me who now being a bona fide coke head spread the stuff over my teeth and gums. Like the marijuana it had little obvious effect on me and I still prefer a bottle of claret any day. Chris was a revelation and I discovered a lot more about Gordon too.

He was about to celebrate his fiftieth birthday and had led a nomadic rebellious life. As youngsters we had a lot in common. He was a working class Glaswegian from the tenements and had been a member of the Militant Tendency, an organisation I briefly flirted with. He worked in Canada illegally for eighteen years and had been to sea. For the previous seven years he had been a TEFL teacher in Saigon fully and unapologetically embracing the kind of sexual hedonistic lifestyle a man of his age could only enjoy in that part of the world. He once told me that he had never had sex with a woman over twenty four as if it was his cardinal rule. I retorted that this meant that any Catherine Zeta-Jones advances would have to be rejected.

Hi Y'all

A couple of days later there was a gathering in the Eucalyptus Club to welcome the half dozen or so new teachers. There were more noisy tales of holiday excess, adventure, and calamity around the cocktail laden tables as the new arrivals nervously found places. Two were tall Texan beauties, one of whom was Genna Jones, who sat across from me and was so beautiful I found it difficult to avert my gaze. She was tall, slim with a wonderful smile and dark flashing eyes matching her lush black hair and of course she had a wonderful sexy Texan drawl. The fact that she was aware and proud of her Welsh ancestry was an obvious ice-breaker. Over the next few months we worked in the same group of classes and fate threw us together regularly. For example several of us went to the theatre to see a mime artist and our tickets sat us next to each other. We got along very well and she seemed to seek me out for daily banter. One night after a function I was heading back to my pad over the river when she called to me, catching me up breathlessly asking if it was ok to walk with me until she got back to her guesthouse which was on the way. Cuenca could be dangerous, especially at night. We sauntered back laughing and chatting then when we got to her place we stood outside continuing to chat and laugh for quite a while. I was confused. It was obvious she liked me a lot but surely in an avuncular sort of way? Apart from her great beauty she was natural and warm. Obviously at my age my interest was purely paternal but my younger self was head over heels.

Tear Gas, Bombs and Revolution

Genna joined our Cuenca supporters club so we introduced her to the Latin American soccer experience. Her initiation wasn't a let down. We all went to see Cuenca play a Brazilian side in the preliminary stages of the South American Cup. On this occasion instead of positioning ourselves close to the "crazies" we actually joined them, playing our part unfurling the huge flag above our, and a few hundred other supporter's, heads. We were handed our toilet rolls to hurl and most of the teachers who had various levels of Spanish under their respective belts sang the songs and chants to the beat of the drums. Just before the kick off hundreds of fire lanterns were launched into the night sky. As the teams entered young athletic supporters climbed the barriers that penned in the crowd and let off extinguishers that sprayed Cuencan coloured powder that eventually fell and covered the crowd. The constant igniting of fire crackers was deafening.

About fifteen minutes into the game events took a sinister turn. A lone character emerged and was about to light what seemed another firecracker, but this time all the local fans started moving away with looks of apprehension on their faces. This man stood in a twenty metre radius of unoccupied terracing as everyone backed off. He lit his incendiary device and threw it in our direction, resulting in a huge bang between Oregon Chris an me. I thought it was just a very loud bang until Chris said "I've been hit". Chris at 6'4" was the archetypal gentle giant and one of the nicest people I've ever met, but he had steel in his eyes as he made his way to the perpetrator who was trying to melt back into the crowd. I went after Chris and grabbed him as he was to launch himself at the bomber, because the result of his revenge attack could have escalated into something more serious.

I went to the toilets with him and he had what can only be described as shrapnel wounds as he picked bits of fragmented wood out of his legs and buttocks. The Red Cross patched him up as the wounds were only superficial. Afterwards we moved away to another part of the ground and watched the remainder of a very good game which ended in a 1-1 draw. Later we started seeing the humorous side of the events. Chris' jeans had about a dozen holes in them which in a way was a positive outcome He went to the game with a $20.00 pair of jeans and as they had become trendy "stressed jeans" they were now worth twice that much. Having seen him in the toilets I informed everyone he had stressed underpants as well.

It would be Cordelia's last match as she had to return to Canada for family reasons. It was sad for her and for me too. We were similar ages which I found comforting but more than that we were friends well met with a lot in common and I would miss her a lot. A few days later we received an e-mail from her, regaling us of a confrontation she had in Guayaquil on her journey home, reminiscent of a famous scene from Crocodile Dundee. It was the scene where the hero is accosted by a knife wielding mugger only for him to produce a more potent weapon reciting the immortal words "Call that a knife? This is a knife mate." Cordelia was always interested in the local culture and she was visiting one of the great ornate cemeteries of Ecuador. She had hired a driver for the afternoon. While wandering through the gravestones, a dark, swarthy hombre appeared from behind a large ornate headstone brandishing a knife and demanding money which must have been terrifying for Cordelia. She then heard a gun cocking behind her. She turned to see her driver, who had wisely followed her, holding a rather large pistol at arm's length. When she turned back again her assailant had fled.

She wrote from the comfort of her Canadian suburban home that she missed the life, passion, colour and culture of South America. This included regular demonstrations and marches organised by young activists wearing Che Guevara t-shirts who would chant and march over the cobbled streets escorted by heavily armed police. They would then assemble in the Parc Calderon where earnest speeches full of, what I assumed, revolutionary rhetoric would be bellowed through a dodgy PA system. On the other side of the Tomibamba where a radical university was located, some of the demonstrations were more violent, with stone throwing at the police who responded with tear gas and baton charges. Often we would arrive at school coughing and spluttering with eyes streaming from the effects of tear gas. This anarchy seemed to be cosmetic because after a demo things returned to Cuenca's normal calm serenity. It was as if the the authorities permitted the regular monthly demo so the students could let off steam and the police could practice crowd control. This balance was maintained until I, and most of the other teachers, were due to leave Ecuador when circumstances contrived to make things very difficult for us.

Blackboard Jungle

They say kids, especially teenagers, are the same the world over but I discovered a marked difference between Saigon and Cuenca. Although both schools were private and the kids hailed from middle class families, the pupils of Cuenca were more streetwise, cynical and spoilt. My teaching experience in Cuenca compared to Saigon was more demanding. The standard of teaching required, despite the poor pay, was of a higher quality in Ecuador. I had three classes, one adult and two teenage, all at intermediate level. The teachers set the mid and end term exams. I failed one of the adults, a large man in his thirties who was apoplectic when informed by me of his failure. He begged me to change the result and had to be tearfully led away. One of my teenage classes was mainly female, were high achievers and were a delight to teach. In fact their commitment and positive attitude was often unnerving as a quiet class dedicated to learning can be as challenging as a noisy one. My third class was made up of a dozen boys and one girl, all about fifteen years old. The boys had such a pack mentality that it verged on being a gang. They could be surly and boisterous and it was obvious after spending a day in their state school that they would've rather been somewhere else.

The one girl in the class was regularly subjected to what in the UK would be judged as sexist jibes. She seemed to accept it as the norm and was perplexed by my protestations on her behalf. The boys had a very macho attitude. When comparing the cultural differences between the USA and Ecuador (it was an American owned school) there were obvious differences. For example I gave them a scenario where the wife was a doctor or lawyer and earned four times more than the husband and I posed the question should the wife work and the husband look after the house and kids. There were hoots of derision and they dismissed the suggestion out of hand. They sought to maintain the role of breadwinner even if it resulted in poverty.

Juan Diago Larriva was the main source of mirth in the class, often at my expense. I unwisely took him on in the banter stakes, a battle I couldn't possibly win, especially as I couldn't speak Spanish. On one occasion I turned to him as the source of a hilarious outburst from the class to find that he had pulled his bobble hat down over his face. In mid syllable, without breaking my stride, I instinctively pulled it off and threw it through a window where it landed three stories below. This silenced the class and Juan was overcome by the loss of his cool headgear. While we continued in near silence Juan kept a close scrutiny on his beloved hat. I won that battle but I knew they would return re-energised with Juan seeking revenge. I returned to the class the following day to find that the whiteboard had my name and "Gay" alongside it in permanent marker. Of course they pleaded innocence and I couldn't prove otherwise. It had the desired affect because throughout the lesson I kept thinking, do they actually think I'm gay, if so, why?

Juan the leader and obvious perpetrator of this dastardly deed insisted on being called Coco Larriva and had designed a very artistic personal logo to represent this which appeared on his books and often on my board. So to get back at him I explained that in English Coco represents a clown which he refused to believe. So I brought in several internet images of Coco the clown and the rest of the class erupted in laughter. I realise that most teenagers do not like to be the butt of such humour especially in public and in Ecuador the effect is more acute especially for a boy. I childishly enjoyed Juan's obvious discomfort as he fell silently into his shell. I took the heat off him later by humiliating one of his fellow conspirators. After answering a difficult question I marched over to Pablo with my arm outstretched to congratulate him by shaking his hand theatrically, then bypassed him leaving him offering his outstretched hand, to shake the hand of the boy behind him. The class fell about in fits of laughter, while the victim boiled with rage.

Despite the few victorious battles, I was losing the war. Although Spanish was not allowed in class they often used it with me as the target. The class continued to be noisy and disruptive. One day Juan took a call on his mobile and when I confronted him he said it was an important message from his mother leaving the class with an expression of great concern. When he got to the door he said something down the line that sent the class into hysterics. I ran to the door grabbed him by the lapels pulled him to his seat and rammed him in his chair. Although teachers can get away with a lot more in Ecuador I knew I had overstepped the mark and this wasn't well thought out class management. I had lost control.

Sanctions in the school existed but the parents were paying customers and the school was a business and often teachers were hung out to dry. Despite this I made a complaint against Juan and his parents were informed. Fortunately the mother was very supportive of school discipline and Juan gave a very good impression of Little Lord Fauntleroy for the rest of the term. If only I had swallowed my pride and done this earlier. I actually liked Juan as he was genuinely funny. In every test or exam with contorted agonising expressions he would call out pleadingly "Teacher, teacher, help me I don't understand." He would be last to leave the exam, often after the bell, as he anguished over his answers. He'd finally offer the paper, then pulled it back to make final amendments. His paper would be a mess of repeated crossings out and arrows pointing to his fourth or attempted final answer. It would always be covered in his Coco logo and he nearly always attained 100%. He was a character and very bright. I did learn an important lesson that it's all about the pupils and I had to learn to swallow my pride and not take things too personally.

Heading Home—The Scenic Route

My vague repatriation plans when I first arrived was to fly from Lima after exploring Peru and Bolivia. I had ticked that box during the unexpectedly long Christmas break. In the meantime I had been inspired by the adventurous spirit shown by young teachers I had met. Shay was a good looking twenty six year old with the wit and charm that is unique to the Irish. I envied his youth and current opportunities to work in exotic places at such a young age. This envy descended into the darkest shade of green when he explained how he arrived at Cuenca to start his job a year earlier. He flew to Rio, travelled north to the mouth of the Amazon then took several boat trips to its source in Peru, crossed into Ecuador before arriving 9.00 am sharp Monday morning for work. How cool is that?

Becky had taught in Nicaragua, travelled alone through Central America, and Penny from South Africa, who was petite, bubbly, and very girlie, but despite all this and to the admiration of many, spent three weeks travelling overland from Buenos Aires to Cuenca, alone.

She used to teach in India although she had a travelling companion on that trip. A group of us were talking about different places one evening as in that company people are keen to hear about places, travel information and experiences. We could chat away without the fear of being accused of name dropping as everyone was interested and mental notes for future travel were logged. Penny had a very interesting tale to tell. She had worked in California, Pennsylvania, and was alone and penniless in New York. She'd also supped Guinness in Dublin and Dun Laoghaire, and she was only 23!!

I had toyed with idea of flying home from Buenos Aires after travelling back through Peru then further into Chile and then across to the Argentine capital. Then because the price of the flights had changed it was more beneficial to travel two weeks after my planned departure so I booked my flight for six weeks after my contract had ended. I had now to plan what to do in this six weeks. I intently studied my Lonely Planets setting and resetting routes and itineraries until I settled on the travel details of my expedition south. I was heading for as far as I could possibly go, Cape Horn on Tierra del Fuego. The planning was always hugely enjoyable especially accompanied by a bottle of wine. My excitement was palpable as I was going to visit places I had never dreamt of even as a kid.

The last week had been hectic with the finals to set and grade plus farewell parties to attend. We collected our final cheques at lunchtime on the last day and headed to the bank, in glorious sunshine, to cash them. Outside the bank we bade our last farewells, and some tears were shed. A highlight of my time in Cuenca had been the quality of the teachers, both as educators and people. Some of the people who I got to know very well weren't there so the final handshake or hug went amiss. It was weird crossing the Rio Tomibamba back to my pad for the last time and passing the shops where I'd been a regular customer for the previous seven months and had become friendly with the staff. The five-a-side soccer court was near my pad and seeing it deserted on a Friday afternoon when for the last few months we had played at this particular time and had so much fun before going for a few beers, was very poignant.

That penultimate afternoon I slowly packed my suitcase. As I was doing so the weather made a dramatic turn for the worse. That happened a lot as venomous, black, pregnant, clouds suddenly appeared from over the mountains. That storm was the worst I had experienced, with torrential rain and deafening claps of thunder that shook the building. The lightening caused temporary loss of power. This went on for hours. As I packed in depressing semi darkness the symbolism was not lost on me. That night the thought of my impending trip to the bottom of the world filled me with a mixture of exhilaration and dread. Why was I doing this to myself. What had fate in store for me?

The following morning I stood for a few moments with Mimi, smoothing and patting her in the post storm freshened air. She seemed to sense my imminent departure especially dragging my wheelie suitcase packed to bursting and a rucksack on my back. I left her without looking back as I couldn't face her standing motionless with that resigned, sad, doleful expression.

Right on cue there was civil unrest throughout the country during the last week. Students with a grievance had attacked vehicles and built road blocks of burning tyres on the main roads. Buses had remained in the terminals. This unrest was throughout Ecuador. Some of the affluent parents of the young American teachers were due to arrive but were stuck in Quito or Guayaquil. Many other teachers were marooned in Cuenca as most roads out were blocked. Fortunately the main road south was clear but Cuenca was cut off from all other directions for many days.

Without a hitch I arrived in Tumbes by late afternoon. There is something uplifting and worldly about checking into a hotel in an obscure part of the world when the manager or receptionist recognises you. This happened in Tumbes on my third stay. It was also quite warming when the owner of my regular breakfast haunt gave me a knowing smile and nod. Tumbes was an unremarkable town but I grew very fond of it. The people were industrious and cheerful and on each time I passed through I had dinner, al fresco, in the main plaza. For the second time I bore witness to a Saturday evening wedding in the church. Like the first, when the nuptials were over the bride and groom, in a horse drawn carriage and to the sound of the church bells, did a few laps of the plaza which was decorated in bunting and balloons. They then entered what seemed like the local municipal hall decked out for the occasion. Extended families and friends happily danced and played in the square to the small but enthusiastic dance band. Their lives seemed simple and happy.

After another twenty four hour journey from Tumbes I arrived in Lima at 7.00am the following morning and once again booked into the wonderful Hotel Espana. I ventured out into the notorious Lima streets totally paranoid looking for predators in all guises. I walked across the main Plaza and was approached by a youth who asked me if I was English. I thought, fuck me I've only been here two minutes and I'm under attack already. He said that he and his accomplices, who stood in the background, were students learning English and could they interview me, a likely story. They looked innocuous enough so I let myself be interviewed on tape by each of them. There were about eight in all and after the interviews they suggested that they all take photographs of the group. When it was my turn, with my guard down, I handed them my brand new camera at their behest. As I posed with the group I realised what I had done so as the photographer inched away to focus I fully expected him to turn and run with all the others scampering in all directions, but he took a photo handed back my camera and thanked me profusely for my time.

I decided to book an evening flight to Tacna on the Chilean border instead of another 20 hour overnight bus journey. I sought out my favourite travel agent, Karla, to put the business her way as some sort of gratitude for her help and kindness the last time I was in Lima. She gave me a smile of recognition and hopefully appreciated the commission of the flight which, although short and internal, was nevertheless quite expensive.

Lima Airport was large, modern and almost deserted. The contrast with Vietnam was marked as the relative cheap flights there ensure the high usage by the indigenous population. In Lima there seemed to be only about a half dozen international plus a handful of internal flights per day. A price revue was well overdue.

Let The Journey Begin

What little of Tacna I saw seemed unremarkable. I arrived at night and took a taxi to the bus station first thing next morning. I purchased my ticket this time knowing my mode of transport was to be a colourful 60's Buick or similar and new exactly where to find it. I was now hurtling towards the Chilean border on the Pan American Highway in a packed sky blue Cadillac, wind in my hair, arm stretched horizontal through the window. I was a laid back easy rider. The driver once again took the hassle out of the border crossing and a few hours later I was on a bus from Arica to Iquique 350 kilometres further south. Up until then I had been on automatic pilot, retracing my steps, using the facilities and knowledge of my previous trip. Now I had to switch back on and concentrate. But first my brain had to absorb the images of the inner reaches of the Atacama Desert. My first trip to Arica was just a brief sampler as we skated past for a few miles at its north westernmost extremities. Travelling into the desert proper I witnessed scenes of uninhabited desolation. There were areas of huge dunes and flat desert disappearing into infinity. The colours varied from dark greys to whiter shades of pale, but dominated by reds and browns of every hue. Where the peerless blue sky met the earth in the distant horizon there was an unidentifiable shimmering no man's land of colour fusion.

After several hours of this uniquely cosmic, isolated void, we cut off the Pan-American highway and headed for Iquique on the coast. Above Iquique is a huge imposing cordella or sand dune. From the top the town looked like a large shunting yard with rows of ugly dark buildings. Apart from the ocean front and a few impressive architectural exceptions Iquique was devoid of any urban planning. In its defence it has to be said that the place was thrown together during the nitrates boom of the nineteenth and early twentieth centuries. Chile was far more expensive than Peru so my ten or fifteen dollar nightly budget realised another small cell in another warren masquerading as a guesthouse. Iquique was for the most part a noisy, ugly, mess of a place. The reason I stopped there was to visit the nearby ghost town of Humberstone.

I travelled in a minibus with a disparate group including two German husbands of Chilean wives. One of the wives explained that she left Chile aged 14 with her family after the overthrow of Allende to avoid the extremes of Pinochet and his henchmen. We drove into the sizzling infinity of the Atacama Desert to seek out this ghost town. On the way we visited an abandoned nitrates works. It appeared like a mirage on the horizon, a sinister black gnarled silhouette fidgeting in the distant heat haze. We clambered over the old rusted workings and in the offices we found many artefacts of another age such as dust covered ancient typewriters, cash registers, huge ledgers and alike. We were informed the nitrates boom came to an abrupt halt in the1930's when the Germans invented a cheaper synthetic version. Fiendishly clever those Nazi scientists. We looked accusingly at our German friends.

Humberstone is the best preserved ghost town of the nitrates boom and became deserted by the 1960's. It's difficult to appreciate the eeriness of the place with tourists wandering around. But with a bit of imagination you can picture what a thriving, bustling, community this must have been, exiled in the middle of the most inhospitable and driest place on the planet. The places that invoked this the most were the well preserved church, hotel, and theatre. At the back of the hotel there was a very large disused swimming pool, with no shallow end and constructed out of steel from a hull of a ship, rivets and all. The black wooden diving boards rotted in the sun. The theatre was very atmospheric. Travelling operas, variety shows, and theatre groups performed in this desert outpost. Movies were also shown. They had posters in the foyer of Charlie Chaplin's, The Engineer, Citizen Kane, Gone with the Wind, and The Wizard of Oz. Perhaps they were placed there after the events for dramatic effect. If that's the case it certainly worked for me. There was also a photograph of Josiah Humberstone. He was the eminent Victorian Englishman who built the place. He looked austere, rotund, with the requisite winged collar, George V goatee, and a dangling Albert pocket watch chain. He looked suitably . . . . eminent.

San Pedro de Atacama

Along my carefully planned route I was eagerly excited about certain anticipated highlights, and a major one was San Pedro de Atacama. It had come recommended by other travellers, and I had read rave notices of it in travel books so after another long bus journey I arrived there late at night. The first thing I noticed was the desert sky. It looked as if someone has thrown a black sequin encrusted ball gown over a glass ceiling. If van Gough had witnessed this, his mind would have been blown in even more. The last time I experienced something like this was when I was posted to RAF Gan in the Maldives. When being transported back to "my" island by motor launch, worse for drink, I would lie, staring up, mesmerized by the teeming myriad of brilliant stars winking at me. Magical.

The following morning I wandered around, booked a couple of trips, and soaked up the atmosphere. The first impressions of San Pedro was of a lazy, sleepy, heat affected, Mexican village. The buildings, for the most part, were single story, fashioned out of the local red terracotta, many of which were whitewashed. Most of the roads were just dirt tracks. There were an inordinate amount of large dogs, made docile by the heat. Those visitors who were not away trekking, horse riding, or on excursions, were drifting about listlessly in the heat, eyeing trinkets, or in various states of repose, reading, or just chilling. The aforementioned dogs were dotted about comatose in various poses of slumber. This whole scenario gave the description "laid back" a euphemistic quality. The distant backdrop was a series of magnificent snow-topped mountains and volcanoes.

At night the whole place came alive. The inadequate street lighting added to the atmosphere. I ducked into any number of weather-beaten hostelries to discovery aesthetically designed interiors that created an ambiance of unique quality. The great variety of cuisine was delicious. The down side was that it was very expensive. I had been used to a US$350 a month salary and searching out $1.50 lunches. I had developed a backpacking mentality and budgeting to match. I was looking for hotels or guesthouses between 7 and 15 dollars per night. I was forced, through circumstance, to use a hotel in Tacna which cost an extortionate $23 for one night. It had a bellhop for God sake! Backpackers and bellhops go together like choc-ice and chips. Here I was offered a single room for $35.00. I was aghast. I settled for a room with two twin bunk beds at $13, and I was the only occupant. Thankfully because of a broken lock I was upgraded to the single room for the same price. So I became a happy camper. I had to admit that my backpacking credentials didn't bear scrutiny. It's true I had a rucksack, but I also had a rather large wheelie suitcase which I incongruously dragged through the rutted streets of San Pedro the previous night. I'm ashamed to describe its contents, but suffice to say that it included three pairs of conservative trousers, five ties, a hairdryer and an iron. I was less Sherpa Tensing more Bertie Wooster.

San Pedro de Atacama was like a Marrakesh in miniature. Marrakesh is known as the pink city because the walls around the city are of that colour. Like Marrakesh you approach San Pedro from the desert and it appears as a red walled community. You could actually walk around it in less than an hour. Apart from its atmosphere and unique nightlife it's perfectly positioned for the amazing natural phenomena in its immediate surround. Despite being about seven thousand feet above sea level it gets very hot during the day but the evenings are lovely and cool.

My first trip outside was to the dramatically named Valley of Death and the Lunar Valley. This included a three hour trek and being driven between destinations. The death bit was because the place was an ancient burial ground not because the skeletons of lost tourist had been discovered in abundance. What you soon realise and the guide explains, is that this part of the desert has great variety, with wildlife, lakes, ponds, plus flora and fauna. The driest part of the desert is further north around Arica and Iquique which I travelled through on the way to Humberstone. It is the part where it had never rained and marks the Atacama Desert out as the driest place in the world. I mentioned van Gogh in connection with the night sky, I also think the subject matter of colour fusion and sandstorms of the north would have interested England's greatest painter, W M Turner. In the vernacular of the Royal Academy he could have filled his boots there.

The Valley of Death was actually much like the Martian landscape. The shapes of the red rock and hardened sand dunes were miscellaneous and haphazard and on an enormous scale, created by erosion and rapid evaporation. Our trek took us around the high volcanic perimeter overlooking the third largest salt lake in the world that stretched out into the distant horizon. We then descended and crunched our way across part of the salt flat. The trip was designed to coincide with the sunset over the Lunar Valley. This valley had many weird and wonderful natural sculptures created over millions of years. To access the best vantage points for the sunset you have to climb an enormous dune. The ascent is like a Freudian nightmare because the sand shifts below your feet giving the impression that you're walking on the spot and making no progress at all. The dune was shaped like an enormous tent and walking across the zenith is reminiscent of a scene from one of the blockbuster movies, I think Lord of the Rings, when we witness human dots making their way across the top of a similar dune.

I rose at the ungodly hour of 4am setting off for the largest geothermal field in the world. The blurb and people who had completed the trip said it was well worth the physical sacrifice of not only the early start but the bone juddering two hour minibus ride. The added discomfort was that at over 13,000 feet before sunrise the temperature was below zero. We arrived to see over 80 geysers each one spouting boiling water and steam. They were surrounded by various sized witches' cauldrons emitting thick opaque steam from boisterous bubbling boiling water. At that altitude water boils at 85 degrees. In Cuenca, after weeks of trial and error and many wasted eggs, I discovered the perfect dippy soldier boiled egg took 7 minutes 15 seconds.

The driver opened up a portable table and proceeded to prepare breakfast. There was cheese and bread available but most got stuck into the hot coffee and saffron cake. There was something eccentrically British about this scenario of a group of people stood shivering in sub-zero temperatures around a table having a 6.00am picnic. We were waiting for the sunrise, not so much because of the aesthetic effect, but more to warm our shivering bones. It duly arrived spectacularly over one of the snow covered volcanoes. It was comical watching the really ardent photographers, with top of the range equipment, tripods and all, trying to capture the random moments of the ejaculating geysers.

We moved on and as it got gradually warmer we shed our layers of clothing like chameleons. We paused to see llamas, alpacas, and vicunas then passed a lake with an abundance of pink flamingos. We then stopped at a smaller more secluded lake where two Wakao ducks had the place to themselves. The guide explained that these beautifully marked, brilliant white and jet black birds were monogamous and when the female lays the eggs the male hatches them. Seeing them swimming in unison, cheek by jowl, around their own lake with the spectacular backdrop in their personal Garden of Eden, I realised I had never seen a better example of natural harmony. Noticing that the whole busload were entranced with this idyllic scene the guide added that when one of the birds dies the other dies almost immediately from a broken heart. This was met with long aaahhhh. Did I detect a mischievous twinkle in his eye?

The next stop was Cactus Valley. Here we had to clamber over rocks to enter the valley where we discovered huge quantities of the largest species of cactus in the world. Also in a picturesque hollow we took advantage of a cooling waterfall. Yes, a waterfall in the driest desert in the world. There is more to the Atacama Desert than people realise. San Pedro lived up to all my expectations but was populated by groups of young backpackers oblivious to a man in his late fifties travelling alone pulling a wheelie suitcase. Apart from trips into the desert I did not register on anyone's radar and wined and dined alone with my thoughts which were still very upbeat and positive.

And It Was All Going So Well

My next journey was to be my longest, twenty hours to Santiago then a connection for the seven hour climb over the Andes to Mendoza, the wine capital of Argentina. I boarded the overnight bus along with the aforementioned and mainly European youth. I was becoming attached to an inanimate yet versatile object and my new best friend, my black hoodie. It was always there when I needed it and never let me down. It accompanied me everywhere stuffed in my bag to be retrieved for the chill winds and the occasional precipitation. I embraced it as my pillow during long arduous bus journeys. One of the reasons I had remained so law abiding throughout my life is that I would never survive a moment in stir. I wouldn't be strong enough to do my time. However after my travels around South America, such was the now in built resilience and calm resignation, I might've just hacked a six month sentence. I began this twenty seven hour ordeal with the shoulder shrugging attitude of an old lag doing another stint of porridge.

After an hour or so I exited at a bus terminal in Calama. Following a two hour wait the Santiago bus pulled in. I'm not sure what happened to my fellow Europeans but I seemed to be the only one to get on. On most of my longer journeys I found myself alone with a busload of doleful Latin Americans. I dozed fitfully between snacks of the ubiquitous cheese and ham sandwiches and coffee or coke. We cruised effortlessly on the clear Pan American Highway through the parched expanses of the southern Atacama. There were strict speed restrictions on buses using the motorways so the bus frustratingly seemed to be stuck in third gear. My chance of making my connection was in the balance. When we stopped for twenty minutes for no apparent reason I was able to relax realising that any chance of me catching the Mendoza bus had gone. But I was cool. I had definitely changed from the hyperventilating, bad tempered, impatient, irrational basket case of months earlier. I had learned to calmly accept what the fickle finger of fate had in store and adjusted accordingly.

We pulled into a large, busy, sprawling bus station in the outer suburbs of Santiago about forty five minutes after the Mendoza bus was due to leave. I hadn't given up hope as our current driver had seen my ticket and my ultimate destination; perhaps they had a system to hold a connecting bus. The driver directed me to my stop so I quickly followed his directions more in hope than expectation, alas to find it deserted. I stood there forlornly as darkness began to fall. Back in my early Saigon days I would now be on the verge of a panic attack but in slow resignation I dug out my Lonely Planet to seek out suitable shelter for the night. After sorting out my ticket I would have to take a cab into downtown Santiago and return the following day. I had become more self contained and self assured, a total transformation from my early Vietnam days. Nothing seemed to bother me now and I felt I could take most setbacks in my stride. As I flipped the pages searching for a guesthouse for the night I felt a tap on my shoulder.

"Senor come, please" was the instruction from a swarthy, leather jacketed, middle age man before he turned and strode away. I stuffed the book back in my bag, grabbed my suitcase and endeavoured to catch him up. He entered a large hallway full of ticket booths, shops and mingling humanity. I could just about see his head bobbing through the crowd and at one point I thought I had lost him. He was stood at an exit with other man to whom I was transferred. I tried to thank this Chilean stranger but he had merged back into the throng within a blink of an eye. My new guide strode back outside before pointing vaguely somewhere at a line of buses and returned back inside. I wandered along from bus to bus until I stood in front of one with its engine ticking over with a sign in big, black, beautiful, and heart-warming letters "MENDOZA." Ten minutes later we were pulling out as I sat snugly and smugly head buried in my best friend as I attempted to catch up on sleep.

The journey from Santiago to Mendoza, is about 200 miles across the Argentina border, and was both spectacular and scary. I thought we would drive through the Andes, instead we drove over them. There was one stage where we zig-zagged up about fourteen levels which was fourteen hairpin bends, each one increasing the drop to which our wheels came perilously too close for comfort. At the top we drove through the high peaks including the highest mountain outside of the Himalayas, Aconcagua, which was, unfortunately, well hidden. We continued down a gentle plain until we viewed the distant conurbation of Mendoza in the breaking dawn.

As I stepped off the bus I was accosted by a taxi driver and ended up in a collectivo with a young backpacking couple. He took us to Base Camp 2 which is a youth hostel with no age barrier. These youth hostels are international and are dotted all over South America. It was cheap and cheerful. All of the rooms were shared dorms and the place was full of music and activities, including trekking and climbing trips in Aconcagua National Park. Nearly all the guests were groups of young people, many carrying guitars and were obviously having a wonderful time. It wasn't my scene and I wished I'd found somewhere more sedate, but decided to spend a couple of nights there and then move on.

Most of what I had read about Mendoza wasn't very complimentary giving the impression of a modern but characterless place where the main attractions were out of town. After the strenuous activities of the desert and long bus journeys I found it to be an ideal place to chill for a few days. I dumped my bags in a room of two bunk beds and walked to the centre in ten minutes. The climate was perfect. In warm spring sunshine, without even a breeze, I sat with the beautiful people in the tree lined cafe society area, enjoying excellent coffee and croissants watching the world go by. I did a bit of shopping in the modern shopping centre. My main purchase was a thick lined waterproof jacket for Tierra del Fuego which would be entering winter by the time I got there. I enjoyed a siesta to catch up on some sleep before dinner.

In the evening I enjoyed a three course meal, again in the vibrant café/restaurant district, that incuded a famed Argentina steak with a bottle of the delicious local Malbec wine, all for US$10. I then went on to The Liverpool Bar which I noticed earlier in the day. This bar was dedicated to the Beatles and Maradona. There were some very artistic and interesting Beatles memorabilia here including a very haunting painting of the Fab Four walking down an alleyway chatting to each other outside the BBC studios. It was their early days and they looked so innocent and such uncomplicated characters. I watched Boco Juniors on television with the locals, consuming several more beers. I returned to my hostel radiating a rosy glow and no doubt went to bed with a contented grin.

It was the next morning that I realised my rucksack was missing. The only thing in it of note was the camera I bought in Cuenca a month earlier. The camera cost US$75 and performed beyond expectations in the demanding conditions of the Atacama desert. I was convinced my bag was stolen from my unlocked room (they gave me the wrong key at reception). I tried to recall what I did during the previous day. I was convinced that I took the bag out once in the morning then on further trips out during the day I left it in the room.

My sub-conscious had become totally redundant and my incapacity for remembering, what at the time, seem unimportant minutiae I had reluctantly come to accept. This combined with a hangover made me doubt that a felon had been committed and that I was complicit in some way. I retraced my steps and investigated to no avail. The camera had 32 shots of the geothermal field of geysers in the Atacama Desert that I rose at 3.30 am to witness. I could handle a mugging on the street but myself inflicted misfortunes were difficult to accept. What exacerbated the situation was that I eventually remembered another shop I had entered and was convinced that was where I had left my rucksack. Unfortunately this flash of recollection took place when I was on the bus that had just left Mendoza. I was consumed by self recrimination and loathing at my own ineptitude. The trip had been going so well and I had been organised and in control. Apart from losing the treasured shots of the Atacama, having purchased an Olympus Trip in Mendoza, I was now on my fourth camera since I arrived in South America. I was still berating myself as the bus pulled into the highly inviting Bariloche.

Move Over Darling

Bariloche was the main holiday destination for the Argentines and young backpackers. It was a holiday resort in the lake district; a beautiful chic town, picturesquely situated overlooking a huge lake that was surrounded by, you've guessed, stunning snow capped mountains. A lot of the young travellers stayed there for at least a week as it was a hive of activity with skiing, snowboarding, paragliding, camping, trekking, horse-riding and a host of water sports. The climate was perfect. The place was a haven for those who were young, active and energetic. I stayed one night and moved on. The night was quite interesting though. In the hostel of my choice there were a couple of expensive single rooms but they were already occupied. I booked into a small room of three single beds in close proximity, the other two including, thankfully, the middle one, had already been occupied. I noticed that one of my roommates was reading "The Tales of Narnia" and the other was reading a book by Kate Mosse. Although I considered myself a liberal anti-homophobic sort of bloke, it's moments like these that bring out the latent prejudices within as I thought "I'll have to sleep with my back to wall, they're a couple of gays!!" I had visions of being pinned down by one of them while the other . . . then I noticed a bangle and some feminine apparel. I realised that this room was mixed. I had heard of mixed dorms but this was the first time I came had across one. I had assumed they would be larger with more privacy, but these beds were almost touching and the space was so confined. I then started to psych myself into acceptable behaviour.

After living alone for over three years I was used to freedom of expression, like shoving my hand down my crotch for a bit of husbandry, realignment and eradicating scrotal irritation. I was used to farting at will, and after consuming a decent curry or similar I'd mastered a version of Trumpet Voluntary. Belching unconsciously had become habit forming. The two girls, who were British post graduates, and very attractive, came in to change before a night on the town, and we had a friendly chat. They were far less concerned about these sleeping arrangements than I was.

In the main plaza I had another wonderful cheap steak from the Pampas washed down with a delicious Malbec. I was accompanied by a group of young lads a lot different to the usual gap year students and we had one thing in common, football. I like to think I enthralled them with tales of games past with George Best, Bobby Charlton, and with a bit of poetic license, my memories of the 1966 World Cup. In hindsight they were probably humouring me.

I climbed into bed about midnight. I was within arm's length of the adjacent bed. Even in advanced years I occasionally wake up with an involuntary lazy lob, or something more dramatic. What if the bedclothes go awry? The wine and beer soon knocked me out. About two I was woken by a pounding din. It was party time somewhere in the building. It was still in full flow at 3am and the noise was deafening. At one stage I got up, put on my jeans and was about to confront the revellers until a bit of common sense took hold. I was in a hostel mainly for young backpackers. It was my behaviour that was odd, not theirs. Then recalling that at their age I was one of the pioneering lager louts of the Taurus Park Complex, Spain, circa '69, the words pot, black, calling, and kettle came to mind. The following morning the three of us got showered and dressed without a break in our incessant chat, instinctively turning our backs at the appropriate times.

The Road To Infinity

I was now on the penultimate leg of my journey south to Ushuaia on Tierra del Fuego. After five hours travelling east I reached Comodoro Rivadavia on the Atlantic coast where I transferred to a coach that would take me to Rio Gallegos. Here I would spend the night before crossing the Straits of Magellan, a sentence I repeated to myself in disbelief. Imagine . . . The Straits of Magellan! The journey was four cheese and ham sandwiches long and although not the longest bus ride of the trip seemed twice as long as any other. The culprit was mother nature, or rather the lack of it. The flatness of eastern Patagonia made Holland look positively Alpine. There was nothing as far as the eye could see, hour upon hour. To increase this sense of inertia the bus seemed to be obeying its own 20mph speed limit. If it was a battered old bus struggling and spewing out black smoke at least it would have seemed like something was happening. On the contrary the bus, like most in South America, verged on luxurious. It silently inched its way south on a mostly deserted and straightest road I had ever experienced that disappeared into infinity, front and back. I did derive a certain sense of perverse satisfaction for this seemingly endless journey. It did provide a great sense of distance that a trip to the bottom of the world should evoke. Flying from Buenos Aires just wouldn't be the same.

On The Whole I'd Rather Be In Philadelphia

The bus terminal was on the outskirts of Rio Gallegos so I took a taxi to a preordained guesthouse. Rio Gallegos was a bland, bleak, grey, chilly town with seemingly no redeeming features. In fact it was featureless. One of the features I had expected such as people or maybe a car were missing. The place was so deserted and bereft of movement, I expected tumbleweed to roll pass me in the bitter wind. The road in was long, wide and deserted, although for a moment I thought I had caught a glimpse of movement in the far distance. There was something more eastern bloc than Latin America about the place. It was how I imagined Ceausescu's Bucharest to be, under a Securitate curfew. I gained entry to my lodgings for the night via a pleasant woman, who, when the formalities were completed disappeared into the back of the building. I never saw her again until my return trip from Ushuaia. The dorm was tiny with four bunk beds, one of which was occupied. I never made the acquaintance of my fellow traveller as he came in late and I left early the following morning. The window faced the main road and was very large with only a net curtain. I felt like a display in high street department store.

Intrigued by this strange place I headed to where I thought I saw a car. After several blocks I came to downtown Rio Gallegos. Reassuringly there were cars, traffic lights and people. I was famished and headed for an inviting Chinese Restaurant, and despite the time of 8.00pm, it was closed. I crossed the road to a busy eatery but it was a glorified burger bar and was full. Down a side street there was steak grill sign so I headed towards it realising as I got closer it had tasteful décor and looked very inviting. I pushed the door in vain. It was locked. I felt I was in a Freudian nightmare, all I wanted was a decent meal. I ended up in a single priced, eat as much as you want, free-for-all. The place was packed with mainly obese members of obese families. I left most of my meal.

The next morning at about 8.00am I headed for the bus station. The wide road which I assumed would be filled with early morning traffic, including lots of taxis, was still deserted. I felt like a refugee from a 1930's Siberian gulag as I trundled my wheelie suitcase up the desolate road. It was then I had one of those "What the fuck am I doing here?" moments. I was getting concerned about missing the bus when I spotted a rare species, a lesser spotted taxi, pulling out of a junction ahead of me. I ran, waving frantically, dragging my case behind me and thankfully he spotted me in his rear view mirror. Ten minutes later I was amongst the throng of excited backpackers boarding the bus and realised that in a few hours I would be crossing the Straits of Magellan. I instantly forgot my earlier moment of doubt. As we queued for the bus I got talking to an English speaking Italian woman in her early thirties, I guess. She had travelled Asia and was now obviously enjoying the Latin American experience. On the coach, along with the signorina, I chatted with a large Argentine young man. The subject of the Falklands came up and not just because he was large, young and I was surrounded by a busload of mainly Argentine people in Argentina, I agreed, as I had since that avoidable war in 1982, that The Malvinas, being in the South Atlantic and only a couple of millimetres from Argentina on a decent map, was rightly theirs. Can you imagine the British allowing Argentina sovereignty over the Isle of Wight because of some medieval treaty?

I'm At The Bottom of The World Ma

Travelling in this southern most part of South America can be frustrating as it has a very complicated, if stunning and beautiful, archipelago exacerbated by strangely positioned borders between Chile and Argentina. The bus trip from Rio Gallegos took fifteen hours, although a lot of time was taken up crossing the border into Chile and then back into Argentina in a very convoluted route. A return journey meant that I had to undergo eight passport and customs checks. To add to this inconvenience, a different country meant a different bus. Eventually, after the first border crossing, we reached the Straits of Magellan. It was at its narrowest point so the other side was visible. We all posed and took shots while waiting for the ferry.

As the ferry moved off I took my turn to climb out of the deep hold. When I reached the top of the metal ladder a swell hit the side of the ferry and a large wave engulfed me. I was saturated from head to toe. Those in front and behind me were relatively unscathed and found my predicament hilarious. It was as if mother nature was waiting for a suitable shmuck for a bit of slap-stick entertainment. I dried off my camera the best I could and returned to the bus in the hold to remove my coat and dry off. We continued through the Land of Fire and reached Ushuaia at 1.00am. Many of the passengers were met by others and the rest of the backpackers quickly disappeared into taxis or just disappeared. I was left alone in the freezing night wind on a desolate street. Mentally I had come along way since my fragility in Vietnam. I was keen to find a warm bed but any sense of panic had been wiped from my psyche. A woman appeared and gave me the "Hotel very cheap" routine and I followed passively. I climbed into the passenger seat of a minivan to discover two young men in the back. Even then I was unfazed. As we drove off into the darkness and up one of the many steep hills of Ushuaia a thought did cross my mind, like, why would three people trouble themselves to pick me up at this ungodly hour for a $10.00 a night room? They knew my money belt, wallet, credit and debit cards, in fact anything of value was on my person so I could have been taken anywhere and mugged. But they didn't and led me to what turned out to be a very cosy, friendly, guesthouse full of backpackers from a great variety of countries.

All these nationalities breakfasted and suppered together with lots of good banter and late night drinking. The lounge/dining room was filled with memorabilia, travel object d'art and photos of previous guests and their travelling exploits including Antarctica, with Ushuaia being the place where expeditions and trips embark. I shared a room with two German PHD students, one of whom became very interested in Welsh culture and was fascinated by the Mabinogion and the Eisteddfod. I promised to e-mail more information and we swapped e-mails over several weeks.

The following morning into the bracing wind I strode down the steep hill into the harbour while staring out to the Beagle Canal. From the Equator I had reached the southernmost town in the world on the verge of Antarctica, which was quite satisfying. Ushuaia looked like a mixture of a Scottish fishing community and Reykjavik. Many of the buildings were made from dark, almost black, weather-beaten stone, but around the centre were brightly coloured wooden houses and buildings, the backdrop being the snow covered Martial mountain range. As I wandered the main street, filled with shops and restaurants, I saw the Italian woman walking toward me and, on seeing me, stopped in her tracks, before turning instantly into a shop which I took as a personal slight. I booked a trip up the Beagle Canal for the following morning.

The Elizabeta was a large modern catamaran filled mainly with Argentines, although there was a sprinkling of other nationalities. I experienced rain for the first time in my three week trip. It was cold, wet, and windy, although I couldn't complain only being six hundred miles from Antarctica in May. Luckily during the afternoon the weather broke into glorious sunshine. During the trip it was comfortable enough for me and a few hardy souls to stay up on deck. There were periods when the wind dropped or we changed direction and the weather became almost spring like in the warm sunshine.

As we headed away from the picturesque port the mountains played tricks with the clouds and swirling mists, creating shafts of cathedral light beaming down at various and changing angles as Ushuaia disappeared from view. We stopped at a small island that had a large colony of seals, some of which swam out to greet us. The next island was populated by a colony of cormorants, then much further on, the highlight of the trip, everybody's favourite bird, the penguin. This colony, used to boatloads of tourists turning up on their doorstep, seemed totally unfazed by these alien daily D-day like beach-landings. It was lovely to see the penguins in their natural habitat.

We were lucky that the weather was so accommodating as it was now almost winter and a reminder of this followed during the next couple of days. It became cold, wet, windy, and generally hostile. I had wanted to visit the Tierra del Fuego National Park but I wasn't hardy enough for this winter onslaught. That was until a young blonde Israeli woman in the guesthouse asked if I would accompany her there as she didn't want to go alone.

"I'll get my coat." I relied. Although the day began in freezing squalls the unpredictability of the local weather patterns meant by lunchtime we were experiencing glorious sunshine. We decided against the "End of the World railway" which was expensive and settled for a shared door to door bus. We followed paths among often stark and wild flora, and wandered off the beaten track through thick, lush and petrified forests to discover huge lakes that were the inlets of the Patagonian Archipelago, some bordering Chile

We chatted as we took photographs. Daniela was a soldier in the Israeli army and was obviously adventurous. She chatted about life in Israel and despite her military involvement was, like most Israelis I've met, quite liberal and had a lot of sympathy for the Palestinians. I was also contemplating the fact that I was alone in an exotic location with a very attractive young woman and wondered if fate was taking the piss as these scenarios never seemed to materialise when I was twenty five. I was pleased that she was comfortable with me and sought safety in my company. This made the attitude of the Italian woman towards me all the more puzzling. The following day I headed north for the first time on this trip.

Camera No. 4?—It's Toast Mate

I had to stop overnight in the dreaded Rio Gallegos on the mainland before heading north west to El Calefate. El Calefate was as picturesque as Rio Gallegos was drab. It was a modern town experiencing huge growth. In 1998 the population was 2,000, in 2006 it was 10,000, and they reckoned it would be 50,000 a few years hence. The growth was fuelled by tourism. The attractions, apart from its perfect climate and position on the shore of Lake Argentina at the foot of snow covered Andes, is its accessibility to the spectacular glaciers ninety minutes away by bus. I booked into a very impressive, newly built, lodge. It was Scandinavian in design with a high pointed roof and built, predominately, of pine and glass throughout. The interior was spacious with groups of young backpackers dotted around. I shared a room in which there were two occupied bunk beds. The place was very modern and spotless. As in all new places if I arrive early enough I dump my bags and go to suss out the local scene. It certainly was a Klondike town, full of new buildings and many more under construction. There seemed to be thoughtful urban planning as the town retained its charm and it was possible to negotiate the centre of El Calefate in a relatively short time. As I ambled down the main street, full of restaurants and shops, she did it again! I caught sight of the Italian woman who, on sight of me, crossed the road. What had I done to deserve this? I only had a brief chat getting on the bus at Rio Galligos and a few words later, all of it bland, run of the mill conversation. Maybe she had a bad experience in Africa or misunderstood an innocent remark. Something I said may have been lost in translation.

When I returned to the lodge I decided to take a snap of the building. I pointed the camera, pressed and . . . nothing. Had my camera hoodoo struck again? I recalled the soaking it received on the Straights of Magellan, but I had used it since then and had snaps developed. As I sat forlornly in the hostel with my stricken camera, four English blokes came bowling in, two of whom were carrying photographic tripods. I asked them if anything could be done about my camera, explaining the events that rendered it unserviceable. One asked me if I had taken out the batteries straight away. A man of my advanced years owning an Olympus Trip, especially in the midst of such natural grandeur, was humiliating enough, but staring up four sets of superior nostrils from my sedentary prone position admitting that I hadn't, made me feel that my inferiority complex was largely due to the fact that I was actually inferior. They looked at each other with knowing smirks and I could almost imagine a communal bubble above their heads with the one uniting thought "What a dick-'ead." One of them, without a hint of sympathy, declared. "It's toast mate."

As they wandered off one said "I got a camera for sale, 300 pesos and it's yours." Feeling out of place and self-conscious with, what for me, was new technology I purchased the said camera simultaneously joining the digital age. My discomfort was not over as he condescendingly gave me instructions on how to use it. In fact his girlfriend was more helpful answering my repeated questions with patience and understanding. These four blokes were the type that would argue and pontificate vociferously about the best route from Milton Keynes to Chipping Sodbury as if was the Gettysburg Address. Later in the evening, while they were discussing macho subjects, I was playing with my new camera hoping to change the topic of conversation where my star would rise in the firmament and I could redeem my flaky image, but finding a link from the specifications of performance cars to the postmodernist approach to Pre-Raphaelite art proved elusive.

I was very lucky to have attempted the failed shot of my then current abode, as if I had gone to the famous Puerto Moreno glacier with a duff camera I would have been rather annoyed. There were pictures of the glacier all over the town so I knew what to expect, although I would have preferred to have had no preconceptions of it at all. I had always imagined glaciers to be D shaped, transparent, solid blocks of ice, rather like large ice-cubes or an inverted Fox's Glacier Mint. In fact from a distance it looked like the white cream topping off a trifle. The front of the glacier had two faces as it was inching its way down diverging paths of the lake. The face of each was 60 metres high (another 85 below the water) and five kilometres wide. The glacier spectacularly backed many miles up two valleys surrounded by classic snow-capped peaks and set against the deep blue water in the crisp pure air it's an awe-inspiring place to be.

We got up close by boat that chugged its way slowly along the huge face stopping occasionally like a commanding officer inspecting the troops. Like The Trooping of the Colour there were occasional collapsing through the heat. The glacier advanced two metres per day. All this sounds serene, however periodically there would be a loud cracking noise followed by a section of the glacier face collapsing into the lake. When a large section collapsed it was equivalent to a fifteen story building disintegrating before your eyes hitting the water explosively. Some of these descending blocks of ice weigh hundreds of tons. The reaction from the onlookers especially American males was "Oh my gaaad that was aaaa-sum."

Photographers, including myself, tried, mostly in vain, to capture these moments on film. Unfortunately because of the pedestrian speed of sound compared to light, the debris was almost in the water before we could locate the area of destruction and take a snap. Also you couldn't predict where or when a collapse would take place. There could be nothing for an hour then three in twenty minutes.

Later we viewed this amazing sight from gangways and viewing areas at different levels. People would be chatting and eating when the cracking sound of the glacier would end conversations abruptly in mid syllable as everyone frantically skimmed the face of the glacier in high alert. Feeling and fumbling for their cameras they were ultimately disappointed by the collapse either beating them to the draw or taking place in an area out of view. This constant battle between the natural forces of the lake and the glacier results in huge ruptures in the glacier that occur every few years. The sound of this cracking is deafening and can be heard fifty miles away.

The following day back in El Calefate a group had assembled at the back of the lodge including the owner, who was about thirty, big and swarthy. He played rugby and we had a long chat about the subject the previous day. He was now kicking a ball about with a few friends in the small field attached to the chill out area where the nerdy technophiles were texting and farting about with their state of the art mobile phones. I joined in the kick about with the Argentines half my age, confident in the skills I honed decades before had not deserted me. After a couple of lengthy spiralling kicks, a reverse spin pass that Gareth Edwards would have been proud of, and the slight of hand that only Welshmen seem capable, I drew admiration from my Puma friends. Out of the corner of my eye I could see I had attracted the attention of the previously condescending geeks. Respect!

The last evening I sauntered down the main street seeking out a restaurant when instinctively I turned sharply into the road and busy traffic, resulting in much horn blowing and consternation from irate drivers. When I got to the other side I dived inside the first bar I saw and ordered a beer, reliving what I had just one. Yet again I had seen the Italian woman and so determined was I to snub her before she snubbed me I instantly turned blindly into the traffic. My subconscious was determined to get my snub in first which could have been fatal. But it wasn't. I got away with it and felt a lot better for it. A crazy logic I know, risking life and limb in a street half way across the world to make a petty gesture to a woman I would never see again.

El Chalten was about 50 kilometres from El Calefate. The attraction there was that close by there is, what is regarded as, one of the most spectacular treks in that part of the world. That part of the Andean chain doesn't have the highest peaks but has the most extraordinary shaped and convoluted evolved arrangements. The highlights are the jagged peaks of Fitz Roy Masiff. Treks, climbs, and camping there are very popular and have various degrees of difficulty and duration. The basic trek lasted for about seven hours. I had hiked for this length of time on the Brecon Beacons and had recently trekked for nearly six hours over undulating terrain in Tierra del Fuego. The combination of the unknown, and organised hiking, when I wouldn't be in control of my progress, plus the recent four days of solid rain in the area were enough to deter me.

Croeso y Chebut

A few months earlier around Christmas time I had a telephone conversation with my eldest brother, Michael, a Welsh Nationalist Plaid Cymru member, who insisted I visit Welsh Patagonia. I told him I had no intention of going that far south. Now I had travelled over a thousand miles north to Chebut, the region where a group of "Welsh" towns were located. The first and largest of these towns was Trelew. The background to the historical connection with Wales is that in 1865 Lewis Jones lead about 150 other Welsh emigrants to that part of Patagonia to escape the English influence on language and religion. The indigenous Telheulche Indians not only provided a warm welcome but also helped and trained the Welsh in the art of hunting and general early survival. The Welsh in turn passed on their farming skills and the area prospered. This is very similar to the scenario that lead to America's most important annual celebration, Thanksgiving. In Trelew (Welsh for "town of Lewis") there is a large statue of Lewis Jones, a Welsh museum, several Welsh chapels, and a building that houses the Association of Saint David. Many of the streets are named after Welshmen, such as Jones, and Roberts.

The most "Welsh" of this little cluster of towns was Gaimen about fifteen miles from Trelew. I arrived there via the local bus about lunch time. It was hot and dusty as I wandered around this small and seemingly deserted hamlet. As I walked down an empty street I saw some movement in another road bearing left from a junction, so I walked wearily in the heat up the hill until I reached that point where I saw the movement. There was nobody around as I stared back to where I had come from and frustratingly there was human activity. I just wanted to speak to someone. There was a small office with the door ajar, so I entered to find two desks with two empty chairs but not a soul around. I located the Welsh museum but it was closed. Despite this calm and inactivity there were a lot of new buildings, others being constructed and obvious growth. Wales was everywhere, but everything, including The Welsh tea rooms and souvenir shops, were closed. Places of business had names like Juan Sebastian Pugh, and Esteban Diego Thomas.

The only way I could get under the skin of the place was to open a few more doors that were ajar. I went into a small place of academia with books, manuscripts and framed pictures of yesterday's men, no doubt the former great and the good, displayed around the walls. The occupants, with good intent, sent me in the wrong direction. I thought I had come across an old Welsh chapel. I entered to find a few elderly people. If there is a Welsh look then the elderly woman who spoke to me had it. She had a presence of an indomitable headmistress with eyes that shone with character, intelligence and intellect. Apart from Spanish she told me she was fluent in Welsh and English then directed me to the Tourist Information Office. There I obtained the information I required. Apparently everything slowly came to life after 4.00pm. The tea rooms opened at tea time which I suppose was logical. I went to the Welsh museum and there met a lovely old woman. She spoke Spanish and Welsh with enough English for us to converse. Her surname was Evans and her Christian names were something like Juanita Maria. Another elderly lady, who was the director of the museum, came in and they greeted each other in Welsh and conversed as if it was their mother tongue. I headed back to Trelew on the evening bus. Apart from the Welsh connection there was little to keep me in this otherwise unremarkable place so I headed for Puerto Madryn the following day. Throughout my time in South America, via e-mails I kept in constant touch with family and friends. One of my friends had informed me that his son, Owen, had a girlfriend, whose acquaintance I had yet to make, and she was currently travelling in South America and I was laughingly to keep an "eye out for her."

Puerto Madryn

In Puerto Madryn I found the road with my chosen hostel address quite easily, the only problem was the number was 798 and the building I was stood in front of was number 5. Thankfully the long trek down the road dragging my wheelie suitcase was worth the effort. The hostel was cheap, and very pleasant, with a really lovely couple, about my age, running it. They informed me that there was a girl from Cardiff staying there. Later that night I met her in the communal kitchen where guests were preparing and eating supper amongst the general chatter. Her name was Anwen and although she was from Cardiganshire she had lived in Cardiff for the previous six years, her house being located in Donald Street off Albany Road which was my "manor" in Cardiff. When she became aware of my intimate knowledge of the area she asked me if I knew Richie Wilkinson.

"About my age, involved with Cardiff Saracens RFC, likes a drink? The very same. She asked me if I knew a pub called . . . .

I interjected with "The Tavistock?" as that's where the "Sarries" hang out. So we had a chat about Cardiff, rugby, and related topics;

what a small world. She drank in the "Tavvie", an old haunt of mine from my youth, The Royal Oak, and The Cryws amongst other recognisable watering holes. She was currently travelling before taking up a voluntary post in Quito. Her sister planned to head out there a few months later to teach Welsh in another Welsh town, Trevelyn, near Esquel in the west of Argentina.

The following day I went on an all day excursion. It was to the Peninsular Valdes which was protected by the World Wildlife Organisation. The wildlife there included, Armadillos, a specie of the ostrich family, penguins, and elephant seals, amongst others. The big attraction though were whales. The Giant Right Whales appear in the bay in October each year to mate and after a twelve month pregnancy return to give birth. It must be a fantastic spectacle. The Orca whales occasionally sneak up onto the beach to poach a seal pup or two. Although the tide was high and the seals were very close to the incoming flow, with an expectant crowd poised with cameras the, Orcas didn't put in an appearance. The last time one did was twelve days previously. I wondered how the disappointed crowd would have reacted to a terrified squealing pup being kidnapped from the midst of the happy family gathering. It was exposed there and bitterly cold so I was glad to get back to the warmth of the guesthouse.

I went to the bus station to book my ticket to Buenos Aires for the following day but the buses for the next two days were fully booked, which turned out to be fortuitous. On the way back to the guesthouse, amongst the din of a busy shopping thoroughfare, I sensed someone was attempting to attract my attention. It was Ruth with Clive in tow. We did some catching up before she suggested we meet up later for a drink. Clive, who up until that point, seemed detached and disinterested, quickly interjected suggesting the lack of time for such a soirée. The disappointment on Ruth's face was palpable. She seemed desperate for some light relaxed conversation. We shook hands and parted. Now I had been guilty of self-pity with regard to my enforced single status but it has given me independence and freedom. To see two people who after forty years cannot see their opposing personality traits has resulted in barely concealed mutual disdain, yet are still inextricably tied to each other, was excruciating to behold.

During the evening Anwen informed me that she was off to Gaimen that night because there was to be a Welsh religious service in the Bethal Chapel. So as I had to kill a day or so I said I would meet her there. On the bus back to Gaimen the following afternoon a classical vision of an English rose among the local dusky maidens jumped on, paid her fare and sat in the opposite seat to me and stared out of the window. She was so obviously British but on the verge of striking up a conversation, with the thoughts of the Italian woman still hovering around in the dark recesses of my mind, I thought better of it.

When we arrived I headed to a bar for a cold beer before going to the Welsh museum where the mystery woman was chatting to an elderly lady in Welsh. When she left I chatted to this lovely old lady in English. She wore a red cardigan to signify her allegiance. Her name was Mrs or Senora Evans and she had visited Wales and learned to speak fluent Welsh while I, a native of the land she obviously loved from a great distance, knew only a handful of words and felt quite guilty. I took some photos including Mrs Evans and bought some souvenirs for my brother including a CD of the Gaimen choir, where the fourteen tracks are equally distributed in Spanish and Welsh including the classic Myfanwy.

I passed a building that looked like a nursery with Welsh writing on the exterior including Croeso y Cymru. The only people I met who spoke Welsh were elderly and I wondered if that was significant. Anwen, being a fluent Welsh speaker, was more confident and assertive than me, so later went into the building and confirmed it was indeed a children's nursery. She was introduced to a class of toddlers who were studying Welsh using their Welsh text books and

Welsh songs were playing in the background. The kids were thrilled to meet an authentic Welsh speaking native of the old country.

I tried to locate Anwen in the guesthouse address she gave me but she wasn't there. It transpired that one of the local matrons invited her to stay in her house. I headed for the Princess Dianna Tea Shop. The place was empty except for the Welsh rose. I took the plunge and asked if she objected to my company. I think she was glad of it. We chatted for a while before we exchanged names. She was from Cardiff and her name was Lynnette, which rang a bell. Well of all the bars and all the Welsh teashops, it was Owen's girlfriend!! What were the odds this chance meeting?

The three of us met up for the 7.00pm service. There was a congregation of about sixty in the archetypal Welsh Baptist church. They were mainly women, middle-aged and older, many wearing red cardigans. The hymn books contained over a 1000 hymns in Welsh. When they discovered I couldn't converse in Welsh I was largely ignored. It wasn't just the Welsh language that was exported to this part of Patagonia, but also the nonconformist Welsh Baptist religion. One of the few men in attendance gave the sermon in Welsh. He looked stern, was dressed in bible black and seemed a throwback to a Dickensian Puritan, full of fire and brimstone. I met Anwen the following day and she told me that her host castigated her for blasphemy. Anwen had a habit of using the exclamation, "Oh God!" or "Oh my God!" which, to the good people of Gaiman, was apparently damning her soul.

Buenos Aires

Anwen, along with many others had raved about Buenos Aires, in fact she went to raves in Buenos Aires including one with DJ Pete Tong no less. I had met travellers who having experienced the delights of the Argentine capital and were heading down to the wintry extremes of Ushuaia, had wished they had organised their trip the other way around. During my incredible six week journey around South America I regularly met fellow travellers who had spent time in Buenos Aires and to a man (and woman) a lasting impression had been left by the Argentine capital. As the last leg of my journey before flying back to the UK after a year away, I entered the city with tingling anticipation.

There are various enticing barrios to base a stay in BA, like chic Recoleta and Palermo or the exotic La Boca, but I headed for San Telmo after some advance research created bohemian images that leapt off the page and beckoned me seductively. It didn't take long for me to fall in love with San Telmo. It became my favourite place on the planet; it was where I belonged and a destination I would be happy to live and spend the rest of my days. It was that place somewhere over the rainbow that actually existed. It was an adult Noddy-land and Trumpton rolled into one: it was that castle in the sky of which you dream.

I discovered this particular barrio on foot, sniffing out its nooks, crannies, and delights. What I loved most about San Telmo was its authenticity. There were many areas where the cobbled streets and little plazas were inundated with the most individually unique and atmospheric bars and restaurants one can imagine. Bass Charringdon could spend millions on refurbishment and not come near to the ambiance of these places. The authentic atmosphere in these buildings had been created over centuries where the imposing walls had soaked up and witnessed carousing, smoke, booze, intimate liaisons, conspiracies, trysts, arguments, political polarisation, revolutions, and the brawls of generations. The objects d'art weren't placed there on the same day as a figment of some art school graduate's imagination, but had evolved over decades. All this history oozed from the pores of the masonry. The bars were generally in old solid buildings with dark wood and restrained lighting. The bartenders and waiters were often middle aged, portly, and wore white aprons. They had the happy medium approach of knowledgeable friendliness without a hint of sycophancy. They were neither condescending nor toadying.

Trees played an important aesthetic role in San Telmo. These trees in many streets provide canopies over the street diners. At night wrought iron lantern and orb street lighting amongst the leaves and branches added to the overall affect. La Boca and San Telmo are renowned for Tango bars. The house dancers kick off proceedings then the punters, self-consciously at first, join in. If it got crowded the dancers spilled out into the warn night air.

I drank and dined at random but one bar I sought out after reading about it in a travel book. It was called Bar Britannico. It sounded like a colonial Union Jack club full of Colonel Blimps in Cravats; it was actually the opposite. The book described it as a place where old men, bohemians and night owls while away the time into the early hours. So I was drawn to it like a magnet.

The bar itself, at first sight, wasn't the least bit attractive. It was on a corner with a huge shop like window on each street and brightly lit. It was similar to Edward Hopper's famous painting, Nighthawks. The big difference was unlike the painting where there were only a few lonely, solitary figures, this place was full and for the most part very animated. In the centre of the bar there was a big group of about a dozen sat around assembled small tables. Most were in their fifties and sixties. The word bohemian was the only description appropriate for that gathering. One, with a mass of thick, grey, wiry hair looked like a cross between an ageing Trotsky and Einstein without his moustache. On show were many beards and John Lennon tinted glasses. There were two attractive women, probably in their fifties, although it was difficult to tell as they had a look of lives led to the full. They belonged to the avant-garde school of feminine beauty and didn't seem to attach much importance to haute couture or personal grooming. One of them in particular must have been stunningly beautiful in her youth but I bet even then she never paid a passing glance at the mirror. I could imagine they both had many lovers, including most of the men around the table. There were one or two younger people involved, including a girl, with the look of an art student, sporting bright red hair. There seemed to be an organised debate going on, with those making a contribution putting up his or her hand. The debate was intense, friendly, and often humorous. I hadn't a clue what they were discussing but my imagination ran rife. It could have been the effect of Dechamp's Readymades on conceptual art or the legacy of Peronist politics. On the other hand they could have been discussing a plot from one of the famously banal South American soap operas. Somehow I don't think it was the latter. They all had one thing in common, which was the look of bookish intelligence. In another place and time they could have been the advanced working party for the Paris Commune. Some may have been involved with the violent politics of the seventies and eighties and may have lost relatives and comrades.

There was an eclectic mix including a conservatively dressed man sat opposite me with whom I assumed to be his wife, although they were laughing and enjoying themselves far too much for a middle aged married couple. There was a strange looking man, grimly poker faced, again middle aged, with his ragged overcoat unnecessarily buttoned up to his throat with a closed book in front of him on the table as he stared unblinkingly into the distance. Despite this clientele the owner seemed to be a bit of a philistine as the décor was basic much like a greasy spoon outlet. I think he relied on his patrons to provide the decoration which they did in the form of many impressive paintings, which I assumed were for sale, hanging around the bar. They were joined by many artistic photographs of the bar and its colourful patrons, mostly in black and white. The waiters were interesting too. The one who, thankfully, served me was again my age with a ponytail. The other looked well into his eighties and as well as looking anaemic, seemed to have been a stroke victim, although it could have been gout. He shuffled very slowly around without his feet ever leaving the ground. He reminded me of a male version of Mrs Overall from Acorn Antiques. Although your meal may be cold and your lager warm by the time he arrived, at least he could guarantee the wine would be at room temperature.

The tree lined cobbled streets of San Telmo were inundated with galleries and bookshops, however the dominant feature of the area was antique shops. I must have come across fifty without covering every street. They weren't poky or bijou, but cavernous with huge inventories of wonderful pieces including chandeliers that would grace the Palace of Versailles. There was a building that housed identical metal cages used for small individual antique shops, each specialising in such items as timepieces, dolls, old wind up phonographs, and trilby hats. There were fifty two of them. I didn't count them, they were numbered. There were also many street markets including several antique stalls. The economics of it all was beyond my comprehension, but these antique shops certainly added to the chic and sophisticated nature of the area.

On the Sunday I headed for the dockland area of La Boca to see the famous brightly coloured shops, restaurants, tango bars and Boca Juniors' Bombarama football stadium famously graced by Maradona. My progress was hindered though as I had to make my way through the San Telmo Sunday market, one of many across the city. You could spend the whole day engrossed in the quality, originality, and diversity of these objects of desire. If I had secured a permanent pad there, and that was a distinct possibility had I managed to land a teaching job, I could've decorated it completely and with genuine artistic originality solely from the produce of this market. There was colourful and often eccentric street entertainment, with all this activity surrounded by well peopled pavement cafes and restaurants. On the way to La Boca I passed the El Britanico Bar. It was full of the usual suspects breakfasting with their Sunday broadsheets and there were several games of speed chess in progress with the ancients hitting the clocks in rapid succession.

I perused the adjacent barrio of El Boca a few miles from San Telmo. This area had a reputation for seediness and you have to be aware of possible dangers. I found it vibrant and friendly amongst the well worn buildings, some of which were architecturally unique and many had the appearance of former glory. There were many split level pavements which could've lead to split level heads. I'd be walking along with other pedestrians and then slowly find myself gradually elevated to about three feet above them only to find the same three feet as a precipice further along. There were steps available but you had to locate them. Walking along the street absentmindedly could be hazardous. Here, as in the rest of South America, the pavements were a minefield of uneven slabs of concrete, potholes, and uncovered manholes. Finding your way home at night three sheets to the wind could be fatal.

I went searching for the Boca Juniors stadium, La Bonbonera, and found it easily enough. I had hoped to get inside and had read there were organised tours. In fact the tour was very professionally organised. Their museum was high tech. To commemorate each year they had won the league, going back to the beginning of the twentieth century, they had three TV screens, one showing the football highlights of that particular year and the other two showed Argentinean and world events of that time. Being a sucker for old newsreel and footage I could have spent hours just watching a century of Argentine and world history. It did delay my entrance into the actual stadium considerably. They had photographs of past great players going back a hundred years, including Rattin, who was famously sent off against England in 1966 in the "animals" game, and a huge blown-up one of their, and Argentina's favourite son, Maradona. I loved the old sepia photos of past heroes of the thirties and forties who probably played against the likes of the Stans, Mathews and Mortenson, when the shorts were worn below the knees. They all seemed to look like Cab Calloway, with the slicked back hair parted in the middle, flashing smile and the devilish moustache. The stadium is famous for its fanatical fans and intimidating atmosphere. Empty, it was hard to imagine squeezing in the sixty thousand capacity. The ground was almost square with seemingly vertical fragile stands reaching up into the sky. They say that these stands sway and vibrate with the cacophonous baying crowd hanging on precariously. This vertical crowd overhang a pitch that is so close to the fans the distance to the corner flag is only two steps, so short, tapped corners must be the only option.

La Boca is alongside the docks and is famed for the pretty bright pastel coloured dockside Tango bars and restaurants along its cobble streets. I lunched there getting high on the atmosphere and cold beer. Unfortunately Boca Juniors were playing away that particular weekend so that evening I headed to the barrio Numez to see Boca's greatest rival, River Plate, at the Estadio Monumental. I was told it was near the airport and headed towards it along the River Plate. On the way I cut through Palermo which is noted for its chic, classy restaurants and middle class residences. The walk was longer than I anticipated as the sight of the airport gave way to River Plate's very impressive stadium which was oval shaped in the typical South American mould.

River Plate and Boco Juniors have legendary rivalry. What irritates the River Plate fans is that as a club it's as big or arguably bigger in many ways than Boca. Their ground, especially the playing surface, is far superior to Boca's, although Boca has a certain unique quality. The superior fame of Boca is down to the status of Maradona who is regarded by Argentineans, and I agree with them, as being the greatest footballer of all time. The capacity at River was 60,000 and I would guess there were about 45,000 there that night.

As the teams came out, the biggest flag I'd ever seen was unfurled from the top to the bottom of the far stands, revealing a huge red and white badge of the River Plate club and must have covered ten thousand souls. Just before kick off the crowd, acting in great unison, magically furled it within seconds. The atmosphere was electric with the singing and chanting continuing throughout with two exceptions; the two conceded goals. It was an excellent game of high quality with Argentina Juniors equalising in injury time with a Beckham style free kick. Although I had witnessed the biggest flag I'd ever seen, I was informed later that Boca had a bigger one. I said the rivalry was intense. Most of Argentina's top players were located in Europe but I did recognise one participant who was Daniel Passarella, the manager of River Plate and the captain of Argentina's World Cup winning side of 1978.

I visited Eva Peron's mausoleum. Even the poor in South America have large ornate headstones, so the rich, great, and the good really express their self-esteem when they pop their clogs. Evita's last resting place is surprisingly restrained. Recoleta Cemetery is full of ostentatious marble neo-classical creations to revere the dear departed and their locations seemed to depend on their status as mortals. I read a biography of Evita many years ago, and although she improved the lot of the poor and underprivileged, she enjoyed a glamorous lifestyle and had delusions of grandeur. When she visited London and Rome she was shocked and slighted when she wasn't allowed to stay at Buckingham Palace and The Vatican. Surprisingly her coffin was in the family vault up an obscure alleyway. Knowing she was dying I wondered if she was complicit in this relative act of humility.

San Telmo is about ten blocks and a pleasant walk from the centre of Buenos Aries. Within twenty minutes I was stood in front of the Casa Rosada in La Plaza del la Mayo, the scene of Eva Peron's most triumphant moments, where she waved from the balcony of the pink palace to her adoring followers. I asked the receptionist in my guesthouse when was the weekly gathering of the "The mothers of the La Plaza del Mayo". She told me between ten and ten fifteen the following morning. So after my twenty minute walk I arrived on time.

These are the mothers of "the disappeared" who were taken during the "Dirty War" under a vicious military dictatorship between1976 and 1983. The mothers had kept vigil ever since in pursuit of the truth. There were a couple of elderly ladies with placards, but many buses were arriving with protesters of all ages alighting. I think this larger demo was concerned with animal welfare. The numerous demonstrations I had witnessed in South America certainly dismissed my preconceived notions of overzealous police and military as they seemed to be very accommodating. Wandering around Buenos Aires in the glorious sunshine my overall impression was that it was a very European looking capital, being more Paris than Madrid. However whereas Paris is condescendingly aware of its glorious existence, BA is not and is a lot more attractive and welcoming as a result. Their recent financial problems and the de-valuation of the peso had the added attraction of being very cheap.

After a week I stretched my umbilical cord from San Telmo across the River Plate to Uruguay a few hours away. I love the historical content of my travels and when I had stood in front of the Casa Rosada I tried to conjure up images of a fifties Peronist rally. Now as this surprisingly elegant ferry set off across the River Plate, I was reminded of the time this stretch of water first came to my attention. I remembered, as a schoolboy, the actor John Gregson (who else) on the Bridge of the Ajax pursuing The Graf Spee in the film "The Battle of the River Plate."

About noon after four hours afloat we landed on Uruguayan soil. I loved the notion of being in Uruguay mainly for the childish reason that it's not on many peoples' "to do" list. My knowledge of Uruguay up until this point was that they had won the first football world cup in 1930, Fray Bentos, of steak and kidney puddings fame, is located there, and Montevideo is my favourite capital city name. Despite five syllables it just rolls off the tongue.

David Lynch Meets Salvador Dahli

Another impressive place name was Colonia del Sacramento the landing point and where I was to spend the night. It turned out to be a blissfully unique, eccentric, anachronistic gem. Most of the passengers travelled straight on to Montevideo leaving a small group of us to find our way around and seek a bed for the night. For ten dollars I booked a lovely serene room with a view, in a lovely serene guesthouse. My bag was dumped and I stepped out into the street which was . . . serene. I wandered along the deserted cobbled stoned street protected from the beating sun by a canopy of tall majestic trees that arched over from either side. In the distance the road led on through the trees where I could see a bright blue watery expanse. Near that bright blue yonder a car crossed the underused thoroughfare at a distant junction. I removed my shades. Was it was a Model T Ford?!

I was aware of some human activity but the overriding impression was of heat, beauty and stillness. I turned into a small street where the cobbles evolved into huge slabs of stone at giddy angles where walking, never mind driving, was extremely challenging. I stopped at a deserted plaza and sat down on the church steps in the shade. I noticed a small group carrying cameras disappearing down a narrow track and decided I would follow them. As I walked across the plaza I noticed, down a side road, two black 1930's saloon cars similar to the one I saw in action earlier. I wandered over. They were both parked on the treacherously uneven road. One had plants inside growing from a tray up through the opened roof. The other had a table for two inserted ready for a romantic dinner. This place seemed like a surreal set from a David Lynch film designed by Salvador Dali. Weird man! I continued to follow the small group of tourists which took me to stone battlements and a cannon used, no doubt, to attempt to repel the Spanish. I wandered around the small peninsular before stopping for a cold beer outside a bar/restaurant. My pulse must have dropped to the thirties, I was so relaxed. I could still be there now. I just didn't want to move, the inertia of the place was contagious.

But move I did and the following day I checked into a large, busy cosmopolitan guesthouse in Montevideo two hours bus drive from Colonia. It had several floors with the buzz of humanity throughout the building but one voice seemed to be more distinctive than the rest of the communal rhubarbs. Some people seem to have a voice that effortlessly permeates space and structures that seem to defy the laws of sound. Adrian was one of these people. I followed his distinctive voice into the next room, up a flight of stairs, down a corridor, through a door and into a well populated common room.

He was dominating a discussion on facets of exploitation, a subject, no doubt, he had introduced as I was to discover his outlook as quite radical. Later that night I engaged him in conversation, which wasn't a difficult task, and despite his inclination to pontificate, he was a colourful character and a likeable one at that. He was in his forties and had bought a bicycle in Mexico City for ten pounds and had ridden it all the way to Montevideo. He had pedalled down the Pan American Highway, sleeping under the stars in the Peruvian desert, had crossed Bolivia and Paraguay and on into Uruguay. He was now attempting to sell his bike for that same ten pounds. I discussed Buenos Aries with him only to be informed that, amazingly, he had no intention of visiting it, other than to catch his flight back to the UK. He said he didn't like big conurbations preferring smaller, more intimate and interesting places. He was a Chemistry supply teacher who worked six months of the year and travelled the rest.

Montevideo is on a peninsular with all three sides being reached within a couple of hours and blessed with plenty of beaches. Overshadowed by its more illustrious neighbour it still has the buzz of a capital city. Although I'm no expert, it was the architecture that immediately attracted my attention. The diversity was astounding.

In the main plaza, Independencia, among the modern glass high-rise offices and department stores was the magnificent 1930s Italian Gothic, Palacio Salvo, that really belonged in Gotham City. Further along on the 18th de Julio Avenue was another magnificent, classical, structure surrounded incongruously by glass monstrosities. A few miles away near the ultra modern, multi-storey, glass panelled telecommunications tower was the long, impressive and imposing derelict 19th century railway station. Apparently moves were afoot to return it to its former glory and reopen it. Then a few miles further away stuck in the middle of nowhere was the Palacio Legislative looking like a giant wedding cake. It was all a bit of planning mess but still wonderful.

After a few days in Montevideo I travelled the two hour journey back to Colonia del Sacramento. I wandered around the sleepy town killing time before the ferry arrived. The silence was interrupted by a recognisable sound in the distance.

"If the Nottinghamshire miners had supported the strike Thatcher would have been defeated and the decimation of manufacturing that emasculated the working class would have been avoided." Adrian was continuing his egalitarian missionary work using his Marxist rhetoric in a building about four blocks away. I wondered if he had sold his bike or ridden there. I followed his voice instinctively like a mesmerised child of Hamlin and passed the building where he was holding court.

"we're led by the noses by the press and big business" he sermonised as I walked past and on towards the ferry.

Music To My Ears

When I arrived back in Buenos Aires I walked for over an hour from the docks to the Plaza de Mayo in the centre of this beautiful metropolis and then carried on further for about eight blocks. The buzz of el centro gave way to the sound of my footsteps echoing down silent darkened streets before I crossed a wide boulevard and into San Telmo. It was like crossing the Severn Bridge into Wales after spell away. I was home. In a few short steps the atmosphere and ambience was transformed into the warm, and the inviting; like returning to the womb. It was about 10.00pm as the welcoming nightspots increased in number with each block I passed. I heard music from one of the plazas and headed in that direction. A few minutes later I turned into the plaza to witness a magical scene. Around the beautiful square were scores dining alfresco under the trees and ornate street lighting. The square, which was a pulsating market a few days previously, was now full of couples dancing cheek to cheek to the crackling atmospheric sound of Carlos Gardel. Above the square on several levels of protruding balconies there was a host of diners and imbibers also bearing witness to the enchanting scene below.

Carlos Gardel is a national icon as the best exponent of the slow tango who died in a plane crash in 1935. His picture, looking like George Raft with a rakish moustache and a trilby at jaunty angle, was dotted around the city. His voice and orchestra were being emitted from speakers lodged in the leafy canopy above the dancers, sounding like original scratched seventy-eights on a wind-up phonograph. I sat in the square with a half bottle of Mendoza's best and soaked up the atmosphere. This was my last night after almost a year in South America before heading back to the UK and I couldn't have choreographed it better. Well with one exception, I'd loved to have joined the dancers but, and I never thought I'd ever use these words in the literal sense; it takes two to tango.

The following morning I stood on a corner near the guesthouse with my baggage and flagged down a taxi. After a few moments I had an unsettling feeling in the pit of my stomach as I realised for the first time that there maybe more than one airport.

"Aeropuerto Internacional por favor" I instructed.

"Si no problemo" the driver reassuringly replied. When we began to hug the River Plate I was reassured further.

"Englaterra?" he said, again confirming the correct airport.

"Si" I nodded and relaxed.

At the airport near the Esatadio Monumental I jumped out, grabbed my bags, paid my smiling chauffeur and I was in good time. This international airport seemed small for a city the size of Buenos Aires I surmised as I showed my e-ticket to a uniformed official who confirmed my worst fears—wrong airport! In a panic I commandeered another taxi and headed out into the sprawling suburbs. It was only at leisure, a while later, that I dwelt on the enormous expanse of outer Buenas Aries, at that particular time I was more concerned with ploughing through it to catch my plane which with every traffic jam seemed more unlikely. An hour before take-off stuck in another gridlock I hadn't even seen a plane in the sky.

With my heart beating and his clock ticking we arrived. My next problem was how to pay this large taxi fare, which I just about managed by completely emptying my pockets of pesos, dollars, and Stirling. Any more and I would've had to hand over my watch. Any further and I would have missed my flight. So without a bean in my pocket I scurried through the gate, last on, and headed back to . . . well that was my next problem. I had no plan as I was just living day to day.

No Country For Old Men

From the outset my lifesaving plan of travel and adventure through the medium of TEFL was based on an estimated two year span. I missed my son and wanted to re-enter his life. I stayed with my sister for a couple of weeks before returning to bed-sit land. I did manage to get a temporary job via an agency while I looked for something permanent. Although I was in the same boat as two years previously and the problem of ageism I would face, being two years older, would be more acute, I was now in far greater spirits. I had achieved what I set out to do, albeit it in an extremely tortuous manner. Not only did I ultimately succeed, I excelled and had new friends around the world. I had been in regular contact with Cindy, Donna, Cordelia and Leanne throughout my travels and continued to do so. I had transformed myself from being a gibbering wreck in both China and Vietnam to being unfazed by anything I confronted in more recent times. I had become self-contained and mentally strong without, I hope, losing my affability.

With my teaching experience I began concentrating on applying for jobs as a teaching assistant. It was now the end of May when the schools began recruiting for the following September. I applied for about eight teaching assistant jobs. None required the degree or teaching experience I had, so I was confident I would soon be employed. My CV, apart from my age, drawn from my lifetime of work, with excellent references, I considered impressive. In the meantime my temporary position via the agency was working for the International Baccalaureate checking marked exam scripts. They had eight team leaders working on large tables of about a dozen per team. They selected me as a team leader which bolstered my confidence, and furthermore we were deemed to be the best performing team. At that moment in time I felt like a master of the universe capable of anything. Towards the end of this part time work the International Baccalaureate advertised for a permanent position in the local press for a less than elevated position at £16,000p.a requiring someone who had a background in printing and publishing. I had spent twenty nine years in varying and responsible positions in the printing industry, had been a co-director of a business called Lakeside Publishing and I had an academic background. On top of that I was in the process of completing a temporary stint as their highest performing team leader. How could I fail? I didn't even receive a reply from yet another time consuming in depth application.

What was more worrying the temporary contract was coming to an end and I hadn't received a reply from any of the schools. I had no intention of returning to a position as a Support Worker. The black capsule scenario reappeared in my subconscious. It would be a better timed exit than four years previously. My self-esteem had rocketed in recent times and maybe fate was telling me it was time to go. Quit while you're ahead. Then I received an official brown envelope with Cathays High School franked on the front; hope at last. It had been such a while since the applications, I had jettisoned all the job descriptions. A group of about ten were to be interviewed of whom three were to be selected. We were shown around the school, then each of us was interviewed throughout the day by a panel of three, including by the deputy head. Securing the interview meant the age barrier had been overcome.

Ten minutes into the interview I realised that the Teaching Assistant position was for the Autistic Spectrum Disorder (ASD) department so I adjusted my answers accordingly. My eighteen month stint as a support worker with experience in dealing with the most violent and extreme aspects of autism had paid dividends. Fate had ensured that my time as a support worker hadn't been totally wasted. I felt that the interview went well but you never know what your fellow candidates have to offer. The blessing with school interviews is that they don't hang about with their response and I was put out of my misery the same evening when the deputy head rang with the good news. I responded calmly until I replaced the receiver. Then it was an emphatic "Yessssss." Although it was a paltry £11,500 salary, which was a pittance compared to what I earned in the printing industry, it was life or death to me . . . literally.

According to The Bard there are seven ages of man and whether I was experiencing the sixth or seventh I wasn't sure, but I was beginning to enjoy it. The things that were important to me in my earlier ages now ceased to have significance. In fact I felt I was living in a parallel universe; on the outside looking in. Advertising in all its guises cease to apply to me. The days of buying carpets, tiles, furniture, poring over mortgage payment options had gone. I lived in comfortable rented accommodation, and walked everywhere or used public transport. As for a significant other, I sort of felt obliged and dabbled occasionally but in their company always felt I'd rather be somewhere else. Some were grandmothers and although I was the same age I felt I'd be slipping towards the Darby and Joan Club.

People of my age seem desperate not to enter old age alone and certainly don't want to face death on their own. I came to realise that my generation were heading towards the arse-end of life with probably pain then ultimate death on the horizon and I would just prefer to manage my own inevitability. I enjoyed living alone and cherished my independence. Now in my sixties and alone for the first time in my life I was enjoying the experience. The main reason for my solo existence is that I saw my destiny growing old with the mother of my children. I'm a simple wife and two point four children kind of bloke, and no other option can distract me from the pain I suffer as a result of being denied this experience that so many take for granted.

Ever since I saw Ken Loach's film "Kes" I had always thought I would have made a good teacher. I definitely would have noticed the bullying and despite being sporty, I think I would have noticed the quiet and vulnerable ones and the kids who were having a hard time in and out of school. At the time I was in my twenties with a few "O" levels so it was a passing fancy. Now I was in amongst the nitty-gritty of an inner-city, non-selective, multi-cultural comprehensive school. I loved it. As a teacher I may not have survived; not because of the challenging pupils, but the curriculum, teaching methods and the overriding priorities set would have been a problem for me. Being a teaching assistant I could adopt methods and strategies to positively affect the behaviour and progress of pupils. I could be informal and deal with the kids in smaller groups and as individuals whereas a teacher rarely has the time or opportunity. They deal with the majority, we deal with the minority. At my age the only cure for the inevitable wearied cynicism was working with the young. It's the perfect job, all the better because with generous school holidays I could backpack during the six week summer breaks and during my first summer term I began planning my trip back to Vientiane in Laos to complete a journey that fate had interrupted two years previously.

Right, So Where Was I?

During the last couple of months of the summer term I planned and continually fine-tuned the itinerary for my return to Asia, although it hardly deviated from the sadly curtailed route I was travelling two years previously. I was determined to make the Knob Chai Food Garden my first port of call so I could rather theatrically whisper to myself over my first beer, "Right, now where was I before I was so rudely interrupted."

I had now experienced several travel expeditions to strange and wonderful places, many off the beaten track and I would guess that 80% of the time it was hassle, stress, and physical hardship of some description. Fortunately the other 20% had been so uplifting and exquisitely sublime it removed all the negative memories in an instant; well until I was about to set out. These expeditions had been planned and booked months in advance with nerve-tingling excitement, but when departure time actually arrived I then became only too conscious of what could go wrong in just attempting to get to the starting destination and the physical and mental punishment I have to undergo. If it wasn't for the financial investment already incurred I would have to be convinced to leave my comfortable sofa and five episodes of Coronation Street a week. It probably affects me more than most as my subconscious continually under-performs, is inefficient, and goes on wildcat strikes without warning. Finding my wallet in the fridge after attempting to pay a bill from the content of cheese sandwich located in my back pocket is good example.

I realised that my outward journey to my first destination, Vientiane in Laos, would be completely exhausting. A fourteen hour flight via Doha in Qatar was to be followed by a twelve hour wait in Bangkok Airport before the short final leg. To make life a little easier I thought I'd book a night in a Gatwick Hotel which seemed a far better option than leaving Cardiff Bus Station at 2.00am. Via the internet The Russ Hill Hotel at £46.00 per night looked reasonable so I booked it.

It was in a rural setting and looked like a grand country manor. Attached to the main building was a row of wooden lodges that actually looked more like large dog kennels. Mine was kennel four. The walls were paper thin and the cobbled thoroughfare outside was brightly lit all night. These bright lights streamed through the full length glass door which was inadequately covered by a three quarter length flimsy red curtain. Wheelie suitcases were constantly rattled across the cobbled surface like intermittent pneumatic drills throughout the night which temporarily eclipsed the sound of the bloke snoring next door. It was also on the main glide-path to Gatwick. The room was so small that with super efficient ergonomic ingenuity they managed to fit a bathroom suite into an area the size of a telephone box. In fact the basin was so close to the bog I had to stand at the side of the throne, form my body into an S-shape and sidle sideways like a prosthetic crab. To this brilliant use of space was added the fact that in a rush I could efficiently shave, clean my teeth and have crap at the same time, I could've had better night sleep on the 2.00am Gatwick special. Day one and I was pissed off already.

The journey out was as knackering as anticipated. In recent years I had become more gregarious which was handy when your travelling alone. In fact I think I was becoming like those weird characters who sit next to you on the bus and bellow in earshot of all the other passengers "I've got 44 cats" ... "I like you" .... "Will you be my friend?" I tried to ingratiate myself into several conversations during the tedious journey but as most of the travellers were half my age I think they assumed (especially as I was on the way to Bangkok) that I was a dirty old man and they politely as possible shunned my pearls of wisdom, wit and repartee. After fourteen hours in the air and twelve waiting at Bangkok airport for my connection, I reached the last leg of the journey; an hours flight from Bangkok to Vientiane.

I was now completely and utterly shagged. My brain had turned to pus and my hand-eye co-ordination resembled someone in the advanced stages of Parkinson's, knocking over drinks and meal cartons with monotonous regularity. My eyelids were so heavy they made Salman Rushdie look like Homer Simpson. As we climbed into the night sky an English speaking and extremely garrulous French architect attempted to engage me in highbrow sophisticated conversation. While he had just left a five star Bangkok hotel in fine fettle after being feted by hotel flunkies, I was one step removed from rig amortise. But I rose to the occasion like a spy being interrogated after sleep deprivation. I matched his well informed multi-syllabic sentences with my own. After an hour of verbal jousting I think I achieved an honourable draw as we landed on Lao soil.

Vientiane must be the quietest and most subdued capital in the world. Arriving there from places like Bangkok and Saigon is like submerging yourself in a crowded noisy swimming pool to seek solace and sanctuary. The population, even the young men, were very quiet, gentle and passive. I was booked into my guesthouse by two young men in their twenties and despite my near state of collapse and my inability to hold a pen, I still felt loud and brash compared my whispering hosts.

Tricky Dickie's Legacy

The following evening after an epic slumber I returned to the Knob Chai Deu Food Garden. Over a beer I recalled sitting at that table two years earlier feeling so crestfallen about my aborted Asian adventure convinced that I had suffered a stroke. Now my mood was totally transformed and my health, both physical and mental, had never been more robust.

After spending a few days recovering from travel exhaustion and jet lag I flew to Xieng Khuang Province from Wattay International Airport. "International" is stretching it a bit as the only regular flights to cross the Laos border were from Bangkok and Hanoi, both an hour away. The only aircraft on the airfield was our 50 seat turbo-prop, so no confusion, panic or lost luggage was experienced on this particular flight. Wattay must be the most relaxed and charming international airport in world. If Trumpton had an airport it would be just like Wattay. On the way in from Bangkok it took me just a few minutes to obtain a visa. Back on track after my 2005 disappointment I was now heading for Phonsavan, the main town in the province, for two particular reasons. One, that it was created from the secret carpet bombing of the Vietnam War, two, I wanted to witness for myself the atmospheric and mysterious Plain of Jars.

Nixon had lied to the American people about the unrelenting bombardment of Xieng Kuang province which was a long way from the Ho Chi Minh Trail. The province contained hundreds of small villages in the sixties but during the bombardment the villagers sought sanctuary by living in the surrounding caves. The villages were destroyed and after the war the villagers came out of the caves to created Phonsavan.

As we descended over the thick, lush Lao jungle and onto the small runway in a clearing, we could see that the wooden shack that was the terminal had filled with excitable locals as this twice a week flight was the major event in their lives. The passengers were pounced upon by prospective guides and I put my faith in a young but wily man called Noi. He drove me into town, changed my money at a very good rate and organised my trip to The Plain of Jars and other places of interest.

Phonsovan was a small remote ramshackle town with just a few dirt tracks dissecting, for the most part, simple wooden homesteads. There was a busy market and an overall air of independence and contentment. I sat in Noi's office which was like a glorified bus shelter opened to the road with an old wooden desk covered with various photocopied excursions, prices negotiable. While the shrewd Noi was relieving me of most of the Laos Kip I had just changed for an all day trip to the local places of interest, I couldn't help but notice that around his office were various examples of ordnance such as grenades, mortar shells, and large bombs. This weaponry was to be the major feature of my visit.

The following day I set out early with the my guide who turned out to be just a monosyllabic driver. In fact during the soaring heat of the day his main concern was seeking out shelter from the unrelenting UV's. We visited the now infamous Tham Piu cave where there is a memorial to the 350 people killed in 1968 from a fighter missile. They weren't even safe in the bowels of the earth.

The Plain of Jars, which should be Plains as there are many sites and fields that cover many square miles, are the location for 650 of the jars. These "jars" were like huge, stone Ali Baba baskets many weighing over six tons, some were in large groups, whereas others were scattered far and wide. They were reckoned to be over 2,500 years old and that's about the only information known. Why they were made and how they got there is still a complete mystery, although there are several local folk tales that, unlike the jars themselves, don't really hold water. Many more jars were destroyed by the bombing and the area is covered by large bomb craters.

As well as the bomb craters, the remnants of villages and temples, other reminders of the war are a constant as shrapnel and ordnance was now a part the local architecture and was used as agricultural equipment. In a bar in Phonsovan I was leaning on the entrance post when I realised it was one of two five foot high shells (defused I assumed). I visited a remote Muang village, an independent tribe of people, who use shell casings for supporting elevated houses, pig's troughs, and growing onions! Many buildings had various weapons of carnage such as mines and cluster bombs as souvenirs.

Some of the lasting memories of travel are what may seem, on the surface, unspectacular, but I like to snatch moments of solitude in the remoter places on the globe. After a charming visit to the remote Muang village, where they made me very welcome and allowed me to crush wheat using a medieval wooden grinding machine, I found myself near an isolated farm several miles away. While my driver was whinging under a tree complaining about the heat, I sat with my feet cooling in a rapid stream feeling overjoyed in the moment of being in the middle of this mysterious, gloriously lush, remote part of Asia, away from anything or anyone I would recognise. During my Wordsworth moment I noticed that the farmer had dammed up part of the stream causing a waterfall of a few feet which was enough to create hydro-electric power from his ingenuous contraption that fed electricity to power an electric light bulb or two inside his rustic farmhouse.

The Vietnamese have forgiven the Americans and rarely refer to their comparatively recent and heroic past. Apologetic Americans are welcomed in Vietnam but are noticeable by their absence in Laos among the mainly German, Scandinavians, Brits and our Antipodean cousins. I asked Noi why the Vietnamese are so forgiving compared to their Lao neighbours. He said it was simple . . . . the Vietnamese won.

After several 24 hour bus journeys in South America the previous year the eight hour jaunt from Phonsovan to Luang Prebang would be a mere bagatelle. Most of the backpacks were stored on top of a jalopy of a bus and the rest were packed into the aisle where passengers clambered over them to get in and out of their seats. At the back a middle-aged Australian couple, a young German couple and a Lao man formed a small English speaking group for the duration. Most of the passengers were Lao, including a uniformed soldier giving orders to all and sundry and a young plain clothed man with a barely concealed rifle under his denim jacket. The mountainous jungle area through which we were about to travel was still home to Pathet Lao guerrillas, although it was explained by our Lao friend that they were now little more than a rag-bag of highwaymen. The armed escort certainly gave the feeling that this was bandit country.

The scowling young armed guard sat unnervingly alongside me across the aisle. The bus climbed, wound, and descended constantly with articles of clothing being added and removed like a Whitehall Farce as the temperature fluctuated dramatically. As it was the monsoon season the heat and the humidity was relieved by torrential downpours that nurtured the lush, dense, and the most vivid green jungle vegetation. At high altitude the journey became a bit hairy because of the precipitous drop at the edge of the road and the driver's propensity to swing into the wrong side of the road to take blind hairpin bends at speed.

Adjacent to this long and winding road were dotted little communities living in basic wooden huts on stilts. They literally lived life on the edge. At the front of their dwellings at the edge of this dangerous road the stilts were about three feet high, at the back because of the steep drop, they were about seven or eight feet. These people must have great confidence in their architectural and building prowess as a miscalculation, a spot of subsidence, or even an attack of woodworm, would send them into the abyss. At the front of these houses on the edge of the road they displayed fruits and lovingly prepared foodstuffs, such as corn wrapped in palm leaves, that they sold for a pittance. I think these were Hmong people whose culture allows a man to take two or three wives which explained why there were kids everywhere. Although the kids seemed happy enough I got the feeling that they were expendable, as toddlers were using machetes and cleavers they could barely lift and we came across a kid about two years old wandering a long way away from his homestead between the edge of this treacherous road and the deep ravine below.

After waking from one of my periodical dozes I found the Kalashnikov pointed right between my eyes. Our guard was also in a state of slumber and his gun had lolled sideways. While hoping the safety catch was on I pondered whether to tap him on the shoulder and request he lay down his arms. Unsure of his instinctive reaction to being suddenly woken and seeming the type to dream of armed combat, I gently moved the rifle away from my direction; in fact it was now pointing at the right ear of the man sat in front of me. I adopted the philosophy of self-preservation, after all it was a jungle out there.

We stopped at a place called Muang Phu Khun for lunch. It was a small, primitive but bustling mountain community and we ate the staple diet there of noodle soup and sticky rice. The eatery was no more than a tin shack and I deliberately avoided any contact with the kitchen on a need to know basis. In these circumstances I fall back on the statistic that, apart from Deli belly when I was pole-axed for about three days, I have never suffered from food poisoning abroad. I broke bread with the very pleasant German couple. She was a teacher and he worked for Lufstansa, hence the exotic, and for them, cheap destinations. The heavens opened once again and the deluge was biblical. We stood staring at the bus thirty metres away as it revved up, with the precipitation acting almost like an opaque

217

curtain between us and the means to our next destination. We made the dash, although we may have sauntered at leisure for all the good it did, as we reached 100% saturation within three strides, but it was a relief to get away from the eardrum bursting, machine-gun clattering of the water bullets on the corrugated roof. We were on the move again through spectacular scenery with international banter and a soundtrack of haunting, evocative oriental music from the radio. These moments make crowded airports, megalomanic customs officials, and 14 hour long haul flights worthwhile. Four hours later we arrived at the jewel of Laos, Luang Prabang.

Luang Prabang

Luang Prabang was lush. I mean that in every sense of the word. Nestled at the confluence of the rivers Nom Ou and the mighty Mekong I could barely make it out as we arrived, camouflaged as it was amongst the tropical rain forest. It's the size of a large village, and is an UNESCO world heritage site. The area is inundated with temples, wats and stupas where visitors mingle at ease with young Buddhists monks amongst the crumbling French colonial buildings. Nothing really happens in Luang Prabang which along with its location is much of its charm. Most of the activities take place in the surrounding countryside and up and down the rivers.

The first morning, to get my bearings, I hired a bicycle. I've never been totally conversant with a bicycle, not having owned one as a kid. My first real experience was at the age of fourteen starting a job as an order boy in Wilson Road in Ely for the Home and Colonial, or was it the Bon Marche or even the Maypole? Well it was one of those now defunct post war grocery outlets. My inability to ride a two-wheeler was matched by my proficiency for physics because the first thing I did was to place a boxed order in the front basket whereby the bike did a perfect forward somersault. After coming off several times I was sacked within a week.

This bike also had a basket, the masculine cross-bar was missing, and it was a pretty shade of blue. Negotiating the contraption down the narrow streets I felt like a nervous Miss Jean Brodie or a district nurse on her first day. I know I should have checked the brakes first but I did have the presence of mind to apply them at the start of a gentle slope before gaining neck-breaking momentum. They had little effect and as I was going too fast to use my feet, I veered towards an inviting bush at the side of the road to cushion my fall. The result was me lying spread-eagle in the bush with the inverted wheel spinning bike next to me. It provided great amusement to a passing group of tourists. I think they were French too. The bike was returned and I reverted to Shank's pony.

Most people ate and hung out on the main drag which was only about 150 metres long. On either side there were bar/restaurants, and internet cafes/tour companies all within the old original buildings. Bar/restaurants along the Mekong were popular too. It's along the main drag you bump into people you've got to know travelling up or on activities. It was all quite friendly and intimate. Despite a large contingent of young people drawn there by the physical activities of the surrounding province, such as three day trekking, caving, canoeing etc . . . , the evenings were quite sedate without any raucous behaviour. Most people were tucked up in bed by eleven.

As well as a trip up river to the Par Ou caves, I went to the Kuang Si waterfall about a half an hour drive away. The waterfall was situated in thick jungle and hence revealed itself in stages from the dense Arcadian splendour. At first an inviting turquoise swimming area was spied through the dense foliage at the foot of a fifty foot waterfall. What wasn't immediately apparent was this was the first stage of increasingly giant steps to the top of the waterfall a few hundred feet above. There were about six steps in all, three of which provided picturesque swimming areas. Also in the forest was a bear and tiger sanctuary.

Me, Two Old Sweats and the Blonde

Have you noticed that many wise adages have opposing and equally sagacious proverbs. "Strike while the iron's hot" can be tempered with "look before you leap" or "act in haste repent at leisure" and "self praise is no recommendation" can be countered with "false modesty is the worst form of conceit" In siding with the latter I would like to state that I have no complaints about the way God or nature had formed me. I may not have been "Hollywood" but nor was I a circus freak. I was given enough to be reasonably successful with the opposite sex. The fact that I hadn't had nothing to do with the hand I was dealt. Out of the biblical five talents in this department I had probably used about one and a half. Part of the explanation is a combination of Catholic guilt, a boys only school and being incarcerated in factories dominated by men in my early youth. My social life again was a male dominated culture of the most extreme kind, rugby. When I first started playing for St. Peters RFC women weren't even allowed in the club.

After a game on a Saturday the post match set routine would be to spend an inordinate time preening myself to suited and booted coiffeured perfection in front of the bathroom mirror humming "Luck be a lady tonight" while Robert Redford stared back at me, moustache and all. About a half dozen of us would meet in the New Market Tavern at eight where we started consuming copious amounts of Dutch courage as we ranged from being awkward and self conscious with the female of the species to downright terrified. By the time we engaged the opposite sex at about 1.00am in Tito's Club, we had consumed about twelve pints of whatever, several

Bacardi and cokes, and being heavy smokers at the time, about 30 cigarettes each. I was oblivious to the fact that as we moved in on groups of typists and comptometer operators dancing around their handbags, in that five hour period I had morphed from Robert Redford into W.C. Fields.

Meeting beautiful women in weird and wonderful places, thrown together by chance rather that the weekly Tito's routine was the stuff of movies; not now. In the previous few years I'd witnessed young people having a ball by travelling and teaching in exotics places, enjoying dalliances and sometimes deeper relationships having been thrown together by fate against backdrops of the type that most could only dream. I was pissed off because I was at least twenty five years too late . . . or was I?

At Wattay airport amongst the sparse, and for the most part, Loa passengers, entered an attractive statuesque blonde woman about thirty. We sat close together in the small café waiting for our flight to Phonsovan without even making eye-contact. I passed her in the street in that one horse town while she was browsing a market stall. Later that night I was having a drink outside a bar sat near four blokes about my age who were getting noisily rat-arsed. Their banter was typical of many of that ilk in Asia, that is foul mouthed and boorish. As I pretended to read my book the blonde happened by and despite there being several other similar bars close by, she smiled at me, came in and sat at the next table. Well she had made the first move and although she opened a book I knew it was impossible to read in the failing light, so I struck up a conversation. She was Swedish working for a few months in their embassy in Vientiane. Despite her presence the raucous foursome continued without deleting the expletives. While I listened to her response to my opening gambit two of the gang of four legged it and the other two asked her to join them at their table; she predictably declined. They offered the invite to me saying we're all mates here; I told them I was happy where

I was and they seemed affronted. I don't think they realised what arse-holes they were and just saw themselves as friends well met.

They looked genuinely insulted so I reluctantly joined them. They had a beer in front of me before I sat down. One of them, Mike, a Kiwi who looked like Eric Clapton during his mullet period, told me he had married a young beautiful Lao girl from a local village, they had a baby daughter and he had been divorced twice. Having met so many like him I felt I already knew. His mate Pete was a sixty year old, pot-bellied, bumptious Australian. I must have said something to which they enthusiastically concurred because they stood up to give me a drunken high five expecting me to respond likewise. Looking like refugees from a Nuremberg rally I felt compelled to meet them half way. How did I get into this? The blonde was still unconvincingly buried in her book. I got my round in and when I came back she was gone. I followed shortly afterwards.

I travelled to the Pak Ou caves which is home for retired Buddha statues of various descriptions about two hours up the Mekong from Luang Prebang. On our small battered boat was a rugby mad retired US diplomat with his Lao diplomat wife. His name was Liam and he was actually born in Ireland, so you can imagine the combination of Irish and American created an expansive, welcoming, and engaging character who knew his rugby and had even coached. He was so well connected he had tickets for the up coming World Cup semi-finals and final. He had been a George McGovern aide and worked in the Watergate building during the Nixon scandal. But even more impressive was the other passenger, Rebecca from Tasmania who was travelling alone to the UK via former Indo-China, Thailand, Hong Kong, Mongolia and Siberia. Apart from being adventurous she was young and attractive, both in looks and personality. We became engrossed in conversation as we chugged along the Mekong. I became lost in time as we chatted and laughed enthusiastically. It was only when I realised that I was unconsciously winding a long nasal hair around my finger in rapt attention, hanging on to her every word, that the spell was broken. I was sixty and she was less than half that. Despite that, at one stage we sort of got lost in a riverbank village on the edge of the jungle after running for cover from another deluge. If only I had invested in an ageing portrait in the attic because as the raindrops were falling on our heads I was Robert Redford again and she was Katherine Ross. Unfortunately I had to come to terms with fact that from her perspective it wasn't the Sundance Kid she was looking at, it was W.C. Fields. When we returned we discovered that fate had us staying at the same guesthouse, but fate also ensured that despite this being a relatively small guesthouse our paths never crossed again, which was probably just as well. To coin another proverb, there's no fool like an old fool.

I only noticed two beggars in Luang Prabang, one was a smiling appreciative, not so old woman with a stick, the other was the scariest Asian I've seen since Dr. Fu Manchu. He was over six feet tall, which is exceptional by Lao standards, and wore little more than a loin-cloth, exposing his lean body exhibiting, in a healthy way, not an ounce of excess fat. He just appeared at a table like a spectre. He had an amazing hypnotic face, with red searing, piercing eyes and a letterbox mouth that revealed haphazard teeth that looked like a vandalised cemetery. From his elbows his arms were outstretched with his fingers waggling like upturned beetles. He hopped from one bare foot to the other like a long jumper at the start of his run-up. He spoke with his eyes as he uttered not a word. His expression said give me money or I will curse you, your children, and your children's children. I refused to be intimidated. Each night as I was eating I would sense a presence and there at the other side of the table, like the ghost of Banquo, appeared his gyrating navel. I refused to lift my gaze. I saw him tap unsuspecting new tourists on their shoulders and the expressions on their faces as they swivelled around was a vision to behold. On my last night I planned to give him a dollar for his picture but he failed to materialise. Finishing my breakfast the morning after, before heading to the airport for my morning flight to

Chang Mai in northern Thailand, he granted me another visitation. I took his photo and intended to offload the last of my Laos kip when the apparition spoke. He said in his death rattle voice, "dollars". So I gave him a dollar. Seeing Thai baht in my wallet he said "baht." A witty Australian on the next table said to tell him that beggars can't be choosers. Without an ounce of gratitude he vanished.

Throughout my time in Luang Prabang I was having a heated debate with myself on the mode of conveyance to my next destination in northern Thailand. After a few beers I leant toward the romantic and adventurous method of the two day boat ride to the Thai border. In a battered old boat a disparate group of travellers would spend two stints of nine hours each side of an over-night stay at a riverbank village. In the sober cold light of day the one hour flight was favourite, especially as I had to pace myself for the privations of Burma. There was the fast boat which took six hours. It was deemed to be quite dangerous and there had been fatalities. Witnessing these options made my decision. The fast boat was like a tin bath with an outboard motor. About eight people were crammed in with their knees under their chins wearing large round safety helmets. From the bank of the Mekong I saw such a craft hurtling up stream with the only visible sight of humanity being the eight large helmets. It looked like a high-speed amphibious egg carton; no thanks. My trip to the Par Ou caves started in glorious sunshine and if it had stayed that way I probably would have chosen this option as my heart tends to rule my head. But this was monsoon season and after experiencing a couple of tropical storms during the journey in a narrow old wooden junk with no windows, I booked my flight as soon as we disembarked.

As a result of trips to Asia I've often witnessed the subjugated role of women. In the guesthouse in Luang Prabang young men in their teens and twenties lounged about watching TV most of the day, begrudgingly shifting themselves to collect or hand out a key. They are more motivated when collecting the rent. During my stay a heavily pregnant woman did my laundry, cooked my breakfasts, and was constantly sweeping and tidying up. Thinking back to the old sweats in Phonsovan, the mystery of their attraction to young Lao women, apart from money, is that compared to the locals they must seem like perfect gentlemen.

Chang Mai and Bangkok

If you're travelling to Asia it's often difficult to avoid Bangkok, unfortunately. In my youth when stationed in RAF Jurong in Singapore I made one of the most exhilarating and exciting trips of my life. In 1970 the two day, third class, steam train ride, packed with many nationalities along with a mate and much live poultry, snaked its way through the rubber plantations of Malaya and into Thailand. This would be exotic now, but back then Benidorm was still a fishing village and Spain was just becoming the destination of choice. I had happy memories of a relatively undiscovered Bangkok, with the Buddhas, Reclining and Golden, the floating market, and yes the exotic bars with the girls with the shiny beads. We met GI's on R & R from that old crazy Asian war. It may have been youthful insensitivity, but I can't remember any sense of guilt about the fact I was having a ball in Singapore and in another part of south east Asia they were experiencing a living hell.

This time I travelled to Bangkok from Chang Mai in the north in a first class sleeper train as result of being 36 years older and the benefits of a booming property market. On this trip Thailand was just a conduit between Laos and Burma. I did like Chang Mai though and appreciate it all the more after I'd been in Bangkok for a few days. My first experience of sampling the world famous Thai cuisine in Chang Mai was not a pleasant one. Outside a bar/restaurant frequented by ex-pats and British travellers I ordered spicy chicken from the menu. Apparently spicy meant hot. So when I slurped the soup-like dish it came as shock that I was actually pouring liquid magma into my digestive system. Traditionally my personal side effects of a good curry is hiccups and snot. I avoided the hiccups but must have lost a third of my body weight in mucus. I used up all the paper napkins on my table and those around me, and poured Tiger beer down my gullet as if I was dousing an inferno. About a third of the way into the contest I sat on my stool and refused to come out. After that I ate mainly at the local street vendors as the dishes are cooked or displayed in front of you, and if you regret your choice, choose something else as it is so cheap. I didn't have any regrets, the food was delicious and it's much more fun sat amongst the happy-go-lucky locals.

Since planning the trip my major concern was obtaining a visa for Myanmar (Burma) which was the main reason I was in Bangkok. I imagined that a visit to the Myanmar Embassy would be a Kafkaesque experience. To get there I had to cross central Bangkok in a tuk-tuk which is not much fun in heavy traffic, although the drivers are very chatty and friendly (once they have out-bargained you on the fare). I went to the embassy entrance marked "Visas" to be told rather aggressively by a uniformed gentleman "closed!" I pointed to the opening times of 9.00am-1.00pm and that it was in fact now 10.00am, but his response was the same and a tad more aggressive. A helpful street vendor, who must act as unofficial Burmese diplomat, explained to me and a couple of others who had gathered, that we should come back in the afternoon and "maybe" it will be open. Imagine having to commute back and forth across a noisy gridlocked Bangkok on the off chance it may be open? Another local mentioned that there would be many police today. I walked around the corner to see cameras being set up. I spoke to a camera-man who explained in very good English that it was the anniversary of the 1988 military coup d'etat by General Saw Maung which had led to the current brutal military dictatorship. It wasn't good timing on my part. After the morning demo the embassy did

open and my visa was processed almost without a hitch. When I went to collect my passport the following day I did have five minutes of trauma while they searched, seemingly in vain, through trays of passports before finally locating it in a draw.

I had thought a lot about the ethics of my trip to Burma. Aung Saw Suu Kye who was elected by 88% of the Burmese electorate in1990 supported an embargo on tourism. She had spent most of the previous sixteen years under house arrest and refused to visit her dying husband exiled in Paris because she would be refused re-entry. There was another pro-democracy group called The Free Burma Coalition who believed the ban was counter-productive. Their motto was "open society cannot be built on isolationism" The argument that western investment, tourism and otherwise, would strengthen the legitimacy of the junta, had lost its appeal because the Chinese who, amongst others, were happy to ignore civil rights abuses, were investing heavily. I had read and been told that westerners were welcomed and greeted warmly by the ordinary Burmese people. I knew that those who disagreed, and I'd met some, took a jaundiced view of my decision and so they should because I was just keen to go. Maybe I'd convinced myself but I didn't regret my decision to go. Apart from the increase in backpackers like me (who can choose where to spend their money) package holiday adverts had appeared in the press. I wanted to travel Kipling's Road to Mandalay (which is more than he did) and witness the wonders of Bagan without distraction and in quiet contemplation before the hordes arrived.

Burma would be a huge contrast to Khou San (cow-san) Road, the backpacker area of Bangkok where I stayed. It was neon-lit, loud, and brash. It wasn't my cup of tea but if I was in my teens or twenties, like the majority, I guess it would've been a hoot.

Burmese Days

I don't think I'd ever been so exhilarated as when flying into Rangoon. Burma's history, so closely tied to Britain and The Raj, had given way to a secretive enslavement of the people by its brutal military dictatorship for over twenty years. This stricken, yet enigmatic country was to be a real adventure of discovery for me. Rangoon Airport was brand new and sadly underused. As I shuffled through passport control and customs I was still nervous of a last minute hitch that would result in an officious hand on my shoulder preventing my entry because of a technical or political problem, so I felt relief and excitement as I headed to the exit.

At the airport the kyat (pronounced chat) was offered at the official government bureau at 450 to the dollar. Luckily I was advised by a Turkish German teacher (honest) back in Luang Prubang to give it a swerve and use the black market. From the airport my taxi driver drove me to a money changer. He drove an ancient dilapidated vehicle with two windows missing and whose manufacturer was a mystery as all identifiable insignias had been vibrated onto the pot-holed road decades earlier. He pulled over, left the vehicle, returning with an unsmiling young man who looked like he whacked people for the mob. He slid into the back seat with a zipped black bag and the exchange took place in great solemnity. I got 125,000 kyats for my two fifty dollar bills. They were all in the highest denomination which was 1000kyats. That's 125 notes which is quite a wedge. His fingers were a blur as he counted them out in about three and half seconds. It wasn't that I didn't trust him of course but mistakes can be made so I double checked while they took a nap.

My journey from the airport took me quite close to where Aung Saw Suu Kye was being held under house arrest. I didn't see any overt signs of violent oppression. Apart from the smart hotels, Rangoon

looked quite battered, The roads and especially the pavements looked as though they had recently experienced a minor earthquake. The city looked busy with lots of activity, much of it commercial. Men conversed and did business sat in tea houses or on the streets sat on tiny stools, chairs and equally tiny tables. I booked into the Mayshan Guesthouse right in the busy centre. The people who ran the guesthouse had ready smiles, were very polite and dignified. Near the more luxurious hotels were ragged waifs and strays who begged or tried to sell junk to the sparsely dotted tourists, usually with some success.

A few weeks earlier in Luang Prabang I had chatted to a middle-aged Australian couple about my impending trip to Burma. She was keen to go but he said he didn't want to go to a place where the army periodically shot homeless people in the street to send the fear of God into the rest. I was a bit sceptical about his claims but my first day or so in Rangoon there seemed that there was some evidence. As I wandered around getting my bearings I noticed faded blood-stains on the pavement where someone seemed to have staggered along bleeding profusely, and further along, a wall was splattered in faded burgundy like the crime scene of the St. Valentine's Day Massacre. Then I realised. Most of the older and quite a few of the younger men had what we would describe as a disgusting habit, that of spitting betel juice. They shoved green betel leaves into their mouths and masticated with the intensity of Alex Ferguson at a penalty shoot-out, which subsequently converts them into a swilling mouthful of scarlet saliva which they then unleash on the general public.

In the film Titanic the scrawny 15 year old Jack incredulously wins the favours of the mature, well rounded, rich and sophisticated Kate Winslett. What was his secret seductive weapon? It was spitting. Remember the scene when he taught her the art of gobbing? Well if that's what turns Kate on, she should get her shapely arse over to Rangoon; the experience would be orgasmic. When they gob there it's like a performing art. They spread their legs, lean forward and using every muscle in their body, extract grotesque amounts of phlegm, then draw it up to the back of the throat. This process takes about eight seconds and sounds like a heavy shovel being dragged over concrete. This collection is honed for a few seconds into an orb of phlegm, snot, carrots, and green gilberts all covered in red betel juice, before being launched, oscillating through the air in its carrier, eventually landing splat in someone's path looking like a 3-D Jackson Pollock miniature. As you step around this blot on the landscape you're reminded of the fact that such is its consistency that apparently it takes on average fourteen and half years to evaporate. To converse with a user compels you to avert your eyes from broken reddened teeth and gums, especially if he has a half a litre of betel juice slushing about. But this is one of the few negatives about my experiences of Burma.

Burma was the poorest country in Asia and one of the poorest in the world. Rangoon is the largest city but had just lost its status as capital to Naypyidaw on the whim its nasty military dictatorship. There are parts of the city that are serene and beautiful such as Kandawgyi and Inya lakes. The main tourist highlight is the stunning Shawadagon Paya which is not just the most important pagoda in Burma but is part of a wider complex of Buddhist shrines and ceremonies. This was the rallying point where the monk led revolt took place a few weeks after I left the country. There were very few visitors with Brits and Americans difficult to find. How were the people coping, and what was the story of their daily existence were my initial main interests.

The centre of Rangoon was a hive of activity with most of the people seeming to have a reason to get up in the morning. There was a thriving black economy and most people seemed to eke out a living of some description. They were helpful and friendly towards visitors and seemed to have a close-knit community spirit. With the modes of transport it's hardly surprising. The buses and pick-ups were crammed with Burmese humanity. Throughout the inner-city there was a multitude of tea-shops where mainly men chat and conduct business. I was taking a photo of such a scenario when a man tapped me on the shoulder and explained, in pretty good English, they were doing gold and gems business. He said "This is how we do it here" before melting back into the crowd. That happened quite a lot; someone appearing at your side for few moments if you were lost or confused then providing much needed advice, smiling and moving on.

One corner in the centre of Rangoon was especially noisy and busy. It was like the floor of the Stock Exchange before the Big Bang with men shouting the odds and gesticulating in coded language. I burrowed through to see what all the fuss was about. At the centre of all this activity was a pile of, what we would describe as, junk with second hand merchandise such as ancient stereos, mobile phones and electronic units, much of which were state-of-the art products twenty ears previously. There was a constant flow of goods transported across the city in various modes of conveyance including, tri-shaws, pick-ups and buses all, to the western eye, dangerously overloaded. The existence of this black market was reassuring to the traveller who wanted to put money into the people's pockets rather than government coffers.

Hit The Road Jack

Jack Kerouac's seminal work "On the Road" is out of date, old hat, anachronistic, passé. That was my drink addled comment to my American mate for the day, Simon, as we ate and drank away the early hours in one of the many bars amongst the street hubbub that was Chinatown, Rangoon. OK it's a classic of the beat generation and influenced the counter culture of the sixties. However it needed to be revisited and up-dated to represent the current crop of young people who want to extract every ounce of adventurous and spontaneous discovery that instinctive youth demands. I met Lisa in Chang Mai while having breakfast on a cafe veranda. She had used TEFL as a means to work, travel, and party in various parts of the world. She had just arrived that morning from India where she had been teaching and was to spend some time in Chang Mai, where she previously worked, to meet up with old friends and party. She was then to head off to Tanzania where another old friend and colleague had fixed her up with a teaching position. In my experience young women dominate this gap year or ten movement travelling, often alone, through dangerous places such as Central and South America. I've asked a few if they could imagine themselves changing nappies and pushing a pram in suburbia. Most say yes, but not yet. They're reluctant to jump off the international roller-coaster. Lisa volunteered the fact she was concerned about her biological clock but could not consider changing her globetrotting lifestyle just yet.

The revellers on Khou San in Bangkok had more predictable, hedonistic goals such as to hit the beaches of Thailand. I met Noel there. He was travelling alone and we went for a beer. He was from rural central Ireland and admitted that he was wet behind the ears on more than one occasion. Even the most trivial event was greeted by raised eyebrows, and a wide eyed.

"B'Jaysus will you look at that? Amazing".

He seemed to view the world with puzzled bemusement. He was the youngest of four with three elder sisters. It was obvious that he was not only mothered but elder sistered too. This innocent abroad was incredibly thirty six years old.

While drinking and chatting with this excitable boy in a man's body, he said that there was a woman on my blind side and that he was convinced she was Irish and had been sat alone for some time. I suggested on a couple of occasions that he invite her over. On the third occasion he said.

"I will, I will, I will." before heading for the toilet.

As she seemed destined to leave I walked over and invited her to join us. She had a shock of cascading red hair and, with uncanny accuracy, using the model of the Maureen O' Hara school of Irish beauties, Noel was spot on, she was Israeli. Leila accepted my invitation on Noel's behalf. When he returned from the toilet his eyebrows disappeared into his hairline and his eyes were like organ stops. He was like a kid at Christmas as he predictably exclaimed

"Well will you look at that now? Amazing." Feeling quite smug at my matchmaking prowess I left them to it.

The following night I was sat in a bar several stories up looking down at the throng along Khou San and listening to a couple of very good live musicians. Travelling alone has its advantages and although watching groups of people chatting and having fun may seem depressing when you're supping ale alone, not everything is as it seems. I found that with older couples they probably needed me more than I need them. It's not that they don't get on but they need a break from each other and away in exotic places even normally reserved people are very gregarious. On this occasion a young couple or rather the girl was quite keen to have a chinwag. She was a young, overly made up, peroxide blonde with a Somerset accent. Their problem was that Debbie was bubbly and Steve, a strapping six foot plus soldier, was the strong silent type. He had completed two tours of Iraq and was currently bored witless in Germany. Most of this information was coming from Debbie, who on occasions was talking about Steve as if he wasn't there. She was speaking on his behalf. I actually got him chatting and it transpired that he was a boy soldier from the age of sixteen. He began opening up about Iraq and as I felt I was getting through to him with my Confucian wisdom and was building up a rapport, Debbie interrupted.

"Is that man calling you?" I looked into the shifting crowds below and it was Noel with his neck craned, his mouth bracketed by his hands as he shouted up "B'Jaysus Dennis is that yourself up there?" Within a thrice he had bounded up the stairs and joined us, cheering everyone with his infectious personality.

Later he left to meet Leila at the appointed time of 10 'o'clock. I ambled past that bar about an hour later and picked them out at one of the tables that spilled out on to the pavement and into the road. The scenario didn't look promising. She was sat at the table flanked by a young, dark, Latino looking bloke while Noel, who was on his knees, elbows on the table, was looking more like a forlorn cuckold than a suitor. It looked like he'd been usurped and was trying to rescue the situation. Judging by her body language I think it was in vain.

Simon was the total antithesis of Noel. He was 22 going on 56, was into books in a big way and was currently reading a Richard Dawkins book (on genetics not religion). He'd just graduated and had been travelling since January before pursuing his PhD in chemistry. He was currently exploring Asia after spending months in Africa. Although he enthused about South Africa he recalled scary moments in places such as Tanzania, Ethiopia and Mozambique.

We met in our Rangoon guesthouse and he decided to join me in my quest for live Premiership football. After dinner my plan was to have a slow expensive beer in a big hotel with cable TV, but we discovered a local watering hole that actually served beer as well as tea with about 150 seats set up in a large adjoining garage facing two ancient, minuscule TV sets. Before it filled up we secured two central seats so that we could watch the two games simultaneously. By half time I looked like Ben Turpin.

Despite being Saturday night the bar closed at 9.00pm. The whole of Rangoon closed at 9.00pm.—except Chinatown. So we headed there. I needed some kind of dessert as I craved for something sweet. Simon said he knew where to satisfy this need on the way. Now I wasn't expecting apple crumble and custard but maybe a few Jammy Dodgers or a Hob-nob or two perhaps. We chatted continually as we headed away from the centre. Simon was very bright, opinionated, and had a latent sense of humour that I did my best to extract. He said he admired Margret Thatcher and modern day Singapore so my animated responses ate up a few of the ten blocks or so we had to cover. Collective consumption goods, such as street lighting, didn't seem to exist in Burma, so our journey to Chinatown took on a spooky and less than corporeal nature. We seemed to be the only people walking in any direction. The tall, battered, crumbling, old colonial buildings on both sides of the wide boulevard created a shadowy backdrop and it became like a scene from the post nuclear nightmare. As we walked from block to block little old ladies sitting alone at the side of the road with small piles of fruit, appeared out of the darkness, raised their heads at the possibility of a sale and as we walked past deep in conversation would lower their heads again and disappear back into the darkness behind us as another appeared out of the gloom in front. They seemed like melancholy souls drifting in purgatory waiting for the call. Simon finally stopped at one, expertly chose and gained complicated entry into one of these obscure fruits which produced a "sweet" pus that he thought would suffice as a dessert; my jammy dodger dream crushed. When asked, I said it tasted delicious whereupon he gave me a further half dozen. I surreptitiously offloaded them one by one down a monsoon drain as we continued our journey. At last in the distance, light and music. Chinatown on a Saturday night was made up of two or three long narrow lanes off the main drag, full of tables and small stools where the Chinese drank, chatted, and generally caroused. We joined them.

Now Dean Moriarty and his freight jumping chums may have thought travelling mob-handed to the likes of Chicago and Minnesota on the way to California the peak of adventurous youthful rebellion from the rat race, but it's hardly Mozambique or Mandalay is it?. They did eventually cross a border into Mexico and found the experience mind-blowing, but the current young "live now pay later" brigade probably feel that their exploits have now been inherited by geriatric caravan and camper-van enthusiasts.

One of the delights of visiting an enigmatic culture such as Burma was the current lack of western influence such as McDonald's or Starbucks. Conversely you have to contend with the fact that the men drink tea all day and all evening, well until 9.00pm when every thing closes down. There were places that sold beer or a decent coffee but they were few and far between. One of the pleasures of travelling, especially in hot humid climates, is to stop for a cold beer whenever you fancy, rest your weary legs and watch the day to day life of a fascinating and alien culture. There were ex-pat places advertised in the travel books where a chap can always get a snifter and experience a few home comforts provided by wallahs in some colonial splendour. I would like to say that I'm not interested in that kind of Victorian Raj mentality, but I'm a sucker for it. Being driven past the The Strand Hotel, which has the same stature and history there as The Raffles Hotel in Singapore, by a pith helmeted tri-shaw driver gave me a little glow. I paid the price for this kind of pathetic nostalgia as I was determined to travel the road to Mandalay rather than fly or take the sleeper train.

Where The Flyin' Fishes Play

My thirteen thousand kyat (six pounds) bus fare ensured that I spent the most tortuous fifteen hours of my life squeezed, knees to nostrils, into a battered jalopy where I happened to be the only non-Asian on board.

I had high expectations of Mandalay and it didn't disappoint. The outer walls of Mandalay Fort and its wide moat were on a scale that I never imagined. The palace and buildings within the walls were destroyed by the RAF in 1945 when Britain wrested it back from the Japanese. At a corner of the fort was the majestic Mandalay Hill which I climbed almost immediately after my wretched and exhausting bus journey, such was my enthusiasm. You are required to climb the many hundreds of steps bare foot despite the many scorpions that inhabit them. The panoramic view from the top was spectacular, looking over Mandalay and beyond to the wide expanse of the Irrawaddy. Despite it being the wet season Mandalay was open, rugged and dusty just as I imagined. Again it was devoid of western influence and apart from the multitude of eager to please tri-shaw drivers there were few discernible signs of an identifiable tourist industry. I had to buy my Mandalay T-shirt when I returned to Rangoon. Mandalay was busy and vibrant. Goods were carted around the city in various modes of transport. It could be a tri-shaw driver peddling an old fridge over the battered and potholed roads on his gearless contraption without complaint or a hint of an expletive. Or one of the many pick-ups carrying any one or all of a car engine, sacks of flour, oil drums, and carpets as well as about fourteen of the human cargo variety.

From Mandalay a seven hour boat journey took us to Bagan which is the biggest attraction in Burma. An eleventh century king in an act of extreme ostentation, to curry favour with Buddha, built thousands of pagodas in a relatively small geographical area. Viewing from the top of a pagoda hundreds can be seen stretching eerily into the panoramic yonder seemingly going on for ever into the distant dry scrubland. I travelled to many of these pagodas quaintly by pony and trap. Sunrise and sunset are particularly spectacular. Some people maintain that Bagan is more impressive than Angkor in Cambodia, but I disagree. Angkor represents the magnificent Khmer empire that stretched over Thailand, Vietnam and Laos about the same time as Bagan was being created. Angkor today still looks imposing, and exudes the almost chilling power of yesteryear.

On the sedate river journey up the Irrawaddy to Bagan we stopped at a riverbank to offload cargo for the local village. Here children appeared out of the undergrowth excitedly looking for any trinkets, pens, soaps, and shampoo. This was common in the poorest parts of Asia, and experienced tourists raid the hotel bathrooms for what are, to these kids, items of luxury. These were angelic children unlike many of the streetwise city urchins hardened by their fate. One particular girl's face still haunts me. Like the others she was in rags with matted hair but she had such a beautiful and intelligent face. She, unlike the others, seemed to know that she was trapped and imprisoned by this dreadful merciless regime that refused to liberate her to realise her obvious but repressed potential.

There were wonderful places around Mandalay to visit, like the ancient cities of Amarpura and Inwa which were visually and atmospherically unique. I was especially impressed by Mingun a couple hours boat ride across and upstream on the Irrawaddy where stands the colossal base or plinth of the unfinished Mingun Paya. I'm a big fan and have a book of paintings of Edward Hopper who painted a lot of atmospheric buildings. Like one of Hopper's creations this mammoth construction has always fascinated me. The pagoda was only a third of its planned size and had been damaged by an earthquake. I saw a picture of it a few years previously in a travel book and found myself staring at it, fascinated, for long periods. When I spotted it in the distance from the boat it had the same effect on me as it stood huge, broken but unbowed, bronzed and magnificent in the strong sunlight. I walked around it, climbed to the top of it, and watched it disappear into the distance as we left. Now I've only got the 437 photos of it as a memento of that aesthetic experience.

The pick-ups travel at break-neck speed whatever the load. In an adventurous frame of mind I decided to travel by pick-up to Pyin U Lwin which is an ex-British garrison town in the mountains. The locals still refer to it by its colonial name of Maymyo after the influential Colonel May. There were a lot of colonial landmarks like the Purcell Clock Tower, reputedly gifted by Queen Victoria.

Maymyo was verging on pretty and looked like a New England town at the turn of the twentieth century with its brightly coloured well maintained ornate wooden buildings. To add to this image, instead of pony and traps, like in Bagan, they used small stagecoaches. I wanted to ride shotgun but my jobs-worth driver made me sit inside and sulk.

After a few days I returned to Mandalay. The trip up the mountain in the pick-up was ok, if a little cramped and uncomfortable, but it was worth it for the novelty of going native. The return trip back down the mountain was a nerve jangling rip roaring affair. For nearly two hours I was terrified and exhilarated in equal measure. Pick-ups drummed up as much business as possible before they set off, which meant there was an excess of humanity crammed inside and non human cargo overloaded on top. The driver then put his foot down to the floorboards and the response of the vehicle depended on its condition and the load, plus or minus gravity. There were two youthful crew hanging on the back to load and unload, and in between times they would try to outdo each other and those in other pick-ups on the road with motorised gymnastics as they clambered all over the vehicle hanging by their fingertips. After a stop they habitually waited until the driver pulled away before leaping on flamboyantly. The pick-ups raced each other, continually honking their horns. We seemed to be travelling at Mach II as we hurtled down the mountain, my cheeks flapping against my ears. Depending on the distance, these vehicles usually have to stop to hose the radiators and cool the engine. In my pick-up clean water was hosed into the steaming radiator which caused it to be returned brown, bubbling and erupting. I reckon it was 80% Radweld.

The Burmese had to live repressed under the brutal military dictatorship. In the areas I travelled there wasn't an obvious military presence. I did witness what seemed like forced labour when young disaffected looking youths seemed to be carrying out some compulsory community work. Armed militia didn't stand on street corners or walk the streets. I didn't see truckloads of uniformed thugs like the Sudanese Janjaweed, or armed soldiers on rooftops as in Lhasa where I subsequently visited. However while I was in Mandalay the demonstrations, which turned into the brave but ultimately futile revolt of 2007 led by the Buddhist monks, were beginning in Rangoon. The world looked on offering only meaningless rhetoric.

In Mandalay I saw a well known vaudeville act called the Moustache Brothers which had, in the past, slipped in anti-government satire and openly supported Aung San Suu Kyi. The leader of this trio was jailed for 7 years hard labour in the 90's for dissent. He was released in 2001 but the group were banned from performing, except inside his own home. So they performed in his lounge for tourists (about a dozen at a time at $6.00 a head). I took this as an acceptance of tourism by this brave troupe.

I had many conversations with fellow travellers and the local Burmese about the ethics of visiting Burma. I didn't hear any negative comments. All the Burmese asked us to entice more people there to help alleviate their poverty. One tri-shaw driver stated that the British and the Americans didn't come because "your government don't like our government" as if they had no say in the matter and that decisions were made above their heads. Another activist Ma Thanegi, who was imprisoned for three years and is a close friend Aung San Suu Kyi, was of the opinion that her leader was too uncompromising and after 20 years of deterioration in the lives of the most vulnerable in Burma it was time to open up tourism and take advantage of the Asian boom. The lives of the poor had been improved dramatically in countries that few would describe as democratic or liberal and whose human rights records are hardly distinguished. This was the view of the majority and every man and woman in the street that I and other travellers spoke to.

Brief Encounter

Any person who has any romance or sense of nostalgia must love train journeys. I travelled by steam as a kid and those times evoke a sense of adventure, espionage and excitement. Even in 2007 travelling overnight from Mandalay to Rangoon was just the most wonderful experience. I arrived at the cavernous station with its long platforms under the distant arched roof to find many hundreds of Burmese of all ages and descriptions sat in groups waiting to board. They were not just sat on platforms but scattered over the rails in small family groups noisily chatting, eating and sitting cross legged on the railway lines and gravel. Uniformed porters and station staff were busying themselves along the one and only huge train.

Although I was very early I decided to find my compartment to offload my backpack. After studying my ticket for some time a very obliging, if slightly perplexed, guard led me to my sleeper. I wasn't impressed by the standard as I had paid top kyat for my first class compartment. This was just a momentary blip as nothing could affect my sense of the aesthetic as I wandered over the populated tracks to a little café where I ate, drank and contemplated this magical scene evocative of a bygone age. I wandered back to my carriage to check on my backpack to find another station guard who was waiting to explain that there had been a mistake and I was to follow him. We wandered alongside the train quite some way until my escort, with an air of puzzlement, stopped to ask the advice of a fellow official, who was equally perplexed and summoned another of a more senior rank. After some discussion and a long reassessment of my ticket, a decision was made and I was lead back along this very long train, this time with more purpose.

Finally I was ensconced in my new sleeper which was little better than the previous one. As I was settling in I was aware that a woman was bent through the window talking and saying goodbye to what looked like her father. When she finished she pulled up the window and turned around. Most Burmese women, although attractive, are quite small but what stood before me was a vision of a natural beauty that only Asian women possess. She had a beautiful olive complexion, dark eyes, cherub lips, and long, black, lustrous hair. She was at least five foot eight, spoke perfect English, moved gracefully, and had the most exquisite smile. She was perfect. In my wildest schoolboy imaginings I could not have envisaged meeting such a heavenly being on the overnight train from Mandalay to Rangoon. I chatted with her transfixed. She was travelling to a new job in Naypyidaw the new capital of Burma hurriedly erected in almost inaccessible jungle between Rangoon and Mandalay. This was a move to isolate the military leadership even further from the population they so brutally exploited. We continued chatting until a station guard entered to inform me that I was still in the wrong compartment and I was to go to an even more luxurious one. Despite my protestations and expressions of inner contentment he insisted that only the best was good enough for me. After reluctantly leaving this vision of beauty I despondently traipsed along the platform until I was relocated. I think the compartment was marginally better, it was difficult to see with four blokes in residence, two of whom were rather large. I reasoned afterwards that because of her destination, breeding and education she was probably close to the ruling elite, but my most clinical analysis was in reminding myself that she was about twenty one and I was sixty. My four companions were very sociable and generous, sharing their drinks and food with me.

The images of Burma are dominated by the peaceful aura of Buddhism with ubiquitous monks in their orange robes, the thousands of pagodas and the unique landscapes. The brutal military dictatorship incongruously bestrode and undermined all this, hopefully on a temporary basis. I, and my fellow travellers, made a lot of Burmese people happy during our visit. The government were keen to develop tourism and had just built a new airport in Rangoon.

The last thing they wanted was hordes of western tourists witnessing or indeed getting involved with demonstrations. Some Burmese were predicting that when the junta's leader was replaced things would improve. Twenty years of isolation hadn't worked. The overnight transfer of power to a democratically elected government seemed highly unlikely, but in recent times there seems to be more hope with the release of Aung San Suu Kyi. She has now been elected to their "parliament" but the real power is still with the military. I would strongly advise anyone to visit Burma, not just because of its unique beauty, yet to be sullied by Western culture, and the warm welcome that awaits, but to help liberate the people from poverty and brutal oppression.

Affection For The Disaffected

Shortly after returning to school from the Far East I secured a promotion to the position of Behavioural Support Supervisor which brought me into contact with those pupils who were internally excluded. They tended to be the most disaffected and disadvantaged of pupils. They would be "sentenced," depending on the gravity of misdemeanour, to a day or several days in the Behavioural Support Base which held up to six pupils who would be strictly supervised, completing exercises from the core subjects. They were cut off from the rest of the school and their friends. This was the punitive side of the job, the other side being pastoral where my colleague and I would support these problem children in lessons, counsel and advise them. This job, especially the pastoral side, gave me enormous satisfaction especially when I witnessed the positive results from the fruits of my labours.

Central America? No Sweat

My next destination during the summer holidays was to be Central America, at the time entering what was regarded as some of the most dangerous places on the planet. If the hurricanes and earthquakes didn't get me I'd still have to survive Malaria and Dengue Fever where Guatemala, in particular, was a hot spot for both. Then there was the fact that there were, on average, 5,000 murders a year in Guatemala, most of which were committed in the capital, Guatemala City. When I booked my flights several months earlier I dismissed such dangers, but on the eve of my departure my arse was beginning to twitch somewhat.

My first port of call was Panama City. I'd booked several days in a hostel called Lunas Castle which was highly recommended. The main attraction was its location in an area called Casco Viejo which apparently had all the charm of old Havana and overlooked the Gulf of Panama. A good place to start especially with a trip through the Panama Canal on offer.

The worst part of these long haul expeditions is getting to that area of the world that's to be the focus of attention for the six week stint. I knew that I would experience some trauma or disappointments, major and minor, while I was there but they're unpredictable and come with the territory. These setbacks would be more than compensated by unexpected positive encounters. But what's more predicable than the Heathrow hassle, and a lot of paranoid officiousness and chaos at Newark International which would result in a four hour delay. I knew I would be physically and mentally knackered by the time I arrived at my hostel at 1.30 am (8.30 am UK time).

The flight from New York to Panama City was actually quite eventful. While flying over the area popularly known as The Bermuda Triangle I thought of Ben when he was younger who had a fascination for the mysterious disappearances in this vicinity. I raised the porthole shutter after a doze in the dark to witness an amazing electrical storm. A gathering of two dimensional dormant clouds were suddenly given three dimensional life by an injection of venomous electrical energy that lit them up across the sky every few seconds like huge light bulbs or illuminated jelly fish with the arcing fork lightening acting as the giant filament. There was no sound and I thought that this spectacular deserved a score specially written. While we were experiencing this spectacle the fire alarm went off in the plane. After a show of concern by the attendants (and us of course) we were informed by the captain that the continuing din was due to the electronics which had been affected by the storm. This was far from reassuring as we were about to land. Anyway we landed safely although the airfield, spookily, just had a few old Dakota turbo props and at the corner of the airfield I thought I spotted a flying boat with Spruce Goose written on the side. What was really peculiar was walking through Arrivals and spotting a calendar on the wall showing 1937.

When I arrived at the hostel Lunas Castle at 1.30am I found a group of young people totally rat-arsed. I enquired about the whereabouts of reception and staff whereupon they informed me, after a fashion, that they were the staff. Eventually one of them roused himself, shuffled to the computer and attempted to key in my details. As both our brains were like melted cheese but for different reasons there was a breakdown in communication. He reminded me of a young hirsute Eliot Gould; thick black hair covered everything but his eyes which were almost totally closed. His slurred speech made communication almost impossible. I was so tired that I just agreed with everything I almost heard him say. So to those at the Lunas Castle and its environs I was known as Derek H. Crockett. If this was what they were like on Mondays what were the weekends like? In their defence I discovered it was a farewell party for a departing member of staff.

The following morning still feeling a bit jet lagged and suffering from sleep deprivation I wandered around Casco Viejo and what a tonic it proved to be. Casco Viejo is a square jawed peninsular jutting out into the Bay of Panama. It was a glorious day and the area, described as being similar to old Havana with cobbled stoned streets and crumbling Spanish colonial architecture, was a great antidote to jet-lag. The locals I passed all wished me "buenos dias" and as I was thinking I needed protection from the beating sun I found myself walking toward a bloke selling, amongst other things, Panama hats. Resplendent in my new acquisition I strolled on. I stopped at a street cafe for liquid refreshment conversing, with some difficulty, with some locals and then moved on. As I turned towards the direction of Lunas Castle down a narrow street one of the locals whistled to me, then shook his head and drew his finger across his throat and suggested I stick to the wider main road. So it seemed that my state of well being and sense of security was false and that I had to keep my wits about me at all times.

At the first opportunity I went to the Minaflores Locks just outside Panama City to see the Panama Canal. Much of the travelling I do now is inspired by my boyhood and teenage imagination. In St. David's Primary School I collected chewing gum cards of national flags including basic information about each country. Panama and its Canal fired my imagination and was placed unconsciously on the back burner for fifty years. The Canal is one of the great modern man made wonders of the world and a heavy human price was paid to complete it, with an estimated 20,000 deaths, mainly from Malaria. There was a very impressive four storey visitors' centre with an elevated viewing gantry, film show, and an excellent museum. In the blazing heat I watched several container ships pass through which became hypnotic as each time I went to leave to visit the museum I kept thinking "just one more ship and then I'm off."

The Lunas Castle Hostel was located in a huge crumbling colonial building with large rooms and dormitories. The place had a hippy atmosphere (bandannas were very popular) with scores of young backpackers passing through to spend a few days chilling as part of their various Central and South American itineraries. Most were just about to go to or had just been to Bocas del Toro on the Caribbean coast where there are great beaches and to dive to pirated wrecks. There was a large kitchen where we cooked pancakes in the morning before plonking ourselves down at a long wooden table ladened with fresh bananas. The chill out rooms contained lots of settees and soft furnishings sometimes used by travellers to crash out if all the beds were taken. On some nights there were great jam sessions when the resident guitars were plucked from the wall, a pair of maracas would appeared from somewhere, and an ancient organ, which I previously assumed was part of the way-out décor, was skilfully put to use. It tended not to be a thrash but gentle unplugged interpretations of the songs we all know and love.

On the first full evening there I sat with a beer on the long balcony which overlooked the Bay of Panama, home to an array of bobbing fishing boats with the backdrop of the silhouetted uptown Panama City across the bay looking like a scaled down Manhattan. I was surrounded by youthful physical beauty and athleticism which was countered by their general inability to string a sentence together. "Holy shit I've run out of beer man" was the typical articulation followed by "awesome man" when the said beer arrived. It was heavy relief to chat with a Turkish bloke, now living in the US, who was the only person not at least three decades younger than me. He was in software, looked bookish and turned out to be a bit of an intellectual. We discussed the religious divides across the globe, Byzantine art, the rise and fall of the Ottoman Empire and alternate energy sources until exhausted I tried to lighten the proceeding by extending the question "Britney or Kylie,-. another beer man?"

I'd already experienced two of what I hoped would be many firm handshakes of the trip. The first was at Newark International while waiting an inordinate time for our baggage. I had quite a long chat with a bloke of about my age from New Jersey and again in Lunas Castle with Tim, a young tree surgeon from Porthcawl in Wales. He'd been travelling for six months around Central America with his girlfriend and convinced me to change my itinerary by not being deterred by horror stories about Guatemala and to venture into southern Mexico and experience the delights San Cristobal de las Casas.

In Lunas Castle I shared a dorm with seven others and I had to struggle up and down a top bunk. There was no hot water, and there was nowhere to hang clothes. Despite being upgraded to business class by Copa Airlines and booking a couple of nights at a hotel in Guatemala City at $45.00 per night, as opposed to $12.00 per night in the Lunas Castle, I still felt I was leaving my comfort zone when leaving Panama for Guatemala City that night, and so it proved.

Bates' Motel

After complimentary wining and dining in the Presidential Suite at Panama's Tucuman International Airport and being fawned over during the two hour flight I got into a battered taxi and headed to the Cantabria Hotel in Zona 1. I selected this hotel at random on the internet after failing to secure accommodation at a few of the places recommended in Lonely Planet which were around the $15-20 mark. They were either full or just didn't get back to me. During this trip I had planned, at certain intervals, to take time out at a few more upmarket establishments rather than the more bohemian crash out places like the Lunas Castle and exchange camaraderie for creature comforts to recharge my batteries.

If you use the human body analogy for Guatemala City the taxi driver was taking me the arsehole route into town. Beyond midnight we veered through spooky, unlit, desolate, and for the most part, boarded up buildings in abandoned streets. Then I spotted signs of life. On several corners there were, in ones and twos, what seemed ghostly ladies of the night until one of them glared straight into our passing cab displaying a grotesquely made up face showing that they weren't ladies at all. "Transvestites" pointed out the driver proudly as if they were objects of civic pride. This was a scary, seedy, twilight world I would have preferred not to have witnessed at the dead of night within twenty minutes of arriving in reputedly one of the most dangerous cities in the world. I was desperate to get to my hotel away from this nightmarish world when the taxi suddenly stopped and the driver declared "Your hotel." I thought there must be some mistake, but there it was, The Cantabria Hotel. For $45.00 per night in Guatemala I was expecting a plush area, a hotel with bellhops and maybe a personal manicurist, but this . . . surely not.

I got out and banged on the door of what seemed just a house. A little old lady appeared after taking an eternity to unbolt. She jabbered nervously in Spanish in one ear, while the taxi driver tried to explain he didn't have change from my $20 note, in the other. I stared at the sky pleadingly "Why has thou forsaken me?" While she was prattling on, the taxi driver, who owned me $8.00 after my tip, offered me a note of local currency stating that it was worth the equivalent of $7. By this time I had moved sharply into cynical mode. A man of my world weary experience knew that crumpled well thumbed notes of a pink hue are never worth more than 20p. Higher denominations have the virile gravitas of blue or green colours. I reluctantly took the note and followed the chattering old lady inside.

It was a house, if rather a large, dark, ornate house. The old dear continued to chatter away nervously as we stood at the small reception desk. We attempted to communicate under a single light surrounded by shadows and increasing degrees of darkness beyond. I had this overriding sense that she and I were the only two people in the building. I signed the register. Mine was the fifth name on the page; so there were at least four others. Even better, the signature above mine was from the USA. Things were looking up. I would have someone with whom I could chat, share information and exchange pleasantries. Then I noticed the date . . . May! I was her first guest in three months! Did she have her son's mummified body secreted in this dimly lit mausoleum?

I slumped despondently on my bed. I was trapped alone in God knows where with no means of communication, and I'd just been conned by a taxi driver. Why didn't I just book a week in Bournemouth? Then I thought, hang on, I wasn't a tourist, I was a traveller. When somebody said to Paul Theroux, the renowned travel writer, before he set off on his Patagonian Express journey which travelled through this part of the world, "Enjoy yourself" he explained that wasn't the point and went on "I craved a little risk, some danger, an untoward event, a vivid discomfort, an experience of my own company, and, in a modest way, the romance of solitude." Well although I wasn't that Spartan, I found this recollection quite comforting.

I slept well until I was woken by the sound of gunfire. It seemed there was a military firing range . . . or squad, close by. I drew the wide curtains which revealed a beautiful second floor veranda. I stepped through the large French windows, sat at an ornate stone table and looked over the city skyline with the backdrop of the most perfectly shaped volcano. It was like a huge isosceles triangle with a bit chopped off the top. I checked the Guatemalan quetzales currency with smug confidence to discover that scruffy pinky notes were actually worth $7.00. At least I gave him a good tip even if it wasn't with good grace.

There had been a TV programme a few years previously about the violence and lawlessness of Guatemala City. The police didn't pursue murder investigations because of a combination of the huge number and apathy. Women were especially vulnerable. Back in Lunas Castle the few who had been there said the threat was exaggerated and you just had to be sensible. My Turkish friend advised me to jettison any sign of being a tourist. Wear long trousers not shorts, keep any ostentation well hidden such as cameras and watches, and don't wear tell-tale T-shirts. So with that in mind I set out to find my way around this den of iniquity. The area was run down but not threatening as it was the previous night. The night people had gone back into their caskets. Eventually I found my way to one of the main plazas wearing jeans, a plain T-shirt, Panama hat, and to make sure I was incognito my rather cool shades. When I got to the corner of the plaza three limb challenged beggars homed in on me. It was like a qualifying heat in the paraplegic games. Well I thought I had blended in quite well but maybe being covered in a thick layer of sun-block, which made me looked like a refugee from the Walking Dead, was a giveaway.

In the evening I went to a Mexican restaurant near the main plaza. I was tucking into, what turned out to be an excellent meal, when I noticed a young, lone, woman, about mid to late twenties, sitting just across from me. I was convinced she was British by her poise, deportment and pale complexion. She was attractive rather than beautiful and had an intelligence about her, not that I was staring of course. She was, or would have been, just my type. The mystery was what was she doing in Guatemala City alone. I was hoping she would say something as I had become too self-conscious of my age to start chatting to strange young women. When I was young and in my prime, thanks mainly to the RAF, I found myself in exotic places but chance meetings like these were at a premium mainly because I was usually with a group of fellow young airmen. The previous year I experienced two brief encounters with mysterious young women both occurring thirty years too late. Earlier in the day I checked the internet to see what Dating Direct had procured since I'd been away, to find two aging Amy Turtle clones, both with the perfunctory GSOH. Oh fate why didst thou mock me?!!

Leaving the restaurant I thought of getting a taxi back, as is generally advised, but I kept walking until the noise of el centro slowly faded behind me and I had about eight dimly lit blocks to go, but inspired by the spirit of Paul Theroux I strode purposefully back to the hotel. In these situations I carry no more than $50.00 which I would gladly hand over, however if I'm carrying my passport and money belt then it's a fight to the death.

I found, wandering around Guatemala City, that although being a poor country, even by Central American standards, the city was vibrant, the people seemed pretty relaxed and were certainly very friendly.

The lady of the house was a sweet old dear of 76 and her bijou hotel was beautiful but in an austere doom-ladened way. Although I wasn't overly aggressive the first night I think she sensed my disquiet. It was blatantly obvious I couldn't understand Spanish and I repeated "No comprende" monotonously. But despite this, every time our paths crossed she engaged in lengthy nervy monologues. When it was plain that I hadn't understood a word she took a deep breath, furrowed her brow and repeated it slowly and with greater intensity as if it would make a difference. Then when this didn't work she searched for another way of expressing herself seemingly totally unaware of the futility of her exertions. I felt my stay had ruffled her feathers and as I left I could see her metaphorically putting her head back under her wing until the next guest arrived, probably in late November.

How To Coban Survive

After some confusion I located the small independent bus company that ran buses to Coban, my next destination. It was secreted away right in the middle of that chaotic city. Amongst the squeeze on the bus, as passengers ferreted away their possessions into nooks and crannies, Dave and I caught sight of each other as the only non Latino passengers. We gravitated towards each other finding adjacent seats. I took an instant liking to him and after days without English conversation we were bursting with banter and repartee. He was a science teacher from Portland, Oregon, and was about forty with a wide eyed childlike enthusiasm for all that he was doing. He had been to Central America before and had done a lot of diving as oceanography was his pet subject. He owned a sort of backpacker's sat. nav., so when he arrived at a new place or was disorientated he'd pull out his sat. nav. and, as he explained to me, used the seven satellites at his disposal (the other seven are on the other side of the world apparently) which would lead him unerringly to his destination.

Coban, a quaint little town in central Guatemala, was a stopping off point to my next destination, Flores, which is in the north east. Flores is a large island in the middle of a huge lake which is accessed by a causeway. This may sound reason enough to visit but the island acts as a village that houses visitors to Tikal just over an hour away. Tikal is the most important and most popular Mayan site in Central America. It has the highest temples and what sets it apart from other sites is that they tower above the thick equatorial jungle canopies which is the habitat and houses the sights and sounds of howler monkeys, toucans, parrots, and tree frogs.

In 2001 I took Ben to the huge music festival, Rock in Rio. It was a snap decision so there was a lot of last minute acquisition of gear and a crash diet on my part so as to look cool posing along Copacabana in my shades. Just before we left I was visited by an affliction due to my lifetime's habit of folding my right leg under my left while sitting on a sofa. It resulted in periodic shots of pain, like an electric shock, shooting up my right leg which led to me leaping in agony, with a simultaneous outburst of expletives. Taking this affliction to Rio was bad enough but within a few days of arriving

I developed a boil the size of a golf ball on the bottom of my left foot which meant I had to limp on tip-toe alongside the odd leap in the air, which I coloured blue. Instead of a cool swagger down Ipanema Beach, it was more of a contorted gyration, a lot like Ratso in Midnight Cowboy. Well on this trip I had brought an Achilles heel problem with me, again the right leg and I had been limping especially after a lot of walking. What had now exacerbated the situation was that the throbbing, pulsating, aggressively sensitive boil had returned, the same size and in exactly the same spot. So during the first few days in Coban I had been limping, with each foot vying for favour. However this time there had been occasions when I had turned my afflictions to my advantage.

Dave and I stayed in the same hostel in Coban where we were shacked up with Ben who was also from Portland, Oregon. In fact they discovered that they lived around the corner from each other but their paths had never crossed until that moment in central Guatemala. They were like chalk and cheese. I heard Ben before I saw him. I thought what's a loudmouth like him doing with a group of girls. I assumed he was with them because I could hear him generating the decibels from their room along the corridor. He was in fact travelling alone like Dave and I. Ben was like a smaller version of Jack Black and had that nerdy lisp that some Americans have, wore a bandanna, and boy was he loud. Coban was full of steep gradients and when Ben began enticing us to check out the local scene Dave actually did something unenthusiastically and went along while I pointed at my feet and declined.

They fell in at about two thirty. Dave explained later that Ben bought a cheap bottle of Guatemalan whiskey in a cantina, slammed it on the table roaring, Jack Black style, "Lets live man!! Dave was up at 6.30am to go caving, swim and tube in underground rivers which are part of the local attractions around Coban. Ben crashed all day on the top bunk, only Dave, out of the pair, was doing any living that day. I explained to Dave that I would have loved to have joined him but my afflictions prevented me. The real reason was my aversion to caves because of my latter day claustrophobia. Later in the day Ben dragged Dave out again to have burgers in a place he'd discovered that sold beer "at only 10 quetzales a bottle man." Again my ailments saved me. Poor old Dave had got the neighbour from hell, if not for life, certainly for the foreseeable future. Actually Ben was ok, very friendly and meant well but he just didn't realise that some people may be a tad different to him and his high octane outlook

A Bit of Slap In Tikal

The following day I bussed it to Flores about six hours further north east. Flores was a beautiful small island 600m x 400m in a huge lake served by a causeway. It was full of cobbled streets, small hotels, eateries, bars, and restaurants all serving the visitors who were there to visit Tikal, the most famous Mayan site, an hour away. Coban was at high altitude so the heat was relatively comfortable, but Flores and the surrounding area was steaming hot with high humidity levels. I was becoming to dread long bus rides because as I age I have to go for a piss seemingly on the hour, every hour. However on this occasion despite consuming copious amounts of liquid the high humidity meant that I very rarely felt nature call.

I hobbled around the Tikal site arriving back at the entrance after just over three hours. I reappeared from the jungle limping, tottering and stumbling, bathed in sweat and constantly slapping at the mosquitoes on various parts of my anatomy. The Mayan ruins are at the centre of a world heritage site and the jungle plays host to many exotic creatures, including jaguars and pumas along with parrots and toucans. The most common sights are of howler monkeys. On the way into the jungle I got chatting to a Guatemalan couple returning for a holiday as they now live in Los Angeles. He was a big boxing fan and as we were chatting about various boxers and fights we heard growling and mighty roars in the distance. We assumed it was a large cat of some kind and moved swiftly on. I discovered, subsequently, it was the sound of howler monkeys who seem to roar more than howl. Later I actually caught sight of them swinging high in the trees and some strange looking insects but not any other creatures, although I knew they were out there because the jungle sounds were as amazing as they were diverse, loud and very piercing. You can arrive at 4.00am if you choose to witness the spectacular sunrise and the jungle creatures are more visible at that time.

I travelled from Flores to Palenque in Mexico. The border crossing from Guatemala to Mexico, like that of Chile to Peru, was as enjoyable as it was unconventional. A relative handful of us were whisked through a nondescript customs building then led through jungle and undergrowth for a few hundred metres to the Rio san Pedro where small boats with outboard motors lay on the bank. The river acts as a border between the two countries. We then chugged our way down river for about fifteen minutes enjoying the sights, sounds and smells of this watery no-man's land before disembarking in Mexico. I then headed to Palenque, an ugly brash town, for an overnight stay before heading to its total antithesis, San Cristobal de las Casas.

Zapatista Revolution

San Cristobal de las Casas does just as it says on the tin or rather in the book; Lonely Planet to be precise. It says that "It's a Spanish colonial wonder." At just under 7,000′ it has a beautiful, warm spring-like climate which was a blessed relief after the heat and humidity of Flores and Palenque. They wear sweaters and jackets at night when it gets a bit chilly. San Cristobal nestles in the Jovel Valley in the south west district of Chiapas and is surrounded by mountainous cloud forests. It's very pretty with adobe hacienda type buildings, narrow cobbled streets and atmospheric plazas. Chiapas is one of the poorest areas of Mexico and is dominated by Mayan culture.

San Cristobal hit the world headlines back in 1994 when a left wing peasant group, the Zapatistas (named after the revered revolutionary Emile Zapata from the early twentieth century) stormed and occupied St. Cristobal to fight for the rights of the poor indigenous people of the area. They wore masks and handmade uniforms. In ensuing battles with government forces lives were lost on both sides. The USA offered the Mexican Government a huge amount of financial aid to put down the uprising. The leader of the Zapatistas was a pipe smoking character called Marcos. He apologised to the tourists for the inconvenience adding "but this *is* a revolution" Many advised the "elimination" of this revolutionary group. In a conciliatory move the government offered Marcos the opportunity to speak to the Mexican Congress but the eccentric and charismatic Marcos allowed a woman called Comandanta Ester the place on the podium. When it was apparent that the Zapatistas didn't seek the overthrow of the government but just sought reforms for the local indigenous people, negotiations took place and a land reform act was passed in 1996. Marcos went on to write children's books and novels. The Zapatistas still exist today as a political party but they have enjoyed their fifteen minutes of fame. Oliver Stone toyed with the idea of making a movie of those events.

I went on an excursion with a group to visit Mayan villages nearby. The tour was led by Carlos, a lively, likeable bloke in his fifties I'd guess. He was twitchy, talkative and had a habit of pulling out his comb at regular intervals to lavish attention on his crowning glory in a flamboyant manner. The expansive follicle attentive narcissists such as Kookie Burns and The Fonze were shrinking violets compared to Carlos. Skrynsey came close though. Peter Skrynes played rugby for Ladymary Sec. Mod., School under 15B team in the sixties. He had a wonderful shock of blond hair which he fashioned into an Elvis quiff and DA (ducks arse) which he kept regularly coiffured so much so that when he broke from his second row position in the scrum, looking dishevelled and covered in mud, he would procure a comb from his shorts' pocket making sure every hair was in place before moving to the next breakdown. If it wasn't for this grooming obsession, not only would have he made the first fifteen, he probably would've got a Welsh Cap. Often in assembly Sharkey (Dickensian headmaster) would badger the kids into rapt attention by comments like "Dunleavey pay attention, Coughlin stop picking your nose, Skrynes how many times have I got to tell you put your comb away!!" But there was something unique about Carlos' grooming; he didn't have any hair. He had joined the famous comb-over brigade along with members such as Gregor Fisher's, The Baldy Man, and footballers Bobby Charlton and Ralph Coates who also attempted to make a little go far.

Not Only Is Your Belch Pardoned, Your Sins Are Too!

I often find guides irritating as they tend to try too hard to impress by overwhelming their group with too much information, but Carlos was invaluable. First we stopped at the Mayan village of San Lorenzo Zinacantan. Here we experienced the usual fare of witnessing local weavers and sharing food with a local family which was enjoyable. Carlos then explained certain aspects of the local culture. Their religion was a mixture of Catholicism and Paganism. He explained that the locals pray that their souls will be cleansed then take a swig from a bottle of alcohol, usually grappa, then a swig from a bottle of coke and with its gaseous elements this provokes a burp. In doing this they belch out their sins. It's a form of confession. No telling the priest your inner most secrets, to be followed by ten Hail Marys, five Our Fathers, and three Glory Bees, just a swig of hooch, a belch and all is forgiven. Your soul is purified. Well we've all heard the adage that we are not responsible for the sins of our fathers, well pity the poor chicken in Mayan culture. As part of their faith the Mayans can offload their sins to a sacrificial chicken. They pray to God to transfer all their sins to the chicken which is then slaughtered and eaten for dinner. All this must take place in church.

With this little local knowledge we travelled to another pueblo called San Juan Chamula. This village was remarkably unique in that it was very independent and suffered outside visitors rather than welcome them. They didn't allow us to photograph them because they believed it removed at least part of their soul and people had been known to be attacked for doing so. I'd met people who had avoided the place because of this perceived hostility. Well they missed a unique experience. The people weren't hostile, especially when you bought something in the market in front of the church. It was a case of mutual respect. We visited a churchyard and prompted by Carlos we stood at a respectful distance and resisted taking photos of an interment that was taking place. Near the church there was an open casket with the dead body into which favourite objects of the deceased were being placed; not just objects apparently. Carlos explained that like many indigenous peoples around the globe some of the Mayan people had a big drink problem leading to premature deaths due to sclerosis of the liver and other alcohol related diseases. He said that often they would get so drunk that their pet dog would have to guide them home at night. Such was their reliability on their canine friend it was shot dead and placed into the casket so that it could guide its master to the pearly gates.

After wending our way through the market throng in the plaza we entered the church. It had a unique wow factor. If Spielberg made an occult movie I could imagine a scene like this, only he could never create its authenticity. The senses of sight, smell, and sound were ignited. The stone floor was covered by scented pine needles and there were thousands of lit candles of various shapes, colours, and sizes. The candles' different colours depicted the various deadly sins committed and commandments that the perpetrator had broken for which they were seeking forgiveness. There were no pews and the vast array of candles were not just down the sides but across the floor as well. The church was full of small knots of people and families squatting and standing in and around the candles. Down the sides of the church were thousands of fresh flowers surrounding large ornate statues of saints. To add to the aroma of smoke, scent and flowers was the wafting of exotic incense by two women shuffling slowly around the church. Through the smoke, incense, and penitents we could make out a distant ornate altar from which hypnotic chanting music was being emitted.

We carefully made our way towards the altar, gingerly stepping over the candles and around the penitents with their hooch and coke bottles. The altar was similar to mainstream Catholic churches with one major fundamental difference. It was dominated by three huge icons, one taking pre-eminence in the middle flanked by two others. The crucified Christ with its typical gruesome Catholic violence was on the right, Mary Magdalene was on the left, but numero uno and centre stage in this Mayan culture was reserved for John the Baptist who, because he baptised Jesus, had the highest status. In front of the altar, the source of the repetitive mesmerizing music, was three blokes who were playing a drum, guitar and an accordion respectively. Amongst the group in front of the altar was a small Indian woman, wrinkled and gnarled from the sun, a hard life and maybe drink, chanting trance-like with her three teenage children. She was holding a very passive hen. Carlos explained that the hen would have its neck rung shortly when the mother was confident

late at night they asked me to walk them to their hotel. During our conversations I often had to quell their fears about the perceived dangers of the area. I think they saw me as wise, mature and felt safe in my company; poor deluded girls. During the third and last leg of our trip we stopped at Panajachel to drop off some and pick up others. One of the new passengers was such a weird and startling character that it was difficult not to stare. He was a white man, over six feet tall, aged about sixty, American (which we discovered subsequently) and sported an impressive head of white hair in dreadlocks. He wore what can only be described as a shaggy pelted loin cloth, carried a staff and was barefoot. He looked like a more robust but haggard Mahatma Gandhi. He was covered with hippy regalia and object d'art dangled from various parts of his body. His state of undress and lack of baggage was worrying because it could get quite chilly and stormy some nights in that neck of the woods.

He sat at the back of the bus with us so I did my best to engaged him in conversation. His skin was cracked and parched and his voice was shot to hell. He was a disciple of Dr. Timothy Leary the self proclaimed leader of the sixties counter-culture movement who has been immortalised through his much quoted proclamation "Turn on, Tune in, and Drop out" and who advocated mind altering drugs like LSD. Our aged hippy friend attended many of Dr. Leary's lectures and seminars in the sixties. We also discovered that until recently he had been living in India and had spent time in Kathmandu. I was hoping to bump into him around town and share a few beers, but it didn't happen. Another new passenger was a 30 year old Dutch woman who had been living in Guatemala City for five years. She worked in some kind of development capacity and was employed by the Dutch government. I asked about the threat to a single blonde woman living in one of the most dangerous cities in the world. She explained as part of her job she worked in the most dangerous parts of the city, and as the people knew her and what she and others were attempting to do they left her alone. She laid the blame for the violence squarely with the Guatemalan government, police, and military who she claimed were totally corrupt.

Panajachel overlooked the Lago de Atitilan and as we drove away up the steep winding road we became agog at the scene leaving us over our shoulders. The village sat on the edge of the lake and two volcanoes bestrode it like the wings of a perched giant bird of prey. To add to the dramatic panorama it was dusk which gave an overall grey sepia affect with thin grey swirling clouds wrapping themselves around the volcanoes like delicate chiffon scarves. Mother nature had provided some wonderful scenes over the previous weeks but this was her masterpiece.

Antigua was like San Cristobal de las Casas but with bells on. It had even more ambiance and the streets were quainter, more cobbled and as a backdrop there was a towering volcano with two others at the other end of town. Wandering these cobbled streets on the first glorious morning I bumped into Onka and Jennifer. We chatted about our immediate plans. They were intent on going to a coffee farm and I had just booked a trip to climb an active volcano. Again they were wary of the dangers. Lonely Planet had described incidents of robbery and rape in the area. Also it had stated that some foolhardy climbers had their shoes burned away suffering serious injuries and that some had actually been killed during the sporadic eruptions that take place. I convinced them to change their minds with my final gambit being "What do you want to tell your kids, you went a coffee farm or you climbed an active volcano?"

We met at 6.00am the following morning. Volcan Pacaya was an hour away by bus. In fact the bus gets you to a sort of base camp where you then climb the last leg. The climb took about an hour and half led up by a guide. They also had horses for the aged, infirm or the generally unfit. My boil had disappeared days previously but I had concerns about my heel and I thought my back would give me problems. Conversely I had great confidence in my legs and lungs that I considered were as strong as a man half my age. I mentioned this to the girls when they suggested I go up on horseback, supporting my case by regaling them of my recent exploits playing seven-a-side touch rugby. There was a gathering of locals with their horses for hire and for some reason they began to head in my direction, so bending my elbows to flex my muscles I sent them away with a flea in their respective ears. We began the ascent which was very steep at first over rough terrain and then the slope became gentler then increased again before we had our first breather. Well my heel was ok and my back was holding up, however my legs were like jelly and I was breathing so heavily that my cheeks were blowing like Dizzie Gillespie's hitting a high note. I persevered hoping to get my second wind. Along the way we passed the locals with their horses looking to provide some profitable assistance to those in distress. When they saw me appear around a corner they were stirred from their stupor and began jockeying (pun intended) for position. But was I a quitter? No!!, well not until the next bend when I saw a prolonged steep incline.

I had tottered and stumbled upwards until I could totter and stumble no more. At that moment I felt a certain affinity with Richard III and with great Shakespearean eloquence I mumbled under my breath. "A horse! a horse! will some fucker get me a horse?" As I turned the next bend, through the sweat that had dripped into my eyes I could see a vision of a shimmering Galadreil holding the golden reins of the mighty Shadowfax. When I wiped away the sweat it was, in fact, a local woman pulling an old nag with piece of string. She didn't have to ask. Now I'd ridden a few elephants and camels in my time but couldn't remember ever going near a horse. Having seen the aging and overweight John Wayne slipping effortlessly into the saddle in True Grit I assumed it was a piece of cake. My short Celtic legs didn't help. Getting my left foot into the stirrup was difficult enough, but my casual, languid, and rather dignified effort to swing my leg over resulted in me kicking the horse up the arse. Obviously more commitment, energy and umph were required. So with a much more determined effort I swung my leg over, which created so much interia that I came close to going straight over the other side, a feat managed by every slapstick comedian since the silent movies. For a full ten seconds I was at the two o'clock position holding on with my ever whitening knuckles before I managed to right myself. It was touch and go. Humiliation heaped upon humiliation. Fortunately this scenario had taken place between groups of climbers who were concealed behind bends at the front and back of me. I was then led around the bend where my group was waiting for me to catch up. I was then paraded through them. There were some, including Onka and Jennifer, with a benign "it's for the best luv" smiles, looks of relief as some were concerned about my wellbeing, others worried that they may have had to give me this kiss of life if I hadn't capitulated, and a few "I told you sos." Most were young but there were a few older ones, including a few flushed middle aged out-of-shape women, who were hacking it. This was the moment I shook hands with my own mortality.

There was temporary release from my feeling of failure when we reached the top as the spectacular panoramic view revealed itself. People were clambering over the waves of solidified lava and the backdrop landscape from on high was Claudian, with Guatemala City off in the distance. Then looking up through the ever changing cloud patterns which added to the overall effect we could see the billowing smoke from the summit of the volcano. When making our way across the lava we could feel the heat being emitted through our footwear so much so that at one stage we toasted marshmallows. I managed to get back down using Shank's pony.

In the evening I wandered into a lively bar/restaurant which seemed quite anglicised. They also sold bottles of Guinness, and then I realized it was called O'Reilly's Bar. I'm sure that if I ever landed on the Sea of Tranquillity there would be an Irish theme pub there to offer their hospitality. I can't complain though as I had delicious and fortifying Irish stew.

Later I moseyed into another bar. There were a few people dotted around and a couple playing pool. The bar itself was long with about a dozen vacant bar stools and I slid onto one of the central ones slipping into my Humphrey Bogart "Gimme a beer Mack" mode. After a while, leaving my beer on the bar and jacket on the stool, I went to the toilet. When I returned a bloke had sat right next to my stool. I thought, "of all the bar stools in all the gin-joints he had to sit right next to mine". I sat down after shifting my stool away a bit so that we weren't actually touching. We both sat in silence although he spoke to the barman in Spanish occasionally. From my sly glances and reflections in the bar mirror his mannerisms convinced me he was gay. He was short, looked seedy and crumpled, reminding me of a rather dishevelled Roman Polanski. Then he turned to me and started chatting. In a perverse way I thought at least I'm still an object of someone's desire. Lacking subtlety I put him in the picture by mentioning my three ex-wives, six children, and my life in the construction business. I needn't have been concerned because for the next couple of hours and with the consumption of many drinks, me and Dave hit it off big-time.

He was American and currently lived in the beautiful Panajachel I mentioned earlier. He was well travelled and had a great sense of history to go along with his geographical escapades. Our politics, outlook, and sense of humour were so similar. He also gave me some interesting information that made me alter my itinerary slightly. It regarded Esteli in northern Nicaragua which was a Sandinista stronghold in the 80's and he told me it was well worth a visit. It was carpet bombed by Somosa's army and attacked by the Contras, financed by Reagan's illegal funding organized by Oliver North. Dave also identified the seat in a hotel in Honduras where North plotted illegal arms deals that resulted in the Irangate scandal. We bade our farewells with a another firm handshake adding to the list. I think pecks on the cheek from Onka and Jennifer counted too.

Copas Ruinas sat just across the border in Honduras and was almost totally concealed in the beautiful mountain forests. Not long after I arrived I took a picture from a vantage point overlooking the pueblo where I could just make out the top of the church and a few red tiled rooftops in the one and only plaza amongst the luxuriant foliage of this delightful little retreat,

TGA By Any Other Name Would Smell

A rose by any other name would smell as sweet. Well that satisfies one of the senses but how about sound? If roses were called sticklebacks or reptilians wouldn't some of the effect be lost? Would Ford have sold as many Mustangs if they were called the Ford Insipid? I don't think so. I'm sorry, as much a fan as I am of The Bard he hasn't fully grasped the point. Johnny Cash emphasises this point by suggesting that having a name like Steve is more preferential than Sue if you're a bloke. Names, especially place names have a resonance with the human imagination and played an important and almost inspirational role in my early life. Like most kids in the fifties I was cowboy mad which is hardly surprising considering the amount of westerns that were on TV and in the movies. The Range Rider, Bronco Lane, Cheyenne Bodie, Sugarfoot, Wagon Train etc . . . My favourite film was "The Fastest Gun Alive" with Glenn Ford and Broderick Crawford as the bad guy, plus the likes of Audie Murphy, Gary Cooper, and Richard Wydmark also mesmerised from the silver screen.

It was the beginning of my, and probably a lot of others', love affair with all things American. Places like Wyoming, El Paso, New Mexico, Colorado, Utah, Montana, The Rio Grande and the place I would have exchanged eternal happiness in heaven for (and this from a devout Catholic boy)—Arizona. I may have grown out the cowboy phase but at the same time I watched the black and white movies of thirties and forties especially the exciting scary roaring twenties gangster movies involving still great favourites of mine, James Cagney, Edward G. Robinson, George Raft and of course Bogie. In my early teens I, along with a couple of my peers, used to ridicule Britain's grey conservative austerity compared with the exciting colourful flamboyance of the USA. They had Elvis we had Cliff; they had JFK and we had Macmillan and the Montgomery Burns look-alike, Alec Douglas Hume. And of course the names, like Chuck Berry who sang about Memphis Tennessee, Sinatra found Chicago and New York his kind of towns, and Tony Bennett lost his heart Frisco. What did we have? . . . . Bud Flanagan singing "Maybe it's because I'm I Londoner", pathetic. Where were the British names that could inspire songwriters? 24 hours from Cleethorpes?, I left my heart in Bognor Regis? Even the Beatles had to sing about Kansas City and probably hadn't clue where it was at the time.

One of the areas that we studied in Geography at school in the early sixties was South America. The images were of the driest deserts, the highest volcanoes, amazing lakes, shifting glaciers, and the densest jungles along with huge spiders, boa constrictors and the like. But did they have the names to match?—with a vengeance. Cotopaxi, Titicaca, The Amazon, La Paz, Quito, Rio, Montevideo, Buenos Aires, and Santiago to mention a few. The imagination ran rife. Because of all this I was very good at place names around the world and my knowledge of capitals was always pretty comprehensive even in primary school.

The reason I mention all this is that I have discovered a couple of anomalies in Central America. The physical and political nature of Central America could not be more exotic, volatile, and tempestuous, forever verging on, or involving in, natural and human violence that seems to be the raison d'etre of these banana republics. Belize has a Caribbean coastline so Reggae, Creole, and Rasta influences add to its other Central American attributes. It has a history of piracy and Captain Henry Morgan pillaged and ransacked the old capital, Belize City, but did not cause as much damage as Hurricane Hattie in the sixties which more or less wiped out the city so much so that a new capital was built further in land. I didn't know the name of the new capital, which was hardly surprising as it had been named . . . BELMOPAN. What?!!. It sounds like a commode room-service for an hotel chain. The only reason I can surmise, is that Belize was British Honduras at the time before Independence in 1981 and today still has the Queen on their postage stamps, so maybe a committee of bowler-hatted Reginald Molehusbands from the Foreign Office were responsible.

The capital of Honduras had also escaped my attention which again is not surprising as it's a five syllable tongue-twisting inappropriate monstrosity called Tegucigalpa (Te-goo-see-gal-pa). I spent an inordinate amount of time trying to master and remember it, but then someone out of the blue ask me where I was heading and I would reply umm. umm Tag . . . . umm. umm, . . . the capital. Linguists have spent less time mastering ancient Sanskrit. I shall now refer to the capital of Honduras using the abbreviation that was printed on my bag label, TGA.

After Guatemala City I had spent several weeks in a beauty competition going from one safe picturesque village to another in Guatemala and Mexico, now I was heading to TGA so it was nitty-gritty time again. For the first half of my trip everything had gone very smoothly which was amazing considering my ability to self-destruct and some of the dodgy places I'd visited. I encountered the first hitches in attempting to travel from Copan Ruinas to TGA. I, along with others, arrived to catch the 9.00am bus and were told that it wouldn't arrive until 2.00pm. The reason given, which turned out to be genuine, was that there was a political demonstration on the Guatemalan side of the border preventing crossings and the buses had to pick up stranded passengers.

The bus actually arrived at 3.30pm. In the meantime I had several conversations, including one with a Honduran chef, who worked in New York City. Lonely Planet stated that the up market district of TGA called Colonia Palmira was generally safe. Downtown was OK in the day but dangerous at night and where the bus station was located, Comayaguela, was just plain dangerous. Bus stations throughout Latin America always seem to be located in gangland areas. It's a chicken and egg situation. Do the dastardly hombres find a habitat where there is a sufficient supply of prey to sustain them or do the bus companies seek out the cheapest real estate, and which came first?

Because of the lateness of the bus it meant that I would arrive at about 11.00 pm on a Saturday night without a hotel reservation. But that would be OK, I'd just get a taxi to the hotel area. However the New York chef said to make sure I write down the taxi's number and ensure the driver is aware as some of them cannot be trusted. He strongly advised me to postponed my journey so I arrived in daylight. Someone else said that if you pay before getting your bags out of the car or boot they will drive off; no worries then. Most of the passengers were getting off at St. Pedro Sula about half way to TGA, so I couldn't rely on the safety of numbers. I made an executive decision to transfer my ticket to 5.00am the following morning. This did not go without a hitch as two hours into the journey there was a hold up (traffic not guns) because a tanker had overturned and caught fire. There were rumours of a stoppage of between one and six hours but we were back on our way within two. The stoppage left us near a roadside cafe which provided an opportunity to have the breakfast we missed because of the early start and to have an enjoyable chat amongst a group of Italian, Spanish, and Americans passengers.

The extra night in Copas Ruinas turned out to be a lively affair. I noticed during the day that scaffolding and platforms were being erected and streets had been cordoned off. I thought it was to be a night market, but it turned out to be a stage for rock bands. There was also a Harley Davidson rally with scores of choppers and greasers in town with some serious partying. All this seemed rather incongruous as this was a sleepy little village in the middle of nowhere. Getting up at 4.00am the following morning wasn't easy.

Arriving in TGA in daylight wasn't plain sailing as I was taken by a young macho taxi driver on the scenic route through some run down barrios to a hotel downtown that I had selected. I lodged my objections and pointed him in the right direction. I knew he was ripping me off, and he knew that I knew he was ripping me off. I paid him the $15 fare which turned out to be twice the correct amount. I was philosophical as I was aware during this detour that he may have driven to an alley where he could have introduced me to some of his amigos. Ten minutes later I was ensconced in a very comfortable room with cable TV, free Internet and coffee, plus the bonus of a rare commodity, a power shower, all for $16.00 per night.

Backpacking, especially in Latin America, has done wonders for my patience in recent years. Even when told about the five hour bus delay in Copas Ruinas, unlike some younger travellers who became quite irate and demanded compensation, I, along with most others just shrugged our shoulders and I took the opportunity to finish the book I was reading.

The Hotel Granada desk was "manned" by two large, formidable middle aged black women: The early shift and the late shift. At first they were unsmiling and uncompromising. The early shift woman was from the Caribbean side of the country, spoke English in a Jamaican accent and reminded me of Lenny Henry's impression of his mother, strict and maternal. I found the formula though, which was to tickle their fancy, make them laugh and after that they were putty in my hands.

TGA was a polluted, gridlocked mess which can describe many cities and capitals in Latin America. But the chaos is part of its charm especially if, like me, you don't have to get anywhere quickly. I spent

271

some time in the main plaza where they had their version of Speaker's Corner and I saw several individuals pontificating to mixed reviews from their respective audiences. It was reassuring to witness such freedom of speech in what I thought would be a typical repressive banana republic. However about a year later the elected president was run out of town by the military and is now in exile; a case of reverting to type. Because of urbanisation new shanty barrios were spreading up the sides of the mountains and volcanoes that surround TGA. Apparently the barrios are a fine example of enterprise, and social mobility. The new arrivals from the countryside build homes from scrap metal, cardboard and alike. After earning some cash in the capital they upgrade to wood, then stone and masonry, which was all very admirable. I spent an extra day in TGA because of the comforts of the hotel, to chill, the power shower, and get my clothes laundered. Next stop Leon in Nicaragua.

Brothers in Arms

Quoting St. Francis of Assisi Margaret Thatcher heralded her landslide election victory with the words "Where there is discord let us bring harmony, where there is despair let us bring hope". She then entered upon a pre-planned, premeditated attack on the most vulnerable members of society using legislation, the judiciary, such as the anti-union Lord Denning, the police, powerful media moguls, sinister national and international right wing organisations and most of all her own intractable iron will to destroy the rights and ultimately the will of the working class. The country was polarised into the go-getting haves of the city along with big business and the growing politically created unemployed have-nots. She created a north-south divide by destroying industrialised areas in the Midlands and the

North. Within a short space of time Toxteth in Liverpool was in flames, and other inner-city areas were rioting.

I was involved with her first serious attack on the unions as she, along with her trusted hit-man Norman "Count Dracula" Tebbit, also described as an untrained pole cat by Dennis Healey, had prepared for battle by creating draconian anti-union legislation. In 1983 they set out to smash the print unions. Yours truly was involved in the battle of Wapping, and volunteered as a flying picket, receiving calls in the early hours to be collected at secret destinations then driven at breakneck speed to some place in Somerset or Gloucester to prevent trucks with newsprint exiting or entering premises. There were many demos in London and Cheltenham GCHQ where unions had been banned by Thatcher. Of course the following year was the historic twelve month miners' strike orchestrated by Thatcher and which still divides communities and families to this day.

Political opposition was in disarray and union leaders, for the most part, were running scared. But there was a little oasis in this desert of despair, Saturday Night Live. Harry Enfield exposed the shallowness of Thatcher's go-getting society with his Loadsofmoney character but it was the besequined Ben Elton's weekly and brilliantly funny rants against all things "Thatch" that helped us unleash our pent-up frustrations by hooting and roaring him on. After a long, loud, word perfect delivery of wonderful comic timing he always finished with "A little bit of politics there, Ladies and Gentlemen". Then we would wake up Monday morning ready for a good right wing kicking. However the reason I regularly found myself incandescent with rage, pounding my fists on tables and screaming abuse at the TV, had little to do with the events taking place in Britain, it was the abuses of power and the scandalous injustices taking place in Nicaragua.

The Somoza family, much like the Duvalier family in Haiti, had for decades and generations used their control of the military to terrorise the population into poverty and subjugation and bled the country dry. The response to opposition was torture, imprisonment, and death. Such military dictatorships were either ignored by the West for Cold War expediency or supported financially and militarily by the USA in particular. In 1972 there was a massive earthquake in the capital Managua leaving 5,000 dead 20,000 injured and 250,000 homeless. 80% of the buildings were damaged. A huge amount of international financial aid was sent. Somoza diverted most of it into his own coffers causing further deaths and suffering. This galvanised a lot of support for the burgeoning Sandinista guerrilla movement. By 1979 after a series of military victories against the US backed Somoza National Guard the Sandinistas were marching on the capital Managua and Somoza fled to Paraguay.

Despite the fact that Somoza had left the economy and infrastructure in tatters the new revolutionary government set about the most radical programme of social and economic reform. Not only did the leader Daniel Ortega receive financial aid from the USSR but Jimmy Carter sent $US75 million to help this ambitious program. Within a short space of time the infant mortality rate was reduced dramatically, and an education programme, which saw teachers sent into the countryside to reach out and educate all members of society, resulted in the literacy rate increasing many fold in an effort to achieve the aim of a fully educated population. Wealth and land distribution programmes were also embarked upon. Gender equality on a scale still being sought in the West was also attained. Although based on a socialist ideology the constitution stated a policy of non alignment. Nicaragua was and still is a strongly independent Catholic country. It would seem that the promised land had been reached and all of the sacrifices and deaths of so many young Sandinistas were worth the pain and suffering.

Tragically following Thatcher's election she was joined by right wing bible punching simpleton Ronald Reagan having his strings pulled by far more sinister characters behind the scenes. A popular effective egalitarian socialist government could be a template for other Latin American countries wishing to rid themselves of US backed military dictatorships, so it had to be nipped in the bud. Using the ex-members of Somoza's hated National Guard and with heavy CIA involvement the Reagan administration financed a counter-revolutionary force (The Contras) to overthrow the new popular Sandinista government. The US even attempted to sabotage Nicaraguan ships in their own docks and was severely reprimanded by The International Court of Justice. Apart from financing a potential invasion force of Contras from inside Honduras the USA set up a blockade in an effort to bankrupt the country. All this was enthusiastically supported by the Thatcher government. In 1985 the US government refused Reagan further aid to the Contras. The Sandinistas had been democratically re-elected again a year earlier. However Reagan ignored his own government and organised by Oliver North, another evangelical bigot, siphoned funds illegally from arms sold to Iran. Known as the Iran-Contra affair it should have meant Reagan going the same way as Nixon and North doing time in a penitentiary. Of course neither happened.

The Catholic Church played a significant role in these dramatic events. On the ground Nicaraguan Catholic priests not only supported the Sandinistas but in some cases held government positions. The hierarchy and the establishment were highly critical of the involvement of priests in politics. Pope John Paul II made an infamous visit to Nicaragua during the height of the Contra onslaught in 1983. At the airport in Managua he was presented to a long row of priests who knelt and kissed his ring in turn. When he came to Fr. Ernesto Cardenal, a Sandinista minister, he publicly berated and humiliated him for his political involvement in front of the watching world. The irony and barefaced hypocrisy was that the Pope at the time was commuting to Poland regularly to effect regime change there and secretly funding Lech Walesa's Solidarity.

A few days later there was a huge open-air mass in the main plaza in Managua. There was a massive congregation. Now we're all aware of the Pope's annual Easter message from Rome. He always makes a meaningless, ineffectual, generalised message for peace. He must say "Peace be with you" a hundred times a day. On this particular day all the congregation of devout Catholics wanted, was him to mention the word "Peace" and he refused. In this instance as the only violent aggressors were the Contras it would have meant something and would sent a powerful message to the US government. The crowd became restless and began chanting "Peace", "Peace." Also seventeen teenagers, ambushed and killed by the Contras, were buried the previous day and the funeral service was on the same same spot as the Pope's mass. The mothers were given a prominent position and cries could be heard for the Pope to acknowledge their loss and say a prayer for them. Again he refused. Sensing the disquiet in the crowd and in the increase in volume of the chanting the Pope lost his cool and angrily commanded them to "Shut up!" and "Be quiet!", but the opposition to his position continued. The mass ended in a shambolic manner before communion was completed. By refusing to mention the word peace the Pope endorsed the murderous Contra attackers and gave support to Reagan to violently overthrow a democratically elected government and replace it with a military dictatorship.

Now I've always opposed the death penalty, but on this occasion I'll make an exception for members of the Somoza family. The Sandinistas were so named after Augusto C. Sandino, a cult figure in Nicaraguan history. During the 20's and 30's he led a guerrilla war against the occupying US forces and although often outnumbered and outgunned he proved to be an elusive fighter and was never caught. Eventually the Americans left, mainly due to financial considerations after the Wall Street crash. The head of what was, unfortunately, to become a Somoza dynasty, Eduardo, then a general invited Sandino for peace talks and to plan for the post American era. However he bushwhacked Sandino having him assassinated as he left the meeting. It took a long time but that act of treachery was avenged two decades later in 1956. A Nicaraguan poet, Rigoberto Lopez Perez, prophesied Somoza's demise in one his poems before surreptitiously obtaining employment as waiter at a function attended by Somoza. At an opportune moment he produced a pistol and shot Somoza dead, signing his own death warrant in the process as he died in a hail of Somoza's henchmen's bullets. He was just twenty six. This happened across the road from where I stayed in Leon.

I was aware of Eduardo Somoza's son, the exiled Anastasio Somoza, was avenged about a year after he fled to Paraguay in 1979. I always assumed that he was shot at traffic lights in the capital, Asuncion. I was corrected by Lucian, a young American graduate, who had been volunteering for the Peace Corps in the area. Apparently Somoza was driving a bullet-proof Mercedes so what actually happened was that a Sandinista assassination squad appeared in front of his limo and blew the car up with a Bazooka . . . even better.

As a group of us clambered off the bus on the outskirts of Leon I think we all felt a good vibe as we headed towards our chosen abodes. I stayed at an attractive, relaxed place aptly called Lazybones. It had a large central courtyard surrounded by lush flora and comfortable lounge areas including hammocks. At the back was a pool and a small bar which was also used to serve breakfast. Leon had a beautiful main plaza with the biggest church in Central America. The church was great fun, as apart from being an imposing and magnificent cathedral, you were allowed, not only to wander around at will and take photos, but clamber around on the roof and in the bell towers which had great vistas of the town and surrounding volcanoes. Leon was a loyal Sandinista town and it wasn't long before I was in the Sandinista museum. It was run by wounded ex-freedom fighters who were now middle-aged and beyond. The museum was mainly old newspaper cuttings and pictures of the fallen. I was greeted warmly by the man at reception who rose from his seat and limped as he guided me towards the main entrance. I have regretted my lack of Spanish often, but not as badly as this day. I think I managed to convey my solidarity with the men and women I met, some of whom showed me their war wounds. There were also murals in the plaza depicting the events of 1979 and beyond. I visited the building (just across the road from Lazybones) where the young poet Perez assassinated the original Somoza in 1956, before being slain.

I left Leon for a few days to visit Esteli three hours away over a very bad road. This is the place where Dave, who I chatted with in a bar in Antigua, suggested I visit as it played a major role in the revolution and the defence of it. During those crucial days many internationalist supporters gathered in Esteli. It is close to the Honduran border, and was carpet bombed by Somoza's, US backed, National Guard and later the Contras. Here I visited the Galeria de Heroes y Martires which exhibited photos, little shrines and clothes of the young men and women who fought and died liberating their country. The Galaeria is run by the mothers of the martyrs and is a very emotive place, as it's the mothers who are left and suffer the most.

I also visited a Sandinista bar. It was a large place with a stage and speakers. Unfortunately there were only a handful of drinkers there as it was midweek afternoon. I was informed that live music was planned for the Saturday. The place was bedecked with Sandinista paraphernalia with much anti-American sentiments. Despite this, a group of young men from the USA were treated with great hospitality amongst the insults that hung from the walls. In the foyer there was a collection of weaponry from the war, just for good measure.

While checking some facts on different websites I read that Thatcher tried to ban the word Sandinista. Well this was news to me, although she had banned so many other democratic institutions in Britain. Another fact of which I was unaware was that there was more opposition in those days than I realised. For example The Clash recorded a triple album called Sandinista! in their honour.

Good ol' Joe Strummer who I'm sure is resting more peacefully than the aforementioned right wing zealots.

Laid Waste in Granada

I caught a chicken bus from Leon to Managua with the intention of grabbing a cab to another bus station across the city to travel on to Granada. Most cities in Latin America have many bus stations catering for the plethora of bus companies serving various destinations. It can be a pain especially when you're loaded up. But as I was alighting the chicken bus a rather large gentleman bellowed into my ear "Granada?" Within a thrice, after being bundled into a minibus shuttle with my backpack and rucksack taking up the last available seat, I was heading for Granada. The reason I didn't spend time in the capital was that apparently there was nothing of aesthetic value to attract a stop-over. After the devastating earthquake of 1972 there had been very little restoration. This was on top of the carnage caused by another huge earthquake in the thirties and another was imminent. The reason the old city was inundated with gutted buildings and rubble was that it was regarded as pointless to rebuild it to its former glory because the chances of further earthquakes are so great. This was another reason to hightail it out of town.

I was also really looking forward to Granada as Lonely Planet was very complimentary about "The Goose that laid Nicaragua's tourism's golden egg" and "the high point of many travellers' trip to Central America" also being a "trip maker" in its own right. Well it didn't do it for me. I can understand the eulogising as the place was in pristine condition because the buildings seemed brand new and they must give them a lick of paint every other week. It wasn't just me, as others described the place as a large wedding cake. The centre of Grenada had perfect symmetry, seemed very contrived and rather kitsch. As in medieval European cities colonial communities in Latin America have their splendour caught up with history. I've visited so many interesting places that have been described with the well coined phrase "fading colonial grandeur" but with Granada the buildings were relatively new and they weren't allowing them to fade. I blame William Walker. Two names seem to dominate the history of certain countries in Central America, Captain Henry Morgan, who was born in Llanrumney Hall (which ended up as a pub on a council estate two hundred metres from where I used to live) and Mr. Walker. What amazing characters they were and what devastation they caused. During the mid nineteenth century the adventurer and filibuster (also doctor, lawyer and journalist) William Walker, from Tennessee of Scottish decent, became, by default, President of Nicaragua before being ejected. On one of his other numerous attempts to find fame and fortune in Central America he was hired by the great and the good of Leon to attack Granada. An obvious devotee of scorched earth policy he burned Granada to the ground on leaving in 1856. Later during another adventurous quest in Central America the British Navy handed him over to the Hondurans who executed him in Trulillo in 1860 where he is now buried. Incredibly he was only thirty six years old. So hence the lack of faded colonial charm.

My fellow compatriot and near neighbour, Captain Morgan, was a seventeenth century pirate and adventurer in the mould of Sir Walter Raleigh, and particularly wreaked havoc in Belize and Panama. He shared his plunder with the monarch, was knighted for his services and was the only one of the trio not to come to a sticky end, living out a full life on his substantial booty.

Granada is near the massive Lake Nicaragua, but despite this I experienced a most oppressive and debilitating heat and humidity. I spent four days shuffling and flopping. I lay on my bed with a fan in my face as the sweat bubbled out of every pore. Even my legs were streaming with sweat. Coincidentally I received an e-mail from

Donna while I was there who had just caught up with my blog. She had taught in many weird and wonderful places, including Granada, and said it was the hottest place she's ever experienced. I doubt if it was much above 30c but it was that kind of heat that drains every ounce of energy.

There was one main highlight though and that was bumping into the phlegmatic Robert again. I first met him in Lazybones in Leon, and our paths crossed a few times after that. Each time he was either dozing in a hammock, sleeping it off, slouched on a sofa with a beer, or with his feet upon a table holding court outside a bar. I'd yet to see him walk. If we meet again, I will walk into a bar and he will be slouched in a corner chatting with whoever: I just know the roles won't be reversed. I saw George Melly, the jazz singer and art critic, perform on several occasions. Often advertised as the Decadent George Melly, he would be carried on stage by his band, lounging on a chaise-long, a cocktail in one hand and a cigarette holder in the other. I could imagine Robert wheeled into a bar in similar fashion. He was forty and had been travelling South and Central America for three years after splitting from his girlfriend, giving up his job and selling his apartment. He was seeking solace from his loss in travel like me. We had a few beers one afternoon in Lazybones with my first impression of him being that of a lounge lizard as he often paused mid syllable for a lecherous leer over my shoulder to give the new female backpacker arrivals the once over. He was slim and gaunt, reminding me of a forty year old Peter O'Toole. He was great company and often I found myself involved in a battle of wits as serious subjects were broached and he was always interested in pushing the boundaries of arguments and debates. He also had a great sense of humour, was extremely bright and informed.

While absentmindedly sauntering up the street heading for a restaurant I heard my name called. Robert was sat at a roadside table, feet up, drink in hand with a stunning female companion. She was an American named Anne and apart from being gorgeous was extremely bright. The first thing she did was translate the political message on my Zapatesta T-shirt. They were drinking black rum on the rocks from a bottle they had just bought. I stuck with beer as I was leaving for San Jose at 5.00am the following morning. Again I enjoyed the funny and provocative banter while the pair of them got slowly pissed. He was also a football fan and got quite excited about the 1978 World Cup which we discussed and argued about at length. As a ten year old it was his first "conscious" tournament, grabbing his imagination and leaving such a lasting impression that the highlight of his trip so far, covering three years, was going to the River Plate stadium, the scene of the 1978 final. We both shared vivid recollections of Mario Kempes scoring Argentina's extra-time winners against perennial runners-up, Holland. Realising for the first time the final was played at the Estadio Monumental added lustre to my experience of watching River Plate there two and a half years previously.

Most of the travellers I'd met shared my opinion of Costa Rica, which is a country you have to travel through to get to Panama or Nicaragua. The irony of course is that it has the most developed tourist industry in Central America. Hence it's full of tourists and has a touch of Miami or Jamaica about it. I spent three uneventful, wet days in the capital San Jose but I did plan to visit a nearby volcano. This one I didn't have to climb as the bus took tourists to a visitor's centre where a path, even I could manage, lead to a platform that overlooked the crater. Apparently it's spectacular. Unfortunately it hardly stopped raining all the time I was in San Jose, so my plans were washed out. I fully expected San Jose to be quite modern and trendy compared to the other capitals but it was quite a drab place with little to recommend it.

Colon: A Critique

After a very long bus journey and with an inordinate amount of ham and cheese sandwiches consumed I arrived back in Panama City staying in the Casco Viejo area again. However this time I opted for the more comfortable and subdued Hospedaje Casco Viejo rather than the more raucous and uncomfortable Lunas Castle.

My plan, for what seemed an attractive excursion, had been stymied after referring to my Lonely Planet. A "luxury" glass topped train journey which followed the Panama Canal from the Pacific to the Caribbean through dense jungle crossing the canal several times was to be a must, until I read about its destination. The end of the line, being on the Caribbean side of the country, would've been an appropriate finishing touch as I'd more or less hugged the Pacific coast for the previous six weeks. The fly in the ointment was that the destination was Colon.

Colon was aptly named as it was the closest place you could get to a shit hole. Here are some of Lonely Planet's descriptions of it. "The mere mention of Colon sends shivers down the spines of hardened travellers and Panamanians alike" "The city had spiralled into the depths of depravity" "Simply put, Panama's most notorious city is a sprawling slum with desperate human existence." It goes on "Colon is a dangerous slum" and "crime is a serious problem even during daylight" Now I thought that when I arrived at Colon I'd dive into a taxi and head for a place of interest such as a botanical garden or museum. Lonely Planet always has a "Places of interest" for each place it describes no matter how small or insignificant, except for Colon, there weren't any. The train arrived in Colon at 9.00am and left at 5.30pm. So what one is supposed to do in the meantime, no suggestions were offered. I had visions of being curled up in a ball in the corner of the platform hoping nobody would notice me for eight hours.

On my last night in Central America during an impromptu party in the guesthouse I got chatting to a large Swedish man in his thirties who did the Colon trip. He said a few minutes after he left the Colon station a concerned local woman stopped him and told him, for his own safety, to get out of town. He hired a taxi to a nearby village where he kicked his heels for seven long hours. At this soirée were a group of European students who had spent the previous weekend in Caracas, Venezuala. They informed us that during those three days there had been fifty seven murders, so I assumed that Guatemala City had lost its title of the most dangerous city in the world.

New York, New York, My Kinda Town

Although I was delayed for four hours at Newark (New Jersey) Airport on the way in I'd never had any problems caused by the likes of strikes, or volcanic ash that had seriously inconvenienced others. My flights, and there had now been many over the years, had been problem free. On this particular trip we broke up from school on the Friday and I was heading across the Atlantic on the Saturday. I was now scheduled to arrive back six weeks later on the Saturday before the term began on the Monday. I fully expected to arrive home on Saturday evening just in time for Match of the Day with my fish and chips TV dinner. Unfortunately the two and half hour leeway for my connection from Newark wasn't enough, especially as we arrived late from Panama City. The baggage collection at this particular airport was the slowest I'd ever experienced. On the way in, especially after a four hour delay, I had plenty of time to relax and witness the chaotic transit area of Newark. Passengers, faces contorted with anxiety, shoes in hand, were frantically dragging their baggage towards their connections and often foolishly arguing with unsympathetic po-faced airport officials and security staff who held up their progress.

I was now experiencing this nightmare. Tension and exasperation pushed my patience to the limit as the USA, with their unique draconian transit regulations, insist we collect our baggage and go back through customs and passport control. I arrived at the Continental Airways transit desk gasping and bent double, being loaded down with my backpack and carrying my shoes. The Continental desk clerk, a young, stern woman with an accusing demeanour in a broad New Jersey accent, snapped "Your Late!!" Before I could catch my breath and respond she added haughtily "You've missed it, the gate closed half an hour go" I snapped back "You seem to be implying the fault is mine; it was your incompetent airline and airport regulations that delayed us!!" I had become aware that the woman stood next to me was in the same boat, well plane, as me. I also quickly realised that I had better tone it down as I was relying on this tough New Jersey broad to get me out of this situation and rearrange my flight. With the realisation that the fault was the airline's her attitude altered not a bit and without hint of an apology or a glimmer of courtesy she rescheduled our flight for 7.00pm the following evening, gave us vouchers and instructions to travel to the nearby Holiday Inn.

My new companion was in her fifties, German, and married to an Englishman who was continuing his stay in the USA. Having located my hotel room I was still annoyed. This night of comparative luxury after Central American guesthouses should have pacified me but I longed for the simple room I had the previous night, with the bare light bulb, single cupboard, a basic mattress and a couple of geckos for company. The room was testing my patience even more as the complicated lighting system, the inability to work out how the curtains were drawn, plus problems with the TV remote were driving me crazy!! Pulling back the bed sheets was a major and complex operation. I had been cut off from such sophistication and was used to the simple life. I was really sulking because I wanted to be high over the Atlantic looking forward to Match of the Day. I eventually managed to master the TV where the newscaster seemed very agitated about the breaking news regarding Lehman Brothers as if it had some kind of historic importance. He seemed to have no sense perspective; so a bank was in a spot of bother, I was to miss Match of the Day!!

I had a pleasant dinner with Margo and we planned to spend the following day in Manhattan. I had been to New York twice, the last time in 1983, so the prospect of a day trip didn't really excite. The following morning brought heavy rain which dampened my spirits further but it began to clear and as the bus swung into the Lincoln Tunnel my spirits suddenly began to rise. We took the tourist open topped-bus around the sights in glorious sunshine while the excitement and magic of Gotham City got right under my skin. I was loving every minute of it. Like a married couple Margo and I had to compromise on the choice of destinations which saw me hanging around the perfume counter in Macy's while she used her woman's prerogative to continually change her mind.

Latin American Fever

After arriving back home on the Sunday I returned to school the following day. My jet-lag was extreme but I felt I couldn't take time off as it was self-inflicted, so I battled on for a few days with blinding headaches. Then I began suffering severe night fevers where my bed clothes were saturate several times during a single night. On the Thursday I could barely open my eyes so I went to the hospital where I was kept in overnight for tests. They confirmed straight away that it wasn't malaria, the correct diagnosis arriving from London six weeks later. I had contacted Dengue Fever. By the time I was informed the worst effects had abated and I was just suffering occasional migraines. My reaction to getting Dengue Fever was elation as I had now acquired a traveller's status symbol. I felt like Dr. Livingstone; I was a proper traveller and adventurer suffering tropical diseases from tropical climes. To add to this kudos there is no prevention or cure and it can be fatal. If you get it twice it's almost certain death. Fortunately I would have to return to the particular region of the fever inducing mosquito bite. The fever has a three week incubation period which would identify Guatemala, a very high risk area, as the source. The consultant explained I would have to travel to the specific area as small as a valley to be in danger. This is why it is a deadly problem for the indigenous population rather than tourists or travellers.

All's Well That Ends Well

My decision to respond to the dark and desolate thoughts of the initial post divorce period by changing my life dramatically had eventually paid dividends. If I had carried on in the printing industry commuting from a rented flat in my home town I wouldn't have survived. During the immediate post divorce years I led a nomadic bohemian existence. I have now settled into a comfortable flat in a quiet area after five different address changes in Cardiff alone. Around the world I had slept in scores of beds. My mind had become occupied by new challenges and problems. I had been confronted by many hurdles, the earlier ones were almost insurmountable and could have been fatal because of my, then unknown, mental fragility. I also fulfilled my ambition and passion to travel. I'm now very fortunate to have landed the kind of job that is so challenging and rewarding that it makes life worth living. Working with kids, many of whom having been dealt a bum hand, prevents me from being tempted to wallow in any kind of self pity.

My generation is blessed. Being born in 1947 was extremely good timing. We were the first beneficiaries of the welfare state. Apart from odd skirmishes in the likes of Aden and Cyprus not only did we avoid wars but National Service too. We enjoyed full employment, growing prosperity and increasing longevity. Many working class baby boomers have lovely homes and properties worth a quarter of a million pounds and more. Macmillan was right when he said that we had never had it so good. Unfortunately it seems that future generations never will. Even the most gifted of the pupils I meet will have a far more challenging life than me or my peers. For perhaps the first time in history the coming generations will be worse off than the previous. So in my quieter moments I realise it's despite my good fortune that I was traumatised by the past.

Although loathed to admit it like many young people, in my teens the prospect of marriage at some point in the future was to be the focal point of my life. I wasn't cut out to be a philanderer or promiscuous. I had a higher ideal. I'd had several girlfriends but when I first met the woman who was to become my wife I realised instinctively that we were meant to be. For me it was love on first date. Now all these years later I find it very difficult to admit I'm divorced. It sticks in my throat. Even in the most bitter divorces most couples can reflect back on the good times when they were young and in love. I can't even do that. My wife's mental fragility created a dominant neurosis that had to be fed at the expense of all else. I made her happy for so long because I protected her, and gave her the security she craved. I mistook this happiness for love. It's only now late in life that I realise objectively, that such were her self-absorbing insecurities she was incapable of loving anyone. It wasn't this realisation that depressed and tormented me the most, it's the fact that the love of a lifetime that most hope for and aspire to with the subsequent home, children, and family life, even for one moment, never existed . . . it just never happened.

"To all those Truth Seekers whom Jesus inflamed to do so."

-1-

Prelude

By Robert Ghanem*

Introducing this book "Jesus Christ that Unknown" wouldn't be easy. The work is colossal, vastly researched, well argued and devised to take the Christian mind in a whirlwind of theology, psychology and philosophy toward a final introduction into the mind of the Son of God; a timely and challenging presentation indeed in this advanced era of knowledge.

---

* Poet and philosopher. Nobel Prize nominee.

1

To *exist* in our times is to me something of a passage through the everlasting human saga. Philosophy in its original essence remains hypothetical while religion reflects personal conviction either innate or inherited. I consider man an intrepid knowledge seeker governed all the time by his corporeal mind that drives him through this materialistic age away from the spiritual realm.

This book comes well-timed to bring the straying, highly ethereal Christian belief through a series of palpable psychological interpretations; a set of guidelines much inherent to our times surprisingly pioneered and adopted by the Master himself who initiated our modern spiritual science; a new illumination indeed on our empirical expectations and a strong ushering of a new faith in this tumultuous, sophisticated social life.

Hadi Eid concentrates with a remarkable simplicity throughout his highly "Christian" book on the elemental, yet essential esoteric knowledge alien to mainstream Christianity. Certainly those who recognized Jesus two millenniums ago are different from today's believers who are immersed in spiritual knowledge and well versed in the powers of the subconscious mind. The elders, including the highly literate Nicodemus failed to grasp the Master's explanations on the "born-again" methodology. The writer explains in a substantiated and convincing style that *cleansing the subconscious* the way we understand it today is exactly what Jesus meant by the "second birth." his updated rationalization of the parables is surprisingly persuasive: a process our churches are so far considerably distant from.

"Your sins are forgiven" is explained in great details by the author as a subconscious cleansing motion the Master would unleash, inducing that mind to generate healing. A "mini renaissance" of sorts coupled by a further indoctrination: "go and sin no more." This and many other psycho-spiritual formulas Jesus practiced were lately discovered and applied by modern science but nowhere to the extent achieved by the Master.

"Go and tell no one," Jesus would direct his disciples following any of his miracles. Secrecy was not the only reason according to the author. During that era entrenched in shallow spirituality such feats could be easily ascribed to charlatanism and trickery. When the mountain Transfiguration took place for instance he commanded his three witnessing disciples "to disclose it to nobody until after the Resurrection;" because only under such a superior significance smaller feats could be believable. In his psychological approach to discern the mind of Christ the author achieved a profundity unattained yet by scholars and philosophers alike. "Jesus Christ that Unknown" is a befitting name to a well researched dissertation unwrapping for the first time the many shrouds that concealed through centuries this divine personality.

Having read the book and *endured* its series of mind boggling topics I reached a better insight on Jesus' personality, the son of man and son of God, and can proclaim to myself as well as to the others that Jesus is no more unknown: Mr. Eid has approached the Scripture with a new twist suitable for our time and place; the time to reclaim Jesus again among our own people so that his updated legacy will be handed on to the next generation throughout this twenty-first century.

-2-

Foreword

"Don't throw a stone on me, before reading the whole book"

The author

Writing a book on Jesus Christ is an absolute challenge. No matter how one is deeply immersed in researching historical, theological and psychological grounds, one remains far from elucidating the enigmatic shrouds surrounding this personality. Even a consummate master of imaginative writing would fail to create a picture of the Son of Man that stirred the whole world and continued through this era of advanced knowledge to stir it again.

Jesus has been considered by many as the most inscrutable and inspirational leader the world has ever known. He toppled kings, enthused millions and founded a new philosophy that did not cease to be controversial; one that springs from and instills the very core of the human mind. His purely spiritual/ human message has been hijacked later by countless rulers and establishments using it to expand their own power. Innumerable attempts to write the lives of Jesus emerged in many countries for a very long time. Beside the forty two or more gospels that only four were deemed reliable and trustworthy, there have been over 60.000 attempts written in the nineteenth century alone. Yet all those writers were unable to dissociate themselves from their own environment, age and level of knowledge; many superposed upon the first Christian century something that belongs to their own time.

This book comes to a great extent as an exception to the rule; it is an updated psycho-spiritual study addressed to the modern, educated reader whose belief is torn between the advanced knowledge and the inherited assumptions. Of course, every period, like history in general, sees Jesus' own saga and stature with its own eyes. But in this age of superior information and swift communications a new reading of Jesus' spellbinding spiritual tapestry that penetrated the foundation of the human spirit is due; a swirl that inculcated the far reaches of that spirit and directed it to the bliss of the positive realm.

Well after the celebration of his 2000th birthday the book in your hands ushers in a modern look at Jesus displaying the old stories with a new twist; a unique source of life, love, joy, and peace of mind. The Son of Man who owned no property, won no medals, never held any political office or commanded an army exceeded by far any man's influence in the human race. His First Coming was prophesied 300 times in the Bible, and those prophecies were fulfilled in Jesus to the letter; his Second Coming is prophesied another 500 times! He made miracles and forgave sins that only God could do! He resurrected from his preordained death to live forever in every human heart.

Many Christians today experience a huge problem: how can they live their lives proclaiming faith in Christ while estranged for lack of proper understanding, of his personality. They do not live his glorious yet simple adventure at work, at home, in the streets . . . the average educated Christian is not a believer but simply fascinated by the story of Christ as one of the most beautiful poetic expressions of the human tragedy. Some believe in it like in a poem or the Passion of Bach. Christ is merely a means of expression best displayed in the many paintings: a man of the people. The objective of this book is to address such modern minds and set aside all the jargons and flimflams that accompanied Jesus' story through centuries, redefine it in a realistic and reasonable fashion to enter Jesus' mind in its full simplicity and make it part of their minds and lives. Entering this mind means coming into the positive realm of love, joy and peace that only Jesus can give and nobody or nothing can take away on this earth.

Perhaps what is essential while combating this alienation is to recognize that Jesus expressed his deepest convictions of positive principles in terms of ideas and language current in his own day. The extreme urgency in the universal situation is to translate these into modern terms. Jesus' statements about the Kingdom of God possess an enormous importance for our present world if we give the resulting definition around which those statements evolved: the Peace of Mind.

One of the worst modern flaws is relativism and standards; an outright contradiction to Jesus' doctrine. Jesus addressed such flaws demonstrating that standards are not relative after all and in the various fields of human endeavor some are good and others bad. This is one of his greatest contributions to our own times. In doing so he showed us what one human being is capable of when following the positive behavioral path. Certainly the Son of Man was on this earth, like other human beings, the product of his age, conditioned by its requirements and limitations

Yet he broke out and away from these negative limitations with such force, he fulfilled an enormous positive role in an unprecedented individual fashion. For in spite of the disconcerting vicissitudes the Church underwent after him, his positive spirituality conquered because of its extraordinary power to reach out. The vast influence exercised by Jesus' philosophy upon past history is an incontrovertible fact that needs no argumentation. This revival can only be explained by its remedial capabilities to the conditions and problems of old as well as our own times. The connection between Jesus' teaching and the circumstances in which we find ourselves placed today is noticeable in our daily lives.

Jesus was a human on this earth who gave us a revelation of the maximum effect that one human being has ever been able to exercise upon others through the positive channels. Anti-religious tones emerge here and there in this ambient, materialistic world and with it man experiences a nostalgic yearning to his *humanism*. Jesus in fact is the most powerful argument demonstrated by none else than his own person of the highest level of attainment human beings have ever proved themselves capable of. His overwhelmingly massive achievement performed by a single individual in spite of adamant, crushing opposition both during and after the ministry permanently remains the most heartening thing that has ever happened to the human race.

Perhaps we can classify writers on Jesus in three categories: the believers, the unbelievers and the independent historians. Almost all such categories are biased into writing with love, hate or pure factual methods rendering belief or unbelief irrelevant. Your writer here is a staunch believer and supportive to what Jesus uttered: "heaven and earth shall pass away: but my words shall not pass away." My support to these words stems from faith in the human mind and spirit that constituted the arena of Jesus' philosophy. His words may only pass away when the last human is wiped out of this planet. In tackling this highly sensitive subject which instills profound feelings it is essential for one to stand up and harbor as much of the truth as possible.

No matter how past writers and historians alienated themselves from the veracity of Jesus' message he did not cease to be a catalyst whose continuous presence forces us to make a decision for or against. Writers of the Gospels may have limited themselves to the facts of prosaic history but they essentially set out to tell us the story of what happened in the ministry of Jesus with a primary spiritual interest where history comes second. Their spiritual line of reasoning did not display the true and profound assessment Jesus meant behind his sayings and parables. Many historians wrote with a moralizing, edifying zest the evangelists would have applauded although their dilemma was: from such meager historical sources how much solid history can be extracted.

Therefore it is expected that many readers find in the following pages an intermingled mixture of facts and fictions, belief and logic, history and psychology. The extensive studies and researches through countless years of information were too wide a bridge to precisely reconstruct the life and philosophy of Jesus. I found many facts that could be fairly well proven and others quite questionable. Some areas did not provide enough evidence to identify factual information. As a result the way the facts are presented was not intended to fill in the gaps with assumptions. These assumptions, especially what relates to Jesus' *lost years* in Qumran were theories fairly easy to identify as facts, and thus the previously unknown truths are made available to those who seek them.

Before launching this document I anticipated that many would regard it as controversial, even heretical. I urge those readers to consider that none of the passages dispute any part of the Scripture's connotations but rather reassess them. The main aim is to provide sustenance not only to what Jesus said but precisely to the hidden meanings of his sayings as narrated by the evangelists many years later. And in as much as I wanted to learn about Jesus and revaluate his teachings through the present-day brainpower, I wished to share this updated knowledge with fellow Christians and many other readers who believe in the power of the human mind. I spent my prime years studying the Scripture and all the ancient literature I could muster about Jesus and his times motivated by his own saying: 'seek the truth . . .' and felt that many believers would want to have access to the *accepted truth* I claim to have found. Since the question of controversy derives from our tradition that we learn about Jesus only from the Scripture, many other ancient documents provided so much additional and useful information. This great body of enlightenment cemented my strong belief in the accuracy of Jesus' mystifying principles heretofore unfathomed; that is what I detailed in the following pages.

In this day and age where many construing minds among historians and philosophers rush to display all faiths as mere fabrications based on the acceptance of imaginative truths offered through metaphor, allegory and amplification, a down to earth synopsis must outline the tolerable truth. Rather than destructing the documents and negating the controversial scriptures a reasonable array of information can be offered to ponder the exceptional life of Jesus. The Bible represents a fundamental guidepost for millions of people on the planet; its metaphors may be a way to help simple human minds process the un-processional; behind those metaphors however stands an important channel of thought between deity and humans so intense to become a major part of the fabric of reality.

Throughout the ages man was seeking a higher power to motivate his spirituality because he was incapable, beyond normal mundane issues, of thinking for himself. He embraced many beliefs and ideologies but remained alien to his own mind. Jesus came with new ideals knocking down various Biblical postulates, enabling man to learn the *truth* about his own mind and the *real God that dwells in this mind*; but first and foremost galvanizing him *to think for himself*.

Unlike the human mind studied and widely portrayed by psychologists the mind of God is far different and difficult to attain. Paul says: "for who has known the *Mind of the Lord*, that he may instruct him? But we have the *Mind of Christ*." (1Cor.2:16.) God reasons *deductively*! He does not need to gather facts to come to a conclusion. He *starts with the conclusion* and *deduces* from there. To say that God reasons inductively (gathering facts in order to come to a conclusion) implies that He does not know the conclusion. God always starts with the answer because He already knows every conclusion. He does not need to go on a fact-finding spree to come up with an answer or conclusion. This simple, straightforward mind does not have the duality of our mind but rather the childlike thinking and deduction. Jesus was not telling us to become immature babies when he asked us to be like children. He was telling us to *believe* as children do without doubting for a very valid reason that psychologists discovered recently: this is exactly how the subconscious mind, our inner motivator, operates.

These things may seem religious deviations as well as beautiful truths. I am not saying them with a proud self-righteous heart; I say them with the unfeigned humility and meekness of a mere listener to Jesus' Sermon of the Mount. Those who attain such high calling will be merciful, loving and forgiving like God, the overall Father. We are the Sons of God in as much as Jesus is. And I know you will not stone me for saying throughout this book in line with Jesus' rediscovered philosophy that we will be made equal to God because God's seed produces nothing less than Himself.

You are introduced here to a different and mature Christian thinking. You will come to know through the upcoming pages that lots of *milky doctrines* have been rightly or wrongly injected in your subconscious mind; these are the catechetic *baby foods* for baby Christians that are no more befitting those who seek perfection. What is needed is the good whole seed or the meat word of God that removes tares with a mighty shove not available to manmade doctrines. In his letter to the Hebrews Paul fully explains this changeover: "for every one that uses milk *is* unskillful in the word of righteousness: for he is a babe. But strong meat belongs to them that are of full age, *even* those who by reason of use *have their senses exercised to discern both good and evil*. Therefore leaving the principles of the doctrine of Christ, let us go on unto *perfection*; not laying again the foundation of repentance from *dead works*, and of faith toward God." (Heb 5:13 . . .)

-3-

Man

"Then the Lord God formed man of dust from the ground, and breathed into his nostrils the breath of life and man became a living being"
(Gen 2:7).

This is how the Bible, using a symbolic language, says that God willed man to be both corporeal and spiritual. All along the Scripture *soul* meant human life or the entire human person. But soul also means man's spiritual principle. The man we have come to recognize as a dualistic combination of body and soul, matter and mind, had gone across his known history through countless intriguing theorizations; many of them were committed to *obsolete* metaphysics and went frustratingly obscure if not directly self-contradictory, others to *absolute* natural phenomenon.

In fact one has to peel back many onion skins and poke through countless orientations to formulate an acceptable definition of the human being; each philosophical, religious or naturalist concept came up with varying perceptions of man.

Within the philosophy domain almost all definitions agree that man is a rational animal, a substance, corporeal, living and sentient. But man's animalism though inseparable, is distinct in nature from his rationality. While neither has an inherent substantial existence, they render man a compound of body and soul. The union between the two is a *substantial* one. The *soul* is a reality capable of a separate existence; the *body* can in no sense be called a substance in its own right. It exists only as determined by a form and if that form is not a human soul then the "body" is not a human body. Such reciprocity of relation between the two determines the principles of the one substantial being.

So, man is a single, individual substance of a rational nature resultant from the determination of matter by a human form capable of reasoning. In Greek and in modern philosophy another celebrated theory laid claim to the *pre-eminence*. For Plato the soul is a spirit that *uses* the body. It is in a non-natural state of union and longs to be freed from its bodily prison. This theory was later reiterated by the controversial, recently published Gospel of Judas. Yet according to Alcher the soul rules the body; "its union with the body is a friendly union though

16

the latter impedes the full and free exercise of its activity; it is devoted to its prison."

These philosophical theories of the nature of man have been explicitly condemned by the Church. The ecclesiastical definitions have reference merely to the union of body and soul and both are referred to as two *substances*. Other pronouncements of the Church merely restate this doctrine: "the soul is not only really and essentially the form of the human body but is also immortal; and the number of souls has been and is to be multiplied according to the number of multiplied bodies." (Pius IX to Cardinal de Geissel, 15 June, 1857).

In the sixteenth century Descartes advanced a doctrine that again separated soul and body and compromised the unity of *consciousness and personality*. While Aquinas avoids the difficulties and contradictions of the "two substances" and asserts: "It is not my soul that thinks or my body that eats. It is 'I' that do both . . ."

The supremacy of the soul however is clear and definite in this union. The human soul does not emerge from the potential of the matter; it rather evolves within that matter but is in no way an arbitrary add-on to an otherwise complete creature. While human behavior exhibits the dimensions of both mind and matter the role of each is different: the matter is intrinsically controlled and directed and the mind *controls and directs*.

The principle of *control and direction* stipulates that everything must have a place and a purpose within the environment. So when a human creature emerges in evolution with a brain too powerful to hold in meaningful stimulation and coordinated response, matter must be integrated directly into the principle of *mind* to direct its energies and draw its identity.

Man's soul is his very essence originating in a mystery. It is not given to him from earth but received from above. It is the *landlord* of the body that originates from earth; a superb apparatus expertly fashioned and just as expertly joined into one single, *organized* aggregate; thus—probably—the *organism*.

This man's organism boasts an array of instruments meshed together to serve his spiritual and worldly needs. Centuries ago man learned to add artificial extensions to these organic instruments beginning with the knife and spoon. Later he learned to replace the loss of bodily members with artificial ones. The art of supplementing naturally endowed organs with artificial ones is constantly expanding in its application. A man at the wheel of a car becomes for a time one entity with his machine. The same can be said of a pilot at the controls of his plane.

On the theological and scriptural side there is a clear differentiation between body, soul, and spirit. To draw this distinction from the scripture we must understand the meaning of certain biblical phrases or terms that are relevant to this topic. When Paul speaks of the "natural man" as in (ICor.2:14,) we must understand that this is a person who is of *body* and *soul*, NO SPIRIT. This person is not a born-again Christian. The only way this person can learn anything is by the brain and the five senses with no *spiritual connection* with God.

We see here a contrast between the spirit of a person and his soul; a topic worth reviewing in details. The soul is the catalyst of life but the spirit is the divine inner person that returns to the divine.

Old traditions and principles maintained that all things came forth from liquid because matter was initially created in liquid form. These principles could have emanated from certain

18

occult books of the Phoenicians that were in turn the books of Moses. This principle seems rational when we note that the Phoenician researcher Thales added *spirit* to water as principal mover. This spirit is mentioned in the most ancient book of all as that which 'was borne over the waters'. The Koran later replicated the same principle: "and from water we created all living things."

The relationships between the electric circuits in the brain and modern circuitry in computing systems are astounding. The architecture of these systems leads to new insights into the circuitry in the human brain equipped with carbon semiconductors made of neurons and *liquid* vessels as well as into other types of brains or logic circuits that abounds in intelligent beings. In addition, we saw the human brain as a broadcasting/receiving station that can interact, motivate and inspire other brains across long distances.

What is the *soul* in this intricate design? Could it be the consciousness or *awareness*, i.e. the functionality of all systems in unison? One theory is almost reasonable: This coupling effect of the soul (consciousness) to body through electromagnetic interactions would rather neatly explain why a *soul* would detach from the body at the moment of death. There would simply be no more of such energy emanating from the physical body so the soul vehicle would become disengaged. But more plausible still is that the soul is awareness on top all human systems' functionality. When those *spiritual* neurons spinning around our heads in coherent patterns decay or weaken so does the soul. The same is true when they dysfunction and die.

Our body is the vehicle for our soul which is in turn the vehicle of our spirit. Our spirit is the eternal part of God. Our soul carries our spirit to experience individuality of existence between the physical and the spiritual realms. The human body evolved for millions of years and it will continue to evolve until it is able to do those things which fully developed people like human Jesus had achieved. At some point millions of years ago spirits descended upon our old ancestors and began influencing them to eventually form societies. Then spirits began inhabiting those early bodies and thus the dawn of humanity arose on this planet.

In the Middle East where the three monolithic religions started, the biblical *breath* that God breathed in Adam's nostrils while still clay and transformed him into a living "soul" is used until this day to call and account for living persons. It is still said for instance that "the Beirut population exceeds 2 million breaths, or Cairo accounts for 12 million breaths. Meaningful also is when a Middle Eastern expresses his ultimate depression saying: "my soul reached my nostrils!" *About to exit from where it came in!*

This is what apostle Paul mentioned when he counted his fellow passengers on the ship over a raging sea: "And we were in all in the ship two hundred threescore and sixteen *souls*." (Act. 27:37.) Paul meant there were 276 "live people" on that ship including himself and Luke. Soul to him depicts the living human body. It denotes that this man is alive.

The Bible is clear in defining the two components. The "soul", "nepesh" in Hebrew/Aramaic and "nephes" in Arabic is in a man that which gives the body its life and vitality. The phrase "breathed into his nostrils" is the figure of speech emblematic to where God attributes human characteristics to Himself. When God put life into Adam He MADE man a living SOUL; *the breath is simply that which gives life to a human body.* As long as a person breathes, he has a soul.

Biologically speaking the soul simply exists when the person is *alive* or fuelled by the breath-life. It ceases to exist in a human when the last breath is taken, and this is of course true to animals as well. While the Old Testament supports this theory the Church considers this illogical and usually teaches that the soul and spirit go back to God. The Scripture notes with a measure of certainty that it is in the blood that passes from generation to another by means of fertilization. "For life of the flesh is in the blood." (Lev.17-11.) so when a sperm impregnates the egg a person can pass his soul-life on to his progeny. A soul of a dead, childless person is simply used up.

When it comes to Creation many clerics retort that on the first day God created this and on the second day God created that and so on. But this is not what the Bible says. In Genesis 1:3, God said, "Let there be light." Why didn't He have to create it? Because He created whatever was needed for light in the beginning when He created the heavens and the earth. All that was ever needed was already created in Genesis 1:1. That is why all God needed to do was to *speak* other things into existence.

After God created the earth and its inhabitants (animals, fish, etc.) He came to His culminating work: man. But God had already formed and made man with body and soul like the rest of the animal world: "so God created man in his *own* image, in the image of God created He him; male and female created He them" (Gen. 1: 27) with body and soul. So what was God doing there? Recreating the man Adam in His own image by simply injecting his spirit—or image within him and accordingly he became Body, Soul *and* Spirit? Certainly: the spirit part makes it possible for God to talk to man and for man to communicate with God.

On the naturalistic side, to please and appease the naturalists namely Darwin's *aficionados*, yes, there were "men" before Adam and Eve among the rest of the animal world. The Bible clearly mentions that "Cain went out from the presence of the Lord and dwelt in the land of Nod where *he knew his wife*" (Gen. 4-16,) and "the sons of God (Adam's sons) saw the daughters of men that *they were fair* and they took them wives" (Gen.6-2.) Certainly, other peoples existed on earth in addition to the *sons of God* and to say or believe that Adam is the first man on earth is a biblical misconception. What will displease the naturalists is that the origin of man is a man not an ape, irrespective of his early forms and propensities.

But why the Bible insists that God created Adam and Eve in person from clay—irrespective of other existing humans? This traditional matter is contradicted by the bible itself. The only acceptable theory is that God picked two humans, Adam and Eve and breathed his *spirit* in their nostrils to become God's *special people* able to interact and commune with Him. The message from the Bible is that when Adam and Eve sinned they lost their *spiritual* connection with God. They had received the spirit upon a condition that they would not disobey God; yet they did and became body and soul without spirit. But is everyone born into this world before them or even today a mere body and soul person?

This is a big question that remains once more a pondering issue: were all men before Adam, around Aden—and certainly over the other continents devoid of God's spirit? We know Adam's children, apparently still blessed irrespective of their parents' "original sin," went out and compatibly married "the fair maidens" of other men. Were these girls devoid of *spirit* thus pertaining to the animal kingdom? Obviously what is intended in the Bible is that a selected breed of people started by Adam and Eve that multiplied later with a well known family tree depicted in the first biblical accounts; formed a human *sample* of sorts to exemplify the rest of the human races and serve as a paradigm of that special man-God relationship.

The ensuing argument here is that man as originally put together surpasses the animal realm because he not only has body and soul but also spirit. Is it discernable that people created by God before Adam whose *fair maidens* were picked by his descendents as wives were not endowed with spirit? These *humans* were surely the same God's creation and the fact that their maidens were "fair" and there were "giants" among them suggests they were a superior people equally endowed with spirit. This muddling issue has been subject to continuous debates in all Catholic theology. The origin of man by creation, as opposed to emanative and evolutionistic pantheism is asserted in the Church's dogmas and definitions. The angelic world was created followed by the universe and afterwards man; the same account is given in the writings of the Fathers and theologians. The early controversies and apologetics of St. Clement of Alexandria defend the theory of creation against

Stoics and neo-Platonists. St. Augustine strenuously combats the pagan schools on this point as on that of the nature and immortality of man's soul. Distinction between the theological and the philosophical has been always a wide crack.

This is a good entrance to the *evolution doctrine and the natural origins of man*. For many people of various faiths support for the scientific theory of evolution has not supplanted their religious belief. And throughout the modern Judeo-Christian tradition leaders have asserted that evolutionary science offers a valid perspective on the natural world. They say that evolution is consistent with religious doctrines and complements, rather than conflicts with religion.

Pope John Paul II stated that the conclusions reached by scientific disciplines cannot be in contradiction with divine revelations and then proceeded to accept the scientific deduction that evolution is a well-established theory. He asserted that science deals with material reality; "while questions of moral conscience, freedom, aesthetic and religious experiences fall within the competence of philosophical analysis and reflection, theology brings out their ultimate meaning according to the Creator's plans." Around 2007 the debate over creation and evolution became conspicuous in America before going global. The theories of Darwin that virtually constitute the base of modern biology gathered momentum though they were challenged many times. Clerical pronouncements on the subject are often couched in careful and sometimes impenetrable theological language. Pope Benedict XVI however asserted that "evolution cannot be conclusively proved; and the manner in which life developed was indicative of a *divine reason* that could not be discerned by scientific methods alone".

Other American denominations outside the Catholic Church advocated that the origin of life was caused by the *intelligent design* initiated by an ingenious Creator. The theory was only accepted as a religious not a scientific one. But Benedict XVI apparently wants to lay down an even stronger line on the status of man as a species produced by divine ordinance, not just random selection. "Man is the only creature on earth that God willed for his own sake," he said. But advocates of the intelligent design or outright creationists are not looking for anyone's endorsement. Their ideas are flourishing and their numbers growing on both sides of the Atlantic. While arguments accepting that scientific descriptions of the universe are valid as far as they go, they are ultimately incomplete as a way of explaining how things came to be.

All students of the theory of evolution from the three monolithic religions however, express their reservations based on their perceived contradiction between belief and theory. Teachers usually address this dilemma almost in the same approach expressed by the Pope. One is that the evolution of organisms is beyond reasonable doubt; so the theory of evolution is accepted in this respect with the same certainty that we attribute to the molecular composition of matter. The second consideration is that science is a very successful way of knowing but not the only way. We acquire knowledge in many other ways such as literature, arts, philosophical reflection and religious experiences. Science has nothing definitive to say about realities beyond its scope and there remain questions of value, purpose, and meaning that belong in the realm of philosophical reflection and spiritual discipline.

On the other hand any honest scientist readily admits that the evolution concept at best might be regarded as an educated guess. It cannot be measured by *scientific methods*, does not meet the verifiability and repeatability requirements for a theory and is devoid of documentary evidence; therefore it should not be classified among the annals of science. Considerable confusion would continue to cloud the true meaning of organic evolution with reference to what it is and what it is not.

A simple concept makes the point: dogs never have kittens or bunnies or monkeys. Dogs reproduce dogs and monkeys reproduce monkeys. To say that monkeys are man's ancestors is enigmatically impossible. It is a presumptuous myth of evolutionists. Monkeys continue to reproduce monkeys and men continue to reproduce men; each organism after its own kind irrespective of the postulations of Darwin in his *Origin of the Species*. This notion is nothing novel since it long antedates Darwin. The cloning magnate Ian Wilmut, *creator* of the history-making lamb *Dolly* said ten years later to Time magazine: "from the point of view of the technique it has been disappointing. Efficiency hasn't changed dramatically and there are a lot of abnormalities."

Yet organic evolution hypothesis championed by Malthus, Wallace and Darwin continue to be published in textbooks and taught by teachers. This contradicts the proven theory that organic evolution is not the growth of an organism. It is not development or variation, or adaptation; nor a reality in embryological development which for years has been used mistakenly to justify the often repeated cliché. The concept alleges that all animals and plants descended from some primordial substance presumably a blob of protoplasm. It holds that lower forms of life without designer or creator and has evolved through a slow, gradual process of mutations into higher forms . . . resultant of man.

For atheists and humanist alike evolution is a system of faith in the doctrine of materialism. It is a dangerous philosophy spreading the seeds of doubt, cheapness of life, abortion, infanticide, euthanasia, murder, unseemly lifestyles, etc. all of which are manifestations of the heathen mentality. Cloaked in the intellectual and scientific garbs, it is probably one of the greatest frauds ever perpetrated on the minds of men in the name of science. Evolutionists have scoured the earth's crust and spent lifetimes searching for the *missing link*. Some have even gone so far as to concoct plausible hoaxes. Yet all their theorizations ended up devoid of evidence or logic.

-4-

Positive and Negative

"The Angel and the Devil are both men's creations."

The author

Electricity has been proclaimed the *subtle* and integral but unseen essence of life and the *soul of the universe.* Wesley the noted theologian/physicist called it back in 1773 the "pure fire". He wrote: ". . . the general principle of all motion in the universe is that from this "pure fire", the vulgar "culinary fire" is kindled. For in truth there is but one kind of fire in nature which exists in all places and in all bodies. And this is subtle and active enough not only to serve the Great Cause or the secondary Cause of Motion, but to produce and sustain life throughout all nature as well in animals and vegetables."

Wesley contended then, and is supported by all scientists today, that the *pure fire* communicates activity and motion through fluids in general and particularly accelerates the circulation of the blood in the human body . . .

During the last half of the eighteenth century many case studies illustrate the variety of both the methods used and the ailments treated by electricity. The majority of the cases were of the nervous, hysteric type. Wesley asserted: "we know it is a thousand medicines in one; in particular that it is the most efficacious medicine in nervous disorders of every kind which has yet been discovered."

It has been equally established in full details that electricity and electromagnetism are forces of nature that can affect the life of beings either beneficially *or* destructively depending on their application. Electromagnetic fields possess inner spiritual qualities that can take hold of and transform the human being completely. And exactly as they display their effectiveness outwardly in physical matter, so they influence inwardly the moral constitution of human beings in the absence of personal control over their negative or positive influences.

The human body is run by an intricate electric circuitry. This low-voltage power directs and regulates many bodily functions including the heart, the brain and the subconscious mind. The body electricity is light in a sub-material state; it is made of streamlined positive and negative currents. Its importance for the inner life of the human being is in the greatest contrast and the constant mixture of good and evil.

Electric power engulfs all human and animal surroundings. Our earth interior emits natural micro-pulsations at approximate rate of 10 oscillations per second. Lightning creates fields in a frequency range of thousands of oscillations per second while a spectrum light is visible with billions of oscillations. Throughout the evolution of human consciousness humans were closely united through physical bodies with this ambient world of matter in relation to thinking, feeling and willing.

In practical applications the greatest danger to the evolving consciousness has always come from substantial forces working through electricity and electromagnetism, influencing thinking and impacting severely on the *will-orientated side* of human nature. In the process *the will that is driven by instincts only* has been in danger where free initiative is concerned if it is not met with the full force of human waking consciousness. Human self-consciousness has always been torn between its built-in morally guiding impulses and *invading* forces from a different *ego* forming an internal *duality.* A destabilizing inner drive constantly seeking a stabilizing support of an ultimate outside force: the Superhuman or Deity.

Humans needed this outside ultimate supporting force to forge courage and achieve peace of mind. Through ages the individualization of human beings as a necessity encountered the repugnance of people who, beset by fear and continuous inner struggles, fight against all human or natural forms because they hamper their all-encompassing desire for life, power and domination. These people, though unaware of the connections between earth electricity and body electricity, used them nonetheless as a weapon against those forms.

It is also a known medical—or demonical fact that human mind can be controlled by means of outside electric impulses. This is a brainwashing and almost a rape of the free will practiced in Soviet Russia when developed by a Spanish Dr. Delgado. He used to stimulate brain activity in his patients with electronic stimulation. The CIA was interested in this form of warfare so they went ahead and financed his project. Delgado was elated of his findings by saying that "movement, emotion and behavior can be controlled by electrical forces, and human beings can be manipulated like robots with the touch of a button."

Enough for external monitoring; there exist in the lower back of the human brain two glands that control the behavioral temperament. The physical organ that forms the memory-image is the pineal gland, while the pituitary gland is the recording part. These cerebral regions house the conscious domain in a human being's life; this is also where the subconscious mind is located. In the natural energy of electricity a spiritual force is hidden that has the tendency to diminish human moral values if injected with negative impulses and attempts to drag human beings down into a morally low and spiritually dark domain. The exact opposite is true with positive impulses. Humans have the option to either consciously develop their morality with the aid of altruistic acts of will regulated by love (positive), or to yield to base inclinations and instincts laced with uninhibited selfishness (negative) that can pour into them.

The electric charges in a human body are entirely composed of positive and negative charged atoms. The electric current is a flow of positive sodium and potassium atoms, negative chlorine, and numerous other more complex positive and negative molecules. The positive atoms flow in one direction while the negative atoms simultaneously flowed in the other: crowds of tiny moving particles with half the dots going in one direction and half in the other without any dots colliding. The negative atoms behave like electrons which drag an entire atom along with them while the positive atoms behave like a proton; but a proton with an entire atom attached.

The flowing negatives and positives are usually not equal and the speed of the positives in one direction is not the same as the speed of the negatives in the other. The human mind using the body functions as we will see shortly, can maximize or minimize at will any of the two components and practically utilize them for his ultimate beatitude . . . or doom.

The human energy field pulsates with a two-way information system generated by the body's biological processes. The energy field extends as far out as the outstretched arms and the full length of the body. It is both an information center and a highly sensitive perceptual system. We are constantly in communication with everything around us through this system which is a kind of *conscious electricity* that transmits and receives messages to and from other people's bodies. These messages from and within the energy field are what intuitively endowed humans perceive.

The human energy field contains and reflects each individual's impulses. It carries the emotional energy created by the internal and external experiences both positive and negative. This emotional force influences the physical tissue within a human's body and the individual biography or the *cumulative experiences* that make up his life becomes his biology. The emotions generated through these experiences develop into an encoded record in his subconscious mind, the central motor of all biological systems and contribute to the formation of cell tissues which then generates a quality of energy that reflects those positive or negative emotions.

A human feels the positive energy as a surge of personal power within his body while negative impulses as an obliteration to this power. In Christ's words this is a *High or Low in Spirit*. Positive and negative experiences register a memory in cell tissues as well as in the energy field. Our emotions reside physically in our subconscious mind and interact with our cells and tissues because the same kinds of cells that manufacture and receive emotional chemistry in the brain are present throughout the body.

Emerson said: "an inevitable dualism bisects nature so that each thing is a half that suggests another thing to make it whole." This is a basic principle of the Newtonian physics: "for every action there is an equal and opposite reaction". Negative and positive are two different aspects of our universe with two different objectives. They resemble day and night and are the angel or devil that carries opposite characteristics. Two features opposite to each other have to join together to form a shape or to reach a goal. So relation of negative and positive is imperative for evolution and generation. One factor is to give life and another to give death that generates new birth. All of us are mortal including land, river, plants, animals, and birds. We all live to die and none is immortal. Some live long and some not but they die. Our souls have to *leave* the body one day. A fresh piece of bread kept for some time will have fungus on it that destroys it; yet this same fungus is the basis to bake fresh bread.

Thus the universal life cycles continues. Negative charges are necessary to the human metabolism; they strengthen the functions of autonomic nerves, reinforce tension-related tissues and fortify the body's immune system. Yet excessive negative impulses can be disastrous and destructive to this metabolism. Nature delivered a human body much more disposed to produce negative ions far exceeding his positive ones. This body's energy is best comparable to a swinging, flowing pendulum, positive on the one end, negative on the other and neutral in the middle. Yet when it stops in this middle, energy ceases, existence is erased and soul *relinquishes* the body.

Human emotional energies are the most complex of all energy types. Each of us contains the capacity for great joys (positive) and great sorrows (negative) plus the *abilities to greatly vary the intensity level of each side*. Emerson comments on this: "actions and feelings go together; if we control the actions that we can (through magnetic will power,) then we control the feelings that we cannot." We differ greatly as individuals: when one of us experiences stress and anger another sees opportunity and finds delight; or one is of a positive nature with uplifting presence and another of a negative nature, brooding and gloomy. This individuality is what makes humans truly unique and superior because each of us has the ability to generate energy of all three polarity designations.

GOD
The Holy Spirit

Positive *(Human power)*	Negative
"ANGEL"	"DEVIL"

Feelings:

Love	Hatred
Joy	Sadness
Belief	Doubt
Kindness	Badness
Compassion	Coldness
Enthusiasm	Apathy
Moderation	Cupidity
Praise (justified)	Criticism
Calm	Anger
Thoughtfulness	Cruelty
Purity	Impurity
Courage	Cowardice
Equanimity	Agitation
Decisiveness	Hesitation
Openness	Reticence
Attractiveness	Repulsiveness
Truthfulness	Dishonesty
Loyalty	Perfidy
Moderation	Greed
Altruism	Selfishness
Contentment	Envy
Wisdom	Foolishness
Etc. . .	Etc. . .

Peace of Mind	Struggle within
"Heaven"	"Hell"

What gives the emotion its positive, neutral or negative energy however is how the emotion is portrayed and interpreted by each individual. Anger for instance, "burns" like fire and, expelled outwardly in a rough manner it becomes negative; yet when harnessed it can be igniting spark for positive change. Love on the other hand is like flowing water that saturates all that it touches and tender loving moments of feelings greatly enrich the human spirit. Love reigns atop all positive human feelings.

Paul's Galatians epistle depicts clearly—even through elementary thinking, the human negative and positive paths: "The acts of the sinful nature are obvious: sexual immorality, impurity and debauchery; idolatry and witchcraft; hatred, discord, jealousy, fits of rage, selfish ambition, dissensions, factions and envy; drunkenness, orgies, and the like. I warn you, as I did before, that they which do such things shall not inherit the Kingdom of God. "But the fruits of the Spirit are love, joy, peace, patience, kindness, goodness, faithfulness gentleness and self-control. Against such things there is no law. Those who belong to Christ Jesus have crucified the sinful nature with its passions and desires. Since we live by the (positive) Spirit, let us keep in step with the Spirit. Let us not become conceited, provoking and envying each other." (5:19.)

Here also the Newtonian laws apply: "whenever one body exerts a force on a second body, the second body exerts an equal and opposite force on the first". In practical application the reaction of released energies, positive or negative, generates additional like amounts of energy though it may not be of the same intensity. Thus the energy generated by a released positive emotion generates a positive energy reaction of the individual receiving this emotion in a like manner. The same laws apply in negative emotions: This is the newly discovered Law of Attraction, a basic constituent of Jesus' Kingdom of Heaven philosophy 2000 years ago.*

Man's internal struggle between his positive/negative currents pushed him to picture them by a more blatant phenomenon: the angel and the devil. He erected mental as well as material temples to glorify or condemn them being the sources of either his bliss or misery.

He made the angels the soldiers of the Almighty who take charge of the human destiny by helping and supporting God's devotees. "For He shall give His angels charge over you, said David, to keep you in all your ways. They shall bear you up in their hands, lest you dash your foot against a stone" (Psa. 91:11.)

Humans bestowed to their own positive powers supernatural figures they cannot see, feel or taste, closing their mind to those heavenly entities that are within them and attributing the little good things that happen to them every day to their prescribed angels.

Many among us have images of angels sitting on clouds, playing harps and smiling down on children; we envisioned them with hard works on their mission to guide us toward the "Light" of which we are all part of. The energy of Angels is all around us, everyday at all times. They never desert us in good and bad. They are there for us always.

---

* Detailed in our new book: "Jesus Christ, Master of the Spiritual Science."

We have classified our angels appointing chiefs among them as well as regulars in the form of Archangels, Angels, Guardian Angels, Elementals or Spirit Guides. They desire nothing more than to guide us toward what is good and protect us from the harm. But because of our right of free will and the principles of positive powers that govern our own life we rendered them unintentionally restricted by what they can do, which is nothing if we do not ask them. The only time an angel may help without being specifically asked is if we are in danger and it is not our time yet to go. By insinuation of our subconscious mind that we only came to know about recently it is not wrong or selfish to ask for our angels' help as the Bible verse above state, "For He shall give His angels *charge* over you, to keep you in all your ways . . ." Thanks to the powers of this subconscious we had been all the way given the gift of angels and through it, we expected them to call upon us when needed: the unfathomed core of Jesus' philosophy.

As to the negative sides, humans depicted demons in many forms. Satan became in many religions an angel, demon, or minor god. Satan plays various roles in the Hebrew Bible, the Apocrypha, the New Testament and the Koran. In the Torah Satan is an angel that God uses to test man for various reasons usually dealing with his level of piety like the test of Adam and Eve in Genesis and the Book of Job and even Jesus' temptation as narrated by the evangelists. Satan is portrayed as an evil, rebellious demon who is the enemy of God and mankind.

This supernatural entity is the central embodiment of evil also commonly known as the Devil, the *Prince of Darkness*, Beelzebub, Belial, Mephistopheles or Lucifer. These different names sometimes refer to a number of different falling angels and demons and there is significant disagreement as to whether any of these "creatures" is actually evil. In Islam Satan is known as Iblis or Shaytan, who was the chief of the Jinn until he disobeyed Allah by refusing to prostrate himself before Adam i.e. refusing to accept *Man* as his superior: a meaningful hint to the power of the human mind. Islam describes Satan as Jinn who inspire poets, an entity made of smokeless fire different from the angels made from light.

The fertile human imagination went wild across centuries depicting its negative features through many satanic peculiarities. They were all hideous, repulsive and vile. Satan was painted in thousands of abhorrent forms to the elders' superficial minds—as well to our children today. The devil has a trim, black body, bowed horns, malicious eyes and a long tail, carries a pitchfork, lives in hell and loves to torture bad ignorant adults as, in our times, little children. Children are not born with these ridiculous beliefs; they learn them from mislead parents who in turn inspire them from the Church. Many use this fear of the devil to persuade children to behave. It is apparently very important to instill fear at an early age; this has unfortunately become a basis in our religion.

To Satan all the dirty tricks, tactics and lies are attributed as well as all the occult practices and deceptions. Demonic activities and deliverance are detailed as well as how to cast out devils; a counter-measure that a true Christian should equip himself with for spiritual warfare and discernment.

This intense and continued positive/negative power struggle within the internal self even pushed man to ascribe to his man-made Satan the power to metamorphose and masquerade as an angel of light to further deceive and swindle people. Paul himself succumbed to this understanding: "For such are false apostles, deceitful workers, transforming themselves into the apostles of Christ. And no marvel; *for Satan himself is transformed into an angel of light.* (2Cor.11:13.) By comparison to what adults are taught seriously through the Scripture, teaching their children about Satan would not appear mere fiction!

While angels are purely spirit beings standing for the purely good aspects in existence within our positive realm, Satan and his descendants represent the purely evil aspects or the human negative products. With man's duality of opposite aspects in his nature, one inclined to good the other to evil, angels represent his good aspect while Satan his evil one. Angels invite him to his purely spiritual, *angelic* facet while Satan tries to seduce him by calling his *devilish* side to do evil. This struggle between positive and negative currents in both man and in the universe around him has been continuing since the beginning of existence. Everyone feels a stimulus calling him to good and evil at the same time. The stimulus calling him to good comes from *angels:* his unpolluted spirit; the stimulus inviting him to evil comes from *Satan,* collaborating with his carnal self which represents his *animal aspect.*

Both angels and devils were mentioned in the Torah and the Koran as existing entities to believe and interact with. Jesus however, maintaining lots of the biblical convictions including angels and devils that became engraved postulates in the minds of people, used them in the figurative sense in order to promulgate his message. Many *devils* that were in reality mental or psychopathic ailments were *exhorted* by him to heal the sick. Typecast clerics still argue that Jesus would exorcise

41

devils out of patients where in reality he was simply prompting their subconscious as we will see to do the healing of the sickness that those patients traditionally believed it as grappling devil! Exorcism, to the amazement of many, is being practiced by Christian Clerics today in many parts of the world. Jesus also invoked multitudes of angels as speech figures to strengthen meanings and illustrate positive *heavenly* forces inherent to the local mentalities.

The *tree of knowledge* in the Garden of Eden was created for Adam and Eve to know the difference between positive and negative or good and evil. We all had to experience the corporeal conscious mind in order to understand it is mostly beset by evil. We know that it is our enemy and it will kill us if we continue to dwell there. Jesus came to differentiate between positive and negative and incited us to embrace that knowledge as well. He was a pre-existing divine being whose utterances were endowed with a grandiose omniscience that seems, even to the modern discerning mind, far removed from his actual approach and practice. He used this omniscience to elevate man to a *truly son of God* status, able to discover his own dual powers as verbalized in the Bible: "and the Lord God said, behold, the man is become as one of us, to know *good and evil*: and now, lest he put forth his hand, and take also of the tree of life, and eat, and *live forever.*" (Gen. 3:22.)

Living for ever in God is what Jesus exemplified in many of his parables and sermons. The *subconscious mind* where God the Father also dwells has been there all along. We have not had any access to it but now it is being revealed. God did not intend to keep His sons from this Tree of Life forever. There is no purpose in hiding it as man has come to recognize the good from the evil, dwell in the good and reject the evil, the path to both is clear and wide open.

Jesus, the catalyst of positivism was bent to bring out to surface from the underlying human currents of mixed energies, the energy type of universal designation. He would draw positive feelings as an emotional energy interaction from those around him. Even when there was no interaction by him to create the event the apparent catalyst effect was always present. This accounts for the reasons why the multitude of his listeners felt they were constantly floating in a pool of goodwill and peace of mind. The laws of energy interaction we call *Law of Attraction* are that you cannot be hit harder than you hit back. You can get only what you give. You cannot touch without being touched: an essence of the Christian credo.

Our main purpose is to highlight and understand this human positive energy. It is the sustainer and provider of life's very essence described by Jesus sometimes verbatim and most of the time through parables for lack of assimilation even among his own disciples. When a human thinks positively he or she generates positive energy instantly transmitted through the electromagnetic field which fills and surrounds the body. It counteracts any negative energy it comes into contact with. The more positive energy is transmitted, the more negative energy is reversed.

When love, the first positive pillar, unleashes its *protons* an electromagnetic wave runs from the source to the receiver. The exchange of energy stimulates the electromagnetic field of the receiver causing his field to literally change the vibration frequency by slowing his pulse and breathing rate. In the rare occasions when the receiver is not able to receive the potent it means that *negative energy is predominant in his field* preventing his soul from accepting the positive energy. If a soul is consumed with negative energy the only way to free it for consumption of protons is to allow it to experience the pain it is causing others.

If a soul is not hungry for love it means it has too much negativity to notice that it is hungry. To *want and not know what* is a very dangerous situation. These *lost souls* are to whom Jesus came. Their only hope then and now was that a super-soul comes across with a positive energy strong enough to overwhelm their negative balance ratio. Without that the soul is at a loss to find strength, hope and forgiveness. Only after a human feels the exchange of love will he remember that is what he sought all along. With no *exchange of protons* the soul merely incarcerates within the body instead of thriving. It yearns to the help of *only one person* to change this soul's path.

The dynamics of energy perform exactly as prescribed by nature: electromagnetic energy is made up of protons (positively charged particles), electrons (negatively charged particles) and neutrons (zero charge or neutral particles). If a soul is emitting positive energy then it is emitting more protons than electrons. If a soul thinks negative or hurtful thoughts the brain emits electrons or negatively charged particles. This energy transmitted by human thoughts has been even measured and considered powerful enough to cross distances and penetrate walls. It changes forms but one can feel such forms and stop or increase them at will.

God may not end this world we know and enjoy. But negative energy will freeze life and its quality. God is not responsible for implanting the negative force for the purpose

44

of empowering the human being with a *whole energy*. Only humans who pursue their negative thoughts, plans and actions are responsible. Negative breeds only negative causing a chain reaction of destructive events not because of some self imposed sentence by God, but because of the consequences of intense negative energy blindly emitted by the human race.

-5-

Man and Deity

'Man, like Deity, creates in his own image.'
Albert Hubbard

Through the earliest known history of man as well as from the oldest relics of antiquity we have been able to unravel, man recognized in every age some deity or deities and worshipped them. Even today every nation from the most primitive to the most advanced believes in and worships some deity. Having a deity and worshipping him is ingrained in the human nature. The constant exertion between negative and positive powers within man's soul forces him to do so.

That struggle however was not the only *thing* that impelled man to follow this trail. Other factors contributed to drive him there. These can be discovered if we look at the position of man in this huge universe. Neither man nor his nature is omnipotent. He is neither self-sufficient nor self-existing; nor is his power limitless. In fact he is weak, frail, needy and destitute.

As early as man started thinking his mind evolved on three unanswered questions: "where do I come from?" "Why am I here?" and "where am I going?" Such questions remain today impenetrable. Every time man attempted to produce a likely explanation skepticism would emanate within him carrying the germs of its downfall. Early man continued through a no-solution path, floundering within the myriad of forces that only today we managed to unmask: the mysteries of gravitation, the chemical atoms, the luminous ether, the electrostatic forces and the greatest mystery of all—his own electrical impulses.

The *ancients* were on the right road somehow as is now demonstrated in Sympathetic Vibratory machinery. They knew of the causal world and *sensed* the unvarying laws of nature almost as all men of science of our time know. They could not fathom but surely *felt* within their beings the positive power which initiates aggregative motion or integration and the negative one which initiates seceding motion or disintegration. Yet those unknown powers in the human organism filled them with fears and disorientations. They feared death; pain and illness; bereavement and loss, personal or natural disasters. The degree of stoicism and resilience was neither within their grasp nor the intellectual daring to accept these things as natural causes not because of some malign supernatural influence they could not appease or control. To gain—or regain equanimity and tranquility they resorted to *mediums* and created their own deities. These *obsessions* did not cease even later with the days of the Apostles on whom the power was conferred to *cast out devils*, or *evil spirits*.

All along the way mankind has always felt the need to worship some kind of higher being. The worshipful varied among the countless Egyptian deities, the Greek gods, the Hindu deities, Buddha and Jupiter, the god of wine or the goddess of beauty . . . Worshiping these beings happened throughout times in individual cultures separated by thousands of miles. These gods aren't necessarily morally or intellectually *higher* or more advanced . . . they just have supernatural powers which are inspirational to their worshippers. The Greek, Roman, and Old Testament gods are examples; yet the human race felt always the need to yield to something superior and better than his self or other peers.

The Greek gods were much more insightful, knowledgeable, and powerful than humans but not infinitely so. Moreover their most distinctive quality is not goodness, but power: power defines a god that represents a type of action, a kind of force. Thus Aphrodite is the force of love and lust; Zeus is the power of the thunderbolt and of kingship; Ares is the power of battle run amok and so on.

They may seem all-too human to us: they get angry over little insults; they let their lusts carry them away (Zeus and Europe); they steal from each other; they engage in petty feuds with one another. Moreover the Greek gods appear to humans and mingle with them, (Cadmus, Europa's brother, had a sumptuous marriage ceremony attended by a host of gods). Unlike men who eat bread and wine the gods eat immortal, uncooked food called *ambrosia* and drink *nectar*. They don't eat cooked meat but savor only the smoke from the altars . . .

Man created those gods to mesh with his aspirations and idealism: humans are *like gods* when they exhibit extraordinary power or resourcefulness or when they possess extraordinary beauty or strength. Humans wanted to imitate the gods' admirable qualities of power and beauty and sometimes, as in the case of Achilles and Helen, excessive behavior to get closer to gods. The Greek human commits a fault not by disobeying divine law as in Hebrew religion, but by exceeding human limits or by trying to outdo, rival or mock the gods.

The Greeks accepted the sad fact that much of life is indeed frail and insubstantial and even the greatest endeavors might fail; but they believed that it could suddenly be enhanced and illuminated and made full and wonderful if they exerted their powers to the utmost and set them harmoniously to work. At such times a man enjoys an exalted happiness—gods willing, along with them in celestial bliss.

This stance is immortalized by a Homer's hymn to Apollo:

And straightway music and singing beguile the immortals.
All the Muses together, voice answering heavenly voice,
Hymn the undying gifts of gods and the sufferings of men,
Who, enduring so much at the hands of the gods everlasting,
Live heedless and helpless, unable to find for themselves
Either a cure for death or a bulwark against old age.

Even when Paul and Barnabas healed the impotent man in Lystra people who saw the miracle "lifted up their voices saying . . . the gods are come down to us in the likeness of men.

And they called Barnabas Jupiter and Paul Mercurius . . . and brought oxen and garlands as sacrifice to them." (Act. 14.11.)

Man always sought to understand his surroundings and when there was a question whose answer was beyond his capacity to understand he created a being in his image with greater competence and capabilities. This is exactly how children act in considering their authoritative parents as the super humans, but once grownups they realize they are mere fallible mortals in need of the support of gods they can communicate with . . . deity and religion.

For ancient Egyptians why does the sun rise and provide light and warmth in an impeccable cycle was too big a question. The sun became to them the life-given god Ra'a to be venerated and worshipped; a mighty god indeed that reflects their human weakness. When other ancient people worshipped various powers of nature fear was their deep-seated inadequacy. The fear syndrome would explain the countless sacrifices that numerous races made to their gods throughout time and the single, most important dreadful event in any human was and remains: death. This is the enigmatic thing that nobody could reconcile himself with and only spirituality could provide the vehicle to embark upon.

With cumulative evolution man endowed with some rationality believed in a more decorous higher being than himself. His psychological needs and human development led him gradually to religious belief and religious institutions. In his paranormal world he created his own gods thoroughly proven to his standards. Religion was an attempt to understand and explain the universe and everything that it encompasses: a primitive form of philosophy.

Hard-wired humans torn within themselves by the negative and positive currents of their hidden power sought out to recognize patterns within what would normally be complete chaos. In this respect French physicist and philosopher Blaise Pascal said: "there is a God-shaped vacuum in the heart of every man which only God can fill and His son Jesus Christ." Because of this, humans tended to attribute seemingly superior patterns to something *more important* than themselves or what they perceived. Many of these patterns are easily explained: humans never liked to be purposeless and would rather let super someone else do the spiritual driving and bestow on them the required tranquility and a sense of purpose in this short, despondent life.

To early Sethian (from Seth, son of Adam) *Gnostic* scholars, the Secret book of John relates the expansion of the divine extending to the realm of electricity defined under various names: eons, luminaries, brilliant clouds, heavens and firmament of the universe. In their same book of John they describe the transcendence of the divine in ethereal expressions:

The One is illimitable, since there is
nothing before it to limit it.
Unfathomable, since there is nothing before it to fathom it.
Immeasurable, since there was nothing
before it to measure it.
Invisible, since nobody has seen it.
Eternal, since it exists eternally.
Unutterable, since nothing could comprehend it to utter it.
Unnamable, since there is nothing
before it to give it a name.

The One is the immeasurable light, pure, holy, immaculate.
It is unutterable, and is perfect in incorruptibility.
Not that it is just perfection, or blessedness,
or divinity: it is much greater.
The One is not corporeal and it is not incorporeal.
The One is not large and it is not small
It is impossible to say.
How much is it?
What (kind is it)?
For no one can understand it. (11.3)

Thus they devoted to Deity all imaginable attributes in the superlative domain; most of them can be listed under the purely *positive* traits we have come to know today. Then came Islam and bestowed to Allah through the overflowing Arabic language 99 names and directed followers to use them when calling Him.

Many of the past celebrated rituals may seem like worship of a higher being. They are more or less suggesting there is beauty and order in the sky and it is awe-inspiring. What *god* meant to ancients is not necessarily the same thing it means to atheists; a lot of philosophers are speaking of the inherent beauty and order of the universe not of a conscious deity. They are awed by the existence of existence; the being of being that it is a complex, regular and great mystery. They have gotten so used to it that we think being atheists makes the mystery disappear under scientific explanation. But all science can do—and it does very well, is describe it. And after all the scientific theories are convincingly laid on the table the metaphysical *question* remains unanswered: an essential part of any human experience. Scientific knowledge failed to reach what is behind its prescribed path; even if it does it will stumble with the mandatory recognition of the non-material world and swing back too feeble to invade its mysteries.

Jesus Christ to the amazement of many has not separated himself from the scientific experience. In fact he came to enhance it and built most of his doctrine on the accomplished art of penetrating man's inner self and directing his faculties to the positive path. The Church and Apostle Paul in particular that sadly did not break through the core of Jesus' philosophy could not as well deviate from that science even if they would; for real Christianity as taught and upheld by Jesus is truthful, positive psychology and the Great Nazarene remains the divine dean of all psychologists of all ages, most certainly in our advanced age today. Pseudoscience has made war on Christianity thanks to the inept Church that may suffer greater penalty in the crumbling away of its many foundation stones.

Paul who did not know Jesus and only reached the peripheral of his philosophy vividly expressed his internal, human struggle in his first letter to the Romans: "for I know that in me dwells no good thing; for the will is present with me; but how to perform that which is good I find not. For the good (positive) that I would I do not; but the evil which I would not: that I do. Now if I do that I would not, it is no more I that do it, but the sin (negative) that dwells in me . . ." (Rom. 7:18.)

"Wise men believe nothing but what is certain and what has been verified by time," men of science retort. But in saying so they fail to comprehend what *belief* means and entails. Until now true science has not been able to verify the wisdom of *The Ancients* by any dynamic apparatus showing how cosmic laws work. Part of this apparatus was explained by Jesus to Judas in his recently salvaged Gospel. It is not yet fully realized that in order to protect science men of learning carried empiricism to its extreme skeptical consequences and thereby cut the ground from under the feet of science sowing seeds of skepticism for many generations. This venomous propagation wafted from one land to another to produce year after year a prolific and ever-increasing crop of negativism, materialism and infidelity, all blossoming into anarchy . . .

Much before science has fostered all the evils by displaying its brilliant and deceiving face, Christ came to rescue man with a system of *spiritual physics* susceptible of proof to the senses. In fact science today started reforming its display with theories like: "a knowledge of scientific theories kills all knowledge of scientific facts;" this *resuscitating* attempt makes it clear to whoever can comprehend it that we are related to the whole universe, and that the fundamental doctrine of *Universal Attraction* is part of the cosmic laws of sympathetic association much sneered at by the ignorant or oblivious men of science.

Such cosmic laws are what we see and feel within our beings in physical form from the creative force that is our mainspring. It is the creative force which man calls God that gives form to his body and shapes his individual world. Were it withdrawn or were anything to interfere sufficiently with its functioning the body would become an inert mass; dead, as we say and likewise its individual world. So the life of an individual man, the individual tributary, opens out into the great sea of life which is its source.

Knowing that the individual life and Power are one with the Infinite Spirit and Power enlarges one's consciousness and gives a wider reception from the Source for that life. It was the flood-gate of this larger reservoir of life that Jesus opened with his supreme aptitude for discerning the issues of the mind and the spirit; it so flooded his own understanding of life that it singled him out to reveal this larger truth to all who would hear and believe his word. It was a great intuitive perception or consciousness which opened the knowledge of this life to his fellow children of God.

This positive cosmic association, the Kingdom of Heaven in Jesus' oversimplification, is the core of the Christian credo that many modern Christians ignore for lack of dwelling deeper into Jesus' teachings. An association using all positive potentials of the human being to establish his peace of mind and elevate him to be a worthy *son of God*; a correlation with the Supreme that haunted man's imagination ever since his stone age.

In this respect the Mormons in the US and the Maronites in Lebanon believe in the evolution of man as a *son of man* walking his perfection road until he shall be a joint heir with Jesus! They both derive this belief from the Gospel based on the Sermon on the Mount: "Be you therefore *perfect*, even as your Father which is in heaven is *perfect*." (Mat. 5:48.) The translation of the Aramaic word *perfect* "Temimo" means accomplished and fully developed; this is the term Jesus chose to communicate the real meaning: *free of all negatives*, without embellishment or trimming. Jesus was a living example in perfecting the son of man he was until full integration with God;

hence the Son of God. Thus Jesus really meant what he said: becoming as our Father in Heaven who in fact dwells within us is a commandment—not just a suggestion. He repeatedly made frequent references to the fact that we are children of and should become like the Father.

Jesus who came to fine-tune the Scripture was certainly aware and supportive of David's quote: "what is man, that You are mindful of him? And the son of man, that You visited him? For You have made him a little lower than the angels, and have crowned him with glory and honor" (Psa.8:4.) And: "I have said, you are gods; and all of you are children of the most High" (Psa. 82:6.) Jesus repeatedly referred to this principle: "He answered them, is it not written in your law, I said, you are gods?" (John 10:34.)

But where is God and what are His features? This perennial question haunted my imagination since my college years. Even before that I was asking my teachers: "exactly *where* or *what* is the secret place of the Most High?" I could not accept He was in Heaven: if so, was He in the atmosphere, the stratosphere, the troposphere or somewhere in the vast firmament? Is He on a throne surrounded by angels as the western imagination depicts Him in countless paintings or is He in the Seventh Heaven or on a throne over the water as Islam narrates? Is He a Soul as in the Scripture? And is that Soul similar in shape to the man himself?

Most of the time my teachers made up a nonspecific answer or gave me some spiritual cliché but nobody was able to give me a direct answer. It was *so very important* for me to find this *secret place* because I wanted to *dwell there*. Is God currently revealing where that is located? To my amazement, these and other questions were plainly answered by Jesus: the *secret place of the Most High* is not in Heaven or *in the Garden of Eden* but in our mind in as much as *the mind of Christ*! True. Jesus referred to God as *the heavenly Father* and even taught us to pray *our Father who is in Heaven* to bestow Him the due eminence and distinction inherent to the human mentality.

Neither the Old Testament nor the Koran could accept a God who is so human. Their great protest is that it is not suitable to speak of God in this way; He must remain pure Majesty full of mercy certainly but full of wrath as well. His mercy should not exceed the point of paying for the faults and sins of His own creatures. Other clerics and philosophers wrote volumes evolving around the big question: "If God exists, why is He hiding?" But God revealed his secrets to his sons and we are His sons as much as Jesus is. We interrelate with our minds and this is where God dwells. Our subconscious mind is the *only* realm of God and this is where we can meet, *see* and interact with Him.

-6-

God: the Holy Spirit

"God is the Truth clothed with Light, the absolute Verity."

Pythagoras

The Holy Spirit is God and God is the Holy Spirit exhibited and imparted to humans. The Scripture abounds with such manifestations: in Acts 5:3, Peter confronts Ananias as to why he had lied to the Holy Spirit and tells him that he did "not lie to men but to God." The Holy Spirit possesses all the attributes and characteristics of God despite the many misconceptions on its identity. Some view the Holy Spirit as a mystical force. Others understand it as the impersonal power God makes available to followers of Christ. The Scripture invariably describes the Holy Spirit as a Person, a Being with a mind, emotions, and a will: the basic traits of the human character.

David, in Ps. 139:7 says: "where can I go from Your Spirit? Or where can I flee from Your presence? If I ascend into heaven, You are there; If I make my bed in hell, behold, You are there." While in 1Cor.2:10 we see the characteristic of omniscience in the Holy Spirit. "But God has revealed them to us through His Spirit. For the Spirit searches all things, yes, and the deep things of God. For what man knows the things of a man except the spirit of the man which is in him? Even so no one knows the things of God except the Spirit of God."

Jesus did not teach that the Holy Ghost was another Person when he said, "The Comforter, which is the Holy Ghost, whom the Father will send in my name, He shall teach you all things . . ." (John 14:26.) Again Jesus said, ". . . if I go not away, the Comforter will not come unto you." (John 16:7.) Also John said, "I will not leave you comfortless: I will come to you." (John 14:18.) A Trinitarian concept contends that the Father, Son and Holy Ghost are one in holiness, love, wisdom and eternal power; but, three in Person. No Scripture can be found to support such a concept but the tradition seems to fit and complement wholeness also the Torah boasts many verses negating it: "I am the Lord . . . and my glory will I not give to another." (Isa. 42:8.)

When the Holy Ghost came on the day of Pentecost 120 disciples were filled and began to speak with tongues as the Spirit gave them utterance. (Act. 2:4.) Peter preached that the

Holy Ghost was the Spirit of God, he said, "It shall come to pass in the last days, says God, and I will pour out of my spirit upon all flesh . . ." (Act.2:17.) As to Paul, he used the terms *Spirit of God* and *Spirit of Christ* as synonymous terms in reference to the Holy Spirit. He said, "You are not in the flesh, but in the Spirit, if so be that the Spirit of God dwell in you. Now if any man has not the Spirit of Christ, he is none of His." (Rom. 8:9.) Thus, only one God manifested in the flesh and received in the hearts of believers. This truth was universally preached by the New Testament Church for many years after Christ.

The Scripture speaks repeatedly of the Holy Spirit known also as the Spirit of God and the Spirit of Christ. It indicates that the Holy Spirit is of the same essence as the Father and the Son. The Holy Spirit is ascribed with the attributes of God, is equated with God and does work that only God does. The New Testament came to further elucidate the relationship between God and His Spirit. It went ahead to even *humanize* the Holy Spirit endowing it with mind, emotions, and will. The Holy Spirit thinks and knows (1Cor. 2:10.) It can be grieved (Eph. 4:30.) It intercedes for us (Rom. 8:26.) The Holy Spirit makes decisions according to His will (1Cor. 12:7.) The Holy Spirit is God, the third *Person* of the Trinity. As God the Holy Spirit can truly function in the same way as the Comforter and Counselor that Jesus promised he would be. These are *the seven qualities* recognized by the Catholic Church.

All the attributes of God are exactly the traits of the Holy Spirit. Holiness is its basic characteristic. The Spirit is so holy that blasphemy against the Spirit cannot be forgiven although blasphemy against Jesus could be (Mat. 12:32.) Insulting the Spirit is just as sinful as trampling the Son of God under foot

(Heb. 10:29.) This indicates that the Spirit is inherently holy in essence. It is eternal: the Holy Spirit, the Comforter, the Consoler, will be with us *forever* (John 14:16.) And the Spirit is *eternal* (Heb. 9:14.) It is omnipresent; existing according to David in *heaven and in hell, in the east and in the west.* It is also omnipotent; the miracles of Jesus were done *by the Spirit* (Mat. 12:28.) In Paul's ministry, the work that "Christ has accomplished" was done *through the power of the Spirit"* (Rom. 15:18.) Last but not least, it is *Omni scientific*: "The Spirit therefore knows all things and is able to *teach* all things (John 14:26.)

Thus the Holy Spirit has a personality. It is the replica of God humanized with mind and will; it speaks and can be spoken to; it acts and intercedes for us. It is our *personal* relationship with God in the sense of possessing our human attributes: it is *intelligent*: the Spirit *knows* (1Cor. 2:11) and is equipped with a mind that is able to make judgments: a decision *seemed good* to the Holy Spirit (Act. 15:28) . . . an inherently distinct human intelligence.

The Holy Spirit executes divine works; it creates, expels demons, beget and the full divinity of the Son implies the full divinity of the Begetter. It begets believers, too: they are born of God (John 1:12) and equally born of the Spirit (John 3:5.) The Spirit gives [eternal] life" (John 6:63.) It is the power by which we will be resurrected (Rom. 8:11.) *It indwells the human mind, it "lives" in us* (Rom. 8:11; 1Cor. 3:16), and because the Spirit lives in us we are able to say that *God lives in us* because the Holy Spirit is God and not His representative or power—God himself lives in us and to deal with the Spirit is to have dealings with the Father and the Son.

This is a good entrance to define the Holy Spirit in our modern understanding: it is the spirit of God the dwells in man's mind whenever he achieves the second renaissance and accost the positive superhighway. It implies intelligence, a concern, and a formal role. Thus the Holy Spirit is not an impersonal or an outlandish power but *an inherent and built-in intelligence that lives within us triggered by the divine helper.*

It is the purity of God. It emanates from the same source that personifies the Mind of God in interaction. When Jesus was baptized in the Jordan River the Holy Spirit fell upon him like a dove, the emblem of purity and gentleness; not like *fire* but like a *dove.* And like the dove of Noah, long did the Holy Ghost hover over this world before He could find a resting-place within the Glorified Body of Jesus. His purity met and meshed favorably with the child-pure mind of the Master. With this purity he opposed all human vicissitudes, all that which is negative, dead, offensive, and only fit for the scavenger. He saw man, every man, in his real state of sin *exactly as God sees him.*

Again, the advent of science—regarded as the enemy of Faith and spirituality, is putting Christian theology today in a credibility crisis; so long as theological extrapolations in matters of nature and earth/human relationships conflict with the human experience the credibility issue intensifies. We need to take seriously the radical truth of Pope John Paul II that heaven is not a "place in the clouds" but rather a *"relationship with God."* A deeper insight into the *scripture* of the universe informs respectful relationship; thus, the case for replacing in religion its static-centrist worldview with the transformational process should be pursued. Until this quantum leap in theology is achieved the frustrating religious wavering will remain.

Jesus proved his divine authority by revealing these ways to his disciples and many audiences to the extent of extraordinary works that he wrought including suspensions of the laws of nature. They are illustrations of the power of mind over matter, of the spirit over the flesh. To recreate such miracles we have the express authority of Jesus himself. Although he ascribed his extraordinary work directly to God but also declared they were wrought by faith; thus basing his authority as a messenger of God not upon any departure from the laws of nature, but upon the power of the very highest law of nature. Therefore Christ was a mediator throughout the remarkable things he has done between the two things which are to be forever most intimately united: science on the one hand and faith on the other. Only Jesus established a palpable truth: the supremacy of spiritual mind over physical matter.

Our bodies are the Tabernacle of God or the House of the Lord. When He *restores our soul* or *renews our minds* then He dwells within us forever. The subconscious is the portion made in the image of the Creator's mind as recorded in Genesis. It is that portion of us that befits the mind of God. It stands apart from anything earthly and only makes its presence known when the soul-self lifts itself up into the vast, expansive level that is God and become part of that oneness. We relate to God by relating to Jesus Christ. That specific relationship is what makes Christians different from followers of other monolithic faiths and what distinctly shapes their approach to ethics, justice and peace, reverence and awe. That is exactly what Paul meant when he said that Christians are supposed to be *in Christ* without really explaining how.

Yet he did explain it to the Corinthians (Cor. 3:16): "You are the Temple of God". He used Solomon's Temple as an illustration and compared each of its rooms and features to our own internal design—our spirit, heart, will, soul and body. The architecture of this Temple included the secret, hidden chambers (*cheder*). This *hidden part* is the subconscious where we hide and bury our hurts, wounds, pleasant and painful memories or the opposite ones. And a very important part of renewing our minds is the cleansing, healing and filling of these hidden chambers so we may make room for the Holy Spirit to dwell there. This *sanctification* process that we go through slowly teaches us that our mind starts functioning as the mind of Christ. There is no mention of the word *subconscious* throughout the Scripture yet that surely was the *hidden place:* our own innermost part.

Many readers would take the ongoing dissertation as mere repetitive Freudian concepts that highlighted the subconscious as the inner human reservoir. Freud did use such insinuations but simply alienated himself from the belief factor that works through the heart of the inner man or woman. It is important therefore for Christians to understand the difference between the "hidden part of man's heart" (1Pet.3:4) and the Freudian psychological approach about the subconscious. While psychological ideas are so rampant in the church as well as in the lives of Christians today we are following here what Jesus discerned two thousand years ago and rephrase it in modern terms and concepts. The intent is to achieve transformation into the image of Christ and bestow God's love that very few can propagate: it is one of the aspects of the Holy Spirit on earth, its pulsations cannot emanate by a negatively plagued subconscious mind.

-7-

The Subconscious Mind

"Enter in the narrow gate, which leads unto life."
Jesus Christ

G od created the mind that we are just beginning to understand its potential. Medical science tells us we only use less than 10% of our brain. There lies a frontier of latent power that heretofore was only harnessed by one man throughout the history of mankind: Jesus Christ.

It was only about two hundred years ago that scientists discovered the subconscious mind and were able to demonstrate the difference between the consciousness and the subconscious.

The two minds have different qualities and abilities. The subconscious mind is very powerful and we have all experienced it knowingly or inadvertently every day of our lives. As we examine it further we perceive its untapped potential and the seemingly impossible things it easily does. For 6000 years we did not even know it existed although Jesus was its pioneer, and only recently we begun to understand its propensities.

There are many divergences between the two: the conscious mind goes to sleep at night but the subconscious never sleeps; in fact it has *never* slept in any human ever since he or she was a mere fetus. This is the tool that reflects our dreams when we sleep and the one that sustains the life functions of our body; it supervises our heartbeat, breathing or even eye blinking. The subconscious mind is in charge of *healing and repairing* the body.

It could be called the *feeling mind.* This part of our brain seems like nothing more than a non-thinking, insensitive, machine-like brute, but is really an incredibly capable computer which never forgets. It does not seem to care how much you hurt if you do. In fact the subconscious mind seems to view all emotions simply as its operating *facts*—just associated items in its database of information. It is only doing its job . . . constantly assimilating what has been *programmed* into it. Hence a human *should be careful* of what he or she chronicles in this computer because he or she would *sooner or later be getting to it.* Everything to the subconscious is cut and dried, black and white, and it will always give the same *emotionally charged* (plus or minus) answer to the same association until its programming or input is changed.

The subconscious houses information from both inherent and inherit knowledge. Inherent knowledge is from our species.

And depending of your rank as naturalist or spiritualist you may call it the human instinct or the soul of God. In the former it is much like the salmon who knows to swim upstream to spawn; in the latter it is the human-held knowledge of this God-created species. Inherit knowledge differs from inherent as to its source. It operates along bloodlines. Talents and abilities possessed without prior learning are many times the result of our inherit knowledge.

An almost equal amount of our subconscious data as inherent and inherit knowledge is our personal memory. Childhood, adolescence, songs, sights, thoughts, ideas, all are stored within our subconscious mind. They affect our conscious mind through hints and suggestion, sometimes sneaking through corridors and circumstances *unknown to us.* Thus an observation made years ago is connected with a statement made two days ago and an idea based on this connection presents itself unexpectedly.

It reasons differently than the conscious mind. It is totally undiscriminating and promiscuous. It welcomes every happenstance, every impression and every realization that rings its doorbell. It will not think over, think through or think twice—because it can't. It is the storehouse of all your thoughts and feelings which together release electrical vibrations. In turn these vibrations through the Law of Attraction or repetition attract into man's experience everything that resonates with his beliefs and convictions. This was discovered in the late 1800's when hypnosis was demonstrated for the first time. Scientist's were able to put the conscious mind of a subject to sleep and then access the subconscious mind. First it was noticed that the hypnotized person was totally *amenable to suggestion.* That means he would *believe* whatever he was told. For example if a person was told it was very cold in a room temperature of 90 degrees, he would believe and begin to shiver. That is the *deductive reasoning*. The conscious mind reasons the exact opposite; it reasons inductively i.e. gathers facts then reasons up to a conclusion. The conscious mind *doubts* everything and must be convinced whilst the subconscious has perfect *faith* and never doubts when indoctrinated with unwavering belief and resolved will!

A subconscious deductive reasoning means giving a picture of reality based on what has been programmed within. It is not locked in time but has one window open to the present time and place and another to the infinity of all time and all space. It is the filter between the finite and the infinite. Its position of being among the two levels gives it the unique capability to function as translator between the two. As such it seems to live in a sort of *spatial* time as opposed to the *linear* time of the conscious mind. This means that time to the subconscious seems to be irrelevant and therefore expandable or shrinkable according to its needs.

Few years back I personally witnessed an American stage hypnotist, Dr. Polcar, who had placed people in the subconscious state of mind. If he told one of them that he could not lift a chair that one could not and vice versa. It was quite entertaining but it demonstrates the fact that the subconscious mind *believes whatever it is told*. The hypnotist then touched his subject's arm with a pencil's eraser inducing it was a red hot one and a blister appeared within seconds. When the subconscious was told the pencil was hot it instantly sent the body into action causing it to blister. Then when he told the person that it was not really hot the blister went away just as fast. This had tremendous implications for us to understand how the subconscious mind works. Jesus Christ did not use a rod to cause a blister but used the Word of God to lift spirits and repair their containers or bodies. Those who did not *believe* in him did not get any benefit because belief is the one and only corridor to the subconscious mind while conscious deductive reasoning creates doubts and leads to negative conclusions.

A modern example is the experience with a Doctor who received a client trying to get rid of excess weight. Despite proper suggestions for changing unhelpful habits nothing occurred. In trying to discover the reason the doctor encountered his childhood experiences and found out he was sickly, exceedingly thin, and had trouble eating. His parents and other relatives were so worried for him they told him many times, "You've got to eat or you'll die!" The power of that suggestion was accepted literally by his subconscious. As he began to recover from his illnesses he began to eat enormous amounts of food thus adding far too much weight to his body. It took (1) regression and releasing methods concerning those early memories; (2) suggestions to the subconscious *child part* that he no longer had to fear dying from not eating and (3) suggestions to the adult self that he was alive and well and could now eat normally. It worked. His subconscious accepted this new fact that became the *new imprint without hypnotism,* through the Doctor's power of suggestion. He was now willing to change his poor habits and began to shed the extra weight.

The subconscious mind has control over the cells of the human body that it started initially from *one single cell* at conception. That single cell began to divide and multiply as monitored by the subconscious according to its DNA register.

Then the cells divided and started to *change form* into bone cells, skin cells, brain cells . . . and so on until they formed the body. It all happened cyclically throughout the formation of the *organism* because *something* was *organizing* everything. The subconscious is that something created by God to perform that complex task. It continues in control of the atoms and the cells of the body and has the ability to create new skin cells when one gets a cut. It can regenerate any organ because it created them *all* from *one single cell* in the first place. The Bible abounds with verses saying the Sons of God will experience a change or a metamorphosis in their bodies. David talks to his soul through God: "and He will regenerate your youth like an eagle."

The subconscious is where *habits* nest and grow and it is as trainable as any domestic pet. It protects itself from change though with emotional—not analytical responses. This is why whenever a person suddenly gets angry or emotional you can then know where his *faith* lies. That can be anything from a scientific theory of evolution to God's stature down to simpler and mundane things. It is deeply ingrained and any force applied to it simply meets an equally forceful emotional response which is not necessarily logical but very, very powerful.

Certainly the electromagnetic signature is deeply seated in the subconscious field. This is now a proven fact that becomes more visible as the world experiences the phenomena associated with this energy. Many scientists over the past two hundred years have reached its various depths calling it various names as the bio-cosmic energy, the animal magnetism and the pyramid energy. Much of their subsequent works has come about as a direct result of their joint experiences confirming that the conscious mind constantly mirrors the infinite reality and what we call spiritual *truth* to the subconscious that in turn shows this to us in dream visions as symbols.

A psychiatrist attempts to remove the *negative mental block*—forgives the sins as in the case of Jesus on a much higher scale—and encourages the patient to adopt a new, positive mental attitude which tends to release a *healing process* flowing through the patient as harmony, health, and peace. The priest asks you to forgive yourself and others and get in tune with the Infinite by letting the positive healing powers of love, peace, and goodness flow through your subconscious mind thereby cleansing many negative patterns that may have lodged there.

Hypnosis reaches underneath the reasoning mind that calculates but does not believe, into the subconscious mind that can understand and believe. The therapist uses altered-state methods to get at that deeper part of the mind which can have the faith to be healed; and just like the disciple he must have faith in order to use hypnosis to help another person be healed. The therapist is not doing the healing, but is *assisting* that person to use more of his own inner resources to absorb what is already given to him. If therapists are not *convinced* that hypnosis can help heal or, more likely, worry that they might be too audacious in suggesting that a client can be healed, then they may betray their own lack of confidence and expectation, and thus influence negatively the confidence and expectation of their clients.

When we *believe* in something our subconscious mind accepts it whether it is real or not. Whatever the conscious mind believes in is accepted as fact by the subconscious. It doesn't differentiate between what is being imagined and what is actually happening and doesn't distinguish between what is real or unreal, true or false. Whatever our subconscious mind accepts as fact will be carried out in our bodies. Hence imagination and emotions have a powerful effect on the body.

The subconscious always reconciles what it got from the conscious and presents the internal harmony or disharmony to us in little symbolic movies or parables many times as we sleep. Dreams can be seen as *real time* readouts on the internal state of either harmony or disharmony between the levels of the individual Self. Dreams could also be called the truly *local*, up-to-the-minute news of the inner condition of the individual. Hence, throughout the Scripture dreams reflected suggestions based on the mental concerns and worries of the people. A dream showed the Pharaohs in Egypt the dreary seven years ahead that was decoded by Joseph, and to Joseph of Nazareth to take Mary and baby Jesus and flee to Egypt. The Angel of God or the *spiritual premonition* was always there to tell what should be done.

Humans are created in three-dimensional manifestations of life, light, and love. A far cry from the triune substance of the Father, the Son and the Holy Spirit and another human-divine unity of the Body, Mind and Spirit. Today science and metaphysics describe human awareness in terms of consciousness (mind), subconscious (soul), and the collective super conscious (spirit).

God, the Father or the Presence of Life inhabits our cleansed subconscious mind and can be an integral part of it. The striking resemblance between the two is almost palpable: the mind of the Lord never sleeps and so does our subconscious; the mind of God reasons deductively and so does our subconscious; the first has perfect faith and so our subconscious; the child-mind of God is displayed in the subconscious functioning. A human's access to his/her subconscious is an access to God. No human can log on his subconscious realm unless he uses the positive narrow door. "Enter in at the strait (positive) gate; Jesus said, wide is the gate, and broad is the (negative) way that leads to destruction and many chose to take it. Because strait is the gate and narrow is the way which leads unto life and *few are those who find it.*" (Mat. 7:13.)

Jesus pioneered and promulgated for the first time in human history the powers of the subconscious that was Omni-present throughout his parables, some of them were solely devoted to explain its characteristics and the way to understand them by "whoever has ears to listen . . ." Here is one: *"The kingdom of God is as if a man should cast seed into the ground; and should sleep, and rise night and day, and the seed should spring and grow up, **he knows not how,** for the earth brings forth fruit of herself; first the blade, then the ear, after that the full corn in the ear; but when the fruit is brought forth, immediately he puts in the sickle, because the harvest is come."* (Mar. 4:26.)

Undoubtedly the power of the subconscious mind is explicitly illustrated in this parable. Any modern psychology professor would not be able to invent a better parable to exemplify it. Our released Thought Forms *germinate* and grow until they can eventually manifest themselves as palpable objects after which they can be harvested and experienced. The "ground" is the *garden* of the Subconscious where the seeds/thoughts are sown either consciously or unconsciously. Jesus' saying: *should sleep, and rise night and day, and the seed should spring and grow up* means that once the *seed* has been sown in that fertile ground that most people are unaware of it will first germinate, then sprout, and finally develop into the vivid experience as a waking certainty.

Jesus gave us another parable on how to cleanse our subconscious and achieve the true renaissance. It has not been understood at his times as well as by many in our churches today but remains very much applicable to this era of advanced knowledge: "the kingdom of heaven is likened unto a man which sowed *Good Seed* in his field; but while men slept, *his enemy* came and sowed tares among the wheat, and went his way. But when the blade was sprung up, and brought forth fruit, then appeared the tares also. So the servants of the householder came and said unto him, Sir, didn't you sow Good Seed in your field? From whence then has it tares? He said unto them, <u>an enemy</u> has done this. The servants said unto him, will you then that we go and gather them up? But he said, *nay*; lest while you gather up the tares, you root up also the wheat with them. Let both grow together until the harvest: and in the time of harvest I will say to the reapers, gather together FIRST the tares, and bind them in bundles to burn them: but gather the wheat into my barn." (Mat. 13:24.)

Jesus wanted the human being to let these unwanted negative implants of his youth to grow along with the positive ones in his subconscious because until he/she grows, one can't distinguish the difference between them. After *growing* it becomes *discernible* to refuse the evil and choose the good. If we weed our garden when we are immature we will pull up the good seed along with the bad. Yet during the time of maturity, *harvest time,* we can remove all the tares that the negative forces—or "enemy," have planted there. This is the first step toward renewing our minds and such is the *renaissance* much heralded by the Master.

This mighty tool that Jesus promulgated 2000 years ago has been withheld from us until we spiritually mature. It is that part of our mind which God has kept virgin, reserved to those who will be able to properly handle its powers and capabilities. The brainpower of Christ has changed in the past and will keep changing everything today. The unexplored periphery of the mind was harnessed by Jesus, the vanguard of human positive power across all ages and he used it to heal others, read their thoughts and even move through a crowd unseen by those around him. He spoke to trees, wind, waves, animals and they responded. He caused withered limbs to straighten out, blind eyes to see and deaf ears to open. Through the Omni powerful mind of Christ he multiplied the loaves and fishes to feed thousands and changed water into wine. He took the severed ear of a soldier and restored it instantly back on his head. He predicted the future with impeccable accuracy telling Peter he would deny him three times before the rooster crowed in the morning. Jesus calmed the wind and seas and walked on water. All these things were done by the power of the mind of Christ charged all the time by the positive command of the Holy Spirit.

It is a fact that probably more than 50 percent of the diseases and disabilities we experience stem from our minds and consequently our minds can also heal us from them. Our minds are greatly involved in letting those *tares* find their way to our subconscious and take over our lives. The other 50% are nature's negative functioning mostly enhanced by modern man to produce viruses and impurities. To counter the first half the negative information in the mind (or old hypnotic spells) has to be reversed through positive hypnotic suggestions and actions. The subconscious responds to our strong impression only if the previous impression is *inferior in strength* and reprogramming with fresh ideas takes place. The process consists of getting rid of the previous imprint (*tares*) and providing sufficient reasons and benefits to the subconscious mind to accept the new imprint. This is what reprogramming is all about.

Ideas can be positively or negatively accepted depending upon previous *programming* and emotions surrounding the ideas whether understood or misunderstood. This delicate method suggests positive ideas which affect the body and cause a positive response; a powerful tool indeed to convince the mind to create a healthy environment outside its electromagnetic shield or inside it. However the *manager of the mind* awaits instructions before getting rid of negative programming. Until then it goes on using the same program unless convincingly told otherwise exactly like a computer which, despite all the hardware cannot run until you enter a program that in turn cannot operate until you touch the keyboard. Entering new human programs is like adding a new dimension to the imagination of the computer or tapping into more of its potential *mind*. Previous natural incarnations in the human mind however maintain their imprints. This is what Jesus meant when asked about the blind man whether his parents sinned or himself in saying: "Neither this man sinned nor his parents, but just to show the acts of God in him." In such a case it is necessary to treat that previous incarnation that went in the human blood through previous generations; what we call DNA history today.

Healing—or killing energy through positive or negative impulses, broadcasts equally as well through the *mechanism* of this amazing subconscious machine. It is comparable to a telephone modem which can connect two or more computers across the world and let them exchange information. This is why *"prayer with belief"*, or *intensive positive purpose*, works much better than reason or argument when attempting to aid own self or even another person when both are resistant to change. Such attempted aid through the will power supported by belief always meets the receptive subconscious that cannot be deceived or tricked. It only yields to the true spiritual ideals and the full natural resonance of the mind that can truthfully penetrate its layers. It is wide open to the positive pattern of truths imprinted in our conscious and delivered with belief and an action of *will*; thus the subconscious does not resist the conscious input but rather listens to it patiently before saying "that does or does not agree with my individual ego's programming". When it does not, the complex problems of reconciling the *opposites*, positives and negatives would emerge; which may engender an *emotional disharmony* and end up through cheating or disbelief expulsing such disharmonies in the outer conscious sphere.

We already possess the same exact mind Jesus had: ". . . But we have the Mind of Christ." (Cor. 2:16.) Only it remains concealed for the moment. It's evident that we need to grow and mature unto the full stature of the measure of Christ. Even though people accept Jesus in their heart/spirit they find they still have a corporeal not spiritual mind to deal with; the difference between the spirit (heart) and the soul (mind). In fact, people use both words thinking they are the same thing. Many Christians cared to seek a deeper walk with God and they try to overcome the corporeal thoughts and desires and few of those are the saints we revere today: "for the corporally minded is death; but to be spiritually minded is life and peace. Because the carnal mind is enmity against God: for it is not subject to the laws of God, neither indeed can be." (Rom 8:6-7).

Jesus Christ sets the pace for us—though misunderstood by our churches, to go the positive spiritual way and adopt his philosophy which is truly "the path, the truth and life" and not the negative and sometime *neutral* attitude that leads to the wrong path, uncertainty and death. Many Christians today want to do the works that Jesus did but the carnal mind persists to take control and does not want to give it up. We all have been led by the carnal mind but we know that those who are led by the spirit are the Sons of God. The saints we glorify and implore were mere humans that discovered Jesus' way and adopted it as a lifestyle. Jesus himself was led by the spirit to overcome his carnal mind. He was tempted in every way that we are yet he did not sin by upholding his spiritual mind alive and well fuelled. The Father, our Father gave him the keys to this powerful mind and Jesus used it unselfishly. He in turn gave those keys to his disciples who were mere fishermen and now to us in this highly sophisticated generation. These same keys are still within our grip as we already possess the mind of Christ but we must *let* it be in control.

How can we make this arduous reprogramming simple? By never attempting to *lie to ourselves* and disorientate our subconscious mind but to follow the truthful path to God that dwells within and be therefore true to ourselves. We can never cheat our subconscious mind: it is God's strength residing within us. We all *know* when we are violating our own ideals i.e. deviating from our positive path. Ideals are the highest forms that we can imagine . . . even if everyone's ideals are slightly different based on their mode of understanding and developmental level of awareness. But to each individual they represent the God-like quality within the self and are the most sacred things that exist. The subconscious of a person who is growing in such awareness is one that is becoming programmed to a new reality that is closer and closer to his or her own higher ideals.

It is every man's possibility that God's thoughts *will become his* thoughts. The mind of Christ contains the thoughts of God and it thinks the same way God does. When the mind of God awakens in us then His thoughts will become our thoughts and His ways our ways. The subconscious is so powerful that it can contain all the knowledge and wisdom that God has in His mind for the bliss of mankind. One man's subconscious has more capacity than all the computers in the world put together. God created the powerful mind of Christ and we have no idea of its full potential except to say that nothing is impossible to those who possess it.

We are powerful beings. Jesus told us "with belief the size of a grain we could move mountains". Life responds to us as we respond to it. The greatest sages and saints had no greater *minds* than us but they knew how to use them. Most of us produce a life of only a fraction of what we want. Yet God does not limit us. It is our own mind which determines our experiences. Our thinking and feeling nature is the cause of this experience. This means that our future may be self-determined depending of our *magnetized will*.

A weakened man's body today can go for months in a coma through supportive medical systems. His conscious is totally dead during such period but his subconscious is alive, giving undetected impulses to his organs to keep on responding. His revival from the coma depends on the degree of instructions he had injected to his subconscious. The exact opposite is true. What happens when we die? A human mind-boggling question that could have a credible answer: the conscious dies with the body and the subconscious leaves the body. The end of life in the body means the same to the rational/volitional system being the conscious and the subconscious that constituted and sustained its awareness, both powered by the body's electrical system. After death our soul body leaves our physical body. As a soul we can then experience in various soul realms as we did every night on earth in our dreams. While in the soul realms our soul body becomes the vehicle of our spirit. Our soul mind functions as our conscious awareness while our spirit plays the role of the subconscious mind. Ultimately, we will want to leave the soul realms and enter into the higher spirit spheres. When that choice is made and the soul actually enters into the light, the soul merges fully with the light and soul body is shed much like the physical body was shed at death. The memories of the soul remain forever in the subconscious mind and the individual is now once again a pure spirit in the spirit realms. As a pure spirit we exist once again in pure thought form in the mind of the one enormous and fantastic power called God.

The subconscious travels into the bio-cosmic environment from whence it emanated to either beatitude or desolation currently known as heaven and hell, depending on the *state of mind* or the last assessment of the total life at the time of death . . . that was *the final programming in that subconscious.*

-8-

The Spiritual Power

*"The Spirit of God speaks to man when he enters
the inner chamber of his mind."*

The author

The existence of an invisible force influencing men and nature in their various activities is felt within every human. The character of this omnipresent force or Universal Spirit is supported by the Bible plainly teaching that God implanted in man His perfect image and likeness with *executive ability* to carry out all His creative plans. Man may arrive to this spiritual understanding that Jesus further spelled out: "My Father works even until now, and I work."

God has implanted Himself and infused freedom in every human. The man is created as diverse as the mind that drives him in life. Every man is king in his own mental domain and his subjects are his thoughts. In this age of scientific achievements people ask why God is not revealing His presence as He did in biblical eras while in real fact He dwells within them and talks to who can grasp His message; the spiritual insight is there only people fail to penetrate their subconscious mind to seize it.

The body is the instrument of the mind and the mind looks to the Spirit for its inspiration. A very little observation shows that *the purer the mind the greater its capacity to receive* and interpret the ideas imparted to it by the Spirit. When Spirit responds to the seeking mind and begins to reveal the magnitude of that undiscovered realm within us we long for a new language with words describing glories beyond all human comparison. Our physical body reveals a radiant, glorified body sitting—as Jesus said 'on the throne of His glory', that interlaces the trillions of cells of the organism and burns as brightly as an electric light. Jesus gave his apostles a glimpse of this radiant body when He was transfigured before them. "And as he was praying, the fashion of his countenance was altered, and his raiment became white and dazzling." (Luk. 9:29.)

Jesus' radiant body—the same body we have, was developed in larger degrees than that of anyone in our race. It glowed "as he was praying" by the intensity of his spiritual devotion; his subconscious mind restored every cell to its innate state of atomic light and power. When John the Baptist was in the state of spiritual devotion he described Jesus' appearance to him saying: "and his eyes were as a flame of fire; and his feet like unto burnished brass."

Spiritually illumined saints in human bodies reflect the illumined existence of the spiritual super-substance. Jesus put this power under control away from all psychic and *spooky* expressions which distort the soul instead of unfolding it under divine beatitude. He further taught us how to gain the mastery of the stored-up riches of the man visible through two parallel avenues: prayer/meditation to reinforce the subconscious and excess oxygen intake to instill the body.

When we pray with positive and unshaken conviction we mentally affirm statements of Truth as positively propagated by Jesus. When we do so we feel *thrills* that last a few moments then pass away; a spiritual experience we can repeat with affirmations. Such thrills intensify with devotion through points in the body and finally become a continuous current throughout the nervous system. Call it *the Spirit* as you will soon find it connected with a universal life force described by Christ through his many parables.

Prayers are our redeemers and contact with life from the negative thinking and living we have so far experienced. Jesus said, "If a man keeps my word (stay positive and alert), he shall never taste death (degeneration of the body)." Why should we believe this claim? Because modern sciences instruct us constantly that the flesh is being broken down every day and its cells regenerate and are transformed into energy and life; thereby a new body is being formed by the *regular* powers of the subconscious mind. Exceptional or increased powers will certainly *supplement* this regeneration.

Meditation and prayer go together. When we pray and meditate we extract ourselves from our mundane apprehensions or *negative zone* and enter the serene realm of confidence. This is the revolving and repeating process of the mind that, when administered with belief, provides entrance to the subconscious mind. Once we reach this state we may begin to give ourselves auto-suggestions. One may enter in a state which is just like day dreaming; there is nothing spooky about this. It's the same state as when the Lord puts his old chosen people into a trance or a deep sleep; there is nothing evil about it as long as it remains within the *positive domain*. The church principles may not accept these things because they did not attain yet this degree of thinking renovation.

In your meditative prayer you *must* dissociate yourself from all the negative suggestions you have associated with words like hypnosis, meditation and spell. These words are all found in the Scripture under older nomenclatures. Jesus used the mind to read other peoples' thoughts; he used his positive psychic powers for the glory of God (the Positive Pinnacle within us) and you can too. In fact we are commanded to meditate positively. Meditation reaches the subconscious mind. It would by no means be a *coincidence* today to rediscover through it Jesus' *real* Kingdom of Heaven and feel it within our own selves!

Without prayer and meditation Jesus himself would not recharge his divine/human battery. And without our deep immersion in this spiritual exercise all his words and sayings would be routine and meaningless. Jesus described this attitude when he addressed the Pharisees: "This people draws unto me with their mouth, and honors me with their lips, but their heart is far from me." (Mat. 15:8.) In the same fashion we utter the repetitive Church prayers that emanates from our mouths; we need therefore to be commended as Joshua was: "This book of the Law shall not depart out of your mouth; but you shall *Meditate therein day and night*, that you may observe to do according to all that is written therein: for then you shall make your way prosperous, and then you shall have good success." (Jos. 1:8.)

Exactly as songs get into our subconscious because we sing them over-and-over so does the positive spiritual thoughts. This is where Jesus wanted to put us through and such was his avenue towards the Kingdom of Heaven. Paul further explains to Timothy: "*Meditate* (revolve) upon these things; give yourself wholly to them; that your profiting may appear to all. Take heeds unto you and unto the doctrine; continue in them: for in doing this you shall both s*ave yourself* and them that hear y*ou*." (1Tim. 4:15.)

Have you ever climbed a steep, solitary hill alone with your own soul whereby you pushed your oxygen intake to the maximum of your lungs capacity? And when you reached the summit you felt your total systems, including your mind, fortified and regenerated? Well, that was a mini-exercise of what Jesus used to do constantly: ". . . And he descended from the mountain, and his disciples followed him" . . . many such statements recur in the Scripture and almost all the major feats were performed *after* his descent from the meditation site. What was Jesus doing, alone, up in the mountain? Surely praying, contemplating and refilling his exhausted *human battery*. Now, next time you do such an exercise, match it with your own positive contemplation eliminating all negatives and implanting positive impulses of joy (within you), love (to those you know) and belief (in many Jesus' teachings you may rediscover in this book). You will see when you reach the summit this time what a new individual you are!

The concepts of *breath, soul, spirit* and *mind* form the basis of the inner human being. They are furthermore the *logos* which we find in the opening chapter of the gospel of St. John—"In the beginning was the Word, and the Word was with God and the Word was God." 'Word' is actually a mistranslation of the 'Logos' which meant in Hellenic 'the Mind of God' and was used in Greek philosophy as the 'overall intellect that runs the universe.' Here Jesus, probably keen to deliver its real meaning, says also: "The *words that I speak unto you, they are spirit, and they are life*"—the Spirit of God from which man receives his breath-of-life. The Spirit of God that speaks to man when he enters the inner chambers of his mind where he finds himself and where he finds God. Each human is a carrier of God's Breath and God's Spirit and God's Mind. How logical to believe that this is the reason why focused breathing and deep relaxation are such powerful tools for healing and maintaining health on a physical, emotional and spiritual level.

Jesus said to his disciples when the sick lady touched his garment and got healed: "I felt a *Power* (electrical) getting out of me". He truly lost part of the power accumulated in his human body and *perceived* it instantly. Such powers were the build-up of his extended mountain retreats. Matthew relates when his disciples failed to cast a persistent "bad spirit": "then came the disciples to Jesus apart and said, why we couldn't cast him out? And Jesus said unto them, because of your *unbelief;* for verily I say unto you, if you have faith as a grain of mustard seed you shall say unto this mountain, remove hence to yonder place; and it shall remove, and nothing shall be impossible unto you. Howbeit this kind *goes not out but* (through a higher positive power) *by prayer and fasting."* (Mat. 17:19.)

Today it is an elementary fact of life that deep breathing is a therapy in which the breath-of-life is accentuated. More and more we see that our breath is the breath-of-life and that we actually inhale the Breath of God. The origin of the word "breath" is in Genesis 2:7, which means "Breath-of-God", "Spirit-of-God" or even "Mind-of-God": "And the Lord God formed man from the dust of the earth and breathed into his nostrils the *breath of life* and man became a living soul". Breathing to a human body is much more indispensable as food and water. The body can go for days without the two latter substances but not for a mere minute without oxygen; it is the Soul of God on this earth also called "the Lord's lamp" in the Bible because in moral sense it is a direct gift from God that enables man to reach his *sublime* conditions.

Today much more than in yesteryears humans subsist In living quarters out of touch with their own nature to the extent that the art of simple living must now be learned from guidebooks. Unlike computers they do not arrive in this world with a "user's manual." Nor do they start life with a clean slate. From birth, the influences of family, race, religion and nationality wash over them like a negative tide of unexamined habits and biases from which they must extricate themselves if they are to pursue the true happiness.

Throughout this pursuit though, they become conscious and creative mirrors reflective of a higher reality in every situation they interact with: the very Kingdom of Heaven Jesus promoted. It may come only in glimpses at first; it may come simply as a gradual release from a lifetime habit of anxiety, fear, or loneliness; we may feel a sense of inner peace or self-confidence; we may discover faith in the rightness of all things; or perhaps there comes to us intuitive and creative responses to life's many challenges. Jesus came to open this humanitarian superhighway knocking down all inherited postulates. He was accused of blasphemy in proclaiming his oneness with God, did he not reply by saying: "Do not your scriptures say, 'You are gods?'" Did he not moreover, exhort his disciples to "Be you therefore *perfect* (free of all negatives), even as your Father which is in *heaven* is perfect"? When asked where *heaven* was, Jesus replied undeniably: "the Kingdom of Heaven is *within* you."

Up in the mountain Jesus practiced intense concentration in the company of God abiding within him. In fact that was the message and example he gave us as God also inhabits us. There he would regain his greatly refined state of awareness that requires a calm, laser-like concentration to perceive and enter into pure super-consciousness, thus dominating his own as well as others' ordinary conscious and subconscious states. Jesus developed through his Qumran years of scrupulous contemplation a keen sense to understand that hidden human power we call today electricity; penetrated the mind and accessed the subconscious. He would be in full awareness of the higher negative energy crippling the human mind in the form of tension, emotions, and restless thoughts: "come unto me, all you that labor and are heavy laden (with negative loads), and I will give you rest. Take my yoke upon you and *learn from me*; for I am meek and lowly of heart (positive), and you shall find rest unto your souls." (Mat. 11:28.) He would bridge from body consciousness to pure Spirit consciousness to receive the subtle energy of Life Force supported by deep breathing, intense feeling and will power. His human body would rearm again with that energy redirected along pathways of muscles, cells, and tissues, upwards to the brain which is the reservoir of Life Force and the seat of pure consciousness, thus preparing the body for the flood-like force of positive Cosmic Power.

Throughout his three-year ministry and for many preparatory years earlier until the day he told his mother in Cana "my hour is not come yet" Jesus was bent into performing this ritual any time he felt *weak in Spirit* i.e. *low in spiritual battery*. Truly, he was subjecting his body to tremendous strain to fuel his spiritual might. In this same context he did not hesitate to deplore the wasted energy he deployed on Galilean cities where most of his mighty works were done and stirred nothing but ingratitude: "Woe unto you, Chorazin! Woe unto you Bethsaida! For if the mighty works, which were done in you, had been done in (idolatrous Phoenician) Tyre and Sidon, they would have repented long ago in sackcloth and ashes. (Mat. 11:21.) This was further illustrated the evening of his crucifixion when he complained for the first time: "the Spirit is strong but the body is weak." That was the hour when he preserved his optimum spiritual power for the mother of all miracles: Resurrection

Jesus asserted that we are spiritual beings capable of spreading the divine Kingdom of Heaven throughout the physical earthly realm. The physical is but a small part of who we really are. It is only vital mainly because it swells the air and light that sustain our body and soul. Physical food is necessary for nourishment but its excess is ultimately detrimental when gleaning cosmic energy and harmful to the other aspects of mental, emotional, and spiritual self. Fasting restores natural balance and health. If degeneration has not been allowed to proceed too far fasting can cure virtually any disease, distress or diversion from optimum health. ". . . Therefore, he told his disciples, I bid you put away anxious thoughts about food to keep you alive and clothes to cover your body. Life is more than food . . ." and "Man cannot live by bread alone . . ."

The strategy for bringing divine powers into your active consciousness lies within the intensity of prayer and contemplation. Intense prayer can bring out miraculous results. It's about dormant energy within us and a capacity to generate a surge of divine power capable of healing you and the people around you. Prayer with faith *can remove a mountain*, irrespective what that mountain is: a physical disability, a broken relationship, a career problem? In reclaiming your Spiritual Power you can confront that mountain knowing you have the authority to do it and knowing that something will follow. True knowledge isn't about intellect as much as it is about spirit; the spirit will show the tremendous power available when you really understand prayer on an intimate level. It is the spiritual dynamite that lies in the subconscious of every human spirit waiting to be instructed with unshakable belief to convert into a Holy Spirit capable of performing miracles.

Chemically speaking, the human body consists of 65% oxygen, 18% carbon, 10% hydrogen, and 3% nitrogen. A total of 96% of the human body is made from these four elements all of which are available in the air we breathe. The awesome oxygen reserve fuels the body's electricity and any extra intake of this *breath of God* means extra electric power in the human body that, when positively carried out, may lead to glowing. Excess carbon is eliminated by the breath in the form of carbon dioxide. One can also say that the body is about 70% water and most of the hydrogen and oxygen atoms are combined in this form of molecule. Atoms do not eat nor do molecules. The human body is capable of transmuting one element from another and of absorbing life force from air and light; such were the main staples of Jesus. He would achieve that through his aptitude to hear and respond to the Spirit of God within him. Most certainly he was conscious of who he was, why he was there, and what he was called for.

". . . When Jesus had come down from the mountain (strong in Spirit), great crowds followed him; and there was a leper who came to him and knelt before him, saying, "Lord, *if you choose* (absolute belief), you can make me clean." He stretched out his hand and touched him, saying, "I do *choose* (positive). Be made clean!" Immediately his leprosy was cleansed. (Mat 8:1.)

Perhaps the most strenuous meditation exercise Jesus went through was after he was baptized by John. The Holy Spirit was then manifested in Jesus the human being. Then He went to the mountain to spend forty days in retreat. He practiced meditation and strengthened that Spirit in order to bring about a *total transformation*. Although it's not recorded in what positions he practiced we can imagine that during forty days all sitting, walking, climbing and deep breathing meditations were performed. He also practiced looking deeply, touching deeply, and nourishing the energy of the Holy Spirit in him. In this process he set the pace for all mankind to attain this spiritual power, reach God within them and enter the realm of the Kingdom of Heaven!

Another perplexing teaching by Jesus haunts the imagination of every Christian pushing him to doubts: "Verily, verily, I say unto you, if a man keeps my saying, (accost the positive highway and achieve total peace of mind) he shall never see death." This was his figurative answer to their saying: "all the apostles are dead! How can you say that God wills to keep us alive from physical death?" (John 8:52.) God planned for us to follow the strict and positive avenue of *glorifying Him in our body* where our Soul lightens as an incandescent bulb: the filament of the bulb may look meager and fragile; but when electricity is passed through it, it glows and becomes red-hot. Our body is like that filament when we are connected to the Holy Spirit within us. Answering another, similar recurrent question he confirmed: "He, who believes in me, shall live even if he *dies*." The living spirit in Christ is thus indestructible.

-9-

Anatomy of a Miracle

"The Father that dwells in me, He does the works,"
Jesus Christ

My attendance in a public gathering to a very entertaining evening of stage hypnotism and mind reading with Dr. Polcar was quite revealing. After he read my thoughts by simply touching my hand and found his purse that, upon his request while hoodwinked, I had hidden in a sack of a lady in the audience; he performed a series of feats through hypnotism where I was an inquisitive witness and medium. One participant, a chain smoker, asked to be healed from his habit; another from biting his nails. Polcar ordered their subconscious minds to do so. Two months after the session both men, well known to me in the community, relinquished their habits!

In a private audience with the mind reader I told him: "you know I misguided you for a minute during your search for the purse", he said: "I knew it, you *thought* my purse was in a shop in downtown Beirut, I sensed your simple misguiding but sure enough you disoriented me for that minute . . ."

I asked him: "can you tell the winning lotto number tomorrow?" He said: "most certainly, only I never think to do it because I trespass the realm of my positivism and lose my power! It would be an impure, negative cheating."

One last question, I told him: "what do you think of Jesus Christ?" He answered: "He is our overall Master; what I do is simply pure psychology using my positive brain power, Jesus did his feats powered by the omnipotent Spirit of God!"

Here is a simple man whose likes are numerous in this world doing what he does through simple psychology. Certainly, the apostles of Jesus did many superhuman feats powered by the Holy Spirit invested on them by Jesus, and the Master himself performed more glorious miracles that no one can match today.

This infinite healing Presence of Life which Jesus called "Father," is the curative catalyst of all diseases whether mental, emotional, or physical. It is in the subconscious mind, and if faithfully directed, can heal the human mind, body . . . and affairs of all illnesses and impediments. This healing power will respond to you regardless of your personal status. It does not care whether you belong to any church or creed as long as Jesus Christ is the basis of your élan. Many "healers" in the Far East and charlatans around the world achieve vast results through the power of mind yet the feats performed by Jesus are unequalled then and now. You have had hundreds of healings since you were a child. You can recall how this healing presence brought curative results to cuts, burns, bruises, contusions, sprains, etc., and in all probability you did not aid the healing in any way by the application of external remedies: your subconscious mind was always there, awake and alert to process your healing.

The scripture abounds with examples of the conscious mind being asleep when God—the Presence of Life, was speaking. When the conscious mind is put to sleep we are in a spell (hypnotism). Why does He put people into a spell? Because the conscious mind or the corporeal mind is the living negative factor! It doubts everything and will try to convince humans that God's word is not true. God puts us into a deep sleep or a spell then speaks directly to the subconscious mind. This is exactly what happened to Paul on the road to Damascus as narrated by none else than himself:

"And it came to pass, that as I made my journey and was come near Damascus about noon, suddenly there shone from heaven a great light round about me. And I fell onto the ground (from his horse: this stark spell was on a par with a harsh, merciless man to shut off his robust consciousness), and heard a voice (directly through the subconscious) saying to me: Saul, Saul, why do you persecute me? And I answered: who are you Lord? And he said unto me: I am Jesus of Nazareth, whom you persecute. And they that were with me saw indeed the light and were *afraid* (a needed brief spell to bar any negative interference), but they heard not the voice of him that spoke to me" (solely directed to Paul's subconscious mind!). (Act. 22:6.)

Paul was subjected later to further *spells*: "And it came to pass, that, when I (Paul) was come again to Jerusalem, even while I prayed in the temple, I was in a spell" (Act. 22:17.) The Greek meaning for *spell* is to *displace the mind*. It is also translated as *amazement* or *astonishment*. But in any translation it implies the state of the conscious mind put to sleep or temporarily disabled.

We also read in the scripture:

. . . "And, behold, men brought in a bed a man which was taken with palsy: and they sought *means* to bring him in, and to lay *him* before him. And when they could not find by what *way* they might bring him in because of the multitude, they went upon the housetop, and let him down through the tiling with *his* couch into the midst before Jesus (a clear symptom of *belief* in the man and his attendants). And when he *saw their faith*, he said unto him, man, your sins are forgiven (subconscious freed of all negative visualizations). And the scribes and the Pharisees began to *reason* (negatively), saying, who is this which speaks blasphemies? Who can forgive sins but God alone? But when Jesus *perceived* their thoughts, he answering said unto them, what *reason* you in your hearts? Whether is easier to say, your sins be forgiven; or to say, rise up and walk? But that you may know that the Son of Man has power upon earth to forgive sins, (stopping momentarily their negative interference, he said unto the sick of the palsy,) I say unto you, arise, and take up your couch and go into your house. And immediately he rose up before them, and took up that whereon he lay, and departed to his own house, glorifying God. And they were all amazed (trance), and they glorified God, and were *filled with fear*, saying, we have seen strange things today." (Luk. 5:18.)

We further read:

. . . "Now Peter and John went up together into the temple at the hour of prayer, being the ninth hour. And a certain man lame from his mother's womb was carried, whom they laid daily at the gate of the temple which is called Beautiful, to ask alms of them that entered into the temple; seeing Peter and John about to go into the temple he asked for alms. And Peter, *fastening his eyes upon him with John*, said, *Look on us*. And he *gave heed* unto them, expecting to receive something of them. Then Peter said, silver and gold have I none; but such as I have I give you: in the name of Jesus Christ of Nazareth rise up and walk. And he took him by the right hand, and lifted *him* up: and immediately his feet and ankle bones received strength. And he leaping up stood, and walked, and entered with them into the temple, walking, and leaping, and praising God. And all the people saw him walking and praising God: and they knew that it was he which sat for alms at the Beautiful Gate of the temple: and they were filled with wonder and *Amazement* (spell) at that which had happened unto him. (Act. 3:1.)

Peter asked the man: "Look on us," and the hypnotist tells his subjects, "Look into my eyes." Both induced the same trance-like state, the man was in a spell as he *fixed his eyes* upon them and his consciousness was temporarily obstructed. Peter spoke to his subconscious mind and it went into immediate action fixing his withered limbs. When Jesus arose from the dead and they went to the place where his body was, the angel (Jesus himself) appeared to them and they went into a spell. As to those who witnessed the healing of the man brought down from the housetop, they were also put into the subconscious realm or in a spell as they saw the man *getting healed,* to keep their conscious minds from creating waves of doubt, the worst of all negative impulses.

Miracles are also called: wonders. A wonder is an act which astonishes the beholder. A miracle is an astonishing event which the beholder cannot trace to any known law or science. As a sign, a miracle is a bewildering wonder which points to something else: the trustworthiness of the performer and speaker of divine truth. "The Jews asked Jesus, what sign do you show?" (John 2:18.) "The Jews said unto Jesus, we would like to see a sign from you." (Mat. 12:38.) The apostles performed miracles with signs. (2Cor.12:12.) These were called *signs of an apostle.* Since he proclaimed himself an apostle the signs should support his claim.

Faith exists in varying degrees: "you, of little faith" said Jesus with a smile mocking his disciples, and: "your faith is great, woman" to the one who touched his cloak, and: "should you have faith the size of a mustard seed you would move this mountain." Through real faith many individuals heal their ulcers and even deep-seated, so-called incurable malignancy. It is as easy for the healing Presence of God to heal a tubercular lung as it is to heal a cut on your finger. The cut on your fingers heals because *you believe* it will; the one of malignancy doesn't because *you don't believe* it would. There is no great or small in God that dwells within us all: "what is not possible for man is easy for God," and with belief, there is no big or little, no hard or easy. Omnipotence is within all men. The prayers of the man laying his hand on another in order to induce a healing simply appeal to the cooperation (belief) of the patient's conscious to access the subconscious, whether he ascribes it to Divine intercession or not a response takes place; for according to the patient's *faith* at the same level it is done unto him.

Atheists and even skeptics attribute miracles stories to accidental accounts during the generally assumed oral gospel transmission period. Some may even go to *deliberate* and/ or *intentional* introduction of elements by the Apostles, and presumably the gospel authors.

Many contemporary *scientists* go yet farther to discuss the possibility of their being *influenced*—without their realizing it by *mythic* elements in their worldview. Before we treat this question let's take a quick look at the 36 recorded miracles ascribed to Jesus in the Gospels, notwithstanding the several *mass healings* performed. That gives us:

1. 17 healing events (cited in all 4 gospels)
2. 7 healings "exorcisms" (cited by all *except John*)
3. 3 precognition (nature, all with fish) miracles (Representatives in all gospels *except Mark*)
4. 3 revivification miracles (cited in all 4 gospels)
5. 6 nature miracles (cited in all 4 gospels)
6. Creation of matter (2 food multiplications)
7. Defiance of gravity (walking on water)
8. Control of thermal energy (calming a storm)
9. Control of metabolic processes (the fig tree)
10. Rearrangement of molecular structure/creation of matter (turning water into wine).

Analyzing the Scripture with a scrutinizing mind to please modern intellectuals and naturalists, we see candid narration with no ulterior motives to dispel the *propaganda uses* of miracles, those were not intended to *convince* others to make any radical behavioral-change or belief-change. They are simply standard accepted literary efforts designed to honor, explain, or further instruct. There would be no other intention on the part of the gospels authors but to portray historical events as they really happened. If a reader came up to them and asked "what part of the lake was Jesus on when he walked on water?" The author would look at them as if they were insane, joking, or grossly uneducated. Many scholars tackled this issue quite meticulously but never came out with a credible data to support the thesis that the disciples fabricated the miracles of Jesus for any plausible reasons . . .

Historians and naturalists had always a different approach using their all dominant inductive mind. They have never approached the power of the subconscious or measured the positive receptivity of belief. Jesus' miracles were invested with a profound spiritual significance and in each event we can discern beyond the full extent of the *miracle* the great symbolical drive to the dawning Kingdom of Heaven. Historians note without explaining that those who witnessed miracles *failed to realize* what had really happened. Furthermore they accuse the disciples of having eyes, but seeing not and describe them as *completely dumbfounded* without explaining why. *They had not understood the incident of the loaves; their minds were closed.* So what in fact did Jesus do? They cannot say for certain. They only rationalize and foist their materialistic interpretations upon the miracles; a process they have been following for hundreds of years. Obviously their reasoning does not traverse the boundaries of their inductive conscious mind where the element of belief is to them an irrational maze.

Historians and naturalists could speculate endlessly about what ailments Jesus cured and how. They compare such acts to those of many *medicine men* practicing sympathetic magic during the Old Testament era as well as his times. Those surface skimmers would not penetrate deeply into the *obscure zone* where many psychosomatic afflictions have been eased by contact with Jesus' exceptionally powerful personality. They fail to grasp how very often *'a power went out of him and cured them all.'* While wondering if Jesus possessed some quite special curative gifts, they refer to true people who refused to *believe* he had accomplished anything whatsoever. In this context the only indication of the truth is the single, paramount criteria: belief.

Jesus' first approach to heal a sick was: "your sins are forgiven" a jump-start to the subconscious to rise and act. He knew quite well the human body and mind are made to be completely whole, completely healthy. They are meant to be continually recreated with new cells and schemes. True, a born lame inherited his handicap from his parents and Jesus concedes that *"nor he neither his parents committed a sin but to show the (natural) works of God in him."* Jesus, mind you, was explaining to uneducated listeners who can only grasp at their limited level of mental picturing; hence his parables option. He could not clarify that a human may be born with an inherited, wrongly programmed subconscious mind; and in the case of the born lame or the born blind reprogramming of their individual subconscious was simply administered.

We read in the scripture:

"And when he was come in, he says unto them, why make you this ado, and weep? The damsel is not dead, but sleeps. And they laughed him to scorn (negative). But when he had *put them all out* (to ward off negative thoughts), he takes the father and the mother of the damsel, and them that were with him (only those who believed), and enters in where the damsel was lying. And he took the damsel by the hand, and said unto her, 'Talitha cumi' (Talitha rise—in Aramaic); and straightaway the damsel arose, and walked; for she was *of the age* of twelve years. And they were astonished (spell) with a great *astonishment*." (Mar. 5:39.)

When negative thoughts and events (sins) block that continuous process of regeneration or misdirect it the body gets all the repercussions. Hence Jesus addresses that part of the mind where some *disconnect* has occurred to release it, so that the healing and regeneration process can continue as nature generally intended it. In fact the healing process consists of calling forth the ability of the subconscious mind to *re-program* itself on operating the body. The disciples copied later the Master's technique in subduing consciousness armed by the omnipotent Holy Spirit as a direct intermediary to anybody's subconscious mind

The contact of inspiration through God, the Power of Life, cannot be done merely by will power working through the conscious mind which is an evolutionary product of the physical realm and perishes with the body. It can only be accomplished through the subconscious. To realize that we can become one with the Creator is a wonderful and awe-inspiring experience. Very few human beings have ever come into such realization and that is why there are so few great saints among us. A man's spirit is not conscious of its powers until it accesses the subconscious. Therefore, to evolve and grow man must learn how to use and develop his own spiritual forces positively.

Any *true* inspiration emanates from our integral Power of Life, our built-in spark of divinity we call the subconscious mind. We can maintain that spark ignited believing in no less authority than Jesus himself who termed it: "The Father *that* dwells in me, He does the works," (John 14:10) and "He that believes me, the works that I do shall he do also, and *greater works than these shall he do.*" Yes. We draw our inspirations from the same power that enabled Jesus to perform his miracles. We call it God, Omnipotence, Divinity, the Creator, etc. It is part of the overall power that created our earth and the whole universe, and Jesus taught us that we can appropriate it for our own reinforcement right here and now and Jesus is very explicit: "ask and it shall be given you, seek and you shall find; knock and it shall be opened unto you."

The Great Nazarene knew that law when he proclaimed: "the branch cannot bear fruit of itself except it abides in the vine." (John 15:4.) No atheist therefore has ever been or will be a great achiever because irrespective of his degree of intelligence and entrepreneurship he operates within the negative, destructive realm. Jesus came not as the great exception but as the great example for us to emulate, creating nothing but divine values and an alliance with the Power of Life. This is the secret of inspiration; which is the ability to synchronize the conscious and subconscious minds just as he did on a much higher level.

In the ancient world where Jesus walked and talked most people accepted that illnesses and disabilities were evidence of God's punishment. Despite the advent of knowledge Jesus remains today the master he was in the ancient time. Because of technology and science the modern world may seem different; yet in terms of human hopes, fears and rivalries today's global community is so similar. Society still stigmatizes and discriminates against groups of people. Jesus is absolutely right when he said: "earth and heaven may disappear but one syllable of my talk shall not." The Divine Healer brings Into the contemporary world the same gospel message of compassion, love, forgiveness and justice as he did two thousand years ago showing us how to live and to help others to live.

Jesus summed up to all humans three distinct steps for healing: the first step is not to be afraid of the manifest condition but to face it with belief and equanimity from the first moment of encounter. The second step is to realize that the condition is only the product of past negative thinking or happening which, save the acts of God, will have no more power to continue its existence. The third step is to exalt mentally the miraculous healing power of God within your subconscious mind. This procedure, craftily indoctrinated into the apostles, will instantly stop the production of all mental poisons in the subconscious (your sins forgiven) in you or in the person for whom you are praying. All Jesus asked us is to live in the embodiment of our positive desires and our thoughts and feelings will soon be made manifest. He warned against allowing ourselves to be swayed by human opinions and worldly fears, but live emotionally in the belief that it is God's irrevocable action in our mind and body.

The Nazarene Master claimed such power and advocated we also should acquire it being his fellow children of God. His masterful penetration through the human subconscious minds was powered by the Supreme Positive Authority that enabled him to perform unattainable miracles. He was rightfully proud of such feats he did not hesitate to evidence them to John the Baptist's inquisitive disciples: "Go and show John again those things which you do hear and see: that the blind receive their sight, and the lame walk, the lepers are cleansed, and the deaf hear, the dead are raised up, and the poor (with much less soiled subconscious) have the gospel preached to them." (Mat. 11:4.)

He further said, "But I have greater witness than that of John: for the works which the Father has given me to finish, the same works that I do, bear witness of me, that the Father has sent me." (John 5:36.) Speaking of his signs of miracles John said, "These are written that you might believe that Jesus is the Christ, the Son of God; and that *believing* you might have life through his name." (John 20:31.) On the question of the healed blind, blindness is an inherited natural happening in the genes that we know full well today and not surely sin-related, but a resulting phenomenon and an occasion for Christ to heal and God to be glorified thereby. (John 11:4; 40-42). Miracles showed God's support to the miracle worker. "You men of Israel—exclaimed Peter—hear these words; Jesus of Nazareth, *a man approved of God* among you by miracles, wonders and signs, which God did by him in the midst of you, as you yourselves also know." (Act. 2:22.) After the lame man was healed by Peter it is said, "All men glorified God for that which was done." (Act. 4:21.)

-10-

The Immaculate Conception

"And Mary said: my soul does magnify the Lord."
Luke

Mary was born and raised in a society where physical and spiritual powers were bestowed to males. Almost the same situation still exists in the Middle East today. Yet Mary, the wonder and pride of all Christians spent her childhood, youth and adult life within the confines of an innate Holy Spirit even when she assumed later the humdrum of marital life with a holy man. Nothing however prevented her from attaining the glory of God, not the weakness of her nature, not the torments of her glorious life in Palestine, Egypt and the Galilee—even Lebanon and not the lack of necessities she always suffered with Joseph in raising the children of Mary her *sister* niece and wife of Cleophas, those the evangelists referred to as Jesus' brothers. Rather all these things served as the bases of her glory. The grace of God was always shrouding her and the pure, childlike and positive conduit was her route and style. To those who say and think that these circumstances and the rest of her mundane occupations create an obstacle to sainthood, she is the proof to free them from their negative debates and to show that they invent pretexts for their failings.

Pope John Paul II was adamant to contradict these when he went ahead in 2004 and sanctified the gynecologist Gianna Beretta Molla, who decided to face death rather than kill her fourth son by miscarriage when she knew she would die during delivery for heart failure, and elevated her to the ranks of saints.

The story of Santa Gianna was a repetition of another married Santa Rita widely worshipped in Lebanon and various parts of the world. On Sundays, I accompany my wife to Mass in a nearby Santa Rita's Maronite church. Her full name was Margarita Lotti; she was married to a bad tempered man called Paolo Mancini and gave birth to her twins: Joachim and Paola. She had a wonderful life with them and later with her husband whom she changed to a stress-free man with her love and affection. When Paolo was assassinated his last words to her were those of love and forgiveness. She went ahead with the authorities and forgave the assassins. Two years later her twins died. With her heart broken, she joined a monastery and consecrated the rest of her life helping the poor and needy.

The chronology of Mary's life on earth started when she was born about 22 BC to Ann and Joachim whereby, a couple of years later, she was presented to the Temple to live her monastic, spiritual life. She later witnessed her betrothal to Joseph and the three most important events of her life: the Annunciation of Christ's Birth, her visitation with Elizabeth and her pregnancy by the Holy Spirit. Then Jesus was born in Bethlehem, his circumcision 8 days later and her purification 40 days after delivery. In this same year the prophecy of Simeon concerning Jesus and Mary took place as well as the statement of old Anna on Jesus (Luk. 2.36,) and the return to Nazareth.

Thereafter, the adoration of the Magi came about followed by the arduous flight with Joseph into Egypt to save Jesus from Herod. They returned after Herod's death and two years later they found Jesus in the Temple at Jerusalem. 29 AD Mary incites and eyewitnesses Jesus to perform his first miracle at the Marriage feast of Cana and accompanies him throughout the early stages of his ministry. She was at hand when he took his trip to Sidon attending to the Phoenician woman's plea, and *waited* for him on a hill called Magdoshee. A basilica was later erected on the site that stands to this day in her name: "Our Lady of the Waiting". Jesus bestowed indirect praise on Mary for her faith and support (Luk. 11:27.) Evangelists though played down her important spiritual role throughout her Son's young life, later ministry and her important leadership to the Church after his Ascension all in line with the existing social tradition of generally ignoring and downgrading women. Our "Lady of Lebanon" has been the Matron Saint of the country. A huge statue over a shrine stands today high over the promontory of Harissa, accessible by cars and cable cars.

The doctrine of the Immaculate Conception remains the paramount issue of her life and the core of the Christian faith. It is important to understand—and believe, that Mary was conceived "by the power of the Holy Spirit," in the way Jesus was. This belief also means that Mary was conceived without the original sin or its stain—that is what "immaculate" means: without stain. The essence of original sin consists in the deprivation of *the sanctifying grace* and its stain is a corrupt nature.

When discussing the Immaculate Conception an implicit reference may be found in the angel's greeting to Mary in a dream-like appearance: the kind of spell God puts his chosen few to interact with them The angel said, "Hail, full of grace, the Lord is with you" (Luk. 1:28.) The phrase "full of grace" is a translation of the Greek word *kecharitomene*. It therefore expresses a characteristic quality of Mary. The traditional translation, "full of grace," is better than the one found in many recent versions of the New Testament, which give something along the lines of "highly favored daughter." Mary was indeed a highly favored by God. This indicates that she was graced in the past but with continuing effects in the present. So, the grace Mary enjoyed was not a result of the angel's visit but the basis of that visit, and it was extended throughout her life.

In this particular state the mind is wide open to positive beatitudes and ready to *uphold its subconscious in a perfectly receptive mood.* It is not hard—as we have seen for the subconscious mind to create new human cells; it does it all the time, exactly as it takes the sperm from the father and the egg from the mother t0 create a new body for the baby. It is the God given power of the soul/mind that produces new life. The Virgin Mary took the word/seed of God and it was her *soul/*

mind, believing what God said, which caused her subconscious mind to act, creating the first physical cells of the baby Jesus!

This is exactly what we read in Luke: "and blessed *is* she that *believed*: for there shall be a *performance* of those things which were told her from the Lord. And Mary said: *my* SOUL does *magnify* the Lord." (Luk.1:45.) Mary's subconscious mind, when ordered: "and, behold, *you shall* conceive in your womb, and bring forth a son, and shall call his name JESUS . . . "Mary doubted with her conscious mind at first when she said, "This can't happen, because I have not 'known' any man."

In today's interpretation her conscious mind was gathering the facts and reasoning inductively. It came up with the conclusion that this was impossible. The angel then *positively* and *irrevocably* confirmed to her that it *is* possible: "for with God *nothing* shall be impossible. And Mary said, Behold, I am the handmaid of the Lord; be it unto me according to your word. And the angel departed from her." (Luk.1:37.)

When Mary *believed beyond any doubt* her subconscious mind took the word/seed of God and began to *magnify* it into a physical fetus. It accepted whatever it was told then went into action. It wouldn't have without Mary's firm *belief*. For today's scientific minds this miraculous feat is questionable. Yet it is far less in magnitude than Jesus' stilling the sea, raising the dead, transfiguring or even resurrecting. We are not talking here about a human subconscious manipulated through psychology but fuelled by the omnipotent Spirit of God. Mary freely and actively cooperated in a unique way with God's plan of salvation (Luk.1:38.)

Like any mother she was never separated from the momentous events of her son or his suffering (Luk. 2:35.) Mary was at the

Cross and later after Jesus' Ascension with the apostles in the cenacle. Mary may have ended her life in Palestine, Lebanon or perhaps in Ephesus where she traveled. However none of those places or any other claimed her remains; there were allegations about possessing her (temporary) tomb but no city claimed the bones of Mary apparently because there weren't any bones to claim and people knew it. Her Assumption to heaven to rejoin her son took place sometime in her late age. This was much in line with his promise: "When I am up, I will draw all . . ." The almost universal consensus is that she did die, but Pope Pius XII acknowledged that Mary, "after the completion of her earthly life was assumed body and soul into the glory of heaven." Here was Mary the most privileged of all the saints, certainly the most saintly. Scripture promises that those who share in the sufferings of Christ will share in his glory (Rom.8:17.) Since she suffered a unique interior martyrdom it was appropriate that Jesus would honor her with a unique glory.

Mary's motherly love and pride bestowed to her son was best manifested in Cana's marriage feast. She *knew* of his spiritual powers not only when he started his ministry at 30 but from his earliest days in Egypt and later at 12 when he was trading dogmatic views with the Doctors of the Temple. Let's read John: "And the third day there was a marriage in Cana of Galilee; and the mother of Jesus was there. And both Jesus and his disciples were called to the marriage. And when they wanted wine, the mother of Jesus *said unto him:* they have no wine. Jesus (perceiving what she is insinuating to him) said unto her, woman, what have I to do with you, my hour is not yet come. His mother (unabashed by his remark and insisting on him to show his powers) said unto the servants: whatsoever he says unto you, do it. And there were set there six water pots of stone, after the manner of purifying of the Jews, containing two or three firkins apiece. Jesus said unto them: fill the water pots with water, and they filled them up to the brim. And then he said unto them, draw out now and bear unto the governor of the feast . . ." (John 2:1.)

As to the controversial issue of her having children later with Joseph after her virginal delivery of Jesus, Christians are split into two factions around this highly emotional subject that never rested to this day. Protestant subdivisions on the one hand, believe she had, while Catholics and Greek Orthodox categorically deny it.

The first camp takes up the scripture verbatim and completely ignores the terms of amiabilities existent—then as well as now—in the Middle East where any friend or relative is called a brother or sister. They base their theory on the following texts and related readings:

"When Joseph woke up, he did what the angel of the Lord had commanded him and took Mary home as his wife. But he had no union with her *until* she gave birth to a son. And he gave him the name Jesus." (Mat. 1:25.) From thence he started this *union*, and later: "While they were there, the time came for the baby to be born, and she gave birth to her *firstborn*, a son. She wrapped him in cloths and placed him in a manger, because there was no room for them in the inn." (Luk.2:4.) *Firstborn* implies other children were also born to her.

"Coming to his hometown, he began teaching the people in their synagogue, and they were amazed: "where did this man get this wisdom and these miraculous powers?" they asked:" isn't this the carpenter's son? Isn't his mother's name Mary, and aren't his *brothers* Jacob, Joseph, Simon and Judas? Aren't all his *sisters* with us? Where then did this man get all these things?" And they took offense at him. But Jesus said to them, "Only in his hometown and in his own house is a prophet without honor." And he did not do many miracles there *because of their lack of faith.*" (Mat. 13:54.)

We further read in John: "Jesus' *brothers* said to him, 'You ought to leave here and go to Judea, so that your disciples may see the miracles you do. No one who wants to become a public figure acts in *secret* (a total departure of Jesus' insistence on secrecy). Since you are doing these things, show yourself to the world.' For even *his own brothers* did not believe in him." (John 7:3;) "Brothers" here may not mean his disciples, or the twelve, or those who *did* believe in him. And: "after this he went down to Capernaum with his mother and *brothers* and his disciples." (John 2:12.)

As to Luke in his second book called "the Acts of Apostles", he clearly distinguished by names between Jesus' disciples and his mother and brothers: "Then they returned unto Jerusalem from the mount called Olivet (the same day of the Ascension witnessed by the disciples, his mother, brothers and many onlookers), which is from Jerusalem a Sabbath day's journey (three permitted hours of march.) And when they were come in, they went up to an upper room, where abode Peter and James, and John, and Andrew, Philip, and Thomas, Bartholomew, and Matthew, James the son of Alpheus, and Simon the Zealot, and

Judas the brother of James. These all continued with one accord of prayer and supplication with women (Mary Magdalene, the other Mary and Salome), and Mary the mother of Jesus and his brothers." (Act.1-13.)

Both Roman Catholic and Greek Orthodox churches are right in rejecting the literal interpretation of the scripture and espousing the spirit of the texts. Accordingly, the metaphorical meaning in the above texts of *brothers* may denote disciples, either the twelve or the seventy and even any other followers. Worth noting here is what Jesus told the Magdalene after his rise from the dead: "Touch me not; for I am not ascended to my Father: but go to my *brothers* and say unto them . . ." what is meant by "brothers" here are the disciples and not his family members as interpreted by the first camp.

Catholic and Orthodox scholars discard the possibility of the Virgin Mary having children from Joseph following her immaculate conception by the Holy Spirit. This assumption would mean return to the original sin and defer the maidenhood of *the Virgin Mary* being a pillar of belief in both churches. On the other hand following the ten-year span in Egypt that provided ample time for Joseph to father children, the scripture did not denote additions to the family and ascertained that only Joseph, Mary and young Jesus returned to Palestine.

The scripture also dropped any notion of children to Joseph when Jesus at 12, missed his clan's caravan and tarried in Jerusalem trading views with the scholars. Only Joseph and Mary returned to find him and take him back home.

John's gospel plainly supports this reckoning and clarifies the ambiguity befalling the Protestant churches: "Now there stood by the cross of Jesus his mother, and his mother's sister, Mary the wife of Cleophas, and Mary Magdalene." (John 19:25). This Mary was not the Virgin's *sister* but her niece that she considered as her sister thanks to the cordiality of their kinship. This *brotherhood* among relatives and friends is difficult to grasp in the West; the Bible however mentioned it repeatedly namely by Abraham. Accordingly Mary considered her niece as her sister and Cleophas' children as her children that she helped raising during the absence of her only son in Qumran. Apparently, Joseph shared her geniality.

What further revokes this canon of the Evangelist churches is a text by Mathews where Jesus' folks in Nazareth listed "Joseph" when naming his "brothers". In the Middle East then and today, a son named after his father is a rare exception to the rule, but usually after his grandfather. Hence, this Joseph cannot be St. Joseph's son but surely Cleophas' along with Jacob and the others. Engaging the spirit of the scripture and not its verbal meaning as we persisted through this volume we see a firm insight in the Catholic/Orthodox interpretation and a solid base of belief in the status of the Immaculate Virgin Mary.

Irrespective of who the *brothers* of Jesus were as expressed by his Nazareth folks we can safely say that Jesus, the Son of God, was not much in unison with his *half brothers and sisters*. Hence when he was told: "your brothers and your mother are out seeking for you, he answered them, saying, who is my mother and my brothers? And he looked round about on them which sat about him and said: behold my mother and my brothers! For whosoever shall do the will of God, the same is my brother, and my sister, and my mother." (Mat. 3:33.) That was a clear cut dissonance with them. First they did not believe in him along with his hometown's residents, secondly the children of Cleophas apparently were not spiritually inclined to understand and assimilate neither the mission of their *brother* nor his Kingdom of Heaven's philosophy. One of them, Jacob, sadly believed in him only after his Resurrection!

-11-

The "Lost Years" of Jesus

*"The Lord your God will raise up unto you a
Prophet from the midst of you, of your brothers,
like unto me; unto him you shall hear."* (Moses)

Deu. 18:15

T he Egyptian period was perhaps the most momentous
love story in the annals of Christianity known as *the
flight into Egypt*, where Joseph did everything he could
to keep Mary and baby Jesus safe away from Herod's wrath.
Joseph's dream is a big part of this story: his subconscious mind
reflecting to him in his sleep what should be done to avoid

this serious threat. It was a similar dream that happened to the Pharaoh in the Old Testament that was clarified by Joseph. Probably the gifts of the three Persian wise men provided enough money for the family to travel on.

When we draw pictures of the journey to Egypt we always seat Mary on the donkey with Joseph walking. In those days most often the husbands rode on the donkeys while their wives walked beside them. Do we believe Joseph was kind enough to have gone against custom for the sake of Mary and the baby? Or probably the donkey was used by both Joseph and Mary alternatively throughout the long journey? With a start in the middle of the night across southern Palestine and through the treacherous, windblown Sinai sands; the 5-day trip was a true adventure in itself.

Baby Jesus may have been oblivious of the outward journey but surely, at probably 9 or 10, he endured its hardships. He said later to Nicodemus: "The wind blows where it wills and you hear the sound of it, but you do not know whence it comes or whither it goes. So it is with everyone born of the spirit." Whatever this passage means it looks like a far reflection of that long trip back to Palestine depicting the human spirit that is prone to radical changes and environments. Jesus was an illustration of this principle; an example of the unpredictability of the human spirit. His life started in Egypt exactly as Moses', nurtured by the splendor of the Nile and the grandeur of the Pharaohs, to blossom later to an example of the heroic, free spirit that lives in each one of us and a statement of the limitless possibilities that abound in all of us.

Until this day there is a special place in the hearts of the Christians of Egypt for the traditions connected with the flight of the Holy Family. For centuries the journey has been celebrated in their liturgy. They have built churches and monasteries over the many sites believed to be visited by the Sacred Family.

The Scripture depicts this event in details: "Now after (the wise men) had left, an angel of the Lord appeared to Joseph in a dream and said, "Get up, take the child and his mother, and flee to Egypt, and remain there until I tell you; for Herod is about to search for the child, to destroy him." Then Joseph got up, took the child and his mother by night and went to Egypt, and remained there until the death of Herod. This was to fulfill what had been spoken by the Lord through the prophet, 'Out of Egypt I have called my son.' When Herod saw that he had been tricked by the wise men he was infuriated and he sent and killed all the children in and around Bethlehem who were two years or under, according to the time that he had learned from the wise men. Then was fulfilled what had been spoken through the prophet Jeremiah: 'A voice was heard in Ramah, wailing and loud lamentation, Rachel weeping for her children; she refused to be consoled, because they are no more.' When Herod died, an angle of the Lord suddenly appeared in a dream to Joseph in Egypt and said, 'Get up, take the child and his mother, and go to the land of Israel, for those who were seeking the child's life are dead.' Then Joseph got up, took the child and his mother, and went to the land of Israel." (Mat. 2:13.)

Matthew's account puts little emphasis on geography. There is considerable mention of place names such as Bethlehem, Egypt, the land of Israel but little is noted of the places that were actually visited by the Holy Family and the period of time spent in Egypt. The contemporary Coptic Church has attempted to reconstruct their actual route. All Christians believe that the

Holy Family traveled to Egypt. A holy man named Apollos fulfilled the prophecy of Isaiah: "Behold the Lord is sitting on a light cloud and is coming to Egypt". Only Jesus did not arrive on a *light cloud* but rather by a more conventional transport, a donkey that was later his same mount on his triumphal entry into Jerusalem. They probably traveled along the Mediterranean coast into Egypt. Of course at that time, Alexandria was very Roman, so they may likely have traveled along the Nile up south. Many locales on this route are marked by churches of great antiquity in commemoration of the Holy Family's treading there. They soon became places of martyrdom where early leaders spread the word of this great religion even at times when it meant their death. They are the monasteries of the earliest Christian monks and the reflection path on the grand edicts that separated the Eastern and Western Christian Churches.

Hermopolis on the north/eastern Nile bank of today's Cairo was an important Egyptian pagan holy center where Jesus' family stayed. It remained an important religious focal point into the Christian era evidenced by archaeological finds including the remains of Christian churches built literally within the ancient pagan temple, along with a monastery dedicated to Saint Severus and at least seven other churches. Apollos insisted on Isaiah's saying: "The idols of Egypt will be shaken by his presence and will fall on the ground". Certainly, the prophecy was fulfilled some 50 years later.

Earlier references to the story of Jesus in Egypt may be found outside the Scripture. The story was a source of controversy for the early Christians in their debates with non-Christians. Two hundred years after the death of Christ, Celsus, a Greek philosopher literally accused Jesus of "having worked for hire in Egypt on account of his poverty and having experimented there with some magical powers in which the Egyptians take great pride." Later, other writers expanded upon this theme claiming that Jesus brought forth "witchcraft from Egypt by means of scratches upon his flesh" and that he "practiced magic and led Israel astray;" an unfair attack on a boy under 10 yet. Associating him with the Egyptians magical arts was a pervasive accusation to disparage the nascent, burgeoning belief. In fact, Jesus learned little in Egypt besides misery, poverty and callous life; the real lonesome life that prepared him for the next 20 years of his career where the edification of his wisdom and spiritual powers were developed to their prime under the contemplative regimen of monastic Qumran.

Palestine witnessed before the appearance of Jesus and after the destruction of the Temple the revival of two major spiritual movements led by Jewish *Ebionim* (Poor). The first was the Essene pioneered by the Torah's *truth-seekers*, those who believed in intense solitary meditation conducive to the penetration of the inner human soul and healing human ailments through that process; hence their nomination: *the therapists*. The second were the Ebionite Nazarines, initiators and followers of the mystique devotion propagated later by their two stalwart and dedicated students, john and Jesus. Their version was that ministered by Jesus and invariably his disciples including Paul. Both movements selected for their central pious retreat scattered caves in the Qumran Mountain near the Dead Sea where the famous *Scrolls* were recently discovered.

Along with the two main sects or schools of Judaism: Pharisees and Sadducees, Essenes and Ebionites were reticent, low profile movements made up of mostly Jewish/Israelites that were concentrated in Palestine and the surrounding regions above the Dead Sea. This is where they led a Sufi, mystique life of prayers and contemplation within a school of puritan spirituality based on the Torah teachings. The Essenes were a nature loving sect that lived in the Qumran wilderness, a district of today's Jordan named Balkaa. They called themselves "The children of light." The many references to light and the Father by Jesus and his disciples indicate that they were influenced by the teachings of the Essenes. This Jewish group who kept themselves apart from the general population—except to teach or trade—in order to follow their own customs. They fathomed the Law of Vibration the way we discovered it recently and sought to keep their vibrant conducts high with healthy life style, pure foods, strong and pure bodies and most essentially, pure thoughts. Cheerfulness was their spiritually uplifting trait. They were highly educated in many fields including the more esoteric mysteries. They spoke a dialect of Aramaic though many among them learned and taught other languages as well. Many went out among the general population of Jews to teach as highly respected Rabbis.

The earlier wave of Essenes totally withdrew from the alluring world to the dreary solitude of Sufism. Using the old Scripture principles they developed their rigorous regimen of mastering the soul through its inner depth or what we call the subconscious mind today. This mastery, sustained by thorough abandonment of worldly desires and intense development of the spirit achieved for them the superiority of mind over matter and soul over body. A school that produced two brilliant disciples who changed the course of humanity: John the Baptist and Jesus Christ.

The Scripture mentions Jesus' *known years*, from birthday to age 12 and from 30 to Resurrection. The *lost 18 years* as a young man vanished to oblivion. Yet the Baptist who shared Jesus the same lost years bluntly displayed his Essene upbringing and way of life: a tough desert man who went "in all the region round about Jordan" wearing "a raiment of camel's hair and a leathern girdle about his loins, feeding on locust and wild honey" and "preaching in the wilderness of Judea that the kingdom of heaven is at hand". In heralding Jesus John epitomized Isaiah's prophecy to "prepare the way of the Lord and make his path straight". This merciless and controversial forerunner who much before Jesus harshly called the Pharisees and Sadducees "a generation of vipers" announced Jesus as: "he that comes after me was mightier than I, whose shoe strings I am not worthy to unloose". He certainly *knew* the spiritual powers of Jesus. He would not know that hadn't he also spent his *lost years* in the company of the Master *round about Jordan!*

The Essenes or *doers of Torah,* who wrote the Dead Sea Scrolls, pioneered certain aspects of this *Way* over 150 years before the birth of Jesus. They were a wilderness, baptizing, new covenant, messianic/apocalyptic group, expecting a *Redemptive Figure,* the Messiah. They saw themselves as the remnant core of God's faithful people preparing the Way for the return of His Glory. Like Ebionites they too referred to themselves as the Way, the Poor, the Saints, the Children of Light, and so forth. Perhaps their most common trait was the brotherhood or community and they referred to themselves as brothers and sisters. They were bitterly opposed to the corrupt priests in Jerusalem and even to the Pharisees whom they saw as compromising with the occupying Roman powers. They had their own ideals and developed aspects which Jesus picked up. They followed one *True Teacher*, the *Teacher of Righteousness* that dwells *in the human mind*; a philosophy that later constituted the core of the Jesus principles modified and disseminated to foster the Kingdom of God through his powerful, prophetic influence as Teacher.

The Pharisees, the Essenes, the Gnostics, and the early Christians were believers in reincarnation (the true bodily *resurrection*) and believers in spiritual renewal (the true spiritual resurrection). The latter were the *esoteric mysteries* and the higher *secret teachings* which Jesus shared only with a few. The public at large in Jesus' day could not understand the difference between the resurrection of the spirit (reincarnation) and the resurrection of the body (being *born of the Spirit*). This is apparent in Jesus' conversation with Nicodemus the Pharisee theologian as narrated by John: "Nicodemus came to Jesus by night and said unto him, Rabbi, we know that you are a teacher come from God: for no man can do these miracles that you do except God be with him. Jesus answered and said unto him, verily, verily I say unto you, except a man is born again, he cannot see the Kingdom of God. Nicodemus said unto him, how can a man be born when he is old? Can he enter the second time into his mother's womb, and be born? Jesus answered, verily, verily; I say unto you, except a man is born of water and of the spirit, he cannot enter the kingdom of God . . ." Nicodemus, the leading Jewish cleric and the low profile Jesus disciple later, could not decipher the Master's philosophy: his argumentations were limited to the conventional Biblical texts far from the new spiritual message.

The last recorded whereabouts of Jesus before he moved to his Qumran retreat probably at the same time as John, his senior by six month, is best narrated by Luke: ". . . and when he was twelve years old, they went up to Jerusalem after the custom of the feast. And when they had fulfilled the days as they returned, the child Jesus tarried behind in Jerusalem; and Joseph and his mother knew not of it. But they, supposing him to have been in the company, went a day's journey; and they sought him among their kinfolks and acquaintance. And they found him not. They turned back again to Jerusalem, seeking him. And it came to pass, that after three days they found him in the Temple, sitting in the midst of the Doctors, both hearing them and asking them questions. And all that heard him were astonished at his understanding and answers. And when they saw him, they were amazed: and his mother said unto him, Son, why have you thus dealt with us? Behold, your father and I have sought you sorrowing. And he said unto them, how is it that you sought me? Didn't you know that I must be about *my father*'s business? And they understood not the saying which he spoke unto them." (Luk. 2:42.)

In Nazareth where he lived with his folks when they returned from Egypt till he was 12, the Essene/Ebionite movement was a committed sect displaying the way of life of the masters in and around Qumran. It was only natural that Jesus picks that spiritual environment to edify his burgeoning religious vocation, ponder through the Torah and try to penetrate the Elders' deep wisdom expressed by means of ethereal poetic prose. He yearned to more profound learning to discover the unfathomable human spirit still too cavernous for his young grasp. The Essenes at Qumran accepted boys at age twelve and older into their Monastery. Also since Nazareth had a little Essene representation, Jesus was accepted along with John into the school. That Essene education included besides the Torah an array of other oriental teachings. Furthermore it was a place of secrecy and seclusion, an optimal hideaway for Jesus and John, remembering that Herod the father tried to find and kill Jesus as a baby.

Their school years furnished an in-depth look at life in the monastery: what they studied, what they discussed, what work they did but most importantly how their beliefs developed. The Essenes had collected all of God's teachings from almost all the great religions of the past and had taken the best of the compilations for their own especially what interconnects with the Mosaic Law. In a very similar manner Jesus took these great lessons, made his very important changes, and created his everlasting teachings.

All geographical factors underline the contention that Jesus and John the Baptist emanated from Qumran. Galilee lacked such spiritual/religious settlements that were mocked and distrusted by the Roman rulers. Some historians minimize the possibility of the Judea Wilderness as a stomping ground for Jesus ostensibly to distance him from Qumran and place his ministry as having taken place predominantly in Galilee. Yet no trusted information denotes any virtual existence of early Essene establishments in Galilee.

True, Galilee was mentioned in the New Testament especially by both Matthew and Mark to assert that Jesus commenced his ministry there. The reason behind that is twofold: one, Jesus was well versed in the Aramaic language that he mastered in

Qumran and found it more expressive than the Hebrew that he also excelled in. This language was his favorite when he prayed or communicated with God. The palpable proof to this theory is his imploring in Aramaic while on the Cross: "Eli, Eli, lima shabaktani" (God, God why did you forsake me). The Galilean area around the sea of Tiberias was highly populated by Aramaic speaking Jews: his best vintage point to disseminate his challenging, profound philosophy. And two, he picked a region with poor, secondary towns where Pharisees and Sadducees displayed a low-profile dogmatic existence. Thus Jesus, the twelve apostles and seventy evangelists spent early exploratory periods preaching in the Galilee. On the other hand, Jesus concentrated on that area initially because John the Baptist was already more active in Judea, preaching the common *Kingdom* philosophy.

To sum up and establish a base position consistent with what many respected scholars assert, John the Baptist was at some stage in his life a member of the Qumran-Essene Community In close association and fellowship with Jesus. This explains their common scheme of the Kingdom of God. It equally explains why early Christianity and the early New Testament had many exclusive features of commonality with the teachings, beliefs, and practices of the Qumran Community.

The texts of the Dead Sea Scrolls did not mention Jesus although they were written sometime before he launched his ministry but surely prefigure someone identifiable with Jesus in the many similarities with the Messianic expectations of the Community and the role fulfilled by Jesus. Only Jesus later embodied the conceived Messiah in the Christian sense: the divine Son of God.

Thus Qumran had its unmistakable cachet throughout Jesus' 3-year ministry. This semi-hermit society rejected all worldly errors and compromises of the other existing religious Jewish groups and maintained a militant, ascetic detachment. The Qumran community had broken away from the central Judaism and embraced the cherished hopes of a more comprehensible, earthly spiritual Kingdom expecting the final event of a *New Covenant* replacing the Covenant bestowed upon Moses to take place soon. The one chiefly inspired by Daniel's prophecy: "may he establish his Kingdom during your life and your days." (Dan. 9:22.)

Such expectations were fervently stimulated by the sudden emergence of John and Jesus as exceptionally gifted students who vowed to undergo the long and arduous schooling regimen and put the Kingdom of God at the very center of their mission; a Kingdom powered by the human Spirit where God dwells to become the Holy Spirit presaged and heralded through the human Mind. All in all a Davidic call proclaimed through his Psalms. The Qumran community provided Jesus the needed biblical knowledge, trained him on the delicate communion with God through strenuous contemplation and rigid spiritual association. Later on his disciples were his new Qumran community carrying the same traits: total immersion in altruistic love, piousness, renouncement of worldly riches and insistence on humility of heart: "blessed are the meek because they shall inherit the earth." (Mat. 5.5.)

Clearly though the Baptist by water differed from his Qumran mate the Baptist by the Holy Spirit. John followed that community's total withdrawal from the world without engaging—except to Herod and the Pharisees—in any controversy with the men of corruption. He was an ascetic from tip to toe deeply influenced by Qumran. Jesus on the other hand who was ingrained in deep contemplation and austere bodily exercises but not ascetics, was in this respect the exact opposite of John. He was harshly disparaged by Jewish critics who objected his sitting and eating in such bad companies. The difference between the two was apparent even to their contemporaries. Jesus who said in defense: "John came neither eating nor drinking, and they say, 'He has a demon'; the Son of man came eating and drinking, and they say, 'Behold, a glutton and a drunkard, a friend of tax collectors and sinners'" (Mat. 11:18.) These pious enthusiasts would not understand how he could usher in the Kingdom of God while keeping away from the sinners. Jesus rebuked them: "Healthy people do not require a doctor, only the sick do." John was in constant hostile resistance against Rome's appointed governors in Palestine (especially Herod the Arab Roman lackey who even Latinized his real Arab name "Hairood" into Herodus), epitomizing not only the spiritual covenant of the community but also its nationalistic drive to independence under the dawning Kingdom of Heaven. Jesus deviated from this move to the strictly human and spiritual side given 'what to Caesar to Caesar' and proclaiming the Kingdom as one 'not from this world.'

In this context, perhaps Jesus, bent to trace the *cause of the cause* and the *reason of the reason* in all his teachings that is evidenced in not addressing the two *sins* of killing and adultery but to the underlying causes of these, did not likewise confront the Roman Empire but conceived a Spiritual Kingdom *not from this world* and not only for the Jews but for *all nations;* a concept that became later the accepted religion by this empire and Rome its spiritual capital.

Many distinctive traits of Qumran were embedded in the core of Jesus' ministry: the vital belief that the end of the world is imminent and only a faithful remnant among Jews will emerge triumphant; the principle of healing psychopathic and other illnesses (believed as demons and bad spirits) through the subconscious mind corridor ; the humility of the *poor in spirit* and the Messianic characters that Jesus fully embodied, prompting John to describe him later as the *one I am not worthy to unloosen his shoe strings.* In addition the Qumran prophesy that the Temple would one day vanish; the rift between the community and the Pharisees and Sadducees that made Jesus resort to open air preaching rather than their dominated synagogues; and last but not least the analogies depicted later through the Gospel of John.

The 18-year Qumran retreat enabled Jesus to rediscover the human mind and the Holy Spirit that we Christians invariably believe in today. God that empowers our mind had empowered his Holy Spirit-born mind to an extent unreachable yet by any human throughout history; the mind of Christ that submits to the spirit in order to be led by the will of God and that unlike human corporeal minds does not die but inherits immortality; the spiritual mind that God empowers and bestows to His Sons. Yes, Jesus rediscovered and differentiated between the conscious *carnal mind* and the *spiritual subconscious mind;* the one that brings death and the other that brings life; the one that doubts everything and the other that believes everything. He distinguished in Qumran that children are born with an unsoiled subconscious mind thus they believe anything they are told but develop a conscious mind soon after and start to disbelieve. Hence he instructed his disciples that "the Kingdom of God is given to them (children)." Later throughout his mission he directed people to the subjective realm of the subconscious and have that *childlike faith* heralded by him in countless occasions.

Many theories and presumptions were given through history about those *lost years* of Jesus. Many advocated that he followed Joseph's footsteps and was a carpenter or a mason. Being a carpenter would not be a very good background for edifying the Messiah legacy. Spending those missing years in a religious school in a monastery hidden from the eyes of everyday people, as well as from the eyes of history provides a much more believable answer. And what a divine option to receive *all the knowledge and wisdom* needed for his ministry than to have the Essenes collect the necessary information and teach it in a formal school setting. The Qumran community had looked for a long time to the fulfillment of the Deuteronomy passage: "the Lord your God will raise up unto you a Prophet from the midst of you, of your brothers, like unto me; unto him you shall hear." (Deu.18:15.) In picking the Qumran retreat Jesus did indeed follow in the will of his Father, the Heavenly Father that he mentioned to his parents when at 12 he was found trading religious theories with the doctors in the Temple . . . certainly not with Joseph.

A candid question arises here from many skeptics: why would Jesus need to *go to school* if he were the Son of God? Here one should take into consideration that God sent him to earth as a *human* and wanted him to live on earth as a human. He was born a human baby, died on the cross as a human and the major part of his *human experience* was to study and learn as a human. Jesus went to school at the Qumran Monastery to spend almost 18 years of his human life studying to accomplish the Messiah he was and to reach the epitome of the human experience through dreary monastic living of prayers and contemplation according to the Torah's pronouncements. Otherwise, *there would be no meaning for a non-human God dying on the cross.* The Qumran Monastery was part of God's plan to elevate the Son of Man into the Son of God status as we understand from Isaiah and Malachi in the Bible.

Not much later a renowned visitor called on Qumran as directed by Hanania, the Essene disciple exiled to Damascus. It was Paul who never met Jesus before he appeared to him on the Damascus road and who wanted to gain more knowledge from the same community that surrounded Jesus' prior to and throughout his ministry. Hanania told Paul after recuperating his sight to withdraw into Qumran where he can "see the Righteous One and listen to him" away from the wrath of Petra's king. During his 3-year stay there, shrouded in secrecy the Essene way, he was ushered into the intricate realm of supremacy of the soul over matter and was taught many of the biblical prophesies announcing the Messiah. He was also enlightened with all Essene values heralded through Jesus' mission. Yet Paul visualized for himself the Messianic message that differed in substance from that of the rest of the Apostles. He also did not agree with many of the Qumran community's ordinances and was later disavowed by them chiefly because he believed Jesus did not come only for the Jews but for all nations as was confirmed later by Mark: "go into *the entire world* and preach the gospel *to every creature*" (Mark 16:15.). He set out north to preach the gospel to both Jews and gentiles alike especially the Greek whose language was within his grasp.

The Ebionite/Essene movement continued strong even after Jesus' Ascension. It consisted largely of followers of Jesus gathered in Jerusalem around his *"brother"* Jacob (the Just). While Peter carried the Gospel to the towns of Judea; James became the head of the now reduced and impoverished church in Jerusalem. Jacob practiced the Law in all its severity and rivaled the Essenes in asceticism; he ate no meats, drank no wine, had only one garment and never cut his hair or beard. For eleven years under his guidance the Christians were left undisturbed. In the year 41 Peter was arrested but miraculously escaped. In 62 Jacob the Just was himself put to death and four years later the Jews revolted against Rome. The Jerusalem Christians, too convinced of the coming *end of the world* to care about politics, left the city and established themselves back around Qumran. From that hour Judaism and Christianity parted. The Jews accused the Christians of treason and cowardice and the Christians hailed the destruction of the Temple by Titus as a fulfillment of Christ's prophecy.

Shortly thereafter the Judaic Christianity waned in number and power and yielded to the new religion as established by the Pauline church and the Greek mind. Remnants of the Christian Ebionite were dispersed across Jordan all the way down to Arabian Hejaz, to emerge some 600 years later as the nucleus of the Islamic faith.

-12-

The Son of Man, Son of God

*". . . till we all come in the unity of the faith,
and of the knowledge of the Son of God, unto a
perfect man, unto the Measure and the Stature
of the Fullness of Christ."*

Paul to the Ephesians

J esus came by the Mosaic Law not to refute that Law but
to straighten it out. Almost all *what has been written* in
the Bible about the Messiah including his predetermined
flight to Egypt fulfilling: "from Egypt, I called my Son," was

sustained and advocated throughout his actions and teachings including the Son of Man title started with Daniel 7.

The phrases containing "son of" *bar enash* in the ancient world had a specific purpose to serve. It carries the meaning of an *heir or successor to royalty* or of a free man of the highest class. Thus *man* here is not just any man but "THE MAN" that is given dominion of the sort that God possesses; the one Jesus was set to elevate to the godly status. The significance of Jesus' *son of man* usage is functionally equivalent to saying that the one like a son of man is *rightful heir* and successor to the divine throne. In this context *Son of Man* is essentially the same as *Son of God*. Jesus did use the phrase consistent with its original meaning; it is a powerful and clear claim to deity.

Furthermore Jesus asserted his divine identity by acquiring the prerogatives of God with the combined honor of being metaphorically seated at His right hand. The *right hand* reference means in a way sharing the highest honor with Him. By using this metaphor Jesus supported the biblical texts describing the *right hand of God* as the place where the splendor and majesty of God comes from (Daniel, Job, Enoch and others.) This is where the righteous are honored by being allowed to *stand*—not sit!—In this context it is noteworthy that Jesus in Acts 7 is still *standing* at God's right hand.

Yet the *bar nasha* in Aramaic was *not* a Biblical Messianic title until Jesus initiated it as such. He identified it to describe the Messianic figure that he was. Many surface skimmers consider it likely that Jesus was using the Son of Man title to keep things under wraps; things related to the clear announcing of his son-ship with God. In fact Jesus was not at all hesitant to publicly identify himself or speak of himself as taking God's prerogative in forgiving sins or altering laws.

With this title Jesus did not mean only himself. While the *son of man* was a typical Aramaic circumlocution for *I* in his times it also refers to the human race in general or any human being as such. The related phrase *son of man* (*bar Adam*) found in Ezekiel also suggests that underlying the Greek version of the Gospels, which says *the* Son of Man there was actually an Aramaic phrase, *a* Son of Man; the change having been made of course to make the idiom look more like a title and to signify a son of the *total mankind* and not in the ordinary sense of the term. Thus Christ the Son of Man became the expression of the total feeling of humanity. Furthermore the term was used by Jesus to mean himself in the third person as well as other humans he called *the Children of God.*

This *human being* approach asserting the Father/son relationship between God of *the heavens* and man where God dwells, characterized Jesus' entire philosophy. It is hardly a characteristic of the race as a whole but to those who uphold and pursue this philosophy: "also I say unto you, whosoever shall confess me before men, him shall the Son of Man also confess before the "angels" of God . . ." (Luk.12:8.) This passage is just a little easier to stretch using our modern understanding of Jesus: 'he, who avoids my teaching, would be alienating himself from my prescribed positive realm.' That was the *only* way to cut through the ancient thinking stupidity and woodenness, otherwise no one would have understood what Jesus meant as many still do not today. This argument may not be digested by scholars and regular Christians who insist on a *straightforward* reading of the texts. But if they consider that literal *blood on*

143

the moon is a mere crass and unsophisticated literalism by the ancients used as metaphors to stir idle spirits, they then accept there was no barrier to Jesus or anyone else using figurative language to refer to a literal event; likewise the parables that cannot be interpreted literally especially when a *log in the eyes* is exemplified.

The *Son of Man* catchphrase repeatedly mentioned in the Bible was not enough influence on Jesus' thoughts but a superficial description. Jesus filled it with greater meaning and depth that do not cease to overwhelm us. It had been meticulously nurtured throughout his Qumran years. In fact Jesus did not have to do much filling in at all since it embodies the nucleus of his mission and person. He used it in a broader way commensurate with his immense salvation mission. One aspect of Daniel 7 description remains valid: the suffering Son of Man. The entire ministry of Jesus including his suffering and resurrection was oriented towards the establishment of "an everlasting dominion, which shall not pass away, and a kingdom that shall not be destroyed." (Dan. 7:14.)

The term *Messiah*—the Anointed—appears about forty times in the Old Testament and always referred to the Savior who would advent the Kingdom of God to Israel. The Jews however expected a grand appearance of a Messianic visitation from above with exceptional worldly glory following the vision of Daniel in his Babylonian exile. They envisioned a terrestrial Messiah, a royal descendant of David, yet a supernatural personage that would be powerful enough to conquer Israel's imperialist enemies. In fact, particular veneration was centered upon John the Baptist; and he was somehow credited with Messianic status by his disciples who reverted later to Jesus following John's heralding as *the one who is to come,* the true embodiment of the Messiah.

Jesus though did not claim to be a Messiah of the earthly, Davidic kind but the supernatural Messiah of another Kingdom *from without this world* powered by the miraculous Holy Spirit. On the level of that spirit he was the Son of God performing his mighty acts culminated by his resurrection from the dead; the ultimate feat that caused even few of his doubtful disciples to fortify their belief in his mission and die defending it.

A perplexing and mysterious observation by Jesus reported by Matthew still baffles clerics and laymen alike: "Everything is entrusted to me by my Father; and no one knows the Son but the Father, and no one knows the Father but the Son and *those to whom the Son may choose to reveal Him.*" (Mat.11:27.) This has been hailed as strong evidence that Jesus announced himself as the Son of God. The underlying meaning that no one knows the Father but the Son whose mind God inhabits and those other *sons of God* the Son may choose and teach to reveal Him as dwelling in their minds has not been noticeable for lack of assimilation.

It sounds like some kind of contradiction at first glance but a scriptural examination reveals that the phrase *Son of Man* carries broad significance. While it is a reference to Jesus' humanity it is not a denial of his deity. By becoming a man and living, drinking, laughing like a man *Jesus exemplified to all mankind that God inhabits the human mind and can lift man up to His status.* The incarnation of Christ did not involve the subtraction of deity but the addition of humanism. In this line of thought the Scripture indicates that Jesus was not denying his deity by referring to himself as the Son of Man. When the

Bible says that only God can forgive sins Jesus as the Son of Man had the power to forgive sins simply because he was able to *identify* those sins, detect their *den* and open their discharge outlet. When Jesus was asked by the high priest whether he was the *Son of God* (Mat. 26:63), he responded affirmatively declaring that he was the *Son of Man* who would come in power and great glory. This signified that Jesus himself used the phrase *Son of Man* to indicate his deity as the Son of God.

In his letter to Ephesians Paul redefined the Son of Man/God in a more simplified format: ". . . till we all come in the unity of the faith, and of the knowledge of the Son of God, unto a perfect man, *unto the Measure and the Stature of the Fullness of Christ.*" (Eph. 4:13.) The Son of Man when imbedded with the fullness of Christ, i.e. possessing the full power of his mind and overcoming all negative forces the way Jesus did becomes a designated Son of God not by any external entity but by the voice of God within him.

The Messianic character assumed by the Son of Man during the Qumran years gained further momentum as a concept later during the three-year mission. Thus the Son of Man/God terms accompanied one another. Jesus pushed the God/Man relation to a filial relationship heretofore unprecedented in Biblical heritage. Thus the Son of God intimacy became presumptuous, even blasphemous to the elders of the Jewish canon. Jesus went even farther by stressing God's fatherhood through the parable of the Prodigal Son and its characteristic intimation. This filial relationship was assigned in a novel sense to the early exclusive followers although the Jewish stance persisted, depicting Jesus as a Jew singled out for a great religious role. Yet most of the Jewish clerics looked down with disdain at this claim. The testimony of the Roman centurion Longinus at the Crucifixion: "Truly this man was Son of God" further alienated the Christian mission from the Jews towards the open Gentiles public.

The Jews failed to understand exactly as Muslims later that Jesus did not claim to be the *only* Son of God but so were all the devotees who accepted and assimilated his message. Hence his prescribed daily prayer addressed in unison to: "Our Father who . . ." Even today questions arise whether the Fatherhood of God was not the core of the experience. Jesus' perception of the Father is something so profound and moving that it should not be spoken about except to those who have shown themselves fitted to hear. The Christian experience with the Father stands upon a rock of intense religious belief that Jesus knows the Father in a way no one else does. He has ever been the supreme reality in the life of Jesus as well as in that of every Christian in whose mind God resides.

-13-

Jesus, the Middle Eastern

". . . Get you behind me, Satan: you are an
offence unto me: for you savor not the things
that be of God, but those that be of men."

Jesus addressing Peter

very time I admire Da Vinci's Last Supper fresco I
wonder at the European superficial knowledge of the
Middle Eastern way of life during the early Christian era.
Jesus did not sit with his disciples on a dining table surrounded
by individual chairs as the famous painting portrays but like
everybody else, except rulers and high priests of those days,

they sat on a ground covered with either woven tapestry or mutton skins with probably two or three 1-foot high tables where food is usually served. In fact the fresco reminds me of another painting I saw in Japan depicting the Holy Family with eyes, hairdos and attires reminiscent of outfitted Geishas . . . and a third sculpture I saw in Peru where the Peruvian artist presented Christ as a brown skinned Peruvian Indian. I also saw him portrayed with sub-Saharan African characteristics by local worshippers or sketched as a short dark haired fellow with no beard in Ancient Roman mosaics . . . Surely religious figures, like beauty, are in the eye of the beholder!

The West had recreated Jesus' looks, way of life and most of his principles in manners readily acceptable to the Western mentality. Thus Jesus is a fair skinned, blue eyed and blond haired personage. A dark haired, brown eyed Messiah won't be digested as a European hue would. These artists also used available models from among their people. It is no wonder that Christ took on a European look especially since the Middle East was no longer a source of Christian art.

The early European church like much of Western Europe came to be dominated by tribes of Germanic or Nordic pagan ancestry. In an effort to convert them to Christianity Christ's image was made to look like them. Since the German-Nordic groups dominated western European kingdoms from Norway to Italy that image went from being as portrayed in Byzantine art, dark haired and eyed, to a classically white western European. This trend in church art continued into modern times as the other great painters of religious art followed this pattern.

But worse than what artists and movie producers have done with the physical characteristic of Jesus is what theologians, church leaders, and historians have done to his character! So much so that many Christians became really at a loss to distinguish the differences between the genuine Jesus and the counterfeit Christ. Through the years believers have depicted Christ as one of their own physical ideals of beauty and compassion. As a Nazarene, Jesus was Jewish and since this was before the days of antiperspirant and stain-removing detergent, his grungy robe probably had huge sweat rings and his curly black hair didn't exactly glisten from a recent hot oil treatment. The historical figure of Jesus probably would have had long, thick and curly brown hair. He would almost certainly have had brown eyes and one of the dusky shades of skin common in the Middle East. From the imposing physical personality detected through the Scripture, he probably had some muscle too, at least enough brawn to bounce the money changers out of the temple on their self-righteous rears. Since he was familiar with the ancient scriptures from a young age you may safely add a striking air of intelligence, imposing manly traits that sometimes his disciples wouldn't look him in the face, and a joyful, yes, joyful and compassionate expression with which Children were drawn to his presence.

We have been grown familiar from Church teachings and art history that Jesus was a sad, cheerless individual. This attribute was more enhanced by the Eastern Orthodox Church showing Jesus and Mary in long, distressed looks throughout their icons. Religious leaders leaning toward formality, sacredness, reverence, rationality and authority have helped develop religious formations that are hierarchical, heavily structured and overly serious. They were leaning all the way on the Gospels that barely attributed any humor to Jesus.

The absence of his joyfulness in the gospels was due to the fact that they were written many years after Jesus' death not for the purpose of setting down an accurate biography. They spoke to a community grappling with the imminent destruction of the Jewish Temple in Jerusalem and a general public feeling of abandonment by God. Following that, Judaism was being reorganized in the absence of a temple and the Pharisees were in competition with Matthew's community of believers. Matthew in his endeavor to display Jesus as the authentic Jewish Messiah cared little about his joyous side let alone his accurate, personal record.

Yet Jesus' ability to laugh in any situation made him more real and accessible. He was an indoctrinator; a challenger of the old ways being done and followed; a prophet recalling the Jewish people to the true ways of the sacred Scripture. A sharp intelligent mind requires good humor to disseminate intelligible issues. Jesus was not a one issue ideologue but an outgoing, masterful communicator who perfected the fine art of joyfully penetrating the minds and spirits to put his listeners at ease.

Many hints however emerge from the Scripture relating joys and laughter to Jesus. It is apparent in Jesus' encounter with Nathaniel; the joke starts with Nathaniel's sarcastic remark: "Can anything good come out of Nazareth?" Whether Nazareth was the butt of humor in Jesus' day or not it is still the same sarcasm in the Middle East today when a rich or famous emerges from a tiny village. Nathaniel's humor was instantly answered by an ironic quip from Jesus: "Here is truly an Israelite in whom there is no deceit!" Nathaniel has just made a snide joke at Jesus' expense that was answered it in the like.

The healing of the Gerasene demoniac (psychopathic sick) carries another of Jesus' sarcasm when he sent into swine the *evil spirits* he named Legion. The swine went nuts, ran into the lake and drowned. *Legion* was a reference to the Roman brigade. A dimension of political satire through which Jesus intended to churn out a good laugh by his Palestinian audience that carried no empathy to the occupiers at the time. This sarcasm had yet another underlying objective: the wrong and long inherited appellations *demons* to all such mental conditions that require exorcism!

Another sign of humor is the way Jesus behaved on the Sabbath; an issue that got him always to trouble with the Pharisees: while walking through a field on the Sabbath Jesus picked few wheat ears from the field and ate them after rubbing the seeds in his hands to eliminate the husk, thereby *doing work*. When questioned about this by the Pharisees he replied sarcastically: "The Sabbath was made for man, not man for the Sabbath."

The most persuasive evidence of good humor is again, Jesus' affinity for children. It is hard to imagine a humorless person enjoying being surrounded by children. Another aspect is the insolent mocking tone Jesus takes when he was questioned sarcastically by Pontius Pilate: "Are you king of the Jews?" and he replied "You have said so."

The conversation between him and his mother when he performed his first public miracle turning water into wine in Cana is quite humorous. Mary tackled him to perform with her power of suggestion: "They have no wine . . ." he retorted humorously: "*Woman*, what have I to do with you, my hour is not yet come." Mary ignored his sarcasm in a motherly manner that *knows* what her son *really* wanted and said to the servants: "Whatsoever he says to you, do it."

The Christian tradition hardly associates laughter to Jesus although he was the forerunner of great joy. Almost all his addresses to his disciples would terminate with the adage: ". . . and your joy will be fulfilled." He certainly valued joy high on his positive ladder and saw in it hope brought to the poor and outcast. He despised sorrow and grief to the point of ordering one of his disciples whose father just died: "let the dead (mournful) bury their dead and follow me (to the joyous life)." He even was mischievous in his pursuit of joy: eating with sinners, feasting when others were fasting, and enjoying life in ways that upset the religious authorities. Jesus advocated that laughter is a positive pinnacle so powerful in connecting people to one another and transforming their lives. He knew joy as a positive ingredient to create magic and send the human spirit soaring on a cloud of bliss and beatitude.

Jesus joked with and teased many of his disciples to cast a positive atmosphere of congeniality. He once mocked Peter, his most entrusted disciple: ". . . get you behind me, *Satan*: you are an offence unto me: for you savor not *the things that be of God*, but those that be of men." (Mat.16:21.) Still in the Middle East today parents jokingly introduce a bright and active child as *a Satan*. And according to the controversial Gospel of Judas he actually mocked and laughed at the disciples as shown in this passage: "When he approached them gathered together and seated and offering a prayer of thanksgiving over the bread, he laughed. The disciples said to him 'Master, why are you laughing at our prayer of thanksgiving? We have done what is right.' He answered and said to them, 'I am laughing at you, you are not doing this because of your own will . . ." meaning they were following blindly an old, conventional practice . . .

Christians down the centuries had conveyed the fear of laughter with a powerful grip. The Church taught that laughter is morally reprehensible and a mockery of truth. The dilemma of laughter hasn't gone away. We do now rarely laugh in church, but that's a recent thing still considered a digression. I personally admire the African Americans who chant, dance and laugh in glorification of God inside their churches. We still don't laugh at the most poignant parts of worship and throughout the Middle East it may be considered irreverence and most priests remain very dour in their sermons. Part of the Church's antipathy towards laughter is because laughter can threaten and mock sincerity. In fact the Church insists on us to know that Jesus was tired, hungry, thirsty and weepy. But when have you ever heard someone say, 'Jesus was truly human; he knew how to laugh,' we hear almost nothing about it in Christian teaching and sometimes it is forbidden or discouraged.

The reason Jesus spoke in parables was in a way because he was not speaking to the learned folk but rather to ordinary people. And as we see today on the lecture circuits, talk shows, interview programs, and in any form of public speech, humor is the lubricant that brings the speaker closer to the audience; humor was also a well-known device of rhetoric in those times. The parables Jesus told were colorful vistas from the human scenes enhanced with everyday images. And it is quite likely he delivered them with a cheerful, non-conformist ways. Even while preaching he broke away from the forms established by the famous rabbis. His own inspiration was all he had needed. When he appealed to the Torah the spontaneity of his words that sometimes contradicted the Old Scripture was hampered by nothing because it sprang from his irresistible inner force. And like the spontaneity of any Middle Eastern then—or even today, we don't find in his sayings the slightest interest in rational or objective knowledge for two obvious reason: such theorizations contradicts his inductive God-mind, and would by no means be perceived by his audience; hence his starting and ending by conclusions.

The most discernible attribute in his messages was exaggeration and over emphasizing; a penchant quite inherent to the Middle Eastern desirous to inject maximum implication in his speech. Unlike the Western exacting, calculating and unemotional mind the one in the Middle East was and remains to this day the exact opposite: an over-viewer, candid and emotive. A mother calls her son my soul, my heart and mostly: *my burier!* A friend tells his pal: my blood is for you, my eyes are yours, I am ready to die for you . . . in fact that is what in this connotation, Peter told Jesus about his readiness to die for him the same night he denied him three times! To people in the Middle East Peter was not an outright liar as taken in the West but simply a courteous flatterer.

In that part of the world people swear by heavens, reserve a place for their enemies in 'the Red Hell' and end their letters with *millions of kisses*. They describe their hand-fed, burly muttons as elephants and their tiny car engines as rockets. While such familiar exaggerations adorn every chat and are taken as mere figurative speech to lubricate an otherwise dry conversation, Jesus adopted the same trend in his time and went high in his allegories. He told Peter who asked him 'how many times one should forgive his brother's mistakes, seven times?' saying: "not seven times, but seventy times seven times." Jesus surely did not mean 490 times but wanted to imply that forgiveness should be a way of life unlimited under all circumstances.

Jesus therefore used exaggerations almost always to make a point in line with the common way of thinking and speaking in his day. He highlighted cutting off a hand or gouging out an eye to dramatize hating to sin. He painted the going of a camel through the eye of the needle to portray impossibility and a beam or timber in one's eye to denote clear judgment. He implied a man should hate his father and mother, wife and children when it comes to the decisive commitment of joining him. But would one think that Jesus really meant that if you want to follow him you would have to hate your family? The *hating your father and mother* in order to be a disciple was meant to show that *you are moving now to a different sphere of thinking and behavior, and unless you relinquish all what you grew accustomed to heretofore, you won't possibly have the sense of obligation nor the power of concentration to become my disciple.* This explains later the many instances where those disciples, to the distress of the Master, could not understand a simple parable like *the sower.*

Within the same perspective and in full contradiction with his overall love message, Jesus dramatized his coming to earth in anything but surprising to his own disciples: "Think not that

I am come to send peace on earth; I came not to send peace, but a sword. For I am come to set a man at variance against his father and the daughter against her mother . . ." (Mat. 10:34.) How else, without such an exaggeration, could he open the ears of *those who have ears* to listen and comprehend a totally new doctrine where man's negative current is evil and his positive one is goodness and where man's mind is or is not, the throne of God! Surely it is a controversial doctrine negating all Old Testament's rulings, capable of setting people apart between knower and snub, believers and doubters.

Hence Jesus' repetitive use of hyperboles; he gave them a respected place in his teaching. We make a grave mistake today when expecting every word Jesus uttered to be *literally* true. What is true is what he said if only we extract ourselves from yesteryear's intellect level of the peasants and fishermen and use our highly educated mind to retrace his meanings; otherwise we will make big mistakes in interpreting the Scripture. In fact, the intelligent reader today keeps wondering: how could Jesus disseminate such convoluted philosophy in such simple words and expressions? Obviously he was constantly finding ways and means within the limited confines of the Aramaic language to highlight his points, he used *poetic options* to create *word pictures* that are not literally factual but they achieve the required meaning in a special, poignant way.

Jesus' message, if taken literally, would certainly fail all the tests of human practice. Furthermore, he did temper with the Bible without compromising its divine inspirations. He critiqued Moses in many ancient edicts and divorce was not the only issue. He introduced himself as *greater than Solomon* and many biblical personages and employed all prophesies heralding the Messiah to full fruition. He did not relinquish though the old biblical idiolects and legends of the ancient Middle East keeping up with demons and angels to highlight man's negative and positive penchants; nor did he relinquish heaven and hell to illustrate the realms of good and evil. Jesus also used many other speech embellishments currently used in his era: brilliant as the Sun, white as the cloud. And, in as much as the local imagination would muster, the second coming of the Son of Man would be over the clouds of heaven . . .

The Bible he tagged along was in itself the most heartrending document to display the maximum of Middle Eastern exaggerations: when Chronicles don't agree on kings or to the number of the king's horses, etc., but is off by thousands or tens of thousands; or when the size of the Israelite armies is more phenomenal than anything historians can possibly imagine, or when Solomon "had seven hundred wives, princesses and three hundred concubines" (1Kin. 11:3,) to settle it on an *even thousand*! Now you call *that* an exaggeration! Further, when the Bible says that Solomon had 81% of the same amount of gold that is currently possessed by the American Treasury: "a hundred thousand talents of gold (that is 3.4 thousand tons), a million talents of silver, quantities of bronze and iron too great to be weighed, and wood and stone," (1Chr. 22:14.) It's difficult to believe today that an ancient king like Solomon ruling over relatively parched and moderately populated lands like Judea, lacking modern methods and machines for gold mining and refining, could have accumulated 81% of what currently lies at Fort Knox. Likely, the author of 1st. Chronicles was inflating the wealth of David and Solomon just as he inflated the numerical sizes of their armies, horses or concubines . . . a deeply innate fancy in every Middle Easter: the passion for exaggeration.

The Scripture is flooded with overstatements of truly *Biblical proportions*. Evangelists adopted the same flamboyance in chronicling Jesus' ministry: "The devil took him up into an exceedingly high mountain, and showed him all the kingdoms of the world, and the glory of them." (Mat. 4:8.) For all we know the highest peak in the area was Mount Harmon—or Gilead from which peak one could see through the naked eye Damascus, Jerusalem and Tyre. But to see *all the kingdoms of the world* is pure amplification. Matthews however was not as lavish as Daniel who presumed a flat earth around the *exceedingly high mountain* when he wrote: "I saw a tree in the midst of the earth, and the height thereof was great. The tree grew, and the height thereof reached unto heaven, and the sight thereof to the end of all the earth." (Dan. 4:10.) Such flagrantly flat-earth verses appear in both the Old and New Testaments. Our cleric reply that such verses are only *apparently difficult* to explain and not the *real truth* as they see it.

Overstatement, especially when seeking attention or arousing interest and sympathy was as it is today, an accomplished art. The embellished story should always take advantage over what *really happened*. When a famous rabbi dies *the stars became visible in broad daylight!* Intended to suggest what a wonderful sage he was. Like other Jews, Jesus often needed more than plain prose to highlight his meaning. His teaching contains indeed many of the formal elements of the Aramaic language: parallelism, rhythm, rhyme, repetition and antithesis. Vigorous metaphors and similes are added to the gnomic diction of the Galilean folklore. This was the ongoing style involving innumerable paradoxes and sharp exaggerations.

Therefore literal understanding of Jesus' expressions would be sometimes disproportionate, even inappropriate. You won't cut your son's hand if he grabs a watch from a department store; and you don't pluck your husband's eye because he had it lustily on another girl. When we understand these same sayings in the daily Middle East language where a good neighbor tells his needy pal: "listen, you won't have to return these loaves, I had been showered by your past bounty . . ." then perhaps we know how to read Jesus.

For it is impossible to any American today who reads: "And there were dwelling at Jerusalem Jews, devout men, out of every nation under heaven," (Act. 2:5,) to imagine that few of the nation of the Sioux Indians in North America were there too! Or when he reads: "A great famine all over the world took place in the reign of Claudius," (Act. 11:28,) to account for Japanese and native Incas who suffered the famine effects. Yet if it was stated "all over the Roman world" the *known* one to the writer, exaggeration could then be contained.

By resorting knowingly to such Hebraic embellishments Jesus not only solidified belief among his listeners but also epitomized his ideas to become eternal symbols: "Then Jesus said unto them, Verily, verily, I say unto you, except you eat the flesh of the Son of Man, and drink his blood, you have no life in you. Whoso eats my flesh, and drinks my blood, has eternal life; and I will raise him up at the last day." (John 6:53.) Through that saying Jesus portrayed the simple bread and wine to symbolize his flesh and blood and permeated them as two of the most sacred rituals in Christianity. He would not do that without his flair for amplification.

Joy and overstatements were most of the time a *positive* mixture to strengthen belief: "The seventy-two returned with *joy* and said, Lord, even the demons submit to us in your name!" He replied, *"I saw Satan* (the overall negative force) *fall like lightning from heaven.* I have given you authority (unshaken belief) to trample on snakes and scorpions and to overcome all the power of the enemy (negative forces); so nothing will harm you. However do not rejoice that the spirits submit to you, *but rejoice* that (the greater reward) your names are written in heaven." (Luk.10:17.) We certainly distinguish today the magnitude of the spiritual thrust these words imparted.

Many other aspects of the oriental daily life and behaviors may seem odd to the Western mind. Jesus used to *break* and bless the bread; the thin bread of the Middle East was always dried out since it was either exposed or wrapped for days in porous material. Bread in that part of the world has a special significance non-existent in the West. It is not just another *food* but sacred life sustenance. We grew up since childhood to pick a dropped piece of bread, kiss it, lift it over our head and deposit it in a clean place for any needy to eat it. Hence Jesus likens bread to his body.

Question marks are drawn and eyebrows are raised in the West over the manner Jesus addressed his Mother: *woman.* In fact Woman in the Middle East is equal to Lady in the West. This is how a man addresses his wife or any female when he really wants to admire her personality and womanhood. The Spaniards inherited this from the Arabs in Andalusia and still acclaim a worthy female as a *Mujer,* from Mura'a in Arabic.

In fact Jesus took a long step towards the rejection of many Jewish attitudes towards women. He even associated himself with them allowing them to play a free role in his life, setting himself sharply apart from the Jewish rabbis. Women have been traditionally taken as inferior to men by nature being created by God only as a second-hand product. They were generally associated with evil and weakness that men sometimes thanked God in synagogues for not being born females!

Jesus was not an ordinary prophet or teacher. He was many times far removed from the *gentle and meek* who turns the other cheek of tolerance and love into a stormy personage with a *mighty vein of granite in his character* giving his opponents as much as he got from them and more. Some of his attacks cannot simply be dismissed as mere oriental verbiage: "You are like tombs covered with whitewash; they look well from outside, but inside they are full of dead men's bones and all kinds of filth . . . . You snakes, you vipers' brood, how can you escape being condemned to hell?" (Mat.23:27.)

This tirade started earlier by the Baptist, may be considered by many a grotesque riposte from the minister of love and compassion. The meek Lamb of God though, who ordained man to return to childhood to become worthy of the Kingdom of Heaven possessed a child's inductive mind, impulsive, spontaneous, non-judgmental and non-restrictive that does not hesitate to call a spade a spade. This same mind of God cannot flatter, cajole or compromise. And exactly as you cannot fool a child with your feelings towards him that is how a child does not hesitate to candidly behave towards you. The Church and many historians were baffled by the romantic picture of Jesus surrounded by children taking his affection for these innocent beings as a feature of his character; obviously they were all unaware of the working of his mind and heart.

The same candid mind of Jesus has been displayed again with the Phoenician woman in Sidon. His initial reaction to her was: "I was sent to the lost sheep of the house of Israel, *and to them alone.*" And when she fell on his feet and appealed for help he replied, probably with an inquisitive smile: "It is not right to take the children's bread and throw it to the dogs." This uncompromising attitude, essential in testing her belief was not encountered by a typical Phoenician maneuvering to consummate a deal: "Lord, yet the dogs under the table eat of the children's crumbs," but by a truly heart-felt belief, *essential to perform the miracle*, that Jesus felt an acted upon: "*For this saying* go your way, the "*demon*" is gone out of your daughter." Here once more, the meek, child-like mind of Jesus acted and behaved.

Throughout his 3-year ministry Jesus interacted with all sorts of behaviors and comportments of the ancient Middle East. Such was his unique approach to network with the existing people's minds and indoctrinate a philosophy that remained to our days of advanced knowledge unfathomed and controversial. The West and many Orientals puzzled with various behavioral incongruities in the Scripture ought to better understand that part of the world in order to achieve fuller comprehension to foster their belief. Today none of the greatest scientists or philosophers of old can be *remembered* in such personal details as can be the Great Nazarene. Across centuries and till today Jesus can be called upon to console, encourage and forgive just as would any human living among us, eating, drinking and breathing!

The spiritual mainstay of the Qumran community was the Bible. The Law of Moses added to the prophets' precepts and foretelling were the guidelines governing all mystical and saintly performances. Jesus charted his three-year ministry based on the biblical references and divinations especially those parts related to him as the Messiah coming from within Israel to its people. Yet he deviated from the biblical theme to reformulate old assumptions to befit the new Kingdom of God. For example it was a Jewish belief that 'all your works should be for the sake of God.' Jesus altered this tradition in his Sermon of the Mount with summons assuring the unfortunate of the happiness to come. His moral injunction: 'set your mind upon His Kingdom and all the rest will come to you as well' was repeatedly the basic message that changed the biblical total reliance on God into man's charting his own destiny with God.

Perhaps the most inspiring Biblical Prophet to Jesus was Isaiah. His prophesies about the Messiah were closely realized. Even Jesus' last eventful hours on the Calvary were foreseen by Isaiah. In his chapter 53 we read: "Surely he took up our infirmities and carried our sorrows, yet we considered him stricken by God, smitten by him, and *afflicted*. But he was *pierced* for our transgressions, he was *crushed* for our iniquities; the punishment that brought us peace was upon him, and by his wounds we are healed. We all, like sheep, have gone astray, each of us has turned to his own way; and the Lord has laid on him the iniquity of us all." Hence, when even these words were meticulously carried out Jesus declared on the Cross his sixth word possibly in a little more than a tortured whisper: "It is fulfilled."

The sequence of events throughout his early life and later ministry unfolded as the Torah predicted him to be. The first announcement of this ministry is a striking biblical message to Israel that the Messiah and the Message were both at hand. Luke tells us that after his baptism and temptation by the *devil*, he "came to Nazareth where he had been brought up; and went to the synagogue as his custom was on the Sabbath day. And he stood up to read." Following the customary rabbinical pattern he took up a scroll of the Hebrew Bible, read it, presumably provided an Aramaic translation, paraphrase of the text and then commented on it. We repeat these words from Isaiah 61:1: "The Spirit of the Lord is upon me, because he has anointed me to preach the gospel to the poor. He has sent me to heal the brokenhearted, to preach deliverance to the captives, and recovering of sight to the blind, to set at liberty those that are bruised, to proclaim the acceptable year of the Lord." (Luk.4:16.)

But instead of doing what a rabbi would normally do: apply the text to the hearers by comparing and contrasting earlier interpretations he declared: "Today this scripture has been fulfilled in your hearing." Although the initial reaction to this audacious declaration was said to be wonderment *at the gracious words which proceeded out of his mouth,* his further explanation created the opposite reaction and everyone was *filled with wrath.* Even the Jews of Galilee who were not as utterly absorbed in religious thoughts as those of Judea Jesus' assertion that this culmination of universal history, this communion of the Kingdom of God which they expected in the future had already begun at that very time and by his own personal action, was startling.

Was Jesus hasty in announcing himself as the Messiah? Definitely so: he was eager to start his compressed, well programmed three-year ministry that he chose to launch first in his own native town of Nazareth knowing full well what the reaction would be for *a prophet in his own country.* Yet this shocking proclamation was needed to prepare his own folks first for his upcoming tribulation. He knew there have been described in the Old Testament 300 prophecies of his first coming as the Messiah and 500 of the second coming all of them made hundreds of years before his birth and must be fulfilled to the letter.

The Jews did not believe him as the predictable Messiah for two main reasons: 1/they expected one that comes with heavenly as well as earthly pomp and solemnity inherent to kings and not a boy born in a manger. 2/they also visualized a mighty one that would mobilize Israel, liberate it from the Roman yoke and propel the Jewish might into nostalgic biblical conquests; not one whose 'kingdom is without this world.' A Messiah from Nazareth though from David's seed frequently prophesized in the Torah was not up to the Hebraic expectations. The majority of them rushed to pronounce him a false prophet pretending to be a righteous Jew who fulfills the Law but at key moments he would turn against certain biblical details in order to make breaches. Jesus rebelled against the authority of the Jewish judges namely the Sanhedrin, believed to be established by Moses and lasted for more than 15 centuries to become a dyed-in-the-wool statute hard to overturn.

Later their distance widened vis-à-vis Jesus who fulfilled all these prophesies to become *king* of the Christian church by changing the original Law, doing away with the Hebrew calendar and the Biblical holidays let alone violating the Sabbath by picking grain or healing the blind! Another major allegation is his disregarding the infinite oneness of God in favor of a new *trinity* that included him. His defense to the rabbis' authority as in Matthew 23:1 is considered an occasional pretension to respect the Law. Nonetheless his sporadic words of piety were meant only to hide his new agenda. Thus a reactionary Jewish move was stirred and a rude awakening initiated to rescue those *lost souls* that mistakenly sought out salvation through the Jesus doctrine.

For many Christians today it has been puzzling to see Jews who across centuries and to this day did not recognize Jesus as the long promised and awaited Messiah. Although the tremendous extent of prophecies in the Scripture most of them fulfilled with no room for forgery or premeditation constitute a convincing rationale for such recognition. The Messiah is in the core and the heart of every Jew . . . He was promised to Abraham, Isaac, Jacob, Moses, David . . . He is an inspiration and hope that runs through every page of the Torah . . . announcing his character, his time of coming, the type and details of his doctrine and ministry.

No doubt, tradition with its big burden of cumulative assumptions took its toll on the programmed Jewish mind. Add to that the severe effects of modern life governed by the daily humdrums of facts and figures that practically eliminate the very inclination to a spiritual thinking, one can reach the answer as to why such debate is shelved, avoided and probably committed to oblivion.

Recently however scholars have put the picture of Jesus back into the setting of first century Judaism and rediscovered the Jadishness of the New Testament in Paul himself. His epistle to the Romans 9-11 is the description of his struggle over the relation between church and synagogue concluding with the prediction and the promise: "And so all Israel will be saved"—as regards election "they are beloved for the sake of their forefathers, for the gifts and the call of God are irrevocable" (Rom. 11:26.) A further reading of the mind of Paul gives special significance to his many references to the name of Jesus as "descended from David according to the flesh . . ." Here Jesus Christ is "of the people of Israel . . . , a Hebrew born of Hebrews" (Phil. 3:5.) The very issue of universality supposedly the distinction between Paul and Judaism necessitates for Paul to consider Jesus a Jew who reinforce the covenant of God with Israel. His irrevocable calling becomes available to all people including the Gentiles who "were grafted in their place to share *the richness of the olive tree*"—namely the people of Israel (Rom. 11:17.) The "Jews for Jesus" association in Los Angeles proclaims the Messiahship of Jesus throughout the Jewish world.

As to their ancestors, Jesus was received by the multitudes that flocked for him with a stormy acclaim: many of them acknowledged him outright as the Son of God and the long-awaited Messiah. But the powerful forces in the Jewish congregation, Pharisees and Sadducees, jealous of his popularity, incensed by his denunciation of some of them and bitterly critical of his disregard for formalism and his willingness to violate some of the minor laws especially for his seemingly heretical claim as the Son of God they repudiated him and conspired to kill him. Their final conspiracy was not after any wrong doing, but after resurrecting a 4-day death: Lazarus! (Jn.12) . . . they saw red!, they could not perceive that he was really the Messiah . . . and eventually they saw him fulfilling the scriptures even when dying on the Cross as he had announced 3 times before. And after learning of his resurrection they persecuted his followers. The most stalwart among their persecutors was Paul before he had his eye opening operation on the Damascus road!

Furthermore the confrontations between Jesus and the representatives of the rabbinical tradition were clearly manifested in his unique approach of teaching as a rabbi. One of the most familiar is the question and answer method with the question often phrased as a teaser. A woman had seven husbands (in series, not in parallel): whose wife will she be in the life to come (Mat. 22:28?) Is it lawful for a devout Jew to pay taxes to the Roman authorities (Mat. 22:17?) What must I do to inherit eternal life (Mark 10:17?) Who is the greatest in the kingdom of heaven (Mat. 18:1?) These were trying questions designed to disconcert and judge Jesus who did not fail every time to drive the point home.

Jesus' deductive and authoritarian mind, God's mind that embraces the conclusion without researching the details was too much innovation to be accepted by the Jewish Doctors. The elevated man investiture that Jesus worked ad infinitum to create among his followers was almost a blasphemy to the Jewish spiritual leaders. What complicated matters was the oscillation between Jesus as Rabbi and his new and unique clout that necessitated additional titles. Hence the Prophet, as in the acclamation on Palm Sunday, was added to the Son of God and the Son of Man all of them objectionable to the rabbinical school of thought.

The New Testament does cite the miracles as substantiation of Jesus' standing as Rabbi-Prophet. That identification was a means to affirm his continuity with the prophets of Israel all the while asserting his superiority over them as the Prophet whose coming they had predicted and to whose authority they had been prepared to yield. God tells Moses and through him the people that he "will raise up for them a prophet like me from among you, to whom the people are to pay heed." The Jewish contention to this was Joshua being the legitimate successor of Moses. Joshua however lived while Moses was still there and could name him overtly for that eminence; Joshua who did not add one word to the Law was clearly chosen for administrative and military functions. Jesus was indeed the one portrayed as the Prophet in whom the teaching of Moses was fulfilled. He ratified the Law of Moses and transcended it; "the law was given through Moses; grace and truth came through Jesus Christ" (John 1:17.) To describe such a revelation of grace and truth the categories of Rabbi and Prophet were necessary though not sufficient.

-14-

Analysis of Belief

"Whether you think you can or whether you think you can't, you're right."

Old wisdom

Belief, also referred to as Faith is by far the most *powerful and creative* force in the human mind; the one that determines all dealings of this mind within its universe. Belief or non-belief in a thing whatever it might be is the basis of the Christian doctrine and the determining factor as to whether one is able or unable to accomplish this thing *regardless* of its size or related circumstances. Through the Power of Belief which causes ANY condition, event or circumstance to manifest, many miraculous occurrences that appear to be out of the realm of human possibility crop up regularly around the world and astound the masses, dependent solely on whether belief is *really* established or not.

In his stressing first and foremost on implanting belief Jesus resorted also to overstatements. Certainly being a disciple of Jesus requires unwavering faith and the apostles were discovering that. They have been overwhelmed by the assurance and authority with which Jesus spoke and acted especially by the way he addressed God as Father; an intimacy they had not met before. To instill unshakable faith in their subconscious minds and respond to their plea: "Lord, increase our faith!" Jesus countered their question indirectly with a noticeable mild reproach: "If you had faith the size of a mustard seed . . . you could say to this mulberry tree, 'be uprooted and planted in the sea,' and it would obey you." He resorted to the bizarre example of the mulberry tree with its extensive root system that would be difficult to uproot let alone plant in deep water, to impress disciples and people with the ensuing miraculous powers.

Jesus taught that absolutely anything conceived by the human mind can or will be brought into physical manifestation. His disciples understandably wanted to have the same conviction and intimacy; they wanted to see things the way Jesus did, acquire his mind and share his outlook. For them perhaps faith could be caught, not taught, and they must certainly have grasped it from his obvious assurance and conviction. But they realized their faith was still weak and fumbling. They had a long way to go before they could know the Father as he did with His will and purposes.

Later they have come to know that faith means that the center of their conviction has to shift, as is the case with Jesus, from their own selves i.e. their corporeal minds, to the Father that dwells in their very spirit: their subconscious. It is one thing to profess having faith and a different matter to *live by faith*. In the first instance we are deeply self-centered, torn between our negative self-related desires wanting it all our way to be served rather than to serve, and in the second, to serve our godly positive ones. Thus the realities of belief as defined by the Bible: "the assurance of things hoped for, the conviction of things not seen" are not discernible to us. "No one has ever seen God," John said, and no one will ever see Him. No one has also seen Jesus in our modern times yet we see and feel him by *faith* in his words: "I am with you always, even to the end of the world." (Mat. 28:20.)

Giving a pure, analytical look into the power of belief we find it the major driving force that can keep an original predominant thought (ideal) manifesting in physical form. Doubt is the exact opposite, a destructive force that directs our minds to perceive failure or the *lack of that physical manifestation process*. Belief is that remarkably powerful rudder of our human ship; it controls the direction and destiny of our lives. Jesus came to embed in all humans a different kind of belief: not that that *knows* and *accepts* our weaknesses but one that can overcome and develop them into strengths. He preached the unshakable faith that is capable when held fast in any human, to realize any physical objective as an irrevocable process of the *creation*; a process that cannot be overwritten.

This creation continues every minute of every day. There is *absolutely nothing* that can hamper its endurance. Exactly as the

175

grass continues to grow when we sleep so does the work of our subconscious mind with all that was indoctrinated through our steadfast belief. Our wants and desires can only be thwarted by a conflicting subconscious stirred by negative emotions that are not aligned with our well defined desires. These are the seeds of doubt that develop negative consequences usually referred to as *unanswered prayers*. The Scripture is full of warnings to those with shaky belief: "So do not throw away your confidence; *it will be* richly rewarded. You have need of patience, that after you have done the (positive) will of God you will receive what he has *promised*." (Heb. 10:35.)

Jesus abridged the process. "*Whatever* you ask through prayer you shall get." He did not draw a line between the possible and the impossible but ushered in the limitless divine power nesting within all humans: "I tell you the truth, if anyone says to this mountain, 'Go, throw yourself into the sea,' and *does not doubt in his heart but believes that what he says will happen,* it will be done for him." (Mar.11:23.) For man to reach this manifestation of the divine within him he has to reclaim his spiritual, positive powers that were lost or spilled through negative acts and thinking. Reclaiming such powers means connecting to the inherent cellular intelligence and activating the dormant powers of the subconscious mind.

Jesus warned us of the negative thinking sowing the seeds of doubt: "the thief (Satan, figuratively the negative prince) comes to steal and kills and destroys (all positive buildups), I have come that they might have life (positive beatitude), and have it to the full (entirely positive)" (John 10:10.) The antidote to this disastrous assault for all believers is "to open their eyes, to turn them from darkness to light and from the power of (negative)

Satan to (positive) God . . ." (Act.26:18.) In this respect, John further assesses Christ's mission: "The reason the Son of God appeared was to destroy the works of the devil."

Jesus recognized that there are people who needed to be monitored and indoctrinated when it comes to questions of faith. Such analytical minds as in the case of Thomas represent *the scientist type* among the disciples and portray many people of our time. When he had the opportunity to test whether in fact Jesus Christ was standing in front of him, Jesus said: "Be not unbelieving, but believer". Thomas was supposed to apply his new experience by pondering honestly and deeply. He was the human type that possesses a corporeal, inquisitive mind that constitutes an impenetrable shield to his subconscious. The root of his doubt disappeared and the truth dawned on him only when the Master managed to penetrate and usher that mind into believing. The fact that Jesus still had to say this afterwards did not mean that Thomas was a skeptic turned *slain* by the external reality and *forced to believe* through fear of punishment. It did however mean that Thomas had still kept his ability to reach new convictions autonomously. Thomas was wanted to learn that there are other ways of arriving at a conviction even without considering the physical facts. Jesus knew what was adequate for Thomas. He did not want to force anybody. There is obviously no intention to provoke anyone into refusing something he was not ready to decide about. To Jesus belief can only be a deliberate, self generated state of mind.

Don't believe it until you see it or *I'll believe it when I see it* . . . these negative, repetitive utterances can have a huge impact on the power of belief and are markedly un-Christian. Jesus said: "blessed are those who believed without seeing". He advocated without explaining (explanation would surely be misunderstood by his lacking audience) that belief instigates the manifestation of things and not the other way around, and that doubt can be especially damaging because the undeniable fact is that you will *never* see any significant events in life until you first believe it! Jesus fought doubt and disbelief imprinted in people's subconscious minds and helped these people come to a perception of how to overwrite such original programming.

His attachment to children stems undoubtedly from the fact that their subconscious is still unperturbed by negative coaching; he knew quite well what dramatic impact such wrong indoctrination has on their long term beliefs during those most impressionable first years. He cared to upkeep people's minds as clean and unsoiled; there lies the *perfect terrain for belief*: "should you not return to become like children, you will not enter the (positive) kingdom of heaven." And: "He took a child, and set him in the midst of them: and when he had taken him in his arms, he said unto them, whosoever will receive one of such children in my name, receives me: and whosoever shall receive me, receives not me, but Him that sent me." (Mar. 9:36.) What Jesus is picturing in this sequence is that the child-mind of God is the greater and is apparent in him as well as in an unspoiled child.

He knew and taught that children work very hard at trying to understand their environment. With their immature brains and limited experience they are great observers but horrible interpreters. As adult role models we have to be aware of what images and concepts we are conveying to the children around us. Mistaken ideas programmed in a child's subconscious become *his truths*. Jesus was adamant in addressing this disastrous, criminal programming: "But whoso shall offend (negatively indoctrinate) these little ones which *believe* in me, it were better for him that a millstone were hanged about his neck, and that he were drowned in the depth of the sea." (Mat. 18:6.)

Jesus was so harsh with the children's negative indoctrinators because he realized they are constantly observing, interpreting and storing information into their amenable subconscious. These billions of thoughts and experiences later become the truths which *run and direct* his or her life. The challenge is to help a child to interpret what he or she sees and hears in ways that can be used later as proof that he or she is capable, loveable and responsible. Today, scores of mistaken beliefs and misconceptions have been stored in the subconscious minds of youngsters who constantly make poor decisions and succumb to self destructive behaviors.

The child-mind of God, omnipresent in the human mind is what Jesus wants to explore, cultivate and safeguard. So great is the crime of evil programming that penetrates the innocent, unblemished young minds that is opposed with such greater punishment. "Woo to those who sow the seeds of doubt" as doubt is the most devastating blow to the mind. "Ask not of those who kill the body, ask for those who kill (the positive powers of) the mind". Shakespeare echoed this later in its simplest format: "Our doubts are our traitors."

Jesus professed throughout his teachings that as time passes and children begin to experience life their belief systems become limited based on what they are taught by those close ones, initially the family. Although this self limiting programming is instilled by those that most care, in the majority of cases it is done totally with the best intention in mind and only comes about from those elders who were wrongly taught and have come to understand to be the truth. Many parents innocently inject in their children seeds of doubts inherited in their own subconscious minds. Jesus was inflexible against this practice which may explain why he told his captured audience when his unbelieving family struggled to see him: "behold my mother and my brothers! For whosoever shall do the will of God (follow my positive guidelines), the same is my brother, my sister, and mother." (Mar. 3:35.)

Many Christian readers may jump on my *unbelieving family* statement especially those ardent Catholic devotees. The truth is Mary, though attached maternally and spiritually to Jesus acquired rudimentary basics of his philosophy as much as a good few of his disciples did. As to his *brothers and sisters*, (Cleophas' children) their belief in him was not much more than that of any fellow resident of Nazareth. Those brothers only *saw* some of his performed miracles but as to *how* those miracles were made was not within their grasp. Hence they incited him, especially after his rejection in his hometown to leave Galilee and *show himself to the world* that was Jerusalem where more educated brains could understand his enigmatic doctrine.

Jesus' sad story with Nazareth we detailed earlier was a vivid example of how faith that permeates the subconscious mind serves as a preamble to miracle works. He carried out a masterful introduction of himself when: "as his custom was, he went into the synagogue on the Sabbath day, and stood up for to read. And there was delivered unto him the book of the prophet Esaias and he announced to them that he was meant to be the Messiah they revoked and started thinking negatively. Reading their minds: "he said unto them, 'you will *surely* say unto me this proverb, physician, heal yourself: whatsoever we have heard done in Capernaum, do also here in your country. But I tell you the truth, many widows were in Israel in the days of Elias (that did not believe him) when the heaven was shut up three years and six months, when great famine was throughout all the land; but unto none of them (unbelievers) was Elias sent, save unto Sarepta, a city of Sidon, unto a (believing) woman that was a widow . . .' And all they in the synagogue when they heard these things were filled with wrath (Phoenicians were always hated by Jews for their wealth and entrepreneurship), and rose up and thrust him out of the city . . ." (Luk. 4:23.)

Jesus read Esaias' verses to explicitly tell his hardened audience that only the poor and the meek receive the Gospel and only the broken hearted receive the healing because their subconscious minds are ready and vibrant with belief and thus receptive. In Nazareth people who knew Jesus, his parents, brothers and sisters had no faith in this *son of the carpenter*. They *challenged* him with overflowing negative waves of doubt to perform the way he did in Capernaum. The Master who could only bestow bread to the *real* hungry could not perform; as a result the people of Nazareth rebuked him but Jesus said unto them, a prophet is not without honor save in his own country, and *in his own house*. And he did not many mighty works there *because of their unbelief.*" (Mat. 13:57.)

Applied psychology discovered today that the subconscious programming received as a child and its resulting thinking processes that became established habits after childhood greatly affect the power of belief. It constitutes a deterrent to the manifestation because of the negative tape loop that is consistently running in that mind. The people of Nazareth have grown up with the firm belief that nothing much could come out of the carpenter's family. This was sarcastically expressed by Nathaniel: "Can anything good come out of Nazareth?" Such underlying (subconscious) negative issues kept the desired things from showing up; they harnessed the true powers of belief. The subconscious has absorbed such issues/statements as *truths* and is only doing the job it was created to do and sending out mixed messages which keep belief shattered. The law of the mind is the law of belief itself; what we believe makes us who we are. Whatever we expect to be true will be so irrespective of whether the object of our belief exists in fact. In the West people have made *the palpable truth* their highest value; this motivation while important, is weak next to the actual power of belief in shaping the human lives. "If you can't believe, all things are possible to him that believes" (Mar. 9:23.)

Unless and until that previous programming is rewritten the results will not change. Based on those negatively established impulses for many years ago a human is literally emitting negative vibrations. Such perturbed mind cannot nurture any seeds of belief and may not achieve goals or be receptive to a healing process. Thus Jesus' first approach to miraculous healing was to cleanse the subconscious from all past tares commonly known as sins: "your sins are forgiven," preparing it to accept the dictates of belief and execute them.

Again, prayer and meditation are the two avenues to keep our subconscious meticulously positive. Jesus practiced meditation and performed prayers in his secluded mountain spots where he was cleansing his subconscious and recharging his human battery. Prayer has a major impediment today in too much intellect and too little devotion. A prayer without intensity and devotion loses the element of belief to take an honest inventory of life and be true to ourselves and others deep in our subconscious mind. In teaching how to pray and meditate Jesus invited us to pray for what we believe to be truly deep in our heart, exactly not what we unknowingly pray for. We don't even have to verbalize that: our subconscious mind sends the messages in accordance with the guidelines we had inplanted there or unwittingly consented to during unguarded moments; and little we know how many unguarded moments we find ourselves guilty of!

Yes. Jesus came 2 millenniums ago to show us how to exercise the power of belief and lead us many steps closer to experiencing the life we were created to enjoy. He is truthfully "the way, the truth and *life*." His message is to assist us in developing a deeper understanding of how to utilize the power of belief to turn our life into a credible and exciting journey filled with Love, Joy, Fulfillment, Inner Peace and Limitless Prosperity. He came to usher us into success and achievement and showed us the ways to ward off negative thoughts of defeat and failure. Christians today are ahead of many non-Christian nations because they use, probably without knowing it, a certain amount of that Christian seed embedded in their souls since childhood. Belief is the strangest secret in life that truly moves mountains and every human has ahead his size of mountains to move whether they are physical, emotional, or spiritual. The principle of decree works across the board if you learn how to tackle the principle. Reclaiming your Spiritual Power will show you how to use it and work it. Everything we say is literally an affirmation either positive or negative, *of what we are driven to.*

To "believe without seeing" is perhaps the most appropriate message in our times: our western culture simply dismisses the possibility of non-visible reality. It is more disregarded than argued against. If there is even a sense of a gap that needs to be filled it is assumed that our churches are not able to fill it by advocating the power of faith. This invisibility of the things of faith must always have been a difficulty that gets more acute in our *times of knowledge.* And let us agree: we cannot help but be affected by this cultural atmosphere; it may tend to unsteady our own faith and certainly make it harder to speak about it to unbelievers. Christ's words however keeps reverberating wherever we live; words that remind us always to spread his good news and believe in the manifestations of our goals much before *seeing* them.

He showed us enough evidence that we largely create our own environment. Our belief systems make a difference on how we relate to life and how we relate to our minds and bodies. We can create a healthy or unhealthy external environment in as much as we create a healthy or unhealthy internal one. It is our thoughts or ideas that create all that. The stories we tell about what happens to us in life are received and inscribed in the hard disc of the subconscious. Positive as well as negative programming has been accepted for one reason or another and it could be considered as *positive or negative hypnotic spells,* in the midst of which the subconscious is disoriented and the person himself is perplexed; as a result: "A double minded man, unstable in all his ways." (Jam.1:8.)

-15-

Philosophy of Death

"Unless a grain of wheat falls into the earth and dies, it remains alone; but if it dies, it bears much fruit"

Jesus Christ

Nature is cyclical, rhythmical and successive. It runs on opposing catalysts to produce viable substances and ensure continuity. Water, the life-given element exists thanks to the fusion of two volatile components, hydrogen and oxygen. The water-laden clouds deliver abundant rains thanks to the synthesis of positive and negative electrical currents that churns out thunder. Electricity can only light a bulb with the blend of positive and negative currents and a human couple can produce children through the interaction of positive love combined with "negative" sex. Yogurt has to *die* or decay into bacteria to reproduce fresh yogurt. Life does come from death for all about us in the physical world. Plant life dies to give seeds for new life. Salmon die after braving the adversity of swimming upstream to spawn their eggs for the production of new lives. They give those lives *knowingly* and willingly to produce fresh ones on this earth. Evidence is now coming to us that even in *outer space* there is the dying of old and the birth of new galaxies.

Many are the examples of this rhythmic regeneration. Life and death like positive and negative are two natural catalysts to warrant permanence. The philosophy of death is obvious and understandable throughout Jesus' ministry: altruism, self-sacrifice and entering *the narrow door* are all acts of bereavement or *transitory deaths* leading to the other opposites: contentment, bliss and bounty. Yet of all the examples and parables he gave to illustrate this philosophy chief among them was *the grain of wheat* worthy indeed of a detailed study.

"The hour has come for the Son of Man to be *glorified*. Truly, *truly*, I say to you, unless a grain of wheat falls into the earth and dies, it remains alone; but if it dies, it bears much fruit" (John 12:23.) Jesus uttered these words to the Greek community through the mediation of his two disciples/ interpreters Andrew and Philip. The message he wanted to convey is simple and direct: with my death comparable to the fall into the earth of a grain of wheat, the hour of my glorification will come. From my death on the cross great fruitfulness will stem. The *dead grain of wheat,* symbol of my crucifixion, will become in the Resurrection bread of life for the world: it will be light for peoples and cultures.

At our times we are not accustomed to finding glory in the death of our champions. Therefore we are enticed to find out how this can be. The people who knew and loved Jesus would see him die on a torture instrument that the Romans had invented to terrorize their enemies. There on the cross he was humiliated with his life taken and before it his dignity. Yet *the hour has come for the Son of Man to be glorified,* says Jesus. We can imagine the puzzled looks on the faces of Philip and Andrew and those innocent Greeks who had come to see Jesus do a miracle, to find instead a man talking in riddles about growing wheat. Certainly only few could figure out what he means and fewer still know about it today!

A grain of wheat has to die; it has to be buried in the good confines of God's earth. Short of that there will be no harvest. There will never be those amber waves of grain without that death and burial. It would be elementary but quite interesting to recall how wheat was sown in Palestine: a farmer first disseminates the seeds evenly on top of the loosened land and then with a pair of strong cows and a tiller he plows the sowed land in a parallel tillage along the field to bury the seeds, whereby the total d soil surface is turned upside down. Then he waits for rain, praying the Lord to do his work and ask nature to cooperate. Amazingly that is how many farmers in the Middle East do today. The single grain lies there in the bosom of the earth gathering moisture and nutrients to itself and after few days of rain it sends tiny root hairs down into the soil and shoots a stem or two upward toward the surface.

The dead seed does not only generate life (in Egypt, the bread is called "Aysh" or *life*); it generates so *much* of it. It is commonly know in agriculture that two bushels of sown seed yield up to eighty bushels or about 2,500 loaves of bread! Jesus said that this is the hour in which the Son of Man will be *glorified!* Still in the Middle East today a farmer is glorified and rejoiced when he watches the final harvest on his round, threshing floor. In fact the meager final harvest in grain is cause to his distress and frustration among his peers, indicative of his neglect and avoidance to deploy the required efforts—the narrow door—while sowing, tilling and picking the right soil.

To some, glory in the cross of Jesus Christ sounds almost grotesque: here is the friend of sinners crucified between his kinds of people in a macabre, God forsaken place. The glory may not be in this ordeal as there is no glory in the farmer's dreary toil; it is in the glorious Resurrection or the magnificent harvest that followed that ordeal. To some historians the Great Nazarene failed both in Galilee and Jerusalem to promulgate the Kingdom of Heaven but turned disaster into triumph through death and Resurrection. They fail to realize that Jesus throughout his three-year ministry was sowing the seeds of the Kingdom that culminated in the death of those seeds and their springing into multitudes of fruits.

To those historians Jesus remains a catalyst whose continuous presence precipitates a crisis of faith in their hearts and forces them to make a decision for or against. They fail to realize that because of God's mighty agriculture the death of Jesus will feed a multitude of nations with the bread of life. Jesus' body sown like a single grain had sent its roots down and its stalk up bursting from the ground to nourish the hungry souls. Thus he was the vivid example of burying his human seed and sprouting it again. He wanted us Christians to share his glory. He took care of the dying part insinuating to us "whosoever saves his life, let him first inter it," to show up for the resurrection and getting a renaissance imprinted in our subconscious minds; hence his asking us to go down into a *death* with all the humility and tribulation that will cause new life to spring up ten-fold while clinging to our *old* life. Jesus compares us to grains of wheat that sprout, develop strains in which the kernels cling to the head; kernels strong enough to withstand the blowing wind. He wants us to assume the miracle of multiplication in cultivating kernels that stick solid to the spike of its old life. We don't get or give life without some *dying*. Jesus himself did not get the glory of Resurrection without dying first.

Perhaps his suffering and humiliation on the cross was not the real tribulation; but the daunting prospect of suffering certainly was: "Now I am troubled. And what should I say: Father, save me from this hour? No, it is *for this reason* that I have come to this hour. Father, glorify your name." (John 12:27.) Still the coming pain is portrayed in the image of the falling grain of wheat, dying in the dark ground to bring up new life and free the world from darkness. Such is the spiritual ordeal that should first cleanse the subconscious of all past tares and prepare the spirit to accept the mind of Jesus, the mind of God. One first and palpable indication for this makeover is the emergence of love, "not in word or speech but in truth and action." (John 3:18.) And once love emerges, "we know that we have passed from *death* to life because we love one another." (John 3:14.)

189

The mind of God is positive and sinless, baby pure. When we call "our Father" we implore purity, love and the life-given power. God who resides in us is the source of life opposed by our everyday trespasses of the boundaries within which He wants us to live. Sin is negative; it bars the way to God and creates a wedge between us and Him. Our sins are the tares that blemish our subconscious and slowly but surely derail us from the life path to the death row. Jesus came to show us how to cleanse our troubled souls and revive our subconscious: "I am the way, and the truth, and the life. No one comes to the Father except through me" (John 14:6.)

Christianity taught by Jesus and the Jerusalem apostles was not centered on the resurrection of the body but primarily on the resurrection of the spirit—subconscious cleansing in our modern understanding—accomplished through the regeneration of our innate Holy Spirit. The early Christian writings emphasize *liberation* from the cycle of reincarnation through a *spiritual awakening* onto knowledge of these higher principles which the public in general during Jesus' ministry, including erudite Nicodemus never grasped. A spiritual awakening is necessary to be able to practice a life of liberation from the desires of the flesh and this alluring world. Reincarnation is the vehicle that allows people to have as many opportunities as necessary to become enlightened and attain liberation. Hell means having to reincarnate and be subjected to death repeatedly without having eternal life. These hidden mysteries of Jesus unraveled today were limited to him and remotely to Judeo-Christianity. They free at last the whole Christian philosophy from its old carapace.

The Easter story is much more than a message of hope for Christians. The disciples were so totally devastated by the brutal murder of their friend and leader. And irrational as it seemed, Mary Magdalene and her two companions went to the tomb early on Sunday morning just to see if by some chance it had all been a bad dream and Jesus was in fact still alive. Later on during the darkest days of the early Church persecution, life was made miserable by those who sought to destroy the burgeoning Christian movement. It is the nature of life however to accost death and to deliver a diehard performance to guarantee survival; a reflection of the reason why the human body is equipped with an immune system. It was therefore no surprise that under the continual threat of death Christians became very creative and found ways, including a behavioral joy in martyrdom, to carve reasons for hope.

The Christian philosophy is radically different from any other kind of belief. Total reliance on the deity preached in Judaism and Islam is the doctrine and procedure. Jesus advocated man's personal conviction in "the way and the truth" he promoted and left to people the choice of saving themselves. Salvation is thus a matter of self-realization in sharp contrast with all other religions. In the Christian faith the saving work of Jesus Christ forms the centre yet not everything is worked through him and depending on him: "*Your* faith has saved you". Jesus shows the way to God in a unique and uncommon approach different from any other faith; he *is* the way that bridges the deep and wide chasm between God and man caused by the latter's negative practices.

The Book of Revelation ascertains that "God's home is now *within* his people . . . and will wipe all tears from their eyes . . ." A true message of hope from *heaven* and a fine reward to the arduous soldiers of inner and outer fights that borders martyrdom; a sense of immortality that became associated with the central theme of early Christians that prevails to this day. It emanates from the central message that Jesus was tortured and crucified but he rose from the dead the third day and ascended into heaven forty days later. An example he set forth for all *sons of God* that can be repeated by any of them on a smaller scale in their earthly lives. Jesus ushered humans into a lesser and more manageable spiritual resurrection, one that impelled those early weak disciples to defy the mighty Roman Empire and establish Christianity, much feared and prosecuted by the Romans after the death of Jesus, as the official religion of that empire. The spiritual resurrection was so powerful and apparent in the lives of the early disciples that the world took notice of it and prepared itself to adopt it as a behavior and way of life.

This renaissance or rebirth or being *born again* is the *liberation* of the spirit from the flesh and the supremacy of the mind over the matter which is also the symbolism behind crucifixion. In such a state of perfected progression humans are liberated from the regular evolutionary cycle mankind has been undergoing much before Adam and Eve. Mankind has been evolving on biological and spiritual levels for millions of years through the succession of birth, death, and natural environments. We have been learning valuable lessons chief among them is the goal for every human to evolve toward perfection in the manner attained by Jesus. His ultimate aim was to see the world filled with perfected human specimens;

that is the time when humans will be able to live as long as they want and perform feats which today we would call *miraculous* like walking on water. Through the practice of unconditional love liberation is attained by *becoming one* with all beings and all people and above all, God.

The liberation Jesus campaigned for calls for evolving from the lower animal nature of the human individuality, that active human *beasts* have been struggling to shed for millions of years. The nature of this stagnant beast within humanity is manifested as selfishness, self-indulgence and self-gratification symbolically identified as *the false gods*, the *devils* and the *beasts*. By practicing unconditional love Jesus wants us to take up his Cross and follow him; in fact he wants us to *crucify* our self-centeredness through self-sacrifice and self-denial and help others follow our example. The Great Nazarene wanted humans to put to death their lower self and animalistic desires to allow their higher self or liberated spirit to come through.

-16-

The Prophet of Love and Joy

"These things I have spoken to you, that my joy may be in you, and that your joy may be full."

Jesus Christ

No less than four million books have been written on the subject of love. Why this tremendous preoccupation about this innate human feeling? Is it because Love is the one thing that the world could really use much more of? Or because it ranks first on top all positive endowments of mankind?

This warm, tender liking; this deep feeling of fondness and friendship; this intense affection and devotion is perhaps the strongest and most fulfilling emotion ever known to man. It is the single, most devastating *positive* approach that can produce magical results in different ways that are strange and wondrous.

It is the elixir that God intends to infuse into our souls and personalities. Even nonbelievers and agnostics can see the power of love and how it has the ability to change individuals and transform lives when it is properly embraced. Its quality is truly universal as it literally transcends peoples, nations and religions. Love is truly the common language of this world, and people from all different walks of life recognize it for what it truly is and understand the power that is in it.

This peak of all positive feelings can make us gentle, patient, caring, humble, appreciative, considerate, understanding, generous and kind. Love is what keeps us from being hateful, unkind, envious, boastful, proud, vain, and rude. It helps us to not insist on having our own way all the time and not be irritable, resentful or malicious.

This heavenly cure-all essence is as critical for our mind and body as oxygen. It's not replaceable and the more we grow immersed in it the healthier we will be both physically and emotionally. Love works its beneficence more directly on the lover than on the loved. It is probably the best antidepressant there is because one of the most common sources of depression is feeling unloved. Most depressed people don't love themselves and they do not feel loved by others. Their self-focusing makes them less attractive to others and deprives them of the ability to interact with them and the opportunities to learn the skills of love.

Jesus may not be the first human who discovered and propagated the power of love but he certainly is the prophet of *universal love*. That unique, unambiguous and boundless feeling that transcends man's closed circles of relatives and friends into the wider universal arena to include enemies and antagonists. It is far from the kind of *love* that our secular society seems to use to cover all sorts of fads where *I love you with all my heart* can be as casual as *I love chocolate ice cream!* It is rather the kind of love that helps us judge with our hearts and not with our minds without being prejudicial or judgmental. The same kind that God who dwells within us possesses and promulgates: it is also the same aspect of pure and authentic love children possess, enjoy and exhibit.

To Jesus believing in and knowing love is not enough. Love must be lived, practiced, experienced, and embodied. This is a very high standard for any human and this is why we are here in this World-School. We are growing to heaven right here on this earth not just to attain heaven but to bring heaven into this world. Unfortunately this may take many lifetimes of soul and bodily development to achieve immortality and, like Jesus did, walk on water, raise the dead and heal the sick. Fortunately however, humanity is evolving and getting closer to this goal.

In a time where the Pharisees of Israel preached scores of human regulations to follow in order to be *righteous*, Jesus had just two: "Love the Lord your God with all your heart and with all your soul and with your entire mind . . . and love your neighbor as yourself." Today we know where Jesus wanted humans to inject their utmost love: to God that dwells within them and motivates their positive moves in life. In loving this God humans can only follow the positive way and knock down all negative failings. Jesus spelled out his second commandment: "Love one another. As I have loved you, so you must love one another. By this all people will know that you are my disciples, if you love one another."

This is the universal love the Great Nazarene wants to disseminate and such is the trait with which he wants all Christians to be identified. With the prevalence of universal love people do not need long legalistic lists of *dos and don'ts* that are being preached and should be subscribed to or end up being condemned. The inner love to God, the Holy Spirit inhabiting us becomes the love of our own higher self; it will automatically eliminate the tares from the wheat of life and provide us a healthy sustenance. Those tares may be easy or tenacious to discard depending on the intensity of our love. We have all been born with these fallen, imperfect and sinful natures. Yet we have the capability to rebel against our negative predilections and become capable of walking in perfect love.

Love and Joy go together. Joy is the exhilaration of love and its natural symptom. Love enables you to literally see everyone as basically good and recognize that the inherent instinct for freedom lives within everyone. Love is contagious because everyone has an instinct for it imbued by God and any loving individual instinctively contains the joy of God that can bubble out of him at any moment. The Joy that helps us to discover this narrow gate that Jesus speaks of and cross with ease. The reason it is perceived by few is simply because of the common belief that the gate that leads to freedom is not here but somewhere else and you have to do something to find it. This is the ego trap causing you to seek something outside your own self that you simply will never find yet it lives in the last place you would think to look: your own heart, again identified by Jesus: "For where your treasure is, there will your heart be also." (Mat.6:21.)

The way is demanding because not anybody can deliver true love. It is a real hard currency especially in our times. Identifying the joy of Jesus is easy and requires no efforts but the way to acquire it is hard simply because it necessitates the deepest surrender which is from the perspective of the mind difficult if not impossible. Surrender is a letting go of everything for a moment to recognize the light of Truth within you at the core and contains the inherent power to reveal itself to you. Joy is a God-given gladness that is not at the mercy of circumstantial happiness. It is the uplift in one's spirit that can coexist with such adversities as pain and suffering as long as love is exerted. It rests on the abiding sense that we are accepted by the Father. Happiness may come and go but joy is not a temporary emotional episode; it is the offspring of divine love and its manifest gift.

There is nothing in life that love and joy cannot change. When we experience them our hearts feel much lighter with that unmistakable feeling of tenderness, warmth and *wholeness* that dissipates our loneliness. They together help us bear hardships without complaint and endure suffering with a smile. Love can change the darkness into day and make things so much brighter. It is a beautiful song that helps to soothe us when everything goes wrong. It makes everything seem so satisfying. It is a reason to want to keep growing and wanting to make ourselves become better. It gives us a goal to work for as it is the only thing that can bring us true joy and peace within ourselves: a reason for living and something to live for. Love is the source of life!

Joy cannot manifest itself without love. Hatred breeds sorrow, distress, grief and an array of distinct products of the somber, negative empire. True love and joy emanate from the child-pure hearts and if you look to see the source that is alive and find it within your own heart you will certainly be at peace with yourself first and with your peers as well. Jesus expresses this sacred phenomenon much better: "Blessed are the pure in heart for they shall see God." (Mat.5.8.) Joy is the nature of God and when you *see* God His joy will naturally arise within you. It is a joy without end. The more your heart opens to this infinite light the deeper you feel this arising joy that is sometimes indescribable . . . It is sheer magic!

The practice of unconditional love is Jesus' main teaching staple. This is the way for any human to attain not only liberation but also a manifestation of the spirit within us and in our lives bringing this spirit into subconscious awareness. This awakening carries out the manifestation of *our holy spirit* within us. And let us confess: it is not easy to be spiritual beings and live in today's material world, but if we live love, manifest love, and become the embodiment of love we find ourselves indulging in a real self-sacrifice and self-denial that would stand us prominent in any society. In this framework we discover all around us the lower nature in humanity; the non-evolved animal nature which humans have been slowly shedding for millions of years through progression and reincarnation. The nature of this beast, to say it once more, is manifested in a series of constant clamoring for ego, symbolically known under devilish names and labeled as "666" in John's Revelations.

"And when one of the scribes came up and heard them disputing with one another and seeing that he answered them well, he asked him, "Which commandment is the first of all?" Jesus answered, "The first is, 'Hear, O Israel: The Lord our God, the Lord is one; and you shall love the Lord your God with all your heart, and with all your soul, and with your entire mind, and with all your strength.' The second is this: You shall love your neighbor as yourself.' There is no other commandment greater than these." And the scribe said to him, "You are right, Teacher; you have truly said that he is one, and there is no other but he; and to love him with all the heart, and with all the understanding, and with all the strength, and to love one's neighbor as oneself, is much more than all whole burnt offerings and sacrifices." And when Jesus *saw* that he answered wisely, he said to him, "You are not *far* from the kingdom of God." And after that no one dared to ask him any question." (Mar.12:29.)

From this conversation with the scribe we can draw two conclusions: first, the scribe agreed with Jesus who *reformulated* the Law into an updated version whereby love is much more illuminated and second, Jesus sensed in the scribe's answer a more verbal than really meant concurrence and advised him he was not *far* from the Kingdom: a big gap of practical application he has yet to fill.

Jesus wanted to enable people to walk in perfect love in their words and actions with other people and learn how to walk in that same Godly love; thus allowing the Holy Spirit to enter their beings and carry out this sanctification process where the Father can then begin to function from the very cores of their personalities. Loving family and friends is easy and comes very natural for many because of the strong bonds already established with them. But learning to love some of your other neighbors whom you have no real special bond with or complete total strangers, let alone your enemies and opponents will be much harder to do, especially with the way our world has become with so many people keeping to themselves and being afraid to trust anyone anymore.

It is amazing how many people we find among us suffering of physical and psychosomatic ailments generated by negative predilections, all derivatives of hatred or at least lack of love. Fundamentally the Truth of Jesus reveals that it is not what happens in your life that causes you to suffer but rather what you think about and store in your subconscious of what happened in your life. Suffering is the root of bondage. Freedom lives beyond the mind's capacity to think. Negative thinking is of the worldly product and the source of all kinds of anguishes and tribulations. Freedom is not of this world and here we approach a bit of ambiguity that Jesus sheds his light upon: *"In the world you have tribulation; but be of good cheer, I have overcome the world."* (John 16:33.) You can become lost in the worldly pain and suffering if you do not look across the distance to see the divine light while still handling your daily humdrums.

Jesus overcame the world by revealing both the Truth of who he is and of who *you are* at the core. He further announces: "Now I am coming to You; and these things I speak in the world, that they may have my joy fulfilled in themselves."

(John 17:13.) He is the uncontested, unmoving light of God that creates endless joy in the yielding human hearts. This is the revelation of the heart of God clearly manifested in the joyful children. Within this child-pure association with Jesus we undergo transformation of our likes and dislikes, what we value and disvalue and even define the very entity that we are. Such change in what we will or want makes us recipient of the universal love that when we start experiencing it, we see our old sad idols fall away to be replaced by that exhilarating joy as *commanded* by Jesus. We are commanded to love as he loves *in order that* our joy may be complete. We have to receive and treasure his love with thanksgiving and love as he loves. This is the way to a devastating joy, the joy of the lord that endures in all circumstances and goes beyond any superficial feeling as depicted by Nehemiah: "the joy of the Lord is your *strength*" (Neh. 8:10.)

The child-pure heart of God did not actually ask us to express our love for Him by worshipping or praying or by acts of fasting and self-sacrifice or by following every rule set forth in His commandments. No! The best way to express our love is by loving other people. This is what Jesus meant when he said, "I desire mercy, and not sacrifice." (Mat. 9:13, 12:7.) He said that God accepts our love for others as if it were love for Him. This is shown in the parable of the sheep and the goats, where he said, "As you did it to one of the least of these my brethren, you did it to me."

Humans in Christ's visualization are all part of one giant Whole. Their individual illusion of separation is the source of many of the problems humanity has faced. He regards us as spiritual beings having a highly evolved human experience and everything on the physical and soul level is slowly progressing toward perfect unity with the Whole. There is no judgment except self-judgment and we should not even do that. The more we fill our void with love for others the more we evolve in the cleansing process of our subconscious. God's love is not a tough love but direct and unbiased wanting anyone to attain a spiritual level that can guide our physical body, the vehicle for our soul, to assume the required driving power as directed by our resuscitated subconscious.

How far many of our Church principals are from the genuine philosophy of Christ! They enjoy being called *Eminence*, *Reverend, Doctors* . . . They relish the sense of honor bestowed by their followers. These are the modern-day status-seeking and ego-centric Pharisees Jesus counseled to become servants, workers and custodians. The true followers of Jesus have a sense of joy and satisfaction in whoever they are and at whatever *level* on the social or ecclesiastical ladder they may find themselves. He also had withering words on the wealthy that oppressed, or simply ignored the poor: "Blessed are you who are poor, for yours is the kingdom of God, but woe to you who are rich, for you have already received your comfort." (Luk.6:20.) Today, take a deep look at any rich man and try to count his many anxieties and preoccupations; you will stop short before you realize why this man is devoid of any real joy: because "his heart settles where his treasure is!"

-17-

The Elevated Man

"But I, when I am lifted up . . . will draw all."
Jesus Christ

Among the three monotheist religions Jesus elevated man from a *slave of God* stature to the *son of God* distinction. The Mosaic Law out of humble and deep submission to the Almighty enslaved man to his creator and established the *slave-master* modus as the only permissible interaction. Islam later echoed the Hebraic belief and even went steps ahead in confirming man's servility to the overall mighty divinity. This servility, meant to imply humbleness among adherents of both religions became false-modesty in real life applications.

Jesus humanized God and raised man to a higher pedestal: "I do not call you servants [or slaves] any longer," he said to his chosen community. In an era where slavery can have many bad names that was indeed welcome news. The larger problem of slaves is that they are *en-slaved* to a blind obedience. They are not given the whole scope of things. They do not make decisions. They merely follow along in a kind of legal obedience to their master. Jesus reversed this cycle and taught that neither he nor the Father is that kind of master. In that new process where the one getting served was not served for the sake of the slaves' own skin a community of love manifested itself: the absolute obedience was transformed into one of a deliberate, joyful covenant.

It is a great tragedy that many non-Christians see the slavery of man before the Almighty as due and appropriate; any alteration to the formula is a clear trespassing by the *created to his Creator*. Many see Christ standing as an angry, exacting judge and condemner of sinners. The exact opposite is true and the words "God sent His Son into the world, not to condemn the world, but that the world might be saved through him," are very much inherent to Jesus' chronicles. He associated himself with sinners despite the reproach of the *good people* of the time just to emphasize his elevating of man to his higher rank out of his sinful slavery. Among his most moving words is the parable of the prodigal son which portrays God as a loving father welcoming home the wayward son who squandered his share of the family fortune. "The slaves," says Jesus, "do not know what the master is doing." That is the deeper malady. He wanted man to be his partner in promoting the Truth and go about it with all the love and exhilaration of that relationship.

Jesus meant this partnership to become a fountain of life watering the soil for an ever-greater human harvest that makes man a joint heir of God. It lights his way and lightens his burden enabling him to live in the consciousness that the Father works within him: "my Father works and I work."

When man realizes this he finds out he is not alone; and the more fully he realizes this the more fully he finds himself conscious of an enlarging reception of life, light, energy and power. Man is born in a consciousness surrounded by countless limitations. This knowledge of a higher consciousness, the consciousness of the spirit of God within him, dissipates slowly but surely such limitations. It is the feeling of being born anew from above; this new birth opens up and makes active in anybody's life possibilities and powers that otherwise lie dormant and dead. It is the nature of the Father to give good gifts unto His children; and those who have faith will attain full realization in life and thereafter.

Jesus raised man to such partnership for yet another, heretofore totally concealed reason: the heavenly Father dwelling in us does not sin. God designs and trails the positive path and wants humans to follow the same trail. A raised man to the deity's order is automatically reminded through the resonance of his subconscious to follow the same positive highway, heave himself from the negative aspects of human feebleness and chart a lifeline prescribed by the sublime impulses of his educated subconscious. This is the leap from slavery to partnership that entails higher responsibilities, renewed dynamism and vigilant alertness. Perhaps for that reason Jesus almost in all his speeches called for such watchfulness to become aware and live up to the commands of the new conscientiousness. Commands that are far from the abiding relationship: a free will bind that has the blessing of the individual self prior to the heavenly one.

The gap was wide between the Jewish Law and Jesus' teachings; it is the fullness of the truth about man and his place in the creation. It is also a morality designed to let people enjoy life and not a constraint of arbitrary laws to show a stringent path to follow. Jesus wanted man to accept the truth about him and reveal his own identity to become truthfully free. Hence: "You will know the truth, and the truth will make you free." Abraham was called *the friend of God*; a well earned tribute to the man who went closer to the Divine than any other human although this expression is not found in the Old Testament. Similarly at the Last Supper Jesus elevated his eleven disciples from *servants* to *friends*. (John 15:13.)

He equally liberated and elevated the woman. Women of Israel were legally defined as personal property totally subjected to the will of their men; Jesus came viewing women as persons of value in their own right. Women are prominent in all four Gospels. From the announcement of Jesus' coming birth to the time of the empty tomb women play roles that no male can assume. Women have been strong links in the chain of Christian witnesses. Without them where might the church be today? Again, many westerners accuse Jesus of looking down at women taking his addressing his own mother with the bare and seemingly degrading name: *Woman*, ignoring that in the Middle East then and now this approach denotes a superior and highly endowed female similar to describing a distinguished male with the all-encompassing appellation: Man.

Before him, Buddha preached that women are jealous, treacherous and vicious creatures. Hindu wives are commended to offer incense to their husbands' big toes and the Judaic Law considered women as minor, irresponsible persons and *in all things inferior to man*. Although Islam came much after Christianity and adopted many of Christ's teachings, it safeguarded both the Judaic and Jahilyah (pre-Islamic era) perspectives towards women. Muhammad addressed one day his twelve wives, the crème of Arab women as "*devoid of reason and creed*." As to Ali the dean of the Shiia he denounced the woman as "*all evil, and the spiteful thing about her is that she is indispensible.*" From such things came Islam's legitimization of polygamy, divorce at will by the husband and slavery.

His special compassion was bestowed on the poor and the oppressed. He did not hold that current suffering is the result of evil deeds or poor performance in earlier life but rather a part of our human experience. Suffering has a number of benefits: it chastens us towards a more holy status; it fits us for the ministry of sympathy; it turns our attention toward positive ideals. But Jesus in healing the sick, restoring the ear of the high priest's servant and in teaching us to show tender mercy and compassion toward those who suffer, teaches us by precept and example to do all we can to help alleviate suffering. He put before the hands of every man the right tools conducive to the path of salvation and left him the choice to determine his fate. He relentlessly showed the key to renewal and growth of every man's positivism that would further lift him above: "But I, when I am lifted up . . . will draw all."

The deeper we search we find that burning purpose of Jesus to make lighter the burdens of common men and women:

"Come unto me, all you that labor and are heavy laden, and I will give you rest. Take my yoke upon you and *learn of me*; for I am meek and lowly of heart; and you shall find rest unto your souls. For my yoke is easy, and my burden is light." (Mat. 11:28.) An open message to all people who had their doubts to face, their problems to meet, their battles to fight and their fears to conquer. This he did in a simple language by showing them primarily that there was nothing to be afraid of; nothing except *their negative doubts and fears* yet in a way far different from the cry of common men today.

He proclaimed this on that opening day of his ministry through the gift of his revealed truth that he longed to reveal to others; the truth that, if they would but *believe* him, would become the veritable gift of God to them. With this high purpose and inflexible faith he taught: "the time is fulfilled, and the Kingdom of God is at hand: repent, and believe the gospel." Repent (cleanse your subconscious minds,) and believe the good news.

The good news is the knowledge of God whom humans have been worshipping as a far off deity and who in reality is within them. He is the life within and the Infinite Spirit of life and power that is behind all, working in and through all: the life of all the life within every human.

Above all Jesus was eager, almost obsessive in lifting the sinners after liberating their subconscious to the chosen ranks. His mingling with drunkards and cheating tax collectors has been a target for his critics. "The healthy would not need a doctor—only the sick do," he would respond. A case in point is Zaccha the tax collector from Jericho. Jesus visited this city expressly to meet and convert this man well regarded but criticized for his excessive cheating. A crowd followed the itinerant preacher heading to see Zaccha for a well known purpose . . . being a short man Zaccha climbed a tree in order to see the Teacher. Jesus approached Zaccha and *fixed his eyes upon him* and the eyes of each person in the crowd looked up too. Jesus smiled and said: "Zaccha, come down right away. I just have to stay at your house today." The man's stomach knotted up with him: how did he know my name and why he wanted to enter my house? Didn't he know? Jesus did very well know and he could hear the crowd mumbling, "He is going to the house of a sinner . . ." Zaccha stood up and said, "Lord, here and now I give half of my possessions to the poor . . . and if I've cheated anybody out of anything, I will pay back four times the amount." "He means it!" muttered one man who was close enough to see it all. "He'll do it!" Few people were able to hear Jesus' words as he hugged the little man: "Today *salvation* has come to this house," he said joyfully, "because this man, too, is a son of Abraham." Jesus looked around to the bewildered crowd and spoke with such conviction and force that it seemed as if he were trying to distill his entire purpose in a single sentence: "The Son of Man came to seek and to save what was lost." "I swear," said one of the disciples watching Zaccha half-walk, half-dance beside Jesus as they made their way to the tax collector's home. "I swear he doesn't look so little, so wizened up after all." He scratched his beard. "He looks to me taller somehow!"

The process of elevating man is a regenerated meaning to humanism in Christianity they don't teach in the church and its related institutions. It relates directly to the power of man. Jesus invoked that power when man was elevated; a power to confront suffering and misery and achieve joy and exhilaration where through that confrontation man can raise himself. Centuries after Adam whose body *was made of dust* and lost its divine interaction as the Torah reports Jesus came to inject spirituality in that body to recreate the *spiritual body.* Paul explains such process in his own way to the Corinthians: "There is a natural body, and there is a spiritual body. And so it is written, 'The first man Adam became a living being.' The last Adam (Jesus) became a life-giving spirit. However, the spiritual is not first, but the natural, and afterward the spiritual. The first man was of the earth, made of dust; the second Man is the Lord from heaven. As was the man of dust, so also are those who are made of dust; and as is the heavenly Man, so also are those who are heavenly. And as we have borne the image of the man of dust, *we shall also bear the image of the heavenly Man."* (1Cor.15:44.)

Jesus went a long way in elevating man thereby expanding the possibilities of our knowing him and in him God the Father. In truth, *it seems that he has gone so far he could not go further.* He even became "a stumbling block to Jews and foolishness to Gentiles," (1Cor. 1:23) precisely because he called God his and our Father and revealed Him so openly in himself to an extent he could only elicit the impression that it was too much. Stereotype protesters who lived the long servility postulates with God were no longer able to tolerate such closeness and thus the remonstrations began. Such dissenters could not comprehend that man who is the only creature on earth which

God willed for Him cannot fully find his own self except through a sincere, divine gift.

Jesus disseminated this divine gift to his disciples. They became staunch seekers and revealers of the truth, free and independent in their thought. No one of them was the representative of any institution or dogma, a chief reason why they all stood so high in estimation and thinking and their thoughts became of real value in the process of enlightenment. Seeking the truth with unbiased minds, they found it in simple clear-cut form and expressed it in similar form. Their reception and understanding of truth were on the one hand similar to those of Jesus; on the other hand their finding and understanding of Jesus were no part of any perplexing or mystifying system that he himself would so thoroughly condemn, even as he condemned the self-seeking purveyors of system woven around and strangling the truth of the prophets before him.

It is an eternal mystery, an unfathomable paradox that man can only truly live for others, mesh and interact with them in the loving relationship Jesus craved hard to promote: "My *prayer is not for them alone. I pray also for those who will believe in me through their message, that all of them may be one, Father, just as you are in me and I am in you. May they also be in us so that the world may believe that you have sent me. I have given them the glory that you gave me, that they may be one as we are one: I in them and you in me. May they be brought to complete unity to let the world know that you sent me and have loved them even as you have loved me"* (John 17:20.)

If we give these words the right interpretation we will but understand that his way is indeed a superb way. In elevating man he made him understand that God to him and to his peers was the Father whose essence is love; the Father that cares for him and us, that revealed Himself to him as well as to us. Jesus insists on the man to develop the same attitude of desire and trust and live in this filial relationship with the Father. And in as much as God rules in the world through established laws thus should He live and rule in the life of man through the channels of man's mind. Here is also an established law.

Perhaps the world is yet to know the genuine Jesus because the universal church is yet far from "complete unity" and a hostile world filled with doctrinal differences still hovers around; hence Paul urged Christians to *make every effort to keep the unity of the Spirit through the bond of peace. There is one body [in Christ] and one Spirit, just as you were called to one hope when you were called one Lord, one faith, one baptism; one God and Father of all."* (Eph. 4:3.)

Emerson epitomizes this theory in regard to the Master in modern, brief and clear-cut form: "Alone in all history he estimated the greatness of man. One man was true to what is in me and you. He saw that God *incarnates Himself in man* who ever more goes forth anew to take possession of the world." The divide in the depth of our souls has been bridged over by Jesus. That inner estrangement so often felt should disappear within those who believe and the whole universe should be part of regenerate man's experience. When that depressing feeling of isolation fades away we become conscious of partaking in that *inner life* common to all of us. One cannot conceive the development of a powerful personality, a deep-rooted and profound mind or a character raising above this world without his having experienced this divine life. That is indeed the main character of Christianity.

Christianity is not merely a belief in some supreme Power nor the establishment of relations of any kind between this supreme Power and man. It is an inner identification with it and the creation of a new life through it. The union of the Divine and human nature is the fundamental truth of this religion and its deepest mystery consists in the fact that the Divine enters into the compass of the human without impairing His Divinity. With this new phase that Jesus promulgated life is completely renewed and elevated. Man becomes immediately conscious of the infinite and eternal that dwells within him which transcends the world. For the first time the love of God becomes the ruling motive of man's life that brings him into an inner relation with the whole scope of reality. It is here that we find a new self: our true spiritual self.

Jesus is a challenger that wants men to follow his steps. He challenged the Law which the Jews considered the ultimate authority, declared that he was above the Law and made statements that caused people to accuse him of blasphemy by equating himself with God. He challenged his own disciples and rebuked them for having too narrow a conception of him and his mission. He braved his mother, *brothers and sisters* when they came to restrain and confine him to their mental image. Jesus opposed the carnal mind imagery that shed *restrictions* for what a human can do. He defied those mental restrictions by walking on water, raising the dead, healing the sick, multiplying the loaves and fishes and performing miraculous acts. All that was done to break the mental barriers and invoke the boundless mind of Christ based on the higher spiritual laws to perform actions that are considered impossible at the human level.

That was also to advocate that God created us as his children and we are meant to be co-creators with God. Jesus told men they were given free will but most of them have used it to descend into the negative abyss by setting aside their positive spiritual powers. Jesus called us to get hold of his mind by "following him and fulfill his testaments" in order to conquer all of the mental limitations that have been programmed into our subconscious and maintain that mind in flawless and transparent format. In this context, we may develop a faith based on the *all you need is love* standpoint away from any historical paradox found in our ongoing Christianity.

-18-

The Kingdom of Heaven

"My kingdom is not of this world: if my kingdom were of this world, then would my servants fight, that I should not be delivered to the Jews."

Jesus answering Pilate

The main theme of Jesus' parables was "the kingdom of God". In fact it is the most prominent subject in Jesus' itinerant ministry. The Kingdom of God and the Kingdom of Heaven are the same. Matthew however who addressed his gospel mainly to the Jews used *the Kingdom of Heaven* because Jews were reluctant out of extreme reverence to use the name of God, and secondly because of the Jewish misconception of the coming Kingdom that many among them anticipated to be a physical one. Matthew used *heaven* to expressly emphasize the spiritual one in line with Jesus' saying "my Kingdom is not from this world".

The term *Kingdom* was used to stress the abstract idea of *reign* or *dominion* not related to a geographical area surrounded by physical boundaries. This is exactly what Jesus promoted: the REIGN or DOMINION of God who is *in heaven* that has always existed as foretold in the time of Daniel (Dan. 2:44) and proclaimed by John the Baptist (Mt. 3:1,) that would manifest itself in spiritual ways within a community of souls where God is recognized as the Sovereign who rules over the hearts.

Throughout his parables Jesus referred always to the Kingdom of Heaven sometimes in its *present* aspects and mostly in its *future* ones. The mysteries of this Kingdom or the way to approach them have never been defined except through parables. One such mystery, the principle of entering the Kingdom, was the need to be born again as revealed to Nicodemus; a new birth of water and spirit (John 3:3,) our modern day subconscious cleansing that prepares men to enter "the tabernacle of God and He will dwell with them, and they shall be His people, and He Himself will be with them and be their God." (Re. 21:3.)

With the belief factor set aside for the sake of the deductive minds historians and theorists proclaim that the Kingdom of God, somewhat incomprehensible but frequently on Jesus' lips, did not occur in the Old Testament as *the Lord's Kingdom* repeatedly did, alluding to an assortment of dynamic kingly rules and sovereign actions of God. This is true when the Old Scripture says: "God is your King, the king of Israel at all times," and when Isaiah relegates this happening where God will show his human hand to the indefinite future; an event Jews still declare daily in their prayers. Daniel, the Psalms of David and earlier the Assumptions of Moses depicted the manifestations of this secret Godly purpose:

> *"Then His Kingdom shall appear through His Creation . . .*
> *For the Heavenly One will arise from His royal throne . . .*
> *And you, Israel, shall be happy . . .*
> *And God will exalt you . . ."*

Such were the hopes of the Jewish Ebionite community which maintained a semi-monastic existence at Qumran and threw considerable light on the background of Jesus' life before he assumed his ministry. Those devotees expected the Kingdom even during their lifetimes. They represented Jews living a miserable life in this world and growing impatient. They had hopes in Daniel's prophecy: "may He establish His Kingdom during your life and your days." Their apocalyptic stance about the end of the world made this occurrence all the more urgent.

Historians overlooked for lack of proper incursion into the Qumran society that John and Jesus would soon emerge to proclaim the Kingdom exactly as depicted in the Torah. John placed it in the center of his mission and assumed the role of the fearless and resolute precursor of the Master. Jesus proclaimed it exactly as John did: "Your Kingdom come, your will be done on earth as it is in heaven" that became the Lord's Prayer. He declined later when asked to specify the date of this coming but explicitly declared that the Kingdom of Heaven has "come near" and whoever wanted to enter it must make every possible preparation for its arrival with full awareness and underpinning: "what I say to you I say to everyone: keep awake."

The reason behind this *watchfulness* Jesus stipulated repeatedly in his parables for a Kingdom of God that became a reality as soon as he announced it is twofold: the need of a human's subconscious mind to be cleansed—spiritual resurrection, and clean of all negative tares comparable to a pure-child's mind and, to *keep it that way* all along in continued expectation. From the first stages of *awakening* and throughout that time of expectation a human is living his fullest life within the positive Realm of God. This contention has caused distress to many theologians. The Anglican J. Duncan wrote as early as in 1870: "Christ either deceived mankind by conscious fraud, or was himself deluded, or he was divine. There is no way out of this trireme." Today we tell him without any self reservation or mental evasion that Jesus did not deceive mankind nor was he deluded, he simply could not explain for lack of understanding among his audience of commoners the working of the human subconscious mind the way he insinuated and as we understand it today; which escaped also Duncan's as well as many other clerics' knowledge. But certainly, he was divine!

This preparedness is further illustrated in the ten virgins' parable: "Then shall the Kingdom of Heavens be likened unto ten virgins who took their lamps, and went forth to meet the bridegroom. And five of them were wise and five were foolish.

They that were foolish took their lamps and took no oil with them. But the wise took oil in their vessels for their lamps. While the bridegroom tarried, they all slumbered and slept. And at midnight there was a cry made, behold, the bridegroom comes; go you out to meet him. Then all those virgins arose, and trimmed their lamps. And the foolish said unto the wise, give us of your oil; for our lamps are gone out. But the wise answered saying, not so; lest there be not enough for us and you; but go rather to them that sell, and buy for yourselves. And while they went to buy, the bridegroom came; and they that were ready went in with him to the marriage: and the door was shut. Afterward came also the other virgins saying, lord, lord, open to us. But he answered and said; verily I say unto you, I know you not." (Mat. 25:1.)

Here is a lesson for our times where wisdom lies in *knowing what to do with knowledge*. We have gained much knowledge of how the subconscious mind works and learned how to plan much ahead to embark in the cleansing process without having any unexpected surprises. Planning ahead is an important part of our continued watchfulness. We need extra oil to maintain our mental lamp enlightened. Our wisdom should be always ahead of our understanding. At our younger times *foolishness* was part of our milk food with which wisdom was not needed to distinguish the good from the bad. When we mature into wisdom and knowledge we begin to feel the need to advance wisdom ahead of understanding: a major prerequisite to enter the Kingdom.

The lesson is that we *can* reprogram the subconscious to transform our body and renew our mind but we must *first* erase all that has been previously recorded there much erasing a CD and re-record it. Jesus said he would send *reapers* at the time of the harvest, our maturity time, to remove the tares of foolishness. Here is the way to be led by the spirit and put on the *mind of Christ*. These things witness deep within our spirit and are no profanation. This is how Jesus wanted really to open the doors to our minds and follow the path of cleaning and regenerating our subconscious.

Jesus did not preach much about himself nor about God but about the Kingdom of God. This teaching is the overall determinant factor of all his discourse. His ethics, theology and discourses regarding himself though cannot be set apart from his interpretation of the Kingdom of God. He labeled the Christian Gospel as the Gospel about the Kingdom of God that was "proclaimed since the time of John the Baptist." (Mat. 3:2,) describing the place of God that settles within every man upon this earth.

The frequent interchangeability between the Kingdom of God and that of Heaven is to refer to the Millennial Kingdom which has been ordained from *heaven*, i.e. from God. Thus, "the Kingdom of Heaven" and *heaven* are not the same. The Kingdom of Heaven is a kingdom *from* heaven not *in* heaven. In line with the repetitive scriptural reference to heaven as the locus of God's authority and the point from which He rules the universe Jesus went along this sublimation although he pointed out many times where God resides and where His siege is: the mind and spirit of people. Heaven therefore refers to the origin of this kingdom and the figurative place from which the Kingdom is coming to bestow on it the heavenly character, not a destination to which we are going. And since the term *Kingdom of God* occurs more frequently in the Bible it remains the preferred, constant slogan when describing the future kingdom in which the sons of men will settle under God, and the phrase that illustrates the genius where the whole Christian faith is concentrated.

In elevating humans to his proportions Jesus wanted to unleash the spiritual power within all and have life respond to us as we respond to it. This is the Law of Attraction he showed to us where a fulfilled life is limited only by our own minds and a future that can really be self-determined. Jesus aimed at synchronizing the human mind with the mind of God through a directive action of the cleansed subconscious. Rather than pleading with the Father he wanted men to turn their positive thoughts in a continuous flow and let "Father" do it without any fear of negativity. Such is the child mind with total receptivity, gratuitous belief and whole-hearted devotion that are keys of admission to the Kingdom. Peter declared on his behalf and the rest of the disciples: 'We have left *everything* to become your followers;' by so doing they had become *pure in heart* and free from the tyranny of the divided self; the major traits for acceptance in the Kingdom of God.

The elemental deep-seated love Jesus called for that has also the child-like purity transcending all aspects of conventional love into loving enemies and turning the other cheek, was far too much to accept by his audience then as well as now. It remains today, a hypothetical practice opposing the human nature and could not be fulfilled. Yet this call is deeply rooted in the Bible when God has said to Moses: 'you shall be holy, because I, the Lord your God, am holy.' In this same spirit Jesus declared: 'There must be no limit to your goodness, as your heavenly Father's goodness knows any bounds.' It is the total positivism for the elevated humans seeking admission to the incipient Kingdom.

'Whoever does not accept the Kingdom of God like a child will never enter it,' another call from Jesus to go back to purity and be able, like children, to *embrace cosmic light and assimilate it into cumulative power*. These are the positive, esoteric metaphysical laws of attraction, expansion and cohesion that contradict the negative ones of repulsion. We attract what we send out; Peter and the disciples received Jesus' doctrine and *left everything* behind them to fully embrace, live and become that doctrine. Ignoring or forgetting it would attract every old vibration associated with it . . . where the tares would mingle again with the wheat . . .

A negative application of the embraced doctrine triggers a sense of guilt that attracts all dormant guilt feelings. Remember the parable of the man whose "unclean spirit" was cast out. He was so lonely and forlorn he contracted seven other spirits more wicked than the first. Guilt is a negative subconscious demand for approval and a pure self-indulgence (it happens in our times to those who relinquish narcotics and undergo rehab.) In the process doubts emerge whether God can really use us for perfection while the road to perfection is simply our choice, not to say our destiny, if we adopt the path of love and forgiveness and adopt the eternal law that we give to receive.

Humans instinctively strive for happiness but rarely find it in their hot pursuit of material things. Material objectives when attained may please mankind temporarily, only to become boring in a short while. The most striking example of unquenchable thirst for happiness was King Solomon. He was so rich (for his time) that all the household utensils in his palaces were made of pure gold! He was so wise that kings, including queen Sheba came from "faraway" lands to hear him. He could easily satisfy any of his whims and it seemed that there was no pleasure that he did not possess or could not obtain. Yet Solomon described his many years of searching for happiness as continual disappointments in his book of Ecclesiastes which he began with the following desolate phrase: *Vanity of vanities, all is vanity.* (Ecc. 1:2.)

Jesus ushered in the Kingdom of God in order to restore in us our lost capacity to spend blissful eternity in communion with God. He revealed to people that only return to simplicity would lead to true happiness. "Look at the lilies of the valley" he told his disciples, "even Solomon in his full glory was not as adorned as any one of them . . ." The road of simplicity is conducive to the Kingdom of Heaven and Jesus was the first who traveled it and showed us how to follow his path: "Whoever desires to come after me, *let him deny himself,* and take up his cross, and follow me (Mar. 8:34.) This *denial* of one's self, its tares, greed and all related negative predilections is clearly the prerequisite for the Kingdom. It was lived and assumed to perfection by Jesus who, when referred to Solomon's grandeur introduced himself to his audience as "One who is greater than Solomon!"

While he did not alienate himself from the Law he insisted on refining it. The Law did not border the 'cause of the cause' that is contributing to the sin but forewarned of the sins themselves. The Law commanded: "You shall not kill" or "you shall not commit adultery", Jesus went down to the causes of such sins: "You have heard that it was said by them of old time, you shall not kill and whosoever shall kill shall be in danger of the judgment. But I say unto you, that whosoever is angry with his brother without a cause shall be in danger of the judgment: and whosoever shall say to his brother, Raca (you ignorant), shall be in danger of the council: but whosoever shall say, you fool, shall be in danger of hell fire" and: "You have heard that it was said by them of old time, you shall not commit adultery: but I say unto you, that whosoever looks on a woman to lust after her has committed adultery with her already in his heart." (Mat. 5:21.)

Cleansing the subconscious of all vicissitudes was, as is always, the shield to succumb to greater crimes. Jesus truly came to fulfill the Law not to destroy it. The translation to fulfillment would have better been *refining* or *updating*. In many instances Jesus *redefined* the Law and fine-tuned it to befit the prerequisites. Killing, adultery and many similar sins tipped off by the Law would vanish from the Kingdom when their initial causes are eliminated, i.e. erased from the human subconscious mind.

In saying: "Anyone who breaks one of the least of these commandments and teaches others to do the same will be called least in the Kingdom of Heaven, but whoever practices and teaches these commands will be called great in the Kingdom of Heaven," Jesus ascertains total adherence to the Law. But when he adds: "For I say unto you, that except your righteousness shall *exceed* the righteousness of the scribes and the Pharisees, you shall in no case enter the Kingdom of Heaven" (Mat. 5:20,) another translation will be order: *'if you don't eliminate the real causes of the sins you are at a loss';* which is illustrated in the gush of explanatory verses following that statement.

Jesus' disciples carried out this philosophy when they started their own ministries. Paul time and again clearly distinguished between *the carnal mind* (conscience) and *the spiritual mind* (subconscious) when he addressed the Romans: "For to be carnally minded is death; but to be spiritually minded is life and peace. Because the Carnal mind (not the child-pure mind of God) is enmity against God: for it is *not subject to the law of God*, neither indeed can be." (Rom. 8:6.)

The Kingdom of Heaven *has already come and was delivered* to mankind throughout Jesus' ministry. It incarnates the Spiritual Deliverance or the Spiritual Truth unveiled and disseminated to whoever can grasp and adopt: "And when he was demanded of the Pharisees, when the kingdom of God should come, he answered them and said, the kingdom of God comes not with observation: neither shall they say, Lo here! Or lo there! For behold, *the kingdom of God is within you.*" (Luk. 17:20.) It is spiritual not carnal, mystical not worldly and divine not material. It is rather what he described to Pilate: "My kingdom is not of this world: if my kingdom were of this world, then would my servants fight, that I should not be delivered to the Jews: but now is my kingdom not from hence." (John 18:36.)

In releasing this Kingdom Jesus first and foremost wanted to unravel this part of our mind that has been veiled and kept barren for millenniums before his appearance on earth. In fact he opened the human mind to the powers of the Father exactly as Sarah's womb was opened in her old age. He unfastened the barren *loins* of our minds to receive the seed of his word and motivated our subconscious to the ability of *believing* this word. There was nothing wrong with Abraham's seed (sperm); the problem was that Sara's *womb was barren*. She was a believer and a receiver but she could not conceive *until God opened her womb at the right time!* The sons of the Kingdom are the *believers/receivers* and they will also *conceive* to bring forth the promised man-child that carries the mind of Jesus. These are the days of discovery where Jesus opened the barrenness of our mind to reveal the narrow door to all the bliss and bounty.

-19-

The Glorified Body

"And greater works than these shall you do."

Jesus Christ

Paul said to the Corinthians: "Glorify God in your body," and questioned: "Know you not that you are the Temple of God, and that the Spirit of God *dwells in you*?" Paul is perhaps the most trusted living man in this context as he bore witness to the strikingly Glorified Body of Christ on his way to Damascus. He also witnessed the splendor of the human body through the many sculptures of the Greek artists. He knew his new converts epitomized *glory* as the condition of a highest achievement or magnificence and wanted to inject his Christian concept on how man is glorified by that spiritual change within his being; the transformation that elevates the body and its owner closer to the glory of God.

Jesus moved on this earth, mingled with different kinds of people, performed his miracles and sustained maximum human sufferings all within a glorified body that kept all its *properties* as identified by St. Thomas: impassibility, subtlety, agility and clarity throughout his mission and after his Ascension from this earth. And to the sole exception of chagrin the night of his Crucifixion when he deliberately relinquished his glorified attributes to undergo the real human pains, he did not suffer any kind of physical evils: death, sorrow, illness, and was free of these maladies which cause so much anguish here in this life. He had the *power to penetrate.* No material objects deterred his glorified body from moving to and fro and his Risen Body was the vivid example of displacing from one place to another unrestricted. His agility was demonstrated in the power of his body to move quickly and effortlessly at the spirit's behest defying gravity and *walking over the sea waves.* Jesus' body shone with an unmistakable brilliance when it transfigured on the mountain with the full splendor, radiance and clarity the soul possesses. St. Thomas further asserts: "Thus in the glorified body the glory of the soul will be known as a liquid contained in a crystal vase."

Paul comments further to the Corinthians: "All of us, with unveiled faces, seeing the glory of the Lord as though reflected in a mirror, are being transformed into the same image from one degree of *glory* to another; for this comes from *the Lord, the Spirit.*" (2Cor.3:18.) Here Paul appears to describe a process that goes on endlessly and is visible anytime not just something that took place in the past or will take place at a certain point in the future. John said: "God is light, and in him there is no darkness at all." From this epistle verse, *Light*, whether interpreted in an allegorical or in a real sense, will always accompany communion with God, and by our very nature we are a receiver of that divine (cosmic) light and when it reaches its pure state we see and feel God saturating our body. The light of God is not therefore restricted to our minds but becomes an active catalyst in the transformation of our entire nature.

When Paul used the term *spiritual body*, he either alluded to the glorified body or offered a description thereof acceptable to his readers. He is not talking about a body made of spirit or an incorporeal body but a corporeal one complete with flesh and bones. The word *spiritual* here is an adjective describing the *body* not negating its meaning. A spiritual body is first and foremost a real body or it would not qualify to be called a body and Paul could have simply put out his differentiation. Hence, Christ's glorified body is in fact a spiritual body that appears and acts most of the time like a regular physical body with the exception of having an array of metaphysical powers beyond normal physical abilities.

Jesus was on this earth *the human incarnation of the Holy Spirit*. His human body is like a bundle of packed conducting wires pervaded all over by the Holy Spirit. Even if you touch its covering garment *with a purpose* an electric shock is given. The events of the sick women and the act of transfiguration are palpable examples of the glorified body. Electricity cannot be separated from Jesus' body; *it's the power of the Holy Spirit in its physical status*. Jesus refers to this Holy Spirit as his Father though he and Father are one and the same. In saying this repeatedly he is referring to a practical reason: every human being repels—or attracts another human being. A man cannot accept another man as God due to jealousy and egoism but would attract another man with love and selflessness. Hence Jesus wanted to be called only as the Son of man when he is introduced to the public or preaching the divine knowledge to this world. Both the body of Jesus and the disciples are instruments of the Holy Spirit chosen for different purposes.

This mystical reality in the technical language of theology: *God is called light,* is not only according to His essence but also to His energy. This array of cosmic energies that is called by its manifested symptom, *light,* is not just by analogy to material light but because of the ineffable reality for which the most suitable name is light. God manifests Himself as light in His dynamic attributes. This divine experience is given to each one according to the worthiness of those who experience it. The perfect vision of divinity becoming perceptible as light, pertains to the few who can open their spirit to embrace it and thus see God face to face. Holy Mary, Mother of Jesus, was one of those individuals. The worthy and eligible to this divine experience are those who are united with God who succeeded in cleansing their subconscious from all negative aspects and becoming worthy to a vision of "the Kingdom of God coming in power," as did the disciples on Mount Harmon.

Mount Harmon, Gilead in the Bible, is the highest mountain (2600M.) in southern Lebanon overlooking all of Galilee. It is described in the Songs of Solomon to allude to stature and majesty. Yet it was a mount connected with earth where the heavenly city coming down from God and connecting its glory to earth took place as depicted by Revelation 21. This is where the Master took his disciples to perform moments of exhilaration and magnificence with his glorified body. The chief hypostasis in the scene up there was the Person of Jesus. The beauty of that Person is the second thing; "His face did shine as the sun" and "His raiment was white as the light" was the third. In Mark it says, "His raiment became shining, exceeding white as snow; so as no fuller on earth can over white them."

White indeed! Unsoiled white that robe! Its mere touching by the women that had an issue of blood healed her. Mark further states: "And she had suffered many things from many physicians, and had spent all she had, and was nothing bettered, but rather grew worse. When she had heard of Jesus, came in the press behind, and touched his garment. For she said, if I may touch but his clothes, I shall be whole. And straightaway the fountain of her blood was dried up; and she felt in her body that she was healed of that plague. And Jesus, immediately knowing in himself that a *virtue has gone out of him*, turned him about in the press and said, who touched my clothes? And his disciples said unto him, you see the multitude thronging you, and you say who touched me? And (because a surge of power has gone out of him) he looked round about to see her that had done this thing. But the woman fearing and trembling, knowing what was done in her, came and fell down before him . . ." (Mar. 5:25.) This surge of power translated as *virtue* was emitted by Jesus' electronic fire body, the mental body receptacle of all cosmic powers; the glorified body constantly permeated with a resurrected subconscious.

Jesus lived in his mental body and he could do phenomenal things. He could walk on water, materialize loaves and fishes, and disappear. Jesus used his atomic body to make soul flights. He could have disappeared from the cross in an instant if he so wanted. In many places the New Testament says that Jesus went "out of sight," which means he was translated or transmuted. To disappear we completely translate our mass into light. This glorified body was *resurrected*' many times when Jesus would feel *low in spirit*. He would leave his disciples and climb up the mountain for few days of prayer and contemplation to refill his cosmic battery and achieve coordination between surrender and physical relaxation. This *resurrection* act was performed by the Master to step up from the emotional-mental tailspin he would endure and conquer among his disciples and followers. The bracing mountain air was the treatment where oxygen, the breath of God, was in abundance. Yet it was more in abundance on Mount Harmon where the Transfiguration took place. Such series of mini-resurrections were preamble exercises performed by Jesus for the ultimate one of all: Resurrection from death.

Transfiguration is the clear phenomenon of the mystic initiation Jesus was subjected to during his Qumran years of retreat and meditation. When Jesus transfigured himself he was a catalyst that recalled and brought together two different substances, Moses and Elijah, and transfigured them into a new, common substance which is *the vibratory rate of balance between the visible and invisible worlds*. His Transfiguration raises the physical cells' vibratory rate from the crude material to the radiant electronic body causing the outer sheath, including its raiment, to *glister* with the White Light. His Transfiguration was his fire body vibration shining through his outer physical casing as all materiality fell from him. His face glistered with the Light from within, visible and brilliant as the sun and his clothes shone. Peter, James and John could see only his white fire body.

Why Jesus took his three elite disciples up to Mount Harmon to witness his Transfiguration? Certainly not for a show off but surely to demonstrate to them that the son of man, anyone of them—as well as us, *can reach* this eminence. He taught them that such achievement may not be accomplished instantly and completely but a bit at a time: whenever they stop negative doubting they resurrect a similar dose of belief and when they and we stop weeping tears of self-pity we erase few tears from this earth. And every time we pray as a true mystic we transfigure in a little light no matter how unseen.

Most certainly, the disciples must have learned the secrets of Jesus' prayers and meditation up in the mountain. Breathing deeply at our age of knowledge is no more confined to the yoga of controlled breath but an exercise practiced by many builders of soul power. When this is coupled by our intensive prayer, similar to Jesus' prayer at the night of his delivery where: "Being in agony (intense meditation) he prayed more earnestly: and his sweat was as it were great drops of blood falling down to the ground" (Luk.22:44,) our prayer draws the life sparks and we disengage toward the Father; light ascends and enters to transfigure our physical body. This is the Holy Spirit, the healer, the purifier and the Light.

Our body will only metamorphose by renewing our mind. Only a renewed mind has the ability to transform the body. Today we know every single cell has in it the complete instructions for our body. A *complete set of instructions* is even contained in a single fingernail cell and may one day create a whole new body! Just as the subconscious mind caused a blister to form on the person who was touched by the pencil erasure (believing it was hot), it can also control the cells of our body to bring the metamorphosis or change that is just short of a resurrection. We are transformed in *our body* by the renaissance of *our mind*. This will happen when the mind of Christ awakens within us. The innermost part of our mind has been kept hidden until now and it has the ability to change the atoms of our body indefinitely. Our subconscious has the power of God in it and it has been kept virgin and unused; it is the womb that can create life, didn't the bible refer to it when it says to gird up the *loins* of your mind?

It certainly strikes us when we visualize that incomparable night scene up on that mountain and then read: "They kept it *close*, and told no man *in those days* any of those things which they had seen"? (Luk.9:36.) Does it not seem strange to you that they should be silenced about this wonderful scene? Jesus asked his disciples as well as the healed individuals not to disclose his miracles to any one for a valid reason: in those days of little belief and limited spiritual education such feats may have been considered sorcery or charlatanisms. "Jesus charged them, saying, tell the vision to no man, until the Son of Man be risen again from the dead." They were temporarily silenced because only in the shadow of the greater Resurrection smaller miracles such as the Transfiguration can be implicitly believed and understood. It was a marvelous, indescribable moment in the dead of that night when they saw the mountain top lit up with the brightest glory. The glorified body of the Son of Man lit up that scene at the time when darkness reigned supreme.

The same light of Jesus' glorified body shone on Apostle Paul this time in the middle of the day on the road to Damascus: "A great light from heaven suddenly shone around me. And I fell to the ground . . . Now those who were with me saw the light . . . I could not see because of the brightness of that light" (Act. 22:6). When Paul said later that "flesh and blood cannot inherit the kingdom of God," he was referring to our flesh and blood *as they are now*: a container of a subconscious mind cursed and under sin. Our resurrected future bodies with a neatly cleansed subconscious—though still physical bodies in the fullest sense will be untouched by sin and indestructible.

A purified subconscious of the Virgin Mary was a seat of God and a dwelling of His grace. Heaven and its *angels* rejoice when a human subconscious long devastated by negative behaviors capitulates to this decontamination process because an extra positive catalyst is recreated on earth. Jesus' parable of the prodigal son embodies this resurrected phenomenon. This is the same reality Teilhard de Chardin explains when he refers in his "Christified Universe," to this *renewed image of God*, into whose likeness Paul says we are being transformed and into the fullness where "the entire creation will be liberated when the sons of God are fully revealed." Teilhard adds a further dimension that Christ already exists as a human example of *glittering, glistening mirror of Divinity,* into which we look and into whose likeness we are being transformed. He adds: *we are all called, like the Cosmic Christ to radiate the divine presence,* implying that some of God's glory is already reflected in our faces and the glory is increasing in us and among us because *glory* is a cosmological term in the Scriptures and here we learn that all the divine glory in the universe has not occurred yet."

The rebirth of the human subconscious consists in changing *the present humiliated state* of its nature enabling it to participate in the divine life. Henceforth by following Christ' example when he spent forty days of contemplation, was tried yet resisted all sorts of *devilish temptations* to consecrate himself as the divine likeness, the sons of men can make such consecration shine forth on this earth. When a person attains this goal he participates in divine life and transforms his very nature. Inside the human body even if it is failing is the blueprint for the glorified, resurrected body. Man may not be satisfied with his current body or mind but he will be thrilled with his resurrecting upgrades that introduce him to enjoy an eternity of wonders awaiting him. This ascension of man reverses the process of the fall and begins to deliver the universe from disorder and corruption into avenues of bliss and contentment. Since the deification attained by the saints constitutes the beginning of the cosmic transformation to come, it refashions and renews our psychosomatic functions turning them into the same functions of a glorified body. This cosmic change is likened to the mingling of a small drop of water being poured into a vast sea of perfume where greater things are stronger than lesser ones and what is divine prevails over what is human. Those *born again*, very dear to Jesus' values become partakers of the divine nature to whom a holy disposition is given, leading to love and righteousness.

The narrow link between body and spirit stretches when consciousness ascends to join the spirit's will. Jesus mated desire to will in his "I AM" assumptions to usher humans into the Way of Righteousness and Life. In doing so he transfigured not only his life but our lives as well resurrecting all the old and opening new brain cells in the process of awakening the subconscious mind. Positive thinking, joy and relaxation are the keys to achieve this resurrection. Jesus propagated these stimulants where the soul becomes a reflecting mirror recording everything on the human brain cells. This is Ascension here and now, changing all physical ills and problems into the new image and likeness of God. Jesus ascertained: *"And greater works than these shall you do."* The Kingdom of Heaven is open to *all* believers depending on how much and how far do they believe!

Our fire body, likewise Jesus', begins to possess the glorified physical aspects: the laws of *vibratory rate of balance* between inner and outer or between *doing* and *being* these laws when we *become amenable and effective* only under genuine, intense prayer. It is one way to pass each test quickly when we believe and stop rationalizing with our corporeal mind under the negative mental-intellectual vibration. Intellectual prayer sinks into the body and our consciousness remains within our skull under the ceiling. The power of the Father descends as individually whirling life sparks to reform and condense still further in their rate of vibration. Kinetic energy is the Universal Christ Principle, his White Light and the potential of his personality. These same whirling life sparks descended on the disciples on Pentecost Day and Jesus' aura filled all of them with this great Light of Life. He lifted as he ascended and the Father bestowed *more* spirit substance upon him. Didn't he tell us: "who he has will be given and added, and who he has not will be taken from?" Jesus was a descended Son of God greater on the cross than anyone who has ever walked this earth. This potential power he called to earth during his ministry is that *Christed* substance we invoke for healing today. We invoke the Power of Jesus' life sparks when we pray and call upon his name and our prayer becomes the power path that establishes our communion with the Father.

But do we really know to what strata we are moving through our intensive prayer? We are actually acquiring a transformation of our whole being not just our mind and soul but our body as well. When we enter into the Father's glory we will be there with our transformed bodies. This is what happened to the many saints who were living among us and who conquered the resurrection of their bodies. This means that even our physical bodies will undergo a transformation like those of the resurrected saints. This is as well what exactly happened to the Virgin Mary.

The light of the Transfiguration was no meteorological phenomenon; it was the light which belongs by nature to God concentrated in the God-Man which appeared clearly to the disciples when their eyes were opened to that glorious mountain scene. At the ultimate heights of holiness the human person becomes in a certain sense able to clothe in the sun and shine. Many saints become luminous in their bodies; St. Sharbel of Lebanon was identified after his death with the constant luminosity radiating from his entombed body which was, besides his numerous healing miracles, the normative sign of his holiness. "You are the light of the world" said—and meant Jesus, and in as much as Moses glowed when he descended from Sinai so there is a light on the faces of the saints who have come close to God. Today's icons that adorn churches convey this phenomenon of light by a halo which is a precise sign in an image of a well-defined event in the spiritual world.

In a glorified body the effect of this illumination can be described to a certain extent by the usual state of dissipation replaced in man by intense, silent prayer where one becomes illuminated by the grace of the Holy Spirit and the entire human being flows like molten lava in a single burst toward God. This is how holiness, *the divine image* was reinstated in the perfect life of Christ. Jesus obliterated all negative powers within the individual and maximized his positivism by his freely accepted passion and led man to realize the task for which he was created: to achieve divine likeness.

-20-

The Death of Jesus

"Father, into your hands I *commend* my spirit."

Luk. 23:46

Perhaps the exact meaning for the Aramaic "Etida'a" used by Jesus in his plea on the Cross "Eli, Bein Edeik Etida'a Nephesh" and commonly translated as 'commend' is hard to get by. While 'commend' means entrust or consign, the Aramaic one connotes: 'entrust a precious item retrievable shortly'. From the verb Etida'a derives "Wadia'a" meaning: a deposited/reclaimed item of value. And that is exactly what Jesus asked God: to deposit his soul in His hands for retrieval in just three days! For the sake of delivering a closer English version let's volunteer the verb: commit.

Jesus announced many times either directly or through insinuations his short 3-day journey to the ambit of death. The 3-day span is emblematic to "Jonah who was three days and three nights in the whale's belly; so shall the Son of man be three days in the heart of the earth." (Mat. 12:40.) This journey was a preordained divine plan much in line with the *narrow door* and the *grain of wheat* philosophy. The false interpretation that he went to death with feeling of despair and abandonment especially when he repeated on the Cross again in Aramaic the words of the Psalm 22, "My God, my God, why have you forsaken me," should be corrected. This Psalm is ultimately a prayer of trust in God despite the evil that surrounds us, and certainly what surrounded Jesus around Golgotha.

Perhaps Jesus' most perceptible declaration was: "The hour has come for the Son of man to be *glorified*. Truly, *truly*, I say to you, unless a grain of wheat falls into the earth and dies, it remains alone; but if it dies, it bears much fruits" (John 12:23.) Many other declarations preceded and followed; the first and meaningful one was when Jesus advised his disciples of his intention to hit the lion's den in Jerusalem after his long exertion in Galilee: "From that time fourth began Jesus to show into his disciples, how that he must go into Jerusalem, and suffer many things of the elders and chief priests and scribes, and *be killed*, and *be raised again* the third day." Meaningful because when Peter took him and rebuked him for mentioning death, "he turned and said into Peter, get you behind me, Satan: you are an offence unto me: for you savor not *the things that be of God*, but those that be of men." (Mat.16:21.) Peter could not fathom this upcoming *ordained* scheme emanating from the Father!

The second announcement was shortly after the Transfiguration while they abode in Galilee, "Jesus said unto them, the Son of man shall be betrayed into the hands of men: and they shall kill him, and the third day he will be raised again. And they were exceedingly sorry." (Mat.17:22.) Other hints to Jesus' passions succeeded when the woman poured the fragrance on his head and he accepted it as a preparation for his burial or when he defied his listeners to destroy *his* temple. John narrates: "Jesus answered and said to them, 'destroy this Temple, and in three days I will raise it up.' The Jews therefore said, 'It took forty-six years to build this Temple, and will you raise it up in three days?' But he was speaking of the temple of his body," (John 2:19.) These notifications served to fulfill the scripture and alert his disciples of the upcoming colossal event and even forewarned them not to disperse and forsake their entrusted mission.

In Jesus' earthly time the Sadducees did not believe in the resurrection of the body. The Pharisees and the Gnostics espoused a vague idea thereof. The Essenes and early Christians were believers in the true bodily *resurrection* through the spiritual renewal or the true *spiritual resurrection* that Jesus advocated. These were the *hidden mysteries* and the *higher secret teachings shared only with a few*. The public at large in those days could not understand the difference between the spiritual reincarnation, subconscious cleansing as we call it today, and the resurrection of the body being *born again of the Spirit*. This is apparent in Jesus' conversation with Nicodemus the Pharisee doctor who praised the powers of Jesus but *failed to understand* his explanations about the spiritual transformation!

What Jesus tried to explain to Nicodemus in our modern terms was that *resurrection* of the body is actually a spiritual regeneration of being *born again* and a total transformation from doctrinal religious thinking toward spirituality; a development to new scientific, metaphysical, and religious foundation into universal spiritual regeneration that starts with water at baptism and culminated at adulthood by subconscious cleansing; an all-important transition—threshold—which we cross to get to our real life in the spiritual realm presided by love and its positive characteristics. This is the true personality of each *born again* with all the requisites for entering the Kingdom of God. Such personality carries an ethereal, glorified body governed and directed by the spirit, the holy spirit of God that moves about like the wind!

Following a compressed, amazingly productive ministry program teaching and healing thousands Jesus *allowed* his work to come to a sudden end. He could have avoided arrest and delude his arraigners as he has done before but he *chose* to die instead of expanding his ministry, although he could have healed thousands more by traveling to the Jews and gentiles who lived in other areas. His teachings and further healings were important but he had come not only to teach and heal but also to die. By applying his own *grain of wheat* parable first on himself he accomplished all objectives the parable entails.

Death was Jesus' most important philosophy throughout the ministry. He was born to die. Death is a crucial part of the Gospel and something all Christians should know. He said, "The Son of Man did not come to be served, but to serve, and to give his life as a ransom for many" (Mat. 20:28.) He came to die so he can give life; this was the primary reason of his earthly sojourn. When he warned his disciples that he would suffer and die they didn't seem to believe it as he was rebuked by Peter. Yet he knew he *must* die as a Messiah in line with the scriptures: "Why then is it written that the Son of man must suffer much and be rejected?" (Mar. 9:12.) "Beginning with Moses and all the Prophets, he explained to them what was said in all the scriptures concerning him . . . . 'This is what is written: The Christ will suffer and rise from the dead on the third day'" (Luk.24:27.) Jesus executed God's ordinance: "Let Your will be done, not mine."

The Jewish leaders certainly thought that Crucifixion would shatter and disperse those disciples and that is almost what happened. But their hopes were dramatically restored when Jesus reappeared to them after his Resurrection, and when at Pentecost the Holy Spirit filled them with new conviction to proclaim salvation in his name. They had unshakable faith in the least likely hero: a crucified Messiah. Herod, Pilate, Judas as well as the Roman soldiers *were all instruments in the grand plan;* hence on the Cross, and for <u>*this very reason*</u> Jesus addressed his executioners: "forgive them Father, as *they don't know* what they do!" In the Garden of Gethsemane Jesus asked if there might be some other way but there was none. (Luk. 22:42.)

Yet Jesus going to his death should not be painted as a passive victim who was blindly fulfilling such pre-ordained divine plan. Far from it; he charted his earthly life decisions in an impeccable way: in the face of uncertainty and risk the human, historical Jesus had an undeviating and immediate access to

247

God's will. He prays that he will come to know and execute the Father's will—God's mind—and make the right decisions in view of his prayer and discernment. Jesus was perfectly aware of all the risks when he had made the crucial decision to take his mission to the heart of Judaism and knew he must live with the consequences of that decision, including his demise.

The recorded events surrounding *the last supper* and *the agony in the garden* show that Jesus went to his death freely and deliberately; not because he actively chose death itself but because he continued to commit himself to the positive mission of the kingdom in the face of all opposition and negativism. The bread and wine at the Last Supper was a final wrapping up of his entire mission lived in loving to serve others. His impending death was the challenge to invigorate and perpetuate this mission. It was marked by the same stratagem that constituted his entire life.

It is hard to comprehend what the pure soul-God experienced in the garden of Gethsemane. Christ knew however that his great sufferings and boundless love would be appreciated by only a few; that the majority of the people would turn away from him with indifference including his disciples: "Couldn't you abide by me *one more hour*?" And that some would reject his teachings and would cruelly persecute those who believed in him. He foresaw many hypocrites among his followers who would turn faith into a means for profit and that there would be false teachers and false prophets who would distort his teachings. He foresaw that false pastors would appear who, because of ambition, would create schisms in the Church. Christ knew not only that many Christians would fail to love God and live righteously but also that they would give themselves to heinous crimes and vices so that by their sins they would even surpass pagans and as a result the Christian faith would be scandalized. Such predicaments haunted his forceful prayer to the point of seeping his sweat like blood droplets to the ground.

Many interpretations targeted Jesus' death. The Jewish tradition is full of stories where the true prophets are killed. The fact that Jesus was killed shows that he is the true prophet-martyr; he sordidly accused Jerusalem of being "the killer of the prophets and the stoner of the emissaries" which ascribes a particular theological significance to Jesus' death as well. Jesus was given by the Jewish elders an accursed death as spelled out in Deut. 21:23: "Anyone who is hung on a tree is under God's curse." Because of this verse Jews considered any crucified person to be condemned by God or "stricken by God" as Isaiah wrote. Those elders probably thought that this would stop Jesus' disciples. And it happened just as they hoped: the crucifixion shattered the disciples' hopes. They were dejected and said, "We had hoped that he was the one who was going to redeem Israel" (Luk. 24:21.) But their faith was spectacularly reinstated in the 'crucified Messiah' when Jesus appeared to them after his resurrection. Later, Peter echoed this understanding when he bravely told the Jewish leaders, "The God of our fathers raised Jesus from the dead—whom you had killed by hanging him on a tree" (Act. 5:30.) By using the word *tree* Peter reminded the leaders of the curse of crucifixion. Only this time the disgrace was not on Jesus; God had reversed the stigma.

Another interpretation focused on the *suffering Son of man* as a renewed example of all rejected and despised previous prophets. Yet Jesus' suffering is read in accordance with the *divine plan of salvation* where it takes a virtuous degree of prominence. The third slant is summarized in the Pauline formula which states that Jesus 'died for us on account of our sins' (Rom.4:25) and considers the death as a *redemptive and atoning act*. These various approaches perceive the struggle between good and evil that brought Jesus' earthly life and mission to such an abrupt end. Yet in all three theories the philosophy of death propagated by Jesus as the *narrow door* for bliss and happiness is ignored as it stands ultimately outside the powers of rational explanation.

Paul wrote: ". . . in Jesus all the fullness of God was pleased to dwell, *and through him to reconcile to himself all things, whether on earth or in heaven, making peace by the blood of his cross*. And you, who once were estranged and *hostile in mind*, doing evil deeds, he has now reconciled in his body of flesh by his death, in order to present you holy and blameless and irreproachable before him." (Col.1:19.) This passage reveals that not only did Jesus take upon himself the sins of mankind when he died on the cross but he also met fully the onslaught of *demons, fallen angels* and all the negative power of evil forces in the heavens as well, disarming all of them completely.

He also wrote: "Since therefore the children share in flesh and blood, he himself likewise partook of the same nature, that through death he might destroy him who has the power of death, that is, the *devil*, and deliver all those who through fear of death were subject to lifelong bondage." (Heb.2:14.) In describing Jesus' victory over man's greatest enemy, death, Paul boldly asserts the overall message of the Crucifixion: liberating man from his *lifelong bondage* under the negative realm.

Before we review the suffering of Jesus on the Cross we should perhaps address the controversial and enigmatic stance of Judas. His baffling figure still confuses Church clerics and historians alike. Many theories and questions were thrown on his betrayal: was he a vehicle in a preordained plan as we assume? As it is apparent that the idea of *Judas the traitor* only developed *after* the Resurrection; his betrayal of Jesus seems odd for two reasons: 1/everyone knows who Jesus was; he was there already if they wanted him and 2/Gethsemane Garden was hardly a hidey-hole for Jesus and his disciples and would be a secret to nobody in a small town like Jerusalem. Another theory advocates that Judas was assigned to provoke disturbance—like Peter cutting one attacker's ear—to speed up the pace . . .

One scenario suggests that in grabbing Jesus there would be a commotion between the attackers and Jesus' followers prompting the Romans to intervene whereby Jesus would show his divine powers and eliminate the faithless of Jerusalem, Palestine and the whole world, especially that cleansing the Temple had shown Jesus had both muscles and temper. But the Master disappointed them all. Violence ensued in the Garden but Jesus quelled it and the high priest's servant had his ear made whole. To Judas this must have been a bitter disappointment seeing the Mighty One really handing himself over. And then too late, in his misery and disillusionment Judas realized why: Jesus was following a master design too complex and intricate for him to understand.

Another scenario was brought up recently upon the discovery of *Judas' Gospel* we frequently referred to representing one of the most unusual and contrarian views among all Gospels. The newly translated document's text begins: "The secret account of the revelation that Jesus spoke in conversation with Judas Iscariot." Whereby the Master told Judas: "You will exceed all of them (disciples); for you will sacrifice *the man that clothes me*," indicating that Judas would help liberate the spiritual self by helping Jesus get rid of his physical flesh. In another passage Jesus told him: "Step away from the others and I shall tell you the mysteries of the Kingdom . . ." Jesus says to Judas singling him out for a special status. ". . . Look, you have been told everything. Lift up your eyes and look at the cloud and the light within it and the stars surrounding it. The star that leads the way is your star." The text ends with Judas turning Jesus over to the high priests and does not include any mention of the crucifixion or resurrection.

In another chapter of this manuscript Jesus allegedly enlightened Judas of the hidden secrets of the cosmos; secrets never revealed to the other disciples. But the big question here is the mere authenticity of this document, written by an unknown scribe some 300 years after Jesus based on oral tradition and long considered as a heresy. Yet it turns Judas' act of betrayal into an act of obedience reflected patchily by the Gospels:

Mathews relates: "And they did eat, he said, verily I say unto you, that one of you shall betray me. And they were exceedingly sorrowful, and begun every one of them to say unto him, Lord, is it I? And he answered and said, he that dips with me in the dish, the same shall betray me. The Son of Man goes *as it is written of him*: but woe unto that man by whom the Son of man is betrayed! It had been good for that man if he had not been born. Then Judas, which betrayed him, answered and said, Master, is it I? He said unto him, you have said it." (Mat. 26:21.)

Mathews, Mark and Luke variably recounted the conspiracy of Judas to deliver his master for thirty pieces of silver. John however shed further light on this issue: "When Jesus had thus said, he was troubled in spirit, and testified, and said, verily, verily, I say onto you, that one of you shall betray me. Then the disciples looked one on another, doubting of whom he spoke. Now there was leaning on Jesus' bosom one of his disciples (John) whom Jesus loved. Simon Peter therefore beckoned to him, that he should ask who it should be of whom he spoke. He then lying on Jesus' breast said unto him, Lord, who is it? Jesus answered, he is to whom I shall give a sop, when I have dipped it. And when he had dipped the sop, he gave it to Judas Iscariot, the son of Simon. And after the sop Satan entered into him. Then said Jesus unto him, *what you do, do quickly.*" (John 13:21.)

The controversy in the role of Judas, the lowest of traitors, one who for a modest sum of money chooses to give over a beloved leader to death and throws away all his ideals in the process, is perhaps elucidated in Jesus' last command to him: "*What you do, do quickly.*" Judas was not bewildered by the spilling of expensive anointment by Mary, sister of Jesus' dear friend Lazarus on the Master's head, nor was he induced by the fact that all those associated with Jesus were in imminent danger and his cowardice was his main impulse. All such arguments correlated with Judas by scholars do not carry any persuasiveness. Jesus though *needed* to be betrayed, even by a disciple that spent a good while in the service of a Master who can penetrate and read the workings of any man's mind at the twinkling of an eye.

We can address this controversy by first revealing who Judas was. His name Iscariot is a derivative of *Ish Kerioth* or the man from Kerioth his native town in southern Judea. He was a proud Judean among the twelve Galilean disciples of Jesus. This alone could have caused him to feel somewhat superior as Judeans considered Galileans to be country dwellers. When Jesus gave him charge of the money box it may have additionally boosted his ego. Furthermore he was identified as a Zealot, an attribute held also by two other disciples, Simon Peter the nationalist and Simon the zealot. Such group of ultra-Zealots known as daggermen in the West carried swords with them at all time to be prepared to assassinate traitors and capitulators. This group believed that if they turned Israel back to God and incited war against the Romans the Messiah would arise to lead them and establish his Kingdom, which led most of them, probably Judas, to misinterpret many foresights concerning Christ's teachings. They totally ignored prophecies regarding his first coming and the eventful ministry he carried out on earth.

Apparently Judas liaised with the Sanhedrin and both Sadducees and Pharisees on the veracity of his Master's message. He was thrilled when the Messiah had chosen him to be among the twelve and started forging high hopes for a prominent position in the new *kingdom*. Yet at some point he came to understand Jesus' message differently and thought he was sacrificing a lot for a spiritual *Kingdom not from this world* especially when Jesus began to tell his disciples that he would die and that this was a main reason for his coming. That disillusioned Judas as a zealot and shattered his materialistic aspirations. The change of heart changed him into a thief; he began to steal from the money box either for his own ends or maybe to fund some of his fellow zealots' activities. Once in Bethany he even complained aloud of his displeasure to Jesus

(John 12:3.) When Jesus gently rebuked him for his comment (Mar. 14:6,) Judas was incensed! Luke (22:3) tells it in his own words: *"Then Satan entered Judas, surnamed Iscariot, who was numbered among the twelve. So he went his way and conferred with the chief priests and captains, how he might betray him to them. And they were glad, and agreed to give him money. Then he promised and sought opportunity to betray him to them in the absence of the multitude."*

Yet the big question remains: Jesus was able to foresee Judas' actions and was completely aware of his betrayal and able to prevent it from the time Judas became a disciple; why he let him go along with it while threatening him with a sordid fate? Is it because Judas was the only non-Galilean *black sheep* among the disciples and the *negative element* in the whole godly positive scheme? Jesus certainly despised and cursed the Sanhedrin with whom Judas, the dishonest servant following the Master's teachings under false pretensions played a double-agent. An astonishing situation ensued and Judas *the negative element* was required to represent the *devil* in the whole scheme. We have to remember that Jesus' death was and remains forever a symbolic, redeeming, challenging and predetermined endeavor. Certainly the *devil* makes Judas do it! Satan, the negative side of the human character was attracted naturally by Judas as flies to a barnyard compost pile. This negative side had his share with Jesus himself during his forty-day fasting. During that exercise Jesus dealt with *"Satan"* with all due understanding exactly as we do daily with our negative postures! With Judas he was as indulgent yet resolute: "What you have to do, do it now!"

Many have wondered how Jesus could have made such a *mistake* choosing Judas in the first place. After all Jesus certainly had greater prudence and power to have easily known that Judas would betray him. The palpable fact is that *Jesus did know* that Judas would long beforehand: "For Jesus knew from the first who those were that did not believe, and who it was that would betray him." (John 6:64.) And, "Did I not choose you, the twelve, and one of you is a *devil?*" He spoke of Judas the son of Simon Iscariot, for he, one of the twelve, was to betray him." (John 6:70.) Jesus was born to die and fulfill the Scripture. He was in fact an absolutely innocent man who was to be betrayed, falsely accused, unlawfully arrested, unjustly convicted, and brutally executed to *fulfill the Scripture.* A naturally corrupt man was required for the role of betrayer and Judas Iscariot was the best available candidate.

Judas was important: there was no option for Jesus not to be executed because without his crucifixion he could not fulfill his undertaking and rise again the 3rd. day. To be executed, though he had to be betrayed to the Jewish authorities, if Judas hadn't done it someone else *should have* in line with the Scripture. This precludes any other conclusion including Judas' greed for money or the anti-Roman rebellion. Judas is important for the gospel authors to rightfully portray the negative element irrespective that Judas acted or not from within the theological assumptions of the Christian system. All of the apostles are depicted as having been unfaithful to Jesus or failing in some manner but at least they were always better than Judas. So much about this controversial disciple . . .

The death of Jesus took place and the Crucifixion was carried out in the normal Roman manner. The fact that he was crucified along with a thief on his left and another on his right further confirms this happening. In ordinary human body Jesus suffered terribly during the long night of his trial. That suffering began with the agony in the garden of Gethsemane when he relinquished his glorified body's characteristics to assume true human sufferings and let out his candid declaration: "The spirit is strong, but the body is weak." The humiliating events of his trial and cruel torture prior to the morning journey to Golgotha took heavy toll on that body.

The worst was yet to come as crucifixion is an especially painful and terrible ordeal. It was common in Roman times for crucified men in good health to hang dying on a cross sometimes for days; yet Scripture records that Jesus died prematurely within six hours' clock time, much ahead of the two other men hence the soldiers, as customary to speed their death resorted to break their legs. This did not happen to Jesus in realization of the Scripture: "No bones of his are broken." Even if he only suffered normal human pain in this ordeal it would have been incredibly severe.

It is meaningful to review the last words of Jesus on the Cross. In his agony he was able to push himself upward to exhale and bring in life-giving oxygen and in between these intakes he uttered the seven short sentences that are recorded: the first was when he saw the Roman soldiers throwing dices for his garment, another biblical fulfillment: "and on my garment they threw dices;" he said: "Father, forgive them for they do not know what they do." Signaling that the soldiers were mere instruments in the master plan, a dilapidated wool garment was not much of a prize to throw dices for; only the fulfillment was taking its course. The second word was addressed to the penitent thief: "Today, you shall be with me in Paradise;" a truly positive injection to the subconscious of the dying man to restore his peace of mind. The third to his mother and the grief-stricken adolescent John: "Woman, behold your son," and to John: "Behold your mother;" a mighty concern that depicts optimum devotion. And the fourth, again in Scripture discharge, from the beginning of Psalm 22: "My God, my God, why have You forsaken me?"

In his following, speechless agony the prophecy in the same Psalm 22 was being achieved: "I am poured out like water, and all my bones are out of joint, my heart is like wax; it is melted in the midst of my bowels." Jesus gasped his fifth cry when his body's dehydrated tissues sent their stimuli to the brain: "I thirst," also in line with Psalm 22: "My strength is dried up like a potsherd; my tongue cleaves to my jaws; and you have brought me into the dust of death." Jesus was offered a sponge soaked with sour wine mixed with myrrh, a mild analgesic, pain-relieving mixture which he refused to drink and at about 3 pm Jesus wills himself to death. He cries "it is fulfilled." This Aramaic phrase actually had a specific meaning in those days of *paid in full* used when people were released by debtors and their unpaid bill was stamped 'paid in full.' With one last surge of strength he once again pressed his torn feet against the nail, straightened his legs, took a deeper breath and uttered his seventh and last cry: "Father, into Your hands *I commit* my soul." In releasing this cry out loud Jesus made it known to himself before his listeners that his passing away has actually taken place and that his soul has been entrusted to God for the span of the next three days: one last command to his *live* subconscious: the mind of God.

Thus Jesus crossed the *narrow door* and suffered on the Cross exactly as any human would. His physical passion began at Gethsemane when the life sparks of potential energy in his glorified body were withdrawn from him. In fact after a long, sleepless night of mockery, humiliation and scourging the 33-year old Jesus stumbled and collapsed under the rough wood of the Cross. He tried to rise but human muscles had been pushed beyond their endurance. The soldiers, anxious to proceed with the crucifixion picked a stalwart North African onlooker, Simon of Cyrene to carry the Cross while Jesus followed until the 650-yard Via Dolorosa from the fortress Antonia to Golgotha was finally completed. On top of the Cross the words *Jesus of Nazareth-king of the Jews* were inscribed in Latin, Hebrew and Aramaic by order of the Roman governor. Pilate probably dictated the title in Latin and the centurion in charge of the execution implemented the edict and its translation into the other languages. The words *King of the Jews* were a public sneer at the Jews by Pilate compounded by his additional taunt that their *king* came from Nazareth, i.e. a despised Galilean.

Hence Jesus sustained a premature passing away ahead of the two thieves sparing the Roman soldiers their resorting to the common method of legs fracture preventing the victim from pushing himself upward so that rapid suffocation occurs to speed up death. The legs of the two thieves were broken but Jesus' bones were not touched. John narrates these significant moments: "Then came the soldiers, and broke the legs of the first, and of the other which was crucified with him. But when they came to Jesus and saw that he was dead already they broke not his legs. But one of the soldiers with a spear pierced his side, and forthwith *came out blood and water. And he that saw it* (John himself) *bare record and his record is true*: and he knows that he says true, that you might believe. For these things were done, that the scripture should be fulfilled, 'a bone of him shall not be broken.' And again another scripture says: they shall look at him whom they pierced." (John 19:32.) The scripture was fulfilled to the letter during the last six hours of Crucifixion; even Pilate and his authorities acted in completion of God's predetermined plan including being anxious to get the body off the cross before sundown.

Jesus put his earthly body in a death slumber or a deep coma by indoctrinating his subconscious power; a recurrence on his own body of a previous happening with his beloved friend Lazarus. John also recites: "Now a certain man was sick, named Lazarus, of Bethany, the town of Mary and her sister Martha . . . therefore his sisters sent unto him saying, Lord, behold, he whom you love is sick. When Jesus heard that he said: *this sickness is not unto death*, but for the glory of God, that the Son of God might be glorified thereby . . . When he had heard therefore that he was sick, *he abode two days still* in the same place where he was. Then after that (when Lazarus was dead and buried) he said to his disciples, let us go into Judea (where he received death threats) again . . . and after that he said unto them: our friend Lazarus *sleeps*; but I go, that I may *awake him out of his sleep*." (John 11:1.) Jesus saw life in Lazarus' body: his sickness *was not unto death*. This is the near-death much talked about in our days when a human body succumbs to a coma for many months in our hospitals while maintaining all its bodily constituents through life support systems. In the case of Lazarus his subconscious mind was in slumber awaiting the catalyst to revive it along with the body it houses back to life. Let us remember other similarities with that son of the widow of Nain and Jairus' daughter. Today's studies of this phenomenon remain controversial. Most analysts approach this highly spiritual issue with their inductive minds and thus fail to enter religious belief structures that cannot be measured scientifically or medically. Yet for many of those people who routinely call the phenomenon a near-death experience the episode is generally viewed as positive and faith-confirming.

Jesus was his own catalyst in his self-afflicted 3-day slumber. His body maintained its components including blood and serum slightly shed by the soldier's spear well after his death; hence John's assertion of this *true and believable record*. This wouldn't happen to any ordinary mortal half an hour after his demise where blood clots and coagulates within its vessels. Such was Jesus' pledge to his Jewish audience and disciples: "Demolish this temple and I rebuild it in three days." He "abode two days still" and let Lazarus go for even four days of coma in his tomb all the while his connection with the dead man's subconscious was controlled through the Holy Spirit. To modern day interpreters we reiterate that the *Solomon Temple* Jesus alluded to his body suggested in its various sections the human temple and mind. Thus, the outside walls and pillars denote the physical body while the secret, storage chambers of Solomon's Temple correspond to our innermost part or the secret place in our soul where we store, hide and bury our wounds, hurts, guilt and memories. These hidden recesses or *cheder* in Hebrew epitomize our *innermost part*; the subconscious mind and mainstay of Jesus' canonical ministry.

Joseph of Arimathea the uncle of Mary, Mother of Jesus was an extremely wealthy and powerful man who according to the Gospels donated his own tomb for the burial of Jesus. He was apparently a famous metal merchant having deals as far as Britain and a member of the Sanhedrin. Joseph was an *honorable counselor, who waited for the Kingdom of God.* Thus he was secretly, along with Nicodemus a disciple of Jesus. As soon as he heard the news of Jesus' death he *went in boldly into Pilate, and craved the body of Jesus.* Reassured by the centurion that death has really taken place Pilate allowed Joseph's request and he immediately purchased fine linen and proceeded to Golgotha to take the body down from the Cross. There, assisted by Nicodemus he wrapped the body sprinkling it with the Myrrh and aloes that Nicodemus has brought (John 19:39.) The body was then conveyed to the new tomb that has been newly hewn for Joseph himself out of the rock in his garden nearby. There they laid it in the presence of "Mary Magdalene, Mary, the Mother of Jesus, and other women, and rolled a great stone to the entrance, and departed." This was done speedily "for the Sabbath was drawing on."

-21-

Resurrection and Ascension

". . . And when he had said this, he showed them both his hands and his side. The disciples therefore rejoiced when they saw the Lord."

John

Historians make the repeated mistake that Jesus' harrowing death terminated a life in complete failure and disaster. The failure took place in Galilee where he dissipated lots of his powers and stamina inconclusively. Their opinion of the event that proved to be wrong was always paradoxical. They came about that conclusion ignoring the small parable disseminated by Jesus, repeated many times in this book and considered to be the crux of his total philosophy: the grain of wheat. If Jesus had remained dead Christianity would be nothing but an empty promise. But three days after his death he rose again from the tomb. This is the miracle of Resurrection that turned historians' alleged failure into enormous triumph. The question of how and why did it happen was a good material for their endless inductive theorizations.

They all ignored that Jesus *sowed* in Galilee his *grains of wheat* and set a condition for those grains to die first in their grounds in order to sprout again and yield bountiful harvests. His Galilean record of mighty events constitutes forever the mainstay of the Christian saga. The purpose was not only the rebirth and dissemination of the faith among believers but also the indoctrination of a basic message that, for lack of proper understanding (as in the parable of the sower), was not totally embraced by the large audience: the spiritual awakening or rebirth of heart (our modern day subconscious), mind and spirit. The public in general during Jesus' days never grasped the knowledge of these higher principles conducive to the spiritual awakening necessary to practice a life liberated from the desires of the flesh. Resurrection is the vehicle which allows people to have as many opportunities as necessary to become enlightened and unchained.

It is fascinating to rediscover today those hidden mysteries that were confined to Jesus who rightfully claimed: "I am the way, the truth and life." These mystical teachings of attaining a human-divine unity were Jesus' roadmap to lift men up to their higher pedestal. They all teach the liberation of the flesh from its carnal mind through the awakening of the spirit within the subconscious. Everyone who becomes *awakened* can distinguish his three-dimensional structure and recognize it again as a manifestation of: life, light and love where the subconscious is the motivator and catalyst.

The next event in eternity for the human spirit of Jesus was his return to reenter his body in the tomb just before dawn on Sunday morning. By means of the mighty power of the Holy Spirit guiding his awakened subconscious he then experienced the complete transformation of his body and his resurrection *out from among the dead*. Joseph of Arimathea knew how to handle his body until he laid it in the tomb. The awakened subconscious held Jesus' body in *due form* and the tomb held its with its full potential energy. The essential earthly elements were kept in this body to reactivate it anew including the bloodstream that they tried to drain by piercing his side on the cross. A big stone was rolled on the door and no one else beside Joseph and Nicodemus touched the body that was not only mass but pure, dormant energy.

Mark reports: "When the Sabbath was over, Mary of Magdala, Mary the mother of(Joseph (and James,) and Salome bought aromatic oils, intending to go and anoint him; and very early on Sunday morning, just after sunrise, they came to the tomb. They were wondering among themselves who would roll away the stone for them from the entrance to the tomb, when they looked up and saw that the stone, huge as it was, had been rolled back already. They went into the tomb, where they saw a youth sitting on the right hand side, wearing a white robe, and they were dumbfounded. But he said to them, 'fear nothing; you are looking for Jesus of Nazareth, who was crucified. He has been raised again; he is not here; look, there is the place where they laid him. But go and give this message to his disciples and Peter: 'He is going on before you into Galilee; there you will see him, as he told you.' Then they went out and ran away from the tomb beside themselves with terror. They said nothing to anybody, for they were afraid." (Mar.16:1.)

Historians again may chose to regard the youthful apparition as unexplainable but they cannot deny the empty tomb witnessed by three women. Mark's narrative about the clear instructions by the mysterious young man to the amazed women disciples gives all the answers. These women saw the empty tomb and the neatly folded burial cloths pointing to them that Jesus is physically alive. Though they flee in fear and *said nothing to anyone* contrary to the young man's demands; their mere witnessing of the empty tomb with a declaration that Jesus has risen and has gone ahead to Galilee to meet his disciples is in itself a valid observation.

Most evangelical scholars agree that Mark is the oldest writer of the Gospel. Although Matthew, Luke and even John leaned upon Mark they all present extended, unduplicated stories of appearances of the resurrected Messiah to his disciples. In the stories the disciples speak with Jesus, eat with him, and touch him. Jesus in turn gives them final instructions and assurances that he has triumphed over death and that he is the Lord of history. After they left the empty tomb the women rush to tell the male disciples and this lead to post-resurrection appearances. But was the young man in a robe the same one who fled when Jesus was arrested or was he Jesus himself in his resurrected, glorified body?

The story of the Master's appearance on the road to Emmaus as told in Luke (24:13) is quite meaningful. Two of Jesus' disciples were walking away from Jerusalem the day after his Resurrection. Luke says Jesus himself drew near and walked with them. The disciples talked with him as a stranger about the happenings in Jerusalem and the Scripture apparently for some time and finally asked him to abide with them for the evening. They ate together but did not recognize Jesus until the breaking of the bread. This event can be a recurrence of what Jesus wanted to know at the outset of his ministry when he asked his disciples: "Who do men say that I the Son of Man am?" This time he wanted to explore the public reaction to his Crucifixion through Cleophas and his friend by means of a jovial and lively exercise all his own: "And he said to them, *what things*? And they said unto him, concerning Jesus of Nazareth, which was a prophet mighty in deed and word before God and all the people; and how the chief priests and our rulers delivered him to be condemned to death, and have crucified him . . . And certain women also of our company made us astonished, which were early in the sepulcher. And when they found not his body, they came, saying, that they had also seen a vision of angels, which said that he was alive . . . Then he said unto them: 'O *fools and slow of heart* to believe all that the prophets have spoken: ought not Christ to have suffered these things and to enter into his glory?' And it came to pass, as he sat at meat with them, he took bread and blessed it, and brake and gave to them. And their eyes were opened, and they knew him; and he *vanished out of their sight!*" (Luk. 24:19.)

Jesus catches up with two of his disciples who are fleeing Jerusalem after his death and resurrection. They fail to recognize him and are amazed that he seems unaware of the major events that have transpired in the capital city. After they inform him

Jesus responds, "How foolish of you, how slow to understand" what has occurred. Jesus then launches into an explanation of the scriptures.

What boggles my mind in this story is Jesus' electing to appear to the three women in a young glorified body. Was he re-enacting what he said that we must be as children to enter the Kingdom of Heaven? On the road to Emmaus not only he looked as a young man but acted as one also. In his other appearances to disciples he regained his regular pre-crucifixion appearance except to the nails and spear scars in his body. Was that appearance a palpable proof to them and especially to Thomas of his identity or did he do that joyfully under motivation of his child-pure mind? As to having vanished from their sight this is an indication that Jesus regained his glorified body that he temporarily relinquished following the Gethsemane prayer.

Speaking of Thomas one cannot tell from the Greek language that Jesus or Thomas was really talking about placing Thomas' finger or hand on Jesus' wounds. Both may just as well have been talking about simply touching the places where the wounds had been. The reason for this test is also unclear to John but according to Luke, it appears that it was probably designed to prove that Jesus was not merely a spirit but truly himself in a resurrected body (Luk. 24:36.) Jesus who *fixed* the ear of his attacker that was taken off by Peter's sword swing in a simple touch, could have easily healed even the marks of his own wounds. Thomas evidently was not satisfied with simply *seeing* the marks but wanted to take up Jesus' offer to *touch* them, perhaps because the others failed to do so. Jesus seemed eager to satisfy Thomas' curiosity and wanted him to believe in this

Resurrection and carry this belief to his fellow Greeks. Many call Thomas the *doubting Thomas*; in fact all of the apostles doubted and ran away and abandoned Jesus. Thomas is the courageous one who knows where to find him. By touching his wounds he begins to understand that the risen Jesus is not a ghost but a true reality and in fact he encountered the authentic and real Jesus. That prompted him to fall to the ground and pronounce a profound act of faith: "My Lord and my God". *Thomas encountered Jesus in all of his humanity and all of his divinity;* the true and same Messiah that died on Calvary and was risen. He came to grasp the reality and gave the example to the disciples who rejoiced at seeing his hands and side. John (20:20) suggests that these wounds had healed. Also those who broke bread with him in Emmaus might be expected to have noticed or commented on such horrible wounds had they seen them on/through his hands.

Resurrection is portrayed in the scripture as involving both fundamental continuity and significant dissimilarity. We should not minimize the dissimilarities as our own glorification can involve a dramatic and marvelous transformation. But the great majority of Christians have underemphasized continuity. They end up thinking of our transformed selves as no longer being ourselves and the transformed Earth as no longer the earth. In some cases they view the glorified Christ as no longer being the same Jesus who walked the earth; a belief that early Christians recognized as heresy. Something similar happened after Jesus' resurrection: the disbelief and uncertainty evidenced by those who saw him reflect an incongruity in the appearance of the newly risen Christ. Slowly they came to recognize him but they still struggled with doubt. At one instance Jesus had to persist on them saying: "See my hands and my feet, that it is I myself; touch me and see for a spirit does not have flesh and bones as you see that I have." (Luk.24:39.)

Let us note here that the son of the widow of Nain, the daughter of Jairus and Lazarus were all brought back to life by Jesus from the slumber of death. Not one of them continued their lives with a glorified body because they were awakened by an extraneous catalyst. The risen Jesus is the same Jesus that regained his physical, glorified reality prior to Gethsemane. He had entrusted his soul (the overall coordinator of his body's functions) to God for a programmed lapse of time and then regained it. He now moves about with the earlier ethereal body not much different from what it once was, transcending the limitations of time and space. His disciples failed to recognize him first because their minds put him already in the realm of oblivion, and secondly because his physical reality, although existing, is no longer subject to time and space.

Undoubtedly fear struck the disciples taking them to further spheres of disbelief: "When therefore it was evening, on that day, the first day of the week, and when the doors were shut where the disciples were, for fear of the Jews, Jesus came and stood in their midst, and said to them, "Peace be with you." And when he had said this, he showed them both his hands and his side. The disciples therefore rejoiced when they saw the Lord," (John 20:19.) Jesus wanted to ascertain to his disciples and through them to the world that he raised *physically*. A *spirit* resurrection is not a revival of the body and without a resurrection of the body of Christ the 3-day death ambit challenge would have not been met and the whole Christian creed would be in vain. Paul capitalized many times in his epistles around this point.

Jesus' subconscious mind reactivated his slumbering body into awakening under an unshakable command energized by the Holy Spirit; this is similar on a much smaller scale to our subconscious waking us up at 4am upon an order given with a meager degree of belief. This simplistic yet grandiose explanation serves to counter the criticisms of the empty tomb tradition and of the appearance stories that are typically given by skeptics and non-believers. Opponents of the resurrection in all ages faced one huge embarrassment anyway: no one has ever produced—besides what you are reading now—a plausible naturalistic explanation of what happened after the crucifixion that measures up with all the accepted scriptural accounts. None of the explanations that have been suggested: wrong tomb, swoon, hallucination, mistaken identity, and myth have any compelling evidence in their favor and many are so weak as to collapse under their own weight once spelled out.

Perhaps the most trusted evidence was the Roman centurion Longinus. His detachment stood watch on Golgotha and he witnessed the awesome portents that appeared at the Cross and confessed before everyone that, "Truly this was the Son of God" (Mat. 27:54.) He also stood watch with his officers at the sepulcher and observed the radiant Resurrection of Christ. The Jews bribed them to bear false witnesses and say that His disciples had stolen away the Body of Christ, but Longinus and two of his comrades refused the Jewish gold. They believed, accepted baptism and decided to forsake military service and preach Jesus in their homeland Cappadocia. The Jewish elders persuaded Pilate to kill Longinus and his comrades. When the soldiers arrived at his village the former centurion came out to meet his old comrades-in-arms and invited them to his home. After a meal the guests revealed the purpose of their arrival and Longinus and his fellows identified themselves and told the surprised soldiers to carry out their duty. They were beheaded.

Resurrection though remained the target of attacks on Christianity by its enemies because the event has been clearly seen as the crux of the matter. A remarkable attack was the one contemplated in 1927 by a young British lawyer, Frank Morrison. Sensing that it was the foundation stone of the Christian faith he decided to do the world a favor by exposing this fraud and superstition. As a lawyer he felt he had the critical faculties to rigidly sift evidence and to admit nothing as evidence which did not meet the same firm criteria for admission into a law court today. However while Morrison was doing his research a remarkable thing happened: the case was not nearly as easy as he had supposed. As a result the title of his book, "*Who Moved the Stone?*" was changed into: "The Book That Refused to Be Written." In it he described how, when examining the evidence he became persuaded against his will of the fact of the bodily resurrection of Christ.

Contestants of the resurrection are further overshadowed by the feat of Jesus' Ascension eye witnessed by many bystanders and all disciples including peter, James and John who witnessed his Transfiguration earlier. It took place atop the Mount of Olives on the fortieth day after this resurrection. Mark, Luke and the first chapter of the Acts of the Apostles narrates this event.

In fact the Ascension presents a problem to all doubters and antagonists of Christianity. If Jesus has not risen from the dead or if he somehow survived the ordeal of the Calvary and died later surely those numerous challengers would have vigorously sought to reclaim his body. Such a *trophy* could have crushed Christianity in its infancy. Those efforts if they occurred were in vain and the lack of evidence indirectly supports the record of the Ascension; *there was no earthly corpse.*

Stealing the body of Christ as usually alleged by assailants is in itself a psychological and ethical impossibility. For one it is something totally foreign to the character of the disciples and all that we know of them. It would mean that they were perpetrators of a deliberate lie which was responsible for the deception and ultimate death of thousands of people. Secondly we know men will die for what they believe to be true. Each of the disciples faced the test of torture and martyrdom for his statements and beliefs. Men and women do not die for what they know is a lie. *If ever a man tells the truth it is on his deathbed.* And if the disciples had taken the body and Christ was still dead we would still have the problem of explaining his physically witnessed appearances.

The Ascension was in fact another fulfilled prophecy by David in his Psalms. A thousand years before Jesus' birth David prophesied his ascension when he announced the Lord's enthronement at the Father's right hand according to Psalm 110:1 frequently quoted in the New Testament to indicate the importance of the event. It was also a pledge and a challenge by Jesus to his Jewish audience. Though the disciples struggled with the concept of Jesus' death he told them plainly that he was going back to the Father (John 14:12.) And while on trial before the Jewish Sanhedrin Jesus announced to the high priest that presently he would be "sitting at the right hand of Power" (Mat. 26:64.) His Ascension was one of the tests of Christ's prophetic credibility. John further relates in 6:62 what Christ told his disciples following his hard talk to the Jews: "Does this offend you? What and if you see the Son of man *ascend* up where he was before?" and in 20:17 he says to Mary Magdalene: "Do not touch me, for I am not yet *ascended* to my Father, but go to my brethren, and say to them: I *ascend* to my Father and to *your* Father, to my God and to your God." Thereafter the Ascension was spoken of as an accepted fact by the apostles namely in Ephesians 4:8, and in Timothy 3:16.

The place of the Ascension would appear from the Acts to have been the Mount of Olives. The disciples are described as returning to Jerusalem after the Ascension from that mount neighboring the city. The site has been since consecrated as the Mount of Ascension and Christian piety has memorialized the event by erecting a basilica over the site. St. Helena built the first memorial which was destroyed by the Persians in 614, rebuilt in the eighth century, to be destroyed again but rebuilt a second time by the crusaders. This one the Moslems also destroyed leaving only the octagonal structure which encloses the stone said to bear the imprint of the feet of Christ that is now used as an oratory.

To modern day's engrossed minds where the several layers of the atmosphere have been invaded by man up to the outer space frontiers, the act of Ascension poses a boggling issue.

Christ's glorified body *did* ascend in space to disappear beyond the clouds. This is emblematic to the elevated man's syndrome itself that Jesus heralded all through. To object to the Ascension issue as implying a childish, outdated theory of the universe is really inconsequential; the change Jesus revealed by the Ascension was not a change of place but a change of state, not local but spiritual. Ever since the dawn of human thinking UP HIGH was always the positive direction to the spirit uplifting and sublimation while DOWN BELOW was the negative domain of doom and misery. Jesus taught us to pray to "Our Father in Heaven" to presage lifting our spirit to this blissful realm above asking us to imply God's will 'on Earth as in Heaven' while he clearly told us where God truly abides: *within our mind*. The language used by the evangelists to describe the Ascension must be interpreted according to the knowledge status of those times. To say that he was taken up or that he ascended does not necessarily imply that they *located* heaven directly above the earth; no more than the words "sits on the right hand of God" mean that this is his actual posture. In disappearing from their view, "he was raised up and a cloud received him out of their sight" (Act. 1:9) and entering into glory he dwells with the Father in the honor and power denoted by the Scripture.

Thus the Ascension of Christ in as much as it was a physical happening is an abiding spiritual significance. Several doctrinal points were established following this event that further reinforced the disciples' belief and bolstered their authority. By ascending his ethereal body Jesus brought to an end his post-resurrection appearances to his disciples, parted from them as to his physical presence and passed to the other world to reappear in spirit—as to Paul—and to the rest of them on several occasions. On Pentecost after arguing for the resurrection and ascension Peter contended valiantly: "Let the whole house of Israel therefore know *assuredly*, that God has made him both Lord and Christ, this Jesus whom you crucified" (Act. 2:36.) The outpouring of the Holy Spirit on the day of Pentecost was a supernatural event that authenticated the establishment of the church of Christ where the Christian regime is divine not human. Ascension further empowered early disciples with miraculous gifts by which the Mind of God was revealed to humanity. This ancient record allows modern students even today to put to the test the credibility of the primitive documents and find them to be trustworthy. Contrary to Jewish expectations the ascension of Christ revealed the reality of the Christian mission on earth that was not to overthrow Rome and establish an earthly, political administration reminiscent of David's setup but a spiritual empire governed by the Holy Spirit of God for the bliss of all mankind.

To take the place of his physical presence Jesus sent the disciples his Holy Spirit as a counselor and guide "to teach you all things and remind you of everything I have said to you." (John 14:26.) He ascended in spirit before the feast of Pentecost which occurred exactly fifty days after the feast of the first fruits that coincided with his resurrection. When he ascended with his other worldly body his Spirit was not meant this time to incarnate into a specific person but was diffusely extended into the human family where everyone who *had faith* would have his share of the spirit for the common good. This is one aspect of Jesus' second coming in the body and Spirit, and this is how any ensuing coming is supposed to be.

The disciples propagated the divine knowledge as they heard it from Jesus. When any of them failed to repeat what the Master exactly preached the Holy Spirit would take over the body of that disciple to relay the message (Mat.10: 20.) Motivated by their experience at Pentecost the discouraged, disappointed men and women were radically transformed by the mighty spiritual power. They turned the world upside down; many lost their lives for their faith, others were terribly persecuted. Their courageous behavior does not make sense apart from their conviction that Jesus Christ was truly raised from the dead: a fact worth dying for!

When Jesus spoke of his second coming in Matthew 24:2, his disciples pointed out to him the splendor of the temple buildings. Since they had spent most of their time in Galilee and only occasionally visited Jerusalem the buildings impressed them very much. Jesus took this opportunity to tell them of the coming events: "Do you see all these things? Verily I say unto you, there shall not be left here one stone upon another that shall not be thrown down" (Luk. 21:6.) Seventy years later that prophecy was fulfilled. Later that same day when the group was at the Mount of Olives these words of Jesus still puzzled them, causing them to ask him a three-part question. "Tell us, when shall these things be? And what shall be the sign of your coming, and of the end of the world?" (Mat. 24:3.) Jesus did not give clearly defined, separate answers to the various parts of this question. Apparently the prophecies he gave were to be applied to both the sooner and the later events.

As discussed earlier, he wanted to keep his believers in constant alertness as to the day of his second advent: "Therefore keep watch, because you do not know on what day your Lord will come." Again let's repeat that keeping watch to any human being means that he has to live a positive life of purity in expectation and therefore readiness. This is best explained in his parable: "The coming of the Son of Man can be compared with that of a man who left home to go on a trip. He gave instructions to each of his employees about the work they were to do, and he told the gatekeeper to watch for his return. So keep a sharp lookout! For you do not know when the homeowner will return—at evening, midnight, early dawn, or late daybreak. Don't let him find you *sleeping* when he arrives without warning." (Mar. 13:34.) Jesus did not want his followers to *do it now and repent later* or *will be ready when I get to it*. Such attitudes mean opening the subconscious to all negative thoughts and deeds with plans to take them out *when the day comes*. To Jesus the *day of reckoning* is not tomorrow or next year but today and every day of a human lifespan. The Master has given his warning that we might not be taken by surprise not only by this great event, but by any fatality or mishap that surprises us in a state of impurity: "Watch out! Don't let my sudden coming catch you unawares; don't let me find you *living in careless ease, carousing and drinking, and occupied with the problems of this life* like all the rest of the world. *Keep a constant watch.*"

Vigilance therefore is what Jesus advocated. Vigilance keeps the subconscious tare-free and indoctrinates a positive awareness to live by. He would stop short to explain this continuous state of watchfulness but in fact he did to those who grasp it using his usual symbolism. The reader should look for a divine interpretation of that symbolism that may be found in the immediate context of this book or elsewhere. If an interpretation is not given symbolism may remain an unsolved mystery and we should not rush to simply acknowledge we do not know what it means. Jesus did not impose his doctrine nor did he provide minute details for its implementation but left it for people to contemplate and consider. Early Christians expected Jesus' second coming during their life span and many of them started asking why is it taking so long? Peter who understood the mind of Christ corrected that understanding. "But don't forget this, dear friends that a day or a thousand years from now is like tomorrow to the Lord. He isn't really being slow about his promised return, even though it sometimes seems that way. But he is waiting, for the good reason that he is not willing that any should perish, and he is giving more time for sinners to repent." (2Pet. 3:8.)

Jesus' second coming, one of the foundations of the Christian faith was inundated with countless false teachings. Many *prediction* books have been written picking the exact day of Jesus' return and others claimed to have been Jesus himself incarnated. The Master warned against such future attempts and stressed not to be fooled about his second coming. "At that time if anyone says to you, 'Look, here is the Christ!' or 'There he is!' do not believe it; for false Christs and false prophets will appear and perform great signs and miracles to deceive even the elect if that were possible. *See, I have told you ahead of time.* So if anyone tells you, 'There he is, out in the desert,' do not go out; or, 'Here he is, in the inner rooms,' do not believe it." (Mat. 24:23.) These books and *personifying actors* may sell many copies and set various stages but they mislead their audience. There's one recommendation to guard against such attempts: as soon as someone predicts the day or time of Jesus' second coming *that prediction is wrong* because only God the Father knows when it will be; Even Jesus doesn't know and he said that to his disciples.

However what Christians and most Muslims ignore is that when talking about the *signs of the hour*, the Koran attributes to Jesus his prior knowledge of *the Hour* of Judgment confirming his second coming that precedes such event: "And Jesus shall be the sign of the hour (of judgment): Therefore, have no doubt about it" (Koran 43:61.)

The answer to the big question whether Jesus is coming back is certainly yes. Not because it is a matter of personal conviction but a context of believing Jesus in any word, promise or pledge he uttered on this earth. This Man-God never failed to fulfill any of his undertakings from raising the dead, healing the sick, defying death, resurrecting and ascending to heaven, down to his promise to Peter to go catch a fish and find 4 Dirhams inside it. His promised second coming is certainly an authentic veracity backed by the credibility of a Prophet that embodied and taught truthfulness. Unfortunately some Christian cults teach that Christ *secretly* returned already. Such a claim is not commensurate with Jesus' known openness and transparency. Jesus fulfilled many of the prophecies of the Messiah during his birth, life, ministry, death, and resurrection. His second coming is the hope of believers that God is in control of all things and Jesus remains as faithful to it as his earlier promises and prophecies.

The Second Coming of Christ will be to fulfill these remaining prophecies. In his first coming Jesus was not only the suffering servant but the *suffering teacher* whose message was obstructed by the walls of ignorance. In his second coming he will be the conquering King, at ease with the advent of knowledge the humanity has evolved to since his physical days on earth. Probably this time he will not resort to parables to disseminate his philosophy of universal love and to take more care of the human children from seven to seventy and remove the tares from their subconscious minds. Yet as in his first coming, he would walk this earth with his known humbleness as the Lamb of God, displaying innate meekness, and not debording caserns of weapons: he will rule the world by conquering simply the hearts of men and women. The Jewish school still insists on the *Conquering Messiah* in this era of nuclear proliferation; they fail to understand that the same Messiah who fulfilled the role of the suffering servant (Isa.53) in his first coming will fulfill the role of the Conquering Messiah as per (Zec.12.) And likewise his first, his *conquest* this time will not be a martial pomp but a spiritual exhilaration.

The "day of the Lord" described by Jesus and Paul later as a fearful day, depicts heavens passing away with a great noise and fire melting the earth and the works of man will be burned up. Paul adds meaning by asking: what kind of people should we be? Jesus knew his fellow Mid-Easters can only be stirred by ceremonial exaggerations as mind openers to take heed and record remembrance, over-emphasized the importance of his second coming as a major event to expect and *be ready* for. Jesus comes after the tribulation of the time of sorrows that we now see humanity walking down to. The intense misery

281

-22-

Afterword

Seek the truth. The truth will make you free."
Jesus Christ

Having written the volume now in your hands I remembered the time when I first became interested in this great subject. As far back as my memory can go I was inquiring, searching and asking all kinds of questions about it. Though I gathered piles of information, the years of maturity found me with but little knowledge concerning it. One day a paragraph in Paul's epistle to the Hebrews struck a chord with a vibrating resonance: "for every one that uses milk

283

is unskillful in the word of righteousness: for he is a babe. But strong meat belongs to them that are of full age, *even* those who by reason of use *have their senses exercised to discern both good and evil.*" (Heb. 5:13.) Paul who renovated Jesus' philosophy to confront the sophisticated Greek intellect prompted me to do a similar share, irrespective of how modest, to bring this philosophy further into the 21st Century human brainpower.

Soon enough I gained access to the works of many men who had written on the subject and with their various aids added to a careful study of the Scripture the fields of Jesus' mind began to break open in my vision. Fourteen years have passed during which time I gave the subject my closest and most extended study yet I regarded myself only a primary student in this course. The more I dug deeper into Jesus' mind the more I would bow before him as Thomas did and declare my profound act of faith: "My Lord and my God!". And having felt thus led by the Master I went ahead and ventured upon the task.

In this period of theological ferment unmatched since the first Christian century we once again have different ways of formulating Jesus' significance and identity while remaining united in the confession of the one faith. We are being called to write the *good news* with a new approach suitable for our time and place. We must reclaim Jesus again among our own people so that his living, updated legacy will be handed on to the next generation throughout this twenty-first century.

This ferment is creating many levels of belief in the story of Jesus that has been handed down to us through ages. Many modern philosophers are linking Jesus' bequest to anything more than mythology ignoring his deepest human longings for the positive traits of peace, justice, joy and love. Today we have to admit that we live within the anonymity of an evolving universe where the ultimate mystery that Jesus identified as our Divine Father is the source and goal of all creation. We cannot be genuinely human if we are not radically related to this divine mystery that pervades the human experience; the one we *live* within its confines as fish live in the sea.

This modern cosmology compels us to revaluate the evolutionary understanding of the Jesus' world in which the human being is called to authentic existence. Once more the pioneering work of Teilhard de Chardin fits in here. He not only saw that the universe is a dynamic unity of matter and spirit; but also recognized that the evolutionary thrust of the universe from matter to spirit was due to the divine empowerment within the creation. He further identifies power with Jesus Christ who is the *alpha* and *omega*, the beginning and end, the origin and culmination of all creation. Jesus represents the climax of divine creation and human history; the one in whom God's plan for the entire universe reaches its peak. Teilhard suggests that the striving for world peace and human community are indications of the power of Christ operating within the created order. Christ saved humanity from endless multiplicity and fragmentation which threaten the evolutionary impulse towards unity. He rescued the human race from the negative realities of sin and evil by the positive, superior power of divine love. Teilhard bridged the world of science with Christian faith and provided a good account to face contemporary views of the human identity and human experience.

Perhaps Jesus is the only *prophet* we can still have a *personal relationship* with that impacts our daily lives today. Because of his resurrection his followers do not honor a dead founder but a creator that is alive in the cosmos and ready to prime his second coming. Jesus lives nowadays and faithfully enriches the lives of all those who trust and abide by him. Throughout centuries multitudes have acknowledged his worthiness including many who have greatly influenced the world.

Numerous Christians and almost all non-Christians disparage Jesus in comparing himself to God: "I and the Father are One." In fact he demonstrated powers over natural forces that could belong only to God, the Supreme Architect of these forces. He stilled a raging storm of wind and waves on the Sea of Galilee. In doing this he provoked from those in the boat the awestruck question, "Who is this? Even the wind and waves obey him!" (Mar. 4:41.) He turned water into wine, fed 5,000 people from five loaves and two fish, gave a grieving widow back her only son by raising him from the dead and brought to life the dead daughter of a shattered father. To an old friend he said, "Lazarus, come forth!" and dramatically raised him from his death slumber. It is most significant that his enemies did not deny this miracle. Rather they tried to kill him for it: "If we let him go on like this, everyone will believe in him" (John 11:48.) Furthermore he demonstrated the Creator's power over sickness and disease. He made the lame to walk, the dumb to speak and the blind to see. Some of his healings were of congenital problems not susceptible to psychosomatic cure. The most outstanding was that of the born-blind man whose case is recorded in John 9. Though the man couldn't answer his speculative questioners his experience was enough to convince them. "One thing I do know. I was blind but now I see!" He was astounded that his friends didn't recognize this healer as the Son of God. "Since the world begun was it not heard that